ECONOMIC GROWTH IN INDIA

Economic Growth in India

History and Prospect

PULAPRE BALAKRISHNAN

OXFORD
UNIVERSITY PRESS

OXFORD
UNIVERSITY PRESS

YMCA Library Building, Jai Singh Road, New Delhi 110 001

Oxford University Press is a department of the University of Oxford. It furthers the University's objective of excellence in research, scholarship, and education by publishing worldwide in

Oxford New York

Auckland Cape Town Dar es Salaam Hong Kong Karachi Kuala Lumpur Madrid Melbourne Mexico City Nairobi New Delhi Shanghai Taipei Toronto

With offices in
Argentina Austria Brazil Chile Czech Republic France Greece Guatemala Hungary Italy Japan Poland Portugal Singapore South Korea Switzerland Thailand Turkey Ukraine Vietnam

Oxford is a registered trademark of Oxford University Press in the UK and in certain other countries

Published in India
by Oxford University Press, New Delhi

First published 2010
Fifth impression 2011

ISBN-13: 978-0-19-806547-0
ISBN-10: 0-19-806547-7

Typeset in Minion Pro 10/12.6
by Sai Graphic Design, New Delhi - 110 055
Printed in India at Anvi Composers, New Delhi 110 063
Published by Oxford University Press
YMCA Library Building, Jai Singh Road, New Delhi 110 001

For Sivakami and Balakrishna Menon
who started me off,
and to the peasants and workers of India
who quickened her economy

Contents

Tables and Figures

Tables

Figures

Foreword

One of the greatest benefits of supervising graduate students is to be able to follow their subsequent careers and see them realize their potential. Pulapre Balakrishnan (Bala) was one of my PhD students at Cambridge in the 1980s. He wrote a fine dissertation on pricing and inflation in India. It was characterized by excellent understanding of the relevant theory, suitable adaption to the Indian case, and sensible use of econometric procedures to test the inferences drawn from the theoretical structure. He exhibited the traits of an excellent all-round economist. In his new book, *Economic Growth in India: History and Prospect*, all these traits are present in their full maturity.

The book is a comprehensive study of growth in post-Independence India. The theory is both subtle and eclectic, drawing on several strands of the relevant literature, and presented in an original narrative by the author. It uses empirical methods to advantage and in the process of examining the several sensibly-defined historical periods, the author tests whether the conventional wisdom on these stands up to close scrutiny. If it does not, he explains why, and also why his carefully presented narrative is a more convincing explanation. In setting out the history of the various phases of growth, Bala is careful to praise the positive aspects, while pointing out clearly and fairly the deficiencies and shortcomings. Most of all, his humane approach always leads him to evaluate how the less well-off have fared and, if they have not gained from the growth in India, as is often the case, what should be done about it.

While reading Bala's new book, I have also been reading the three volumes of the late A.K. Dasgupta's *Collected Works* (New Delhi, Oxford

University Press, 2009). I was struck by the similarity of their approaches, both in setting out economic theory and applying it. Their findings are explained in clear distinguished prose, bringing out the economic intuition of their analysis while unobtrusively, but clearly, supplying the necessary technical back-up to their results. Bala's book is a major contribution, which is destined to have a proper impact on the profession's understanding of recent Indian economic history and on what may be learned from it.

It is a privilege to write the foreword to this excellent book and to be able to pay a tribute to a former student and a firm friend.

G.C. Harcourt
Jesus College
University of Cambridge

Acknowledgements

This work was fully funded by a Senior Fellowship of the Nehru Memorial Museum and Library (NMML), New Delhi. Therefore, the first and largest part of the gratitude that I would like to express for the support that I have received in completing it goes to this unique national foundation. Its lavish award alone afforded me the leisure so central to such an undertaking. Apart from funding my research, the Library also waived for me its mandatory residence requirement, allowing me to remain at Kozhikode, which has considerably furthered my research and writing. This special dispensation was due to the high-mindedness of K. Jayakumar and N. Balakrishnan, the Acting Director and Deputy Director, respectively, at the time of my assuming the Fellowship in March 2006. The understanding was magnanimously maintained by Mridula Mukherjee who was to take over as the full-time Director a little later. Since for the economist, material outcomes can never be wished away, I am relieved to note that their judgement paid for itself in the form of this book! Subsequently at the NMML, P. Chandramohan, Deepa Bhatnagar, Aruna Tandan, and the staff of the Library and the Administration all facilitated my research in various ways.

A study as wide-ranging as this could not have been accomplished without the assistance of many individuals, and it gives me great pleasure to acknowledge their inputs. Foremost among them are M. Parameswaran and M. Suresh Babu. Parameswaran generously agreed to my use in this book of our joint work and updated the statistical exercises as more data and better methods became available. Suresh Babu read the entire manuscript, suggested how my arguments could be improved, chased up the data needed to support them, and assisted with the graphics. These two young economists exhibit an understanding of the economy and a sense for the right methodology in applied work that far exceed their years in the profession. I have been the beneficiary of these rare capabilities.

Among the persons with whom I have had the privilege of discussing my ideas as they appear here are Bharat Ramaswami, Arunava Sen, Aditya Bhattacharjea, Amitava Bose, Balaram Menon, Venugopal Menon, K. Pushpangadan, E. Sridharan, Rajagopal Natarajan, D.J. Bangara, C. Selvaraj, Jairam Ramesh, Murkoth Ramunni, Ramachandra Guha, Francine Frankel, Ruchira and Ajit Kumar Ghose, Ravi Arvind Palat, V.N. and Ahalya Balasubramanyan, Govinda Rao, S.K. Rao, Abhijit 'Manik' Sen, Ashok Soota, K.P. Sankaran, K. Saradamoni, Arunima Gopinath, Prem Shankar Jha, Majid Siddiqui, Partha Dutta, R. Nagaraj, Mahesh Rangarajan, Dilip Mookherjee, Amrit Tandon, Debraj Ray, Mukesh Eswaran, Sushil Kumar Pillai, K.C. Mohan, Ashok Kotwal, T.N. Srinivasan, Aditya and Mridula Mukherjee, Tirthankar Roy, N.R. Nanda Kishore, Surajit Das, Anit Mukherjee, K.R.S. Murthy, N. Chandramohan, M.P. Chandrashekaran, Sanjaya Baru, Rakesh Mohan, the late Amaresh Bagchi, C.T. Kurien, K.L. Krishna, A.R. Vasavi, Preeti Bahadur, Jayati Ghosh, Tapas Sen, V.R. Panchamukhi, Deb Kusum Das, Abdul Azeez, N.J. Kurien, Peter de Souza, Ram Manohar Reddy, Vijay Shankar, V.K. Natraj, P.V. Shenoy, Rajeswari and Dhruv Raina, Ajit Mozoomdar, Shovan Ray, Prakash Upadhyaya, R. Govinda, Guilherme Vaz, S. Venkitaramanan, Manmohan Agarwal, Gurbachan Singh and Ritesh Jain. All of them have been generous with their time and advice even when they have disagreed with me, at times strongly. Finally, the comments and suggestions of two anonymous referees have improved the argument and the structure of the book. Of course, I remain responsible for the views expressed here.

Selected parts of this book have been presented at seminars or lectures at the NMML, Centre for Development Studies at Thiruvananthapuram, National Institute for Advanced Studies at Bengaluru, Indira Gandhi Institute of Development Research at Mumbai, Centre for Policy Research and the National Institute for Public Finance and Policy at New Delhi, Centre for International Trade and Development of the Jawaharlal Nehru University, Institute of Economic Growth of the University of Delhi, Centre for Studies in the Social Sciences at Kolkata, and Vivekananda College in Chennai. I have benefited from the interaction with the audience present on these occasions.

Parts of the material here have appeared as publications in journals or as monographs. Thus, parts of Chapter 1 have appeared in the *Economic and Political Weekly* and the *Indian Economic Journal*, and the econometric exercise undergirding the argument in Chapter 3 has appeared in the former. I thank the editors Ram Manohar Reddy and V.R. Panchamukhi, respectively, for graciously according me the privilege of publishing this material here. Also, the section on 'The Agriculture Quotient' in Chapter 4 is largely based on research funded by the Reserve Bank of India and published as Development Research Group Study No. 27 of its Department of Economic Analysis and Policy. I am grateful to the Bank for granting me permission to publish it here and to my co-authors Ramesh Golait and Pankaj Kumar for their substantial input.

Apart from the NMML, some other institutions have strongly supported my work. Principal among them are the Centre for Development Studies at Thiruvananthapuram and the National Institute for Public Finance and Policy at New Delhi. Here my work was nurtured and I was given unrestricted access to their extraordinary resources of libraries, guest houses, and faculty. This was entirely due to the active encouragement of my project by their respective Directors, K. Narayanan Nair and M. Govinda Rao. In addition I have received much assistance there from Navin Bhalla, Siva Chidambaram, Anil Kumar Sharma, R. Surendran, Jai Mohan Pandit, Hari Shankar, Naveen Singh, Soman Nair, and Anil Kumar. At the Indian Institute of Management Kozhikode, where the early parts of the book were written, K. Kunhikrishnan, Chief Administrative Officer; M.G. Sreekumar, Librarian; Ashok Pathak, Manager of the Computer Centre; and their staff always welcomed me back even after I had moved on.

Finally, it is both a pleasure and a privilege to acknowledge the contribution of the Oxford University Press India team at New Delhi. The professionalism that has accompanied their every response and the civility that has permeated our every interaction as the book was being produced has made the experience memorable even for this second-time author with the Press.

Writing a book is both a solitary and uncertain business, but this has been compensated for me by living in so hospitable a city. Kozhikode's balmy air, easy commerce, plural streets, and cosmopolitanism that dwarfs its size, all combine in my mind to come close to being what Michel Foucault must have imagined as a social space of difference. Away from the predatory logic of corporations and the distractions of state-sponsored politics, it was the perfect setting to contemplate the past and future of economic growth in India, a topic that can evoke both wonder and dreariness. This city's recent history does not parallel that of India. Once a port unrivalled in the Indian Ocean World, its fortunes declined as power was to get concentrated in Delhi after 1947. But India herself was to rise, through means explained in this book, and by the end of the first decade of the twenty-first century she began to leave a mark on the world stage. From the playing fields of cricket to the climate-change negotiations at Copenhagen, the world has suddenly become a happy hunting ground for her increasingly confident elites. There can be no doubt that this is the result of its rising economic power as a political entity. While this must cheer the patriot, she cannot but be aware that even as India joyously competes globally, we remain severely challenged at home. To a large number of Indians the recent and unexpected ascent of India is small comfort as they struggle with the lack of employment and, even more, with public institutions without a mandate to serve them. It is by now clear to anyone choosing to see things as they are that the type of growth we have had since 1991 cannot erase this deficit. While greater integration with the rest of the world is entirely to be pursued, and even for its own sake, by itself it is not a solution to the challenge of inclusion. I believe that this book establishes why this is so. But even more, I believe that it succeeds in showing that these hardships are no longer necessary, for India has by now the intellectual and material resources to create for all her citizens the opportunity to engage with life, liberty, and the pursuit of happiness.

PULAPRE BALAKRISHNAN
Kozhikode

Abbreviations

ASER	Annual State of Education Report
BIC	Bayesian Information Criteria
CPI	Communist Party of India
CSO	Central Statistical Organisation
EFA	education for all
FDI	foreign direct investment
FERA	Foreign Exchange Regulation Act
FYP	Five Year Plan
GDP	gross domestic product
GNP	gross national product
HYV	high-yielding varieties
ILO	International Labour Organization
IMF	International Monetary Fund
ISI	import-substituting industrialization
ITES	information technology–enabled services
LPG	liberalization, privatization, globalization
MRTP	Monopolies and Restrictive Trade Practices
NREGS	National Rural Employment Guarantee Scheme
OECD	Organisation for Economic Co-operation and Development
PISA	Programme for International Student Assessment
R&D	research and development
SIA	Secretariat for Industrial Approvals
SSI	small-scale industry
TFP	total factor productivity
TIMSS	Trends in International Mathematics and Science Study

Introduction

> *Sooner or later, it is ideas, not vested interests, which are dangerous for good or evil.*
>
> —J.M. Keynes (1936)

IDEAS, EVENTS, AND THE ECONOMY

It is a measure of the youthfulness of economics as a discipline that a full two centuries past the appearance of Adam Smith's landmark treatise *The Wealth of Nations* an economist has posed the question 'How do economies grow?'[1] Far from being seen as a sign of weakness, it ought to be seen as one of strength that the economics profession entertains a periodic reappraisal of its central ideas. However, even as the awareness of such candid self-examination may be flattering to a practitioner of the Dismal Science, it does also speak of an unsettled issue at its core. This study of economic growth in India is intended as a response to the question posed. As economic history, it surveys the six decades from Independence to the present; as prognosis, it conveys what we may expect in the near future.

This narrative was written at a time of some turbulence in the world of economic ideas, one that could hardly have been anticipated even a decade ago. The 1990s had appeared to be a final turning point with respect to ideas about the economy, a turn that was largely driven by political events, the more far-reaching of which had been the crumbling of the Berlin Wall in the summer of 1989. The Wall itself was symbolic of the allegedly unbridgeable divide between the two great politico-economic systems of the twentieth century. Since the Second World War, a fierce competition had been unleashed for an allegiance of the public to one of either state-directedness or free markets as the organizing principle underlying the economic arrangements for a society. The fact that to most intelligent observers this had always appeared to be a false dichotomy made little difference as to how the end of the Cold War, following the implosion of the Soviet Union, was interpreted by the survivors in the contest over economic ideas. The triumphalism of those who had all along claimed the superiority of the free-market system said it all. Adding to their sense of self-satisfaction, the world was now globalizing, which promised not just more of the market, but actually a market on a global scale. In the world of economic policy this had led to the purveying of a 'Washington Consensus'. This was a set of economic policy prescriptions intended to serve as benchmark for the so-called 'emerging market' economies. The prefix itself referred to the fact that the US was now the sole superpower and, therefore, Washington, D.C. the epicentre of this ascending school of thought. But 'consensus' was somewhat of a misnomer—as we were to discover only later—for the original reference was merely to the views held by the United States Treasury and the Bretton Woods institutions over which the former has always wielded an influence. All these, among the world's most powerful economic bodies, are based in Washington, D.C. Of course, this was not lost on the author (Williamson 1990) of the expression who had titled the article where it had first appeared 'What Washington Means by Policy Reform', implying that there was room for other interpretations! Williamson's original listing of the ingredients of a sound economic policy package had contained: (i) fiscal discipline, (ii) re-orientation of public expenditure, (iii) tax reform, (iv) financial liberalization, (v) unified and competitive exchange rates, (vi) trade liberalization, (vii) openness to foreign direct investment, (viii) privatization, (ix) deregulation, and (x) secure property rights. Dani Rodrik (2006) has helpfully summarized this list to read: 'Stabilize, Privatize, Liberalize'! While this may come across as somewhat of a caricature, it is the case that this brief agenda had enjoyed unrivalled prestige in the world of economic ideas during the final decade of the twentieth century. It seems that, while Keynes had thought of economics as a difficult subject, the dramatic end of the Soviet Union had emboldened some to make it appear easy. In any case, the so-called Consensus did not think much of state-directedness. On the other hand, its recommendations seemed to imply that the sole objective of policy reform was to carve out space for the untrammelled functioning of markets.

It appears, however, that a decade is a long time even in the sedate world of academic economists! The Washington Consensus was itself to disappear, though like the grin of the Cheshire Cat its votaries have been left behind. The events responsible for its final exit could not have been within their imagination though. In 2008 the icons of American capitalism from the investment bank Lehman Brothers to the giant insurance company AIG were to go under, dragging along with them some of the other big names in global finance, and the corporate sector had to be fed by the very hand that it had once scorned. The world was staring at the prospect of another Great Depression. By early 2009 the original Keynesian prescription for stabilization of the private-enterprise system, mocking which had become fair game for academic economists for at least three decades, was now hastily resorted to in the form of the most spectacular economic stimulus package the world has ever seen.

There are some lessons to be learned by the professional economist from this episode. First, as John Hicks was wont to emphasize, economics ought to be seen as a discipline and not a science, as closer to history than to astronomy, as it were. While it remains a most powerful language to organize our thoughts on the production and distribution of wealth alright, to assert that the immutable laws that govern the economy in perpetuity have been discovered would not be credible. Hubris of this kind has afflicted the two contrasting socio-economic experiments in the Eastern Europe of the communists and the Anglo-America of Thatcher and Reagan, respectively. Second, economics was meant to be a serious subject. Shorn of groundedness, especially when used to make prescriptions, it no longer remains so.

Given this country's age-old tradition of pluralism in thought, it was only natural that debates among economists in India have followed the global pattern of division, with individuals aligning themselves with one or the other of the two extremes. However, in the early decades after Independence there was also another cohort, one comprising those less convinced of the unquestioned superiority of either the state or the market to solve the problems of the Indian economy on their own. Their worldview, it appears, was shaped by the realization that India's economy is both complex and heterogeneous, and that in any case you need to understand it before you attempt to change it according to some first principles of *etatisme* or market fundamentalism. These pioneers were neither enamoured of the practice of theory for theory's sake nor moved instantly by the provenance of an idea. Unfortunately, this line of practice—kept alive by vigorous empirical research and a questing temperament—went into a decline over time. As a result, for at least a couple of decades now, India has been in the recipient mode as far as ideas on the economy, and much else, are concerned. More than ever before, it is bombarded with ideas from the highly developed West and reminders of its backwardness from a rapidly developing East. For India, at this moment, it is possible to make her own way in the world only if there is also a production of knowledge at home.

This work engages with the present conjuncture in the evolution of economic ideas as I have described it. It is aimed at getting a steady picture of the functioning of the economy when the theory that has hitherto been applied to the task is in a state of flux. It attempts to be an investigative account of growth and its future in India, one informed by theory and guided by method. Its aim is to contribute to a conversation about how the economy works, though focused on the process of economic growth. However, while in its concerns and emphasis it may be seen as a book aimed at the fellow economist, I hope that it will also attract the intelligent reader interested in India's recent economic history and the prospects for our common future. After all, the economy is one of the pillars on which a civilized society must rest.

Economic Growth in India: What is to Be Explained

In the first decade of the twenty-first century, for five years continuously from 2003–4, India has been among the fastest growing economies of the world. At least two aspects of this growth may be highlighted. First, the rate of growth itself—at a simple average of over 8 per cent per annum—would be found to be high in an international historical comparison. Very few countries are growing at a similar rate currently and, for instance, the economy of the UK, the first industrial nation, has seldom grown at more than 3 per cent per annum ever since records have been kept from the early eighteenth century.[2] Five years of unprecedented performance had made for an 'India growth story' which came to be the cynosure of all eyes.

Second, the nature of that growth is interesting in itself. While the rise, and rise, of the software industry had been its motif, more recently the most dynamic segments of the Indian economy have actually been in the manufacturing sector and are driven by foreign direct investment. From motor cars to mobile phones, India exudes a potential to emerge as a global manufacturing hub. However, as the folk saying goes, 'It wasn't always so'. For about three decades after a programme for industrialization was launched, Indian manufacturing was a byword for poor quality at high cost. As for growth itself, in the late 1960s the Indian economy had appeared to be stuck in a quagmire which was the making of its policymakers. Industrial growth had slowed significantly and the spectre of food shortage was back in the public consciousness. With hindsight though, this was set to change within about a decade.

From the late 1970s on, the rate of growth of the economy accelerated. Interestingly, that development appears to have caught most economists unawares. Upon reflection, it had to do with a tendency within the profession in India to be largely guided by, if not theoretical models of growth, the idea that growth is determined by the policy regime. And for the policy regime itself to be, somewhat myopically, identified with the trade and industrial policies of the country's central government. Thus, in the 1970s the outlook of a section of the profession had coalesced around the critique of India's economic strategy as an 'inward-looking industrialization'. Naturally, it was to leave them ill-prepared to recognize a quickening of the economy while the policy regime remained unchanged. Not a dog had barked as the elephant deftly shifted gear to quicken her pace *circa* 1980.

A similar mindset is evident in some of the appraisals of economic performance in India during the 1990s, only now the academic economist's priors were of a resurgent growth. Having observed the dramatic changes to the trade and industrial policy regime in 1991, some appear to have simply assumed the arrival of faster growth. However, this has not inevitably been the trajectory of the economy. First, from a statistical point of view, the acceleration of growth after 1991 has taken a while coming, getting established only if the very high growth rates post-2003 are included. Second, there is a sectoral twist to the growth story in that it is the services sector that has been the most expansionary. This is significant in the context, as services have not particularly been the focus of the reform measures. This less-than-immediate acceleration, not to mention the sectorally-skewed growth, in an economy that was expected to respond with alacrity to the liberalizing reforms of 1991 are not what tend to get attention in the 'India growth story'. However, it should be a matter of some interest to growth economists. Nevertheless, these details are by now history, so to speak.

While the trajectory of economic growth in India thus far is of interest, what can get overlooked when focusing on the recent past is that despite being one of the world's fastest growing economies currently, it remains one of the world's poorest. It has a long way to go before approaching the global average per capita income. Now, the prospects for growth in India, and its relation to the reforms currently underway, assume as much interest as the nature and extent of growth since 1991. Accordingly, this study also aims to offer a prognosis of growth in India in the immediate future.

Generally, while the future offers the researcher a *tabula rasa*, or a clean slate, the past is a trodden ground. This is as true in a study of economic growth, and the new entrant must define his/her position in relation to others. While I shall take care to do so at every relevant stage, one major break from established practice made in this study may be pointed out at the very outset. It is customary in accounts of growth in India to commence with Indian Independence and to partition the period since into phases of growth, allegedly on some objective basis. At some level, this would appear natural as a procedure, for India became a political entity in 1947 and a coherent economic policy for growth emerges only from then on. Usually the researcher identifies an acceleration of the growth rate from around 1980 and possibly again in the twenty-first century. In a recent study, the latter acceleration has even been hailed as a 'growth miracle'.[3] Some caution is advisable in the adoption of this approach to the study of growth in India. It is indeed true that India's rate of growth since 2003–4 has been very high, placing it at the very top of an international league-table for growth. However, a longer viewing of the data yields evidence of other equally interesting episodes to the growth economist. For instance, we can now assert with confidence that the dominant break in the gross domestic product (GDP) series for India actually occurs mid-twentieth century,[4] in the sense that the acceleration of growth in the 1950s dwarfs all subsequent accelerations. That moment now presents itself to the growth economist as a most significant one in India's economic history, and an explanation of that transition must figure prominently in a study of economic growth in this country for it to be taken seriously. So, I shall devote some time to this acceleration.

Two other stylized facts require explaining, and have therefore been placed centrally on the agenda here. These are the by now widely acknowledged acceleration *circa* 1980 and the gradual acceleration of growth following the policy reforms commencing 1991. Methodologically, these two histories can be explained within the framework for analysing growth and development foregrounded early on in this study. To run ahead a little, our investigation reveals at least one of the factors underlying faster growth in the 1980s to be absent from the scene after 1991. That factor is a buoyant agriculture.

The phases of growth referred to earlier have been identified through an econometric estimation of breaks in GDP growth and tests for their statistical significance. The methodology and the assumptions underlying its implementation are outlined in the Appendix. Familiarity with its strengths and weaknesses is strongly recommended for a better appreciation of this study. For now, however, it need only be emphasized that this methodology of estimation and testing for multiple structural breaks in a time series, due to Bai and Perron (1998), is notable for excluding the researchers' priors on the timing of the break. It was first applied in my joint work with M. Parameswaran[5] to identify growth regimes in India, and has now been applied to a longer sample in this book. Though the Bai–Perron method is not without its limitations, it is arguably the approach most suited to the problem of delineating the phases of growth in the economy. Nevertheless, it is advisable to treat the results as indicative rather than definitive.

Figure 1 plots the time series of (the logarithm of) GDP since the year 1900 with the quadrant space having been partitioned according to the results of the econometric exercise referred to earlier. The length of the time series enables a view longer than usually allowed for in studies of growth in India. This graph may be seen as setting the minimum agenda for an investigation of growth in the country. The three main phases of growth that are on view are the striking reversal of the early 1950s, and accelerations at shortening intervals thereafter.[6] A longer view of Indian economic growth needs to be alert to this pacing of the economy and not see the high growth of the twenty-first century in isolation.

While I have already stated what this study is about, it may help to expand upon the statement. Essentially, drawing upon the distinction in philosophy between descriptive and normative analysis, this one falls squarely within the former type. It is mostly an account of how things are, or 'were' when we deal with history. There are, of course, passages where I devote attention to some major lapses in policy. However, even as I believe that some fundamental lapses in Indian economic policy, avoiding which could have altered in a major way the course of the economy, are identified this book is not mainly about these lapses. It is, on the other hand, an attempt to both understand the past and to reflect upon the likely future of growth in India by identifying what in a global

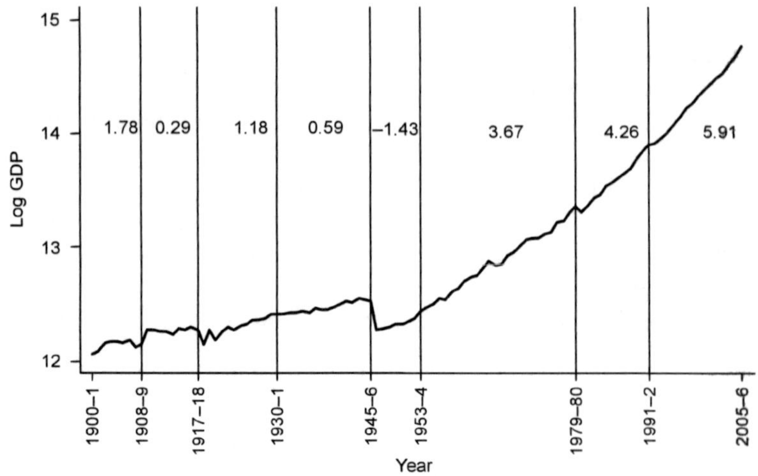

Figure 1 Economic Growth in India, 1900–1 to 2005–6

comparison is missing in its economy. It is not a book about how things could have been. There is a reason for this choice of emphasis, which is that even as I pursue the history of growth in India I remain interested in making sense of the body of economic literature that may be referred to as 'thinking about growth'.[7]

Lately this has included more than just the theoretical growth models of academic economists. It includes, very significantly, the ideas held by global multilateral institutions ranging from the Bretton Woods bodies to the UN agencies. As these bodies have access to unprecedented funding, they have not been constrained by commercial considerations. Their ideas[8] about the structuring of economies in general and about growth in particular hold a significant sway over the destinies of the poor countries of the world, not to mention the worldview of academic economists. It is fully evident by now that the policies that have emanated from the activity of these international bodies are not always optimal. As we come to grips with the history of growth in a market economy of sub-continental proportions which is also a democracy, as is India, we are in a position to evaluate the policy pronouncements of these agencies and the predictions from the theoretical models of growth which have enjoyed somewhat of a renaissance since the mid-1980s.

A better understanding of the past also helps us evaluate the extant evaluations of economic policy in India. An example should help here. Two highly influential and independently-made critiques of India's economic policy over the long haul are that it neglected foreign trade and that no radical redistribution of land was attempted. The reconstruction of the past in this study—of the conditions prevailing in the world economy in the 1950s and the recent history of agricultural growth in India, respectively—enables us to make sense of these critiques. It may as well be stated that I find these grand critiques of Indian economic policy as lacking in empirical foundations. The purpose of this study is to try and unearth the foundations of economic growth in India so that a stronger critique of economic policy may be mounted. Precisely because this study is about how things actually were in the past, it offers a natural beginning for visualizing how things ought to be for a better tomorrow, albeit in the specific sense of a growth that is sustained and broad-based. Towards that end, this study aims to uncover the mechanics of growth in India.

Finally, politics. Politics has undoubtedly influenced the course of economic growth in the country. To state this should come as no surprise as it is widely believed in this country that political considerations have stymied India's economic development. Some of this belief is correct in its assessment. However, it is also true that politics—in the sense of actions chosen deliberately by government—is responsible for some of the achievements with respect to growth in India. This does not imply, however, that economic policy could not have been better structured by far or that the course correction needed should not have been applied much earlier than it was, both of which must be treated as major lapses in a democracy. Far from having been inevitable, these failures reflect the influence of special interests and the tendency of governments to seek short-term political advantage over long-term economic growth when catering to them. While the thrust of the explanation in this study must *per force* be in terms of economic determinants, an effort has been made to factor-in the role of politics in shaping growth, especially during the interregnum of 1965–91. However, I am aware that in the end this study can yet only aspire to be an economic rather than a fully political account of growth in India.

Our Conclusions and Their Significance

For the purpose of this study of the history of and prospects for growth in India, the following three-way partitioning of time has been adopted, namely, 1950–64, 1965–91, and after 1991. This is founded partly on the policy regime prevailing and partly on the political configuration as both these evolved. The bearing of the latter on the economy is considerable in a democracy, a feature often overlooked in studies of economic growth in India. Thus, the choice for separate study of the first period is based not only on the radically new economic policy regime that was instituted in 1950 but also on the political consideration that the Indian state then was more autonomous than it has been since.

Following from this, the choice of the period 1965–91 for separate study is defensible on the ground that while the policy regime remained more or less unchanged, the nature of politics in India underwent an almost tectonic shift after the exit of Jawaharlal Nehru. The Congress Party was first to split and then to decline, gradually making way for government by a coalition of parties, with a direct implication for economic policy and thus growth. At the same time, powerful new actors arrived on the scene with a determination to shift economic policy in their favour. The main casualty was the public sector which rapidly lost its mandate for performance, and therefore its resource-mobilizing capacity, with an immediate consequence for public investment. This was to delay the acceleration which would now finally come only in the late 1970s, actually following a revival of public investment. So while the policy regime as observed by economists, say the control of private investment and closure to trade, may not have altered at all, the politics did change, and in an economy in which public investment was a force for growth, its constriction was inevitably to slow things down. For this reason the period 1965–91 has been hived-off for separate study here.

The period 1965–91 is also marked by a series of exogenous supply shocks of a kind not witnessed before, or since. These had ranged from droughts to oil-price shocks, requiring hitherto unanticipated responses in the form of adjustment policies. Overall, at least in its early days, the period saw an approach to economic management that favoured more controls and more stringent, and often arbitrary, application of the regulatory apparatus. If this period had been marked by a shift in the political regime compared to the Nehru era, by comparison with it, the period after 1991 is marked more by a shift in the economic-policy regime than in the political. And, while not as wide-ranging as often made out, in the areas of actual change, namely, the trade and industrial policy regimes, the shift has been markedly in the direction of liberalization.

Though our periodization, as outlined earlier, is compatible with the demands of the history of growth to be explained, that is, each period must contain one of the three growth transitions post-Independence indicated in Figure 1, the narrative for the period since 1991 has been approached a little differently from those for the previous two. There I have mainly focused on the foundations for accelerated growth in the *future*. This has been motivated by the judgement that the history of growth in India since 1991 is both so recent as to be easily recalled and that it has been quite heavily documented anyway. On the other hand, there have been less of serious evaluations of its prospects, particularly following the onset of high growth from 2003–4. The strategy pursued in trying to formulate the immediate future of growth in India is the following. First, I have drawn upon the cross-country record to establish the main factors associated with the growth of nations over long periods. Then, I have appraised the extent of their presence in India today. From this exercise, the factors essential for a sustained acceleration of growth are identified.

The main body of this volume has been arranged in four chapters. Here, as if in a preview, I discuss briefly their contents and the conclusions, conveying the significance of the latter. The two parts of Chapter 1 provide a critical exposition of some prominent theoretical representations of growth and a historical perspective on its drivers, respectively. Among the former, two are taken up, namely, the neo-classical approach based on the idea of a production function and the methodology of 'growth accounting' which derives from it, and the one based on the idea of growth as endogenous cumulative change.[9] It is argued that growth accounting is not only a non-starter as an explanation—for an explanation is more than accounting—but also potentially misleading as it is based on some questionable assumptions. Thus we find no reason to revise Moses Abramovitz's early assessment of the output of growth accounting—the estimated total factor productivity (TFP)—as no more than 'a measure of our ignorance' (Abramovitz 1956). Moreover, the discovery by Alwyn Young (1995) of very low TFP growth in the fast-growing economies of East Asia clearly suggests that TFP may not even be a driver of growth anyway, as economists have made it out to be. The continued attempt to 'explain' growth using growth accounting really amounts to the proverbial search under the lamp post for the key that a late-night reveller could have dropped anywhere on the street. And these considerations are even prior to the implications of the Cambridge Critique[10] of the aggregate production function, the pillar of the neo-classical approach to growth upon which the practice of economy-wide growth accounting rests.

The vision of growth through 'circular and cumulative causation' in a market economy is taken up next. In this representation, growth in the system is seen as being, at the same time, an impulse to further growth and a response to the impulse. This makes for a circular causation. When increasing returns, originally imagined by Young (1928) as due to specialization but later taken by Kaldor (1966) to mean 'dynamic' economies of scale, are thrown into the mix, both the impulse and the response are greater in each successive round. *Growth begets growth* and increasing returns make for an accelerating growth rate, at least until the process is derailed by exogenous shocks. For this insight alone, the idea of circular and cumulative causation is of value in a study of growth in India, as now the finding of a growth acceleration taking place even as the policy regime is unchanged is no longer a mystery as has been proposed (Rodrik and Subramanian 2005).

The second part of Chapter 1 is an attempt to isolate the main drivers of growth in a cross-country historical comparison. Both an eyeballing of the data assembled and subsequent statistical tests point to a very strong association between the ranking of countries in our sample when using GDP and their ranking according to investment or agricultural growth. For educational attainment, however, the rank correlation test turned in a statistically insignificant association. However, this does not lead us to reject a role for education. First, we may not be correlating growth with the appropriate measure of education in the context. And second, the global evidence on the presence of strong educational foundations in countries of varying histories united in having high incomes is far too strong to overlook.

Guided by our evaluation of the alternative representations of growth in theory and understanding gained of the drivers of growth in history, we embark on a growth narrative for India since 1950. The period is studied in the three phases outlined in the previous section, the rationale for which has been set out there.

The principal conclusion in Chapter 2, where the period 1950–64 is studied, is that it is the public policy pursued in the Nehru era that contributed to the recovery of the Indian economy after half a century of stagnation under British Raj. This was a period of unprecedented growth. An explanation of this is provided by drawing a parallel between the Nehru–Mahalanobis Strategy and the Big Push of development economics. In an evaluation of the Strategy itself, it is pointed out that a more or less similar strategy was pursued in East Asia, except that the state in India was not up to the task of disciplining either private capital or organized labour, including the employees of the public sector. On the other hand, this task had been performed, with some panache, by the repressive regimes to the east of India.[11] The positive evaluation of public policy in the Nehru era, at least as far as growth is concerned, is likely to assume piquancy only for academic economists. Economic historians have shown a greater awareness of the significance for the future of the Indian economy of the public policy of this period [12] In my evaluation of the Nehru–Mahalanobis Strategy I argue that critics may have overstated the closure to imports as a source of weakness and understated the long-term debilitating consequences of the failure to have built human capital, in the first instance via the rapid spreading of primary education. It is this that distinguishes the Indian economic strategy over the long term from that pursued in East Asia. Actually, by the late 1950s the Indian state had even tried its hand at export promotion, though perhaps half-heartedly. However, primary education appears to have received no more than lip-service. This has been missed in critiques of the Indian economic strategy delivered from both the left and the right of the political spectrum.

In Chapter 3, I study the period 1965–91. As mentioned already, what is distinctive about this period is that while the policy regime had remained more or less unchanged, the rate of growth of the economy accelerated. This has intrigued those economists who had harboured the belief that faster growth is a function of a more liberal policy regime. Such a prior is a reflection of an ahistorical approach to the economy. An economist aware of the growth transition of 1950s would not have committed the mistake of looking for a liberalization episode to understand the growth acceleration circa 1980. My own explanation is in terms of the wider impact of the Green Revolution. Initiated with renewed vigour in the mid-1960s, this intervention not only raised permanently the rate of growth of agriculture, notably food production, but via forward and backward linkages energized the rest of the economy. This account is found to be valid in an econometric investigation of inter-sectoral growth relations prior to and inclusive of the transition date.

To take another approach to the transition *circa* 1980, if we are prepared to look at the three decades from 1950 as a whole, then we can imagine a 'circular and cumulative causation' at work whereby the growth dynamic set off in the early 1950s begat the growth acceleration that was to follow. However, the Green Revolution stands out as an intervention exogenous to this quite plausible aspect of an ongoing growth process and needs to be recognized as an independent force making for the acceleration of the economy-wide growth rate later on. Though the foundations for raising the rate of growth of agriculture were laid in the 1950s, a significant intervention had taken place in the mid-1960s. The politics of this episode are at least as interesting as the economics and are outlined briefly in the chapter. The significance of our explanation of the growth acceleration circa 1980 is that it trumps stories of a growth resurgence due to attitudinal shifts, whether on the part of the government or of the private sector, a line of argument that has been put forward to account for the event.[13] The title of the chapter itself—'Second Wind, 1965–91'—has been chosen to make explicit the feature of long-term growth in India that the transition that occurred during the period 1965–91 was only the second since 1947, the first having taken place in the early 1950s. By this stage of the book the reader should have got the message that, discrediting claims to the contrary, planned economic development has contributed to the growth of the economy and its acceleration. This is far from arguing that the outcome was optimal. However, the positive portrayal of the contribution of planning in India should equip the reader to at least make up her own mind on the question of what was missing in the Nehru–Mahalanobis Strategy, and thus to separate the wheat from the chaff in critiques of economic policy in this country.

Finally, with Chapter 4 we come closer to the time and place in which we live, that is, India since 1991. I commence with a brief statement on the nature of the economic reforms initiated in that year and after. I then sift through the arguments of political scientists regarding the politics of these reforms. These are of value in that the political scientists often display greater acuity in their characterization of the reforms than the economists who, perhaps by focusing on the details of the policy changes, tend to miss the big picture. I conclude that the guiding principle of the reforms of 1991 was to integrate the Indian economy with the rest of the world. The decisiveness of the move in this direction sets it apart from any of the other liberalization episodes starting from the mid-1960s. As far as its impact on growth is concerned, the success of this strategy would depend upon the validity of its premise that growth in India is constrained by lack of interaction with the rest of the world, largely via trade but also via capital and technology transfer. Next, I evaluate the evidence for an acceleration of growth after 1991 on the basis of the econometric investigation in this study. Two findings emerge. First, there is evidence of faster growth but an acceleration is detected only when the high-growth phase from 2003–4 is included. Second, at around 6 per cent, the average annual compound rate of growth of the Indian economy over 1991–2006 is less than per capita growth of GDP in Korea over 1965–96.[14] More pertinently, it is below the double-digit growth rate considered necessary by Prime Minister Manmohan Singh to eradicate poverty in India.[15] The obvious question that arises out of this then is why the growth acceleration anticipated to follow the reforms of 1991 has been so slow in coming. The rest of the chapter may be treated as an answer to this question while at the same time proposing what is needed to permanently raise the growth rate to the levels aspired to by the Indian leadership.

As I see it, the central contribution of this study to the discourse on growth in India is that policy regimes, alternatively dubbed 'socialist' and 'liberal', have been less directly relevant for growth transitions than the specific interventions that have been made from time to time. At the academic level far too much effort has been expended to account for the transition of *circa* 1980 by identifying a liberalizing shift in policy or at least in attitude on the part of government. Outside academia in the 1950s much time was spent in debating the merits of socialism versus capitalism when what the economy had most needed was a focus on building human capital and improving the delivery of public systems, without either of which even the most perfectly joined policy regime itself would be rendered quite irrelevant. The most cursory engagement with the histories of developing economies of today such as India and the recently developed such as those of East Asia strongly suggests that it is the growth of production of food per capita and the spread of basic education that distinguishes them.[16]

The rest of Chapter 4 is devoted to an investigation of the constraints on accelerating agricultural growth and the general state of educational preparedness for faster overall growth in India. A difference in methods adopted between these two investigations may be noted. The constraints on agricultural growth are attempted to be isolated by a study of the actual performance of agriculture since 1991. The approach also enables us to evaluate the sufficiency of the reforms for the task of accelerating agricultural growth. On the other hand, when it comes to the question of educational preparedness, my method is mainly to investigate the provision for education in India in relation to the rest of the world, especially the more developed. However, a look has also been taken at outcome indicators such as quality, though the necessary evaluation of this usually ignored aspect of education is constrained by the availability of data.

The principal conclusion of this chapter is that 'more reforms', taken to mean expanding the reach of markets, are by themselves likely to be insufficient for accelerating permanently the rate of growth of the Indian economy. A far stronger agricultural and human capital base would be necessary for that. In the attainment of these foundations the financial capacity of the government may no longer be the binding constraint. That constraint, our analysis suggests, is governance, being in this instance the ability to enforce the performance required to ensure that the public intervention works as intended. This is demonstrated by the use of two examples. First, I present data from the recent history of irrigation, identified by researchers as fundamental to faster agricultural growth. Specifically, a near doubling of real expenditure on irrigation since the late 1990s is shown to co-exist with stagnation in the area irrigated. Next, I refer to the experience from the sphere of education, where, we have reason to believe, the very substantial expansion of expenditure on primary education in recent years has yet not resulted in better learning outcomes. A rise in the tax-to-GDP ratio has contributed to a reversal of fortunes, as it were, with the central government now witnessing an accretion of current revenues unimaginable even in the recent past. As stated, finances—including in the specific form of foreign exchange—no longer constrain the state in India. Arguably, however, a wage-goods constraint may not have been eliminated. While food availability is by now less pressing in quantitative terms, India has not been able to lower the real price of food, an important ingredient of growth as witnessed across countries over time. India's challenges in the fields of agriculture and education indicate that everyday governance continues to elude her even as democracy in the form of periodic elections thrives.

The book ends with a brief consideration of the issue of inclusive growth. This issue takes on importance due to the centrality it has assumed in the political discourse on the economy recently. As the discourse itself is marked by a certain lack of clarity on what is meant by inclusive growth, I start by proposing two criteria according to which it may be identified. I then argue that satisfaction of these two criteria would in turn require faster agricultural growth than we have had since 1991 and superior educational preparedness of the population than is the case presently, especially in rural India. As I had in Chapter 4 also proposed these as the conditions for faster growth, I conclude that inclusion and growth go together. Indeed, as one cannot be sustained without the other, we must view with some concern the privileging of welfare programmes over the creation of public assets that is increasingly marking out economic policy in India today.

NOTES

1. See Scott (1997).
2. See Maddison (1995).
3. See the 'Introduction' by the editors in Bhagwati and Calomiris (2008).
4. Originally demonstrated by Hatekar and Dongre (2005), and replicated in this study.
5. See Balakrishnan and Parameswaran (2007).
6. The numbers in Figure 1 refer to the trend rate of growth for each phase.
7. See Abramovitz (1989).
8. See, for instance, World Bank (2008).
9. Not to be mistaken for the more recent 'endogenous growth theory'.
10. See Harcourt (1972).
11. See Kohli (2004) for a discussion with reference to the literature on growth in East Asia.
12. See Sivasubramonian (2000).
13. See Rodrik and Subramanian (2005).
14. The year 2005–6 was the last date for which final estimates of GDP were available when this volume went to press. The average rate of growth of the Indian economy is higher when the sample is extended up to 2008 using provisional data. However, it must be borne in mind that for two years following 2008, the growth rate has declined due to the global recession. See Chapter 4 for a full discussion of the growth of the economy since 1991 and Table 1.4 for evidence on long-term growth in Korea. The reference to Korea itself is motivated by the indication that the Indian leadership set itself East Asian targets for growth (see Planning Commission 2006).
15. See Singh, M. (2008).
16. See Chapter 1: Table 1.4.

1 Understanding Economic Growth

Progress is not and cannot be continuous. The next important step forward is often initially costly, and cannot be undertaken until a certain quantum of prospective advantages are accumulated.

—**Allyn Young (1928)**

The claim of an economic phenomenon understood is necessarily circumscribed by the framework of analysis. Often, this framework is not even made explicit, there having been merely an application to the data of some methodological tool or the other without due concern for its relevance. This is a practice also encountered in the field of empirical growth studies. Naturally, we would wish to avoid this in our study. At a minimum this would require of us the adoption of a credible and capacious analytical framework and methods that do not yield misleading conclusions. With this in view, this chapter first appraises some leading representations of growth in economic theory. Next it turns to the empirics of growth with a view to extracting from some cross-country historical data an idea of its main drivers.

Representations of Growth

The Production Function and Growth Accounting

The production function is a construct with a substantial presence in modern macroeconomic theory and, consequently, in empirical studies of growth. It specifies the maximum production feasible from the application of current inputs and is commonly stated in equation form as

$Y = AF(K, L)$. In an economy-wide conception, Y would stand for domestic output, K for the aggregate capital stock, L for the total employment, and A for a scale factor measuring the efficiency of conversion of the combined inputs into output. A is conventionally referred to as total factor productivity (TFP).

Growth accounting is an application to the time-series data on output and input growth of the idea of economic activity as represented by the production function. Being a method widely used in empirical analysis of growth today, it is appropriate to make sense of it, as it would be a candidate for application in any prospective study of growth in India. Growth accounting claims to decompose an observed growth in output into the contributions due to the increase in inputs and that due to the change in the efficiency with which they are used, respectively. While the idea underlying growth accounting[1] is intuitive enough, its implementation has required resort to some highly simplifying assumptions. This becomes fully apparent in the mathematical exposition due to Solow (1957). Solow had commenced with an economy-wide, or 'aggregate', production function displaying constant returns to scale and Hicks-neutral technical change, of the form

$$Y = AF(K, L) \tag{1.1}$$

where A is the Hicksian efficiency parameter, changes in which are taken to represent technical progress. Solow's solution had proceeded as follows: total differentiation of the logarithm of 1.1 with respect to time yields

$$\frac{\dot{Y}}{Y} = \frac{\delta F}{\delta K}\frac{K}{Y} \cdot \frac{\dot{K}}{K} + \frac{\delta F}{\delta L}\frac{L}{Y} \cdot \frac{\dot{L}}{L} + \frac{\dot{A}}{A} \tag{1.2}$$

where the dot over the variable denotes its time derivative. In 1.2 the rate of growth of output is written as the sum of the growth rates of capital and labour, both weighted by their respective elasticities, and the rate of change of the Hicksian efficiency parameter. With this, the growth in output is decomposed into the growth in inputs and the contemporaneous growth of TFP.[2] Assuming perfect competition, the real prices of the factors may be substituted for their marginal products and the unobserved elasticities converted into observable factor-income shares s^k and s^l. Now TFP growth, the 'Solow residual', may be written as

$$\frac{\dot{A}}{A} = \frac{\dot{Y}}{Y} - s^k \frac{\dot{K}}{K} - s^l \frac{\dot{L}}{L} \tag{1.3}$$

Under constant returns to scale, when factors are paid their marginal products, the factor shares must sum to one. This facilitates their measurement, the actual practice being to start with the share of labour from the national accounts and treating the residual as the share of capital.

One can see why growth accounting has attracted many economists. It is easy to implement and bears the intuitive message that growth of output is a combination of the increase in inputs and the change in the efficiency with which they are used, termed 'technical change'. However, the considerable elegance of the Solow procedure should not blind us to the fact that the output of growth accounting is no more than a residual and even when it is asserted that it stands for technical change, the representation of technical change is *sui generis*. When technical progress is Hicks-neutral, TFP estimated by growth accounting is potentially equal to the rate of growth of the Hicksian efficiency parameter. The potentiality needs to be stressed, for we can see from the demonstration earlier that as a residual it contains the components due to measurement error, omitted variables, aggregation bias, and model specification. While the content of the residual raises crucial questions of interpretation, I shall focus on the implications for growth accounting of the assumption of the Hicks-neutrality of technical progress. Consider, for a moment, that technical progress is instead factor-augmenting in nature. Accordingly, the production function is now re-specified as

$$Y = F(aK, bL) \tag{1.1'}$$

where a and b are the augmentation factors. Replicating the earlier procedure now yields the following expression for TFP growth:

$$TFPG = s^k \frac{\dot{a}}{a} + s^l \frac{\dot{b}}{b} \tag{1.3'}$$

The residual yet measures the rate of change of TFP, but note that it is now the share-weighted average of the rates of factor augmentation. When the rates of factor augmentation are equal and the shares constant, we are back in the world of Hicks-neutral technical change. When these rates are unequal, we have 'Hicks-biased technical change'; TFPG depends on the factor shares and the rates of factor augmentation. It implies that a change in the factor shares can lead to a change in TFPG even when the underlying rates of technical progress are unchanged. It only reinforces the basic point that productivity growth is not the same as technical change. Clearly, sustaining the interpretation of the growth of TFP as technical change is dependent upon the assumption of Hicks neutrality.[3]

In a problem generic to the production of knowledge, growth accounting too is vulnerable to its results being shaped by the method employed. As was pointed out by Nelson (1973), the attractiveness of growth accounting derives from the feature that it can ostensibly be implemented without prior knowledge of the underlying technology. However, as he was to demonstrate, the form of the production function and the nature of technical change crucially impinge upon the decomposition of output growth into the contributions of input accumulation and technical change. Two alternative combinations were considered, namely, a Cobb–Douglas production function—implying elasticity of substitution of one—with Hicks-neutral technical change and a production function of elasticity less than one combined with capital-using technical change. It is intuitive that for equivalent increase in the capital-intensity the contribution of technical change to an observed unit increase in output would be lower in the latter case. As Nelson's demonstration was graphic, it is not reproduced here, but we can see that its implications are far-reaching. Growth accounting undertaken without ascertaining the form of the production function underlying the data can be misleading. This is almost never done in practice, the default mode being to work with a Cobb–Douglas production function assuming Hicks-neutral technical progress. We can now see the 'fundamental arbitrariness' (Nelson 1973: 462) of the techniques that have been employed to distinguish between factor accumulation and technical change in empirical analyses based on growth accounting.

Once the importance of knowing in advance the form of the technology is acknowledged, the question of the very existence of an aggregate production function cannot be far behind. Intensely debated in the 1960s by the profession's leading theorists, the matter had been resolved when Fisher (1969)[4] demonstrated that the aggregate production function exists only under some very restrictive assumptions, notably that the micro production units in the economy—that is, plants, firms, and industries—all have production functions that are identical up to some constant multiplier. In the context, to paraphrase Hulten (2000: 15), if the aggregation conditions fail, the meaning of the term A in equation (1.1) is ambiguous.

Finally, there is yet another assumption regarding technical change that is implicit in the Solow solution which appears to be the preferred form of growth accounting. This is the assumption of costless technical progress, aptly described as descending upon earth like 'manna from heaven'. When the development of technology is paid for, it must be entered on the right hand side of the growth accountant's equation. I shall postpone the implication of this requirement till I have first discussed the results of some applications of growth accounting.

Calculating TFP growth using some version of the simple formula in equation (1.3) has kept economists busy for the past half century. However, the outcome has not always squared with our intuition. The earliest applications of this methodology, which were to growth over the long term in the United States, had invariably yielded a bewildering result. In almost all of these studies it was found that only a small fraction of the output growth could be attributed to input growth, with the overwhelming portion left unaccounted for. For this reason the remainder was appropriately termed the 'residual'. Over time, it may have taken on the more respectable title of 'total factor productivity', but this would hardly alleviate doubts regarding its pedigree.

Abramovitz (1989) has pointed out that the earliest growth accountants were less sanguine about the residual and were more than aware that this component as estimated must include the contribution of elements that may have gone unmeasured. The more obvious ones among these were recognized to be:

1. The growth of human capital: the accumulation of human capital tends to raise the effectiveness of labour exactly as physical capital does;

2. Economies of scale: one way of seeing this in context is in terms of the Smithian notion that 'the division of labour is limited by the extent of the market'. Now output per unit input, which we term TFP, will *ceteris paribus* show an increase along with the volume of production; and

3. Organizational improvement: we can conceive of this as superior resource allocation due to better management of resources, including time.

Abramovitz had raised two other issues. Generally, enhancing the productiveness of factors and the introduction of superior management practices involves expenditure. Hence it is easy to see that explicit accounting for this expenditure would lower the value of the residual. Further, as the value of TFP thrown up by growth accounting is merely the difference in the measured growth rates of output and of total factor input, any errors in the measurement of the data would be incorporated into the residual. Perhaps it is for this reason that at the moment of its emergence into the literature on empirical growth analysis, Abramovitz (1956) had cannily dubbed it as 'some sort of measure of our ignorance about the causes of economic growth'.

To appreciate more fully the potential of growth accounting as a means to understanding growth, it is instructive to study the results of some representative instances of its application. The best known among these are for the United States and have been surveyed by Abramovitz (1989). In one of them, the 'primitive' residual amounted to a whopping 99 per cent of output growth, implying that measured input growth accounted for only 1 per cent! When adjustments were made for the rising quality of labour and the other factors outlined earlier, as these may be expected to affect output, it had left a much reduced residual but one that yet amounted to 51 per cent of the growth rate. This was treated as the contribution to growth of 'the advance of knowledge'. Note, however, that the attribution made is indirect. This is intrinsic to the practice of growth accounting, leaving the interpretation of TFP thus arrived at always open to the construction that it is no more than a measure of our ignorance.

As in any exercise of measurement in economics, the outcome of growth accounting can vary according to the data used and the definitions adopted for the variables. Some of the issues that invariably arise are the following. Should production be measured net of the allowance for depreciation? An answer to this will determine our measure of the product. *How to deal with obsolescence?* This will influence the measured capital stock. *Do earnings differentials measure the 'quality' of different classes of the factors labour and capital?* On the answer to this question hinges the procedure to be adopted for aggregation of inputs. *How should income earned by proprietors of incorporated firms be divided between labour and capital?* Such a division is necessary for determining the shares of the two main factors of production.

In a review of growth accounting using US data, Abramovitz (1989) has pointed out that alternative definitions of output and capital, in particular, result in greatly differing estimates of the contribution made by capital and TFP, respectively. However, while the recognition that alternative definitions of variables can lead to differing estimates alerts us to the problems encountered in the application of growth accounting, other problems are less easily resolved. These are of two types, once again, those problems related to measurement and those that arise in the interpretation of the growth accounts. I shall here ignore the former set, as they are resolvable in principle, instead moving on to a consideration of the latter aspect alone.

The Implicit Premise of Growth Accounting: Independence of the Sources of Growth

The objective of growth accounting is to measure the proximate sources of the increase in output.[5] Its received interpretation is that whatever may be the underlying causes of growth, 'they act through the sources identified in the accounts with a force that the accounts measure' (Abramovitz 1989: 23). For example, if the measured contribution[6] of the growth in employment is 4 percentage points, growth accounting implies that aggregate output growth would have been 2 percentage points less if employment growth was only half as fast as it actually was. Similarly, if the contribution assigned to 'the advance of knowledge' is 2 percentage points, according to the principle of growth accounting, output growth would have been 2 percentage points lower had technology not progressed at all. We can see in these interpretations the maintained hypothesis that the sources of growth, namely, factor input growth and the advance of knowledge, act independently of one another, thus enabling the extraction of their individual contributions. This is a questionable assumption, as it would be more natural to imagine the sources of growth feeding off one another. For instance, viewing the advance of knowledge as technical progress, we can easily visualize an interaction between technical progress, capital accumulation, and the growth of human capital via education and training. Though, as suggested here, each of these sources is likely to interact with each of the other two, we confine possibilities only to the interaction of technical progress with the accumulation of each of physical and human capital. An understanding of these interactions will serve not only to evaluate the implicit premise of growth accounting but also to further our understanding of how growth progresses.

Technical Progress and Capital Accumulation

An interaction between technical progress and capital accumulation may well be imagined. Consider first the impulses that run from capital accumulation to technical progress. While advances in knowledge can improve work organization and managerial quality, showing up as a rise in the residual of growth accounting, at least some of the advance can be incorporated into production only via new capital equipment. This is the case of 'embodied' technical progress. In this case, a quickening of capital accumulation allows for a faster incorporation of the advance of knowledge. Embodied technical progress implies that the rate of growth of the capital stock would be binding, in that it determines the extent of technical progress. Consider, for instance, a motivation for fresh investment to take advantage of emerging potential economies of scale. This usually requires larger, and perhaps more specialized, firms. Here the pace of technical progress is dependent upon the rate of capital accumulation. Significantly, the rate of capital accumulation need not only determine the rate of technical progress but it can actually be part of the process of acquiring new knowledge. Arrow's model of 'learning by doing' envisaged a lower unit cost of production as capital accumulates (Arrow 1962). Another instance arises from the relation between research and development (R&D) and the size of the market. The incentive for investing in R&D, say for improving a product, depends upon the size of the market for it. In the case of capital goods, the size of the market for its product is determined by the economy-wide level of investment. Now the rate of growth of capital accumulation fully drives the rate of growth of technical advance. But this relationship is by no means one-sided.

Technical progress can both influence the growth of the capital stock and determine the contribution of capital to output. After all, the anticipated returns to an investment depend upon the efficiency of production and the ability to offer better products to consumers. It is easy to imagine that technical progress may influence both these outcomes, with capital accumulation and the returns to capital depending upon technical progress. This view is strengthened by inference from historical experience. In the US economy, which remains the most studied in the context, the rate of expansion of the capital stock has far exceeded that of employment, resulting in a rising capital–labour ratio. Standard economic reasoning would lead us to expect a consequent lowering of the return to capital, in turn bringing capital accumulation to a halt. That this has not happened renders plausible the inference that continuous technical progress has enabled investment to be effective in lowering the cost of production continuously, thus sustaining the contribution of capital to growth. Clearly in this episode technical progress has been 'capital using', driving the demand for capital relative to labour. And we would be right to presume that capital accumulation has been supported by technical progress even if not fully determined by it.

Technical Progress, Education, and Human Capital

As with physical capital accumulation, there is an interaction between technical progress and the accumulation of human capital too. This is best understood by taking the specific case of the expansion of education which is entered as a separate input in some growth accounting exercises.

The level of education in a country determines the pace at which advances in knowledge can be commercially exploited. This is so whether we consider scientific, technical, and other forms of professional training such as managerial or just plain schooling in the '3 Rs'—reading, writing, and arithmetic. The first three matter for technical progress at the frontier as well as when it comes to acquiring and exploiting technology already in use elsewhere. Firms seeking to borrow technology must have the capability to first recognize its potential, to appraise its commercial value, and to then adapt it to their own conditions. As new technology and products require setting up new firms, reorganizing and relocating old ones, designing facilities, training workers, implementing a marketing strategy, and activating a supply chain, the acquisition of new technology depends upon the availability of professionals other than scientists. The required competencies encompass engineering, managerial, administrative, legal, and accounting skills. At the production end are required appropriate capabilities of workers, mainly manual, so that they are able to respond to the demands of new technology. Schooling is a minimum requirement here. It is difficult to imagine the operation of advanced capital equipment if the workers are not acquainted with basic mathematics, for instance. Further, on-the-job training is crucial to the application of new technology as it becomes commercially viable. So, we have good reason to believe that education and human capital accumulation drive technical progress.

As with physical capital accumulation, there is also an impulse running from technical progress to the accumulation of human capital in an economy. Technical progress raises the premium on education and thus governs the growth of education via the demand for it. Firms value personnel with technical and general education for the qualities with which such an education endows them. The demand for educated workers rises in a growing economy. Thus, even if technical progress affects growth directly, it would, very likely with a lag, also affect it indirectly by raising the skill level of the workforce. The rising demand for engineering education in India following the emergence of information technology is a clear instance of technical progress driving the acquisition of skills, thus determining the 'effective', that is, education-weighted, labour input.

The Implication of Interdependence among the Sources of Growth

The existence of a mutual feedback between the progress of technology and the growth of factor inputs points to the limitation of growth accounting as a method. It can no longer be claimed that its application identifies the putatively independent sources of growth if the accumulation of the inputs and the progress of technology actually interact. When they influence each other, it is only appropriate to hold that they make joint rather than separate contributions. Now the standard interpretation of the results of growth accounting would be misleading. This has been stated quite precisely by Abramovitz as follows: '[T]he contribution of any one of these sources, as this is measured in the accounts, may be too small because it does not give adequate weight to its effect in generating the contributions of the others. Or it may be too large because it makes no allowance for the effect of the others in supporting its own' (1989: 28).

All in all, it appears then that we would be justified in entertaining a healthy scepticism regarding the value of growth accounting. While definitional and measurement issues abound, the scepticism is addressed to more than merely the problem of quantification. It relates to the interpretation of the 'accounts' and impinges upon the use of growth accounting as a means to understanding growth. This has long been known. A particularly strong statement on the underlying premise of the methodology had come from Kaldor. Recall that Solow (1957) had demonstrated that, under certain conditions, output growth could be decomposed into factor input growth and an exogenous technical progress. Graphically, his method may be described in terms of its capacity to distinguish the shift in the production function from a movement along it. However, within a year of the publication of Solow's result, Kaldor (1958 [1961]: 207) had observed that:

> [T]he rate of shift of the production function due to the changing state of 'knowledge' cannot be treated as an independent function of (chronological) time, but depends on the rate of accumulation of capital itself. Since improved knowledge is largely, if not entirely, infused into the economy through the introduction of new equipment, the rate of shift to the curve will itself depend upon the *speed of movement* along the curve, which makes any attempt to isolate the one from the other the more nonsensical. (emphasis original)

The arbitrariness of the procedure whereby growth is decomposed into movement along the production function and the shift in the function itself is best described in the language of the post-modernist thinkers as bereft of a 'meta narrative'.

I now return to the treatment of technical progress in growth accounting. As flagged, growth accounting is usually undertaken assuming that technical progress is costless. We know, however, that this is far from correct. Most advances in knowledge have to be compensated. When this is accounted for explicitly, part of the return to innovation reimburses development expenditure and must show up as an offsetting input cost in the growth accountant's equation. Now, it could be that very low TFP growth is observed. However, it would hardly do to conclude that the future of growth is in doubt as technical progress is dying out. We are now able to make sense of the observation by Lipsey and Carlaw (2004: 1142) that 'It is conceptually possible, therefore, to have sustained, technologically driven, economic growth with zero changes in TFP'. On the use of growth accounting for understanding growth in various contexts, the authors caution against the use of TFP measures to support assertions that range from the non-arrival of the 'New Economy' based on Information and Communication Technology to the lack of technological dynamism at the time of the First Industrial Revolution and the precarious future[7] of growth among the East Asian Tigers. On the value of TFP as a route to understanding growth, an early warning signal had been set off by Schultz (1970), who had observed

What is the economic meaning of an index of productivity? Leave aside any particular factor productivity indexes, that is for land or labor, and consider only an index of the productivity of total inputs used by a sector, or the economy as a whole. Suppose such a sectoral index shows a gain in agricultural productivity between two periods, namely, that measured output increases more than the measured aggregate of inputs, what economic inferences are permissible from these measurements? The implication would seem to be that the economic value of the output has increased more than the economic value of the inputs over such a period. If so, to farmer-entrepreneurs in the second period would presumably accrue a windfall gain relative to the profitability of farming in the first period. Suppose, however, that the agricultural sector were in equilibrium in each of these two periods and that profits were normal and identical, the economic value of the output in each period would be equal to the value of the productive services of the inputs plus normal profits during each of the two periods. In this sense, an index of total factor (inputs) productivity is an anomaly; it is inconsistent with economic theory. Thus, we cannot infer from a gain in productivity which is revealed by such an index that farming has become more profitable, that the value of output exceeds the value of the productive services of the inputs, that the increase in output attributed to the gain in productivity was obtained at no cost or cheaply, or that the investment in achieving the additional outputs was in accordance with priorities set by the relative rates of return. (Schultz 1970: xv–xvii)

Schultz's example may be somewhat artificial but it serves to remind us that the interpretation of TFP, even when it has been properly measured, is a tricky business. Investment decisions of firms are guided by expected profits, and the changing profitability of production would be a better guide for the empirical growth economist. To see this, one need look no further than East Asia where low TFP growth has combined with some of the most dramatic growth rates ever achieved.[8]

The foundational weakness of growth accounting must lead us to look elsewhere for a means to understand the factors driving the growth of an economy. May it then be assumed that the mainstream models of growth from Solow to Romer can be of use? While it is true that these at least remain economic models as opposed to the mere tools, as represented by growth accounting, they remain quite limited in their applicability. The main concern is that they are essentially supply-side models, leaving them alike in this respect, despite the belief that the 'endogenous growth theory' pioneered by Romer (1986) is a major advance.

Recall that in the Solow model, output just courses along the production function, as it were, so long as the savings rate exceeds the sum of the rates of depreciation and population growth. In the steady state, where capital accumulation is just sufficient to offset these demands, leaving capital per worker constant, only faster technical progress can shift the economy onto a higher growth path. This process had been labelled 'exogenous growth' as Solow had left the source of technical progress unspecified. Romer (1990) had endogenized this pivotal variable by resort to profit-maximizing agents motivated by the super-normal profits assured by patents for their inventions. However, the models are similar to the extent that they ignore the demand factor entirely. This can be seen more clearly in the Solow model as he was working with a framework amenable to standard macroeconomic analysis. We find that there all savings are assumed to be automatically invested, the hallmark of pre-Keynesian economics. Romer's model is less amenable to a similar macroeconomic analysis, revolving as it does around an aggregate production function with all the action, so to speak, centred on the technical progress component. Of course, technical progress is endogenized, making for an advance in terms of the canons of theoretical modelling. However, it is not clear by how much the Romer model per se advances our understanding in situations where growth is not entirely driven by technological progress at the frontier. Endogenous growth models have been criticized, of course. In particular, it has been pointed out that they have no role for the institutions of capitalism, including more recognizable firms. However, it is significant that an agenda for growth theory recently drawn up by a leader of the profession does not mention the role of demand.[9]

Outside the spare theoretical models of the phenomenon, growth may be seen as the outcome of a process of both the creation of the capacity to produce and the growth of demand for the product. It is this that gives capital accumulation a special role in the growth process, for as investment takes place it both creates capacity to produce and generates aggregate demand. Further, as we have seen, it is also a conduit for technical progress. This by itself would lead us to assign a special role to investment in the empirical analysis of growth. Empirical approaches to growth have related investment spending to the regime of macroeconomic and microeconomic policies, including those concerning foreign trade and thus wider competition.[10] While physical investment is no doubt important, there is also clearly a role for education which has only relatively recently[11] come into the mainstream analysis of growth.

Education matters not only by making a literate and numerate workforce more productive on the job but also by facilitating the absorption and diffusion of new technology, both effects having been flagged here already. Usually these two functions are distinct. Arguably, education is more important for the latter which requires a continuous adaptation of the agent to change.[12] In growth accounting, education is usually admitted by entering labour in 'effective' units which is a weighted index of the number of workers, the weight assigned to each worker being an increasing function of educational attainment. However, the production function, which is the basis of growth accounting, relates the maximum attainable output to current capital services and the number of workers in routinized jobs. Note that the second of the two functions of education flagged earlier is not taken into account here. For this reason Nelson and Phelps (1966: 75) have suggested that 'the insertion of some index of educational attainment in the production function may constitute a gross misspecification of the relation between education and the dynamics of production'. We need a more nuanced understanding of the contribution of education than is allowed for within the framework of growth accounting.

It tends to get overlooked that the advance of knowledge deeply affects the demand side of the economy. New technology increases output by expanding demand in existing lines of production via cost reduction and by creating the demand for hitherto unimagined products. We can think up many instances of this historically, such as machine-spun cloth, the motor car, plastics, and, more recently, personal computers. Historically, new products which are initially affordable to only a few end up becoming items of mass consumption. Technology both brings forth these goods and continuously contributes to their increasing accessibility via cost reduction. The generic growth model based on a production function cannot help us imagine this process of development of markets which has been the hallmark of growth across countries over centuries. A vision of growth that is alive to the role of demand was already in the work of Smith. Though the view itself was specific to a productivity-enhancing 'division of labour' rather than output growth per se, Smith ultimately privileged demand by asserting that these innovations are 'limited by the extent of the market'. The late Classicals saw the demand constraint as pervasive, and in Malthus's 'theory of gluts' this took on a particularly pessimistic vision. It took over a century for economists to return to a more optimistic view of the future, yet based on demand, as contained in the work of Young, which was to be refined by Myrdal and Kaldor. Before turning to a critical review of this perspective, some concluding remarks on the representation of growth by a production function would be in order.

Even if it is granted that the production function is meant to capture only the *proximate* rather than the *deeper* causes of growth, there is a tautological ring to an explanation of growth based on its use. Internal to its logic, the implied answer to the question 'Why is there growth?' would be 'Because the inputs have grown'. Equally, to the question, 'And why did the inputs grow?' the answer must be 'Because production has increased'. This self-referential element in the explanation of growth intrinsic to reliance on the production function is unsatisfactory. To see this better, note that there are growth models—either in terms of investment or exports—free of such circularity, at least by assumption of exogeneity of the growth drivers. Instances of the use of the production function in empirical growth analysis illustrate the contention by Romer (1996) that ahistorical explanations are more often a test of growth models rather than explanations of growth. Clearly, for an understanding of the mechanisms underlying growth[13] in India we cannot rely on the methodology of growth accounting. In the context, it may also be mentioned that the claim that we have understood the drivers of growth having established from cross-country regressions that the growth of output is explained[14] by differences in TFP is particularly vulnerable once we entertain the claim that the Solow residual is only a measure of our ignorance. Such an explanation is tantamount to acknowledging that we do not know the source of the difference in the growth rate between countries.

We now move to an alternative representation of economic growth.

Growth as Endogenous Cumulative Change

Myrdal had propounded 'the principle of circular and cumulative causation' as more than just an approach to the growth of the economy. He had seen it as a general theory of development and underdevelopment. It does, however, contain a vision of change that has an immediate application to growth. To exposit circularity of causation, Myrdal (1957) had taken recourse to Nurkse's idea of the 'vicious cycle of poverty'. Thus, it is possible to imagine a poor individual not having enough to eat, leaving him/her undernourished. Poor health affects capacity for work, lowering his/her earning power. This leaves him/her poor. The idea of the vicious cycle of poverty extended to the level of the economy was expressed as 'a country is poor because it is poor'. At the time when it was proposed this insight was dismissed as a tautology but this is a mistaken view of the idea of a 'vicious cycle', which was essentially a proposition regarding how a constellation of forces tending to act upon one another could pin down an economic equilibrium.

The circularity of causation has the implication that if a prevailing constellation of forces is shocked, the system may be expected to remain in continuous motion unless shocked again in the opposite direction. To see this, let us go back to our example of poverty. If a positive shock is applied to any link in the chain, the levels of all the constituent forces improve. Consider an improvement in healthcare facilities in a poor country. This may be expected to lead to greater worker productivity. This raises the workers' income, leading them to eat better, improving productivity and aggregate income further. Whether this change is perpetual cannot of course be asserted, and for a variety of reasons. Among these are that tastes and preferences intervene, the labour-supply curve may be 'backward bending', and very likely there are upper bounds on the capacity to work. But we get the message of a circular causation from this example. The circularity also implies that the impact of the initial shock is cumulative, for a shock to the system sets off forces for change that return to drive the source of the original impulse ensuring that at the beginning of the second round the renewed impulse, being the accumulated effect of all preceding changes, is stronger than it was the first time round. Or, to put it differently, the circularity sets up cumulative causation in a process of change, for, an initial impulse 'returns' to move the system with renewed vigour after having been fed through it once already.

Interestingly, Myrdal had thought of his 'principle' as a characteristic of 'social change' in general, first applying it to a study of the condition of African-Americans in the United States of the 1940s. He had divined the following implication of his principle:

> [I]n the normal case, there is no such tendency towards automatic self-stabilisation in the social system. The system is by itself not moving towards any sort of balance between forces, but is constantly on the move away from such a situation. In the normal case a change does not call forth countervailing changes but, instead, supporting changes, which move the system in the same direction as the first change but much further. Because of such circular causation a social process tends to become more cumulative and often gather speed *at an accelerating rate* (Myrdal 1957: 13; emphasis mine).

Four points may be noted about Myrdal's idea of change as applied to growth. First, as far as the economy—as opposed to society—was concerned, Myrdal had used the idea of circular and cumulative causation to account for the growing divergence that could result when economies were integrated through trade, capital flows, and migration. Indeed, it was envisaged, in the event of such an integration, the free flow of market forces could actually spur a cumulative causation downwards in the poorer regions. So, Myrdal thought of his 'principle' as containing the germ of a 'general theory of development and underdevelopment'.

Second, circular and cumulative causation has the implication that once change gets going—for which, of course, a shock to the prevailing arrangement of forces is required—it springs from within the system. Now growth is truly endogenous as 'growth begets growth', so to speak. By comparison, the claim to the endogeneity of growth in the Romer (1990) model is only that the source of growth, that is, technical progress, is accounted for within the model. From this point of view, despite its prestige, New Growth Theory does not offer an original vision of growth.

Third, Myrdal did not claim that change once initiated would be perpetual. In fact, he had visualized secondary effects, again internally generated, that could stymie the movement initiated. I choose not to dwell on this issue here, though the author himself had thought of them as potentially significant. Finally, though Myrdal had allowed for a change to be reversed, he had imagined that the movement would accelerate so long as the momentum lasts. When it came to the cause of the acceleration, though, he was not to specify a uniquely economic mechanism. However, in the discussion of the unequalizing nature of economic development due to the principle of circular and cumulative causation, he did refer to increasing returns.

The possibility of growth once set off accelerating due to increasing returns was central to the vision of growth due to Allyn Young (1928). For the author, increasing returns themselves were related to the division of labour that proceeds apace with the expansion of the market. While acknowledging a debt to Smith, Young took care to also state that by the division of labour he meant something broader in scope than that splitting up of occupations and development of specialized crafts which Adam Smith had had in mind. It is instructive to quote him here:

> It is generally agreed that Adam Smith, when he suggested that the division of labour leads to inventions because workmen engaged in specialised routine operations come to see better ways of accomplishing the same results, missed the main point. The important thing, of course, is that with the division of labour a group of complex processes is transformed into a succession of simpler processes, some of which, at least, lend themselves to the use of machinery. In the use of machinery and the adoption of indirect processes there is a further division of labour, the economies of which are again limited by the extent of the market. It would be wasteful to make a hammer to drive a single nail; it would be better to use whatever awkward implement lies conveniently at hand. It would be wasteful to furnish a factory with an elaborate equipment of specially constructed jigs, gauges, lathes, drills, presses and conveyors to build a hundred automobiles; it would be better to rely mostly upon tools and machines of standard types, so as to make a relatively larger use of directly applied and a relatively smaller use of indirectly-applied labour. Mr. Ford's methods would be absurdly uneconomical if his output were very small, and would be unprofitable even if his output were what many other manufacturers of automobiles would call large (Young 1928: 530).

The division of labour was seen as generating increasing returns via two developments, namely, the growth of indirect or roundabout methods of production and the division of labour across industries, mechanisms that were imagined as being interdependent. The economies of roundabout, or 'capitalistic', methods of production are the principal economies that manifest themselves as increasing returns. Such methods usually require the use of more capital-intensive methods with the specialized tasks now being undertaken using specialized capital equipment, themselves designed to perform only a limited range of functions. In the aforementioned quote Young had shown how the degree of roundaboutness would depend upon the extent of the market. For the division of labour across industries—essentially specialization of production, which was the second source of increasing returns for Young—he had used the expression 'industrial differentiation'. This was seen as occurring in the intermediate and capital goods sectors more than in the market for consumer goods. As a larger market permits the use of specialized intermediate and capital goods, it also promotes the specialized supply of these goods which, being capital intensive, was believed to be subject to significant scale economies. Now we would have specialized intermediate and capital goods that lower the cost or production of final goods, with these also becoming cheaper themselves as the market for these final goods expands. Young had provided a detailed account of this process of specialization across industries with a demonstration from the printing industry with which he was familiar, interestingly enough, having actually worked there.[15]

Two points may be noted before we proceed to Young's view of growth. First, as increasing returns arise from 'industrial differentiation', it is possible to reconcile his vision of growth with competitive markets. The economies being largely external to the firm, increasing returns do not inevitably lead to the concentration of production within a few firms. Second, within the scheme of things, the role of competition is to ensure that the cost reductions that ensue from the productivity improvement due to increasing returns actually accrue to consumers and producers across the economy. Young's vision of growth itself is organized around the idea of growing productivity based on increasing returns arising out of the processes described earlier. The potential for realizing increasing returns is determined by the extent of the market, which Young took care to state is defined by the 'volume of production'.[16] These building blocks are then turned into a story of continuing growth by arguing that increasing returns which depend upon the extent of the market also have the effect of increasing the size of the market itself. Young had expressed the idea succinctly thus: '[T]he division of labour depends upon the extent of the market, but the extent of the market also depends upon the division of labour' (1928: 529). The implication of this interrelationship is that there is a positive feedback among two aspects central to an economy. It led Young to visualize that due to increasing returns, change in an economy, which he termed 'economic progress' but we may as well interpret as growth, 'becomes progressive and propagates itself in a cumulative way' (Ibid.: 533).[17]

Young's view of a virtually boundless growth once the economy was in motion stemmed from a view of economic activity ultimately consisting of the exchange of goods for goods, implying that every increase in the supply of goods enlarges, at least potentially, the market for other commodities. However, something that would ensure that an increase in supply emanating in one part of the economy has a stimulating effect on production in other parts is required. Only if this something is present, can growth be viewed as a continuing process of interaction between demand increases which have been increased by increase in supply and increases in supply which have been evoked by increases in demand. While this is a plausible idea, Young appears to have simply assumed the existence of the necessary and sufficient condition for this to occur. The condition itself was stated as follows: '[T]he demand for each commodity is elastic, in the special sense that a small increase in supply will be attended by an increase in the amounts of other commodities which can be had in exchange for it' (Young 1928: 533–4).

Note that Young's is a somewhat unconventional use of the term 'elasticity of demand'. In an appraisal of Young's view of growth, Kaldor (1972) was to argue that if by this term we mean something that reflects the *elasticity of substitution* in consumption, the increase in the purchasing power of the producers of commodity *a* following upon the increase in its production must have resulted from a diversion of expenditure to commodity *a* from all other commodities. Now the rise in income of the producers of *a* would be matched by a reduction in the income of the producers of other commodities. This is significant, for, the elasticity of demand for each commodity taken individually may be greater than unity but this would be insufficient for a chain reaction of the type envisaged by Young, whereby increased aggregate production is followed by rising demand, followed by increased production, and so on. This, as Kaldor (1972: 1247) had pointed out, requires that: '[T]otal income measured in terms of money is rising as well, which in turn presupposes that total expenditure, and not just expenditure on a particular commodity, rises in response to a rise in production'. We can see that this requires a theory of the determination of income, or *macroeconomics*, which was not available to Young as he was writing before the appearance of the General Theory. Kaldor's solution of the problem of translating increase in aggregate production to an increase in aggregate expenditure is to resort to the mechanism of 'induced investment'. Induced investment takes place as traders add to their stocks when supply exceeds demand and run down these stocks when the reverse situation prevails. A distinction is drawn by Kaldor between the markets for commodities and that of manufactures, but this need not detain us. The point is that induced investment in the form of stock adjustment is the mechanism whereby an increase in production is translated into an increase in income, a necessary condition for Young's vision of the growth process to be plausible.

As Young had only considered a barter economy, and had actually relied on J-B Say's Law of Markets, it meant that he would overlook the peculiarity of a monetary economy which can generate Keynesian aggregate-demand failure. Even Kaldor's ingenious device of imagining induced investment cannot negate this possibility entirely, as potentially fluctuating autonomous investment must be allowed for. However, the idea of growth through cumulative causation originated by Young has relevance to the empirical analysis of growth. First, it alerts us to the idea that growth begets growth. Second, the presence of increasing returns and the interdependence between productivity growth and the growth of the total volume of production—the 'extent of the market'—has a specific implication. As it is the growth of the market that encourages the roundaboutness of production and indivisibilities of investment have to be overcome in the transition to more specialized production, growth is unlikely to proceed in a smooth or linear way. In short, growth takes place in historical—or in today's parlance 'real'—and not the 'logical' time of economic theory. Young had read the implications of his vision most clearly to state: '[P]rogress is not and cannot be continuous. The next important step forward is often initially costly, and cannot be undertaken until a certain quantum of prospective advantages are accumulated' (Young 1928: 535).

Young's vision appears to hold out contradictory implications when considered as a framework for the study of a developing economy. On the one hand, it appears to speak exclusively of a highly industrialized economy in full flight surveying a future of only boundless growth. Where are the structural impediments in the form of the agrarian constraint or absent social and physical infrastructures which can set a limit to the maximum growth that can be attained by an underdeveloped economy? On the other hand, the idea of the discontinuity of growth, the hint of thresholds imposed by indivisibilities of physical investment, and the necessity of accumulating certain advantages before being able to initiate successive rounds of growth are all major insights of immediate relevance to understanding the likely growth path of such an economy. It is in terms of these insights that it can be of use in the study of the history and prospects of growth in India on which we are embarking. But more generally, the vision of growth through cumulative causation developed by Young, Myrdal, and Kaldor is unparalleled in its imaginativeness. As has been noted (see Toner 1999: 29), it achieves a balance by emphasizing both supply and demand factors—privileging neither—focuses on production organization, emphasizes the feature of manufacturing as the one economic activity given to increasing returns, regards technological change as largely endogenous, identifies capital accumulation as a key element in growth, and implies a never-ending search by firms for new markets as the driving force in capitalist economies. Among alternative representations of growth, it holds out the most promise as a framework for the empirical growth analysis on which we are now ready to embark.

We turn next to the empirics of growth with a view to identifying its most prominent drivers as revealed by its global history.

GROWTH IN HISTORY

The Stylized Facts

Growth is typically understood as a quantitative summary of the change that has taken place in an economy over a period. We are so used to dealing exclusively with this index of change that we overlook other conceptions, say, qualitative ones. One such is the 'development' of an economy that accompanies its growth.[18] The history of growth across countries suggests that development as a transformation of the structure of an economy is the key. In this section we try to understand why development thus defined may be necessary for sustained growth.

Over forty years ago, Simon Kuznets had brought to the attention of his fellow economists a stylized fact of what he had characterized as 'modern economic growth'.[19] This fact had to do with the relationship between the growth of per capita income and the structure of the economy. Kuznets observed that long-term growth, especially of the industrialized countries, was associated with a certain structural transformation. The structure in question here is the distribution of activity across an economy, with the activity itself comprising both production and employment. The transformation identified as central was of the composition of output and the distribution of the workforce across sectors of the economy.

Principally, it was observed that rising per capita income is associated with a rising share of non-agricultural activity, that is, industry and services, in national income. A sequence had been noted too. This was that the rising non-agricultural activity would first be concentrated in manufacturing and only later spread to services. The pattern was believed to conform to our idea of 'a hierarchy of needs' with material consumption, and food within it, coming before services. A mature economy would therefore be characterized by a very high share of services in output, followed by industry, with agriculture bringing up the rear by constituting the smallest part of the whole. Some decades after the findings announced by Kuznets, this developmental pattern accompanying growth was identified across a wider range of economies by Chenery and Syrquin (1975).

As non-agricultural activity comes to dominate a growing economy, so it has been observed, does labour shift out of agriculture to support the new activity. This corresponding development has also been confirmed by economists; that is, as per capita income rises, the share of the labour force in agriculture declines sharply, mirroring the changing composition of output, in particular the declining share of agriculture. As growth proceeds, it was noticed, the share of agriculture in both aggregate output and the labour force will become very low indeed. For instance, in the United States in the late 1980s, these shares were both around 2 per cent.[20] The United States was at that time among the richest countries in terms of per capita income. The decline in the share of agriculture in the labour force is strongly captured in Kuznets' work. Having analysed the evidence on the shift of the (male) labour force from agriculture to the rest of the economy based on the estimates of the International Labour Organization (ILO) for seventy-two market economies over the period 1950–70, Kuznets (1982) had reported the following: (i) the difference in the levels of shares of the labour force in agriculture is negatively and significantly related to the difference in the level of product per capita, and (ii) among the less developed market economies, the difference among the sub-groups in the magnitude of the shift of the labour force from agriculture is significantly positively associated with differences in the growth rate of per capita income.

The Lewis Model (Lewis 1954) was designed to provide a theoretical account of the transformation that accompanies growth. It may be described as follows. Underdeveloped economies are characterized by disguised unemployment in agriculture, the 'traditional' sector. Here custom and tradition ensure that food is shared equally. The marginal product of labour in agriculture is less than the fixed institutional wage and lower than the marginal product in industry, the 'modern' sector. If offered the institutional wage, it is assumed, some agricultural workers would move to industry. The implied labour supply curve to the modern sector would remain horizontal till such time as there is a surplus—'unlimited supplies'—of labour in agriculture. After that the agricultural wage would no longer be institutionally determined, but would move along labour's marginal productivity schedule. This turning point marks the transition from the traditional to the modern economy.

Lewis' model is 'classical' in the sense of Keynes, in that there is no story of how demand for industry arises. Moreover, the faint suggestion that workers carry their lunch packs with them when they migrate to the modern sector underestimates the importance of a marketed surplus of food. However, as observed of the model by Papola (2005: 7): '[I]t emphatically makes the point that economic development of an underdeveloped economy not only involves but requires shift of labour from agriculture to industry'. As, by assumption, the marginal product of labour in the modern sector is higher than what it is in agriculture, the solution to the problem of low income which characterizes underdevelopment lay in shifting labour out of agriculture, which would raise the per capita income of the economy. This Lewisian mechanism, we find, is broadly in accord with the observed change in the sectoral distribution of labour that accompanies growth.

Even outside the world of pure economic models, the transformation of the economy with growth constitutes a stylized fact of economic development that has a reasonable degree of acceptance among economists. It would therefore serve as a yardstick by which to evaluate the extent of development in India en route to an assessment of the growth prospects of its economy, which is our objective. However, prior to proceeding towards this, a consideration of the dynamics of the development of an economy would be appropriate.

We have reason to believe that the association between rising per capita income and changing economic structure is not unidirectional, as may be assumed. The shift in labour to the non-agricultural sectors is enabled by a rise in labour productivity in agriculture. For, if this productivity does not rise, the labour shifted to non-agriculture cannot be fed, as agricultural output—including that of food—will decline as some labour exits. Constant output with labour migrating out is feasible only in the presence of disguised unemployment in agriculture. Now, while this establishes the vital role of rising labour productivity in agriculture, the latter is in turn enabled by the growth of the non-agricultural sectors making available both intermediate inputs and new technology. This is what is implied by the expression 'science-based agriculture'[21] or even 'industrial agriculture', as much of agriculture in western Europe and North America might appear by comparison with the agriculture of South Asia. Over time, it may be expected that the industrial and service sectors are able to provide cheaper and better, that is, yield-increasing, intermediate inputs to agriculture as productivity growth, including new products, rises in the non-agricultural sector. Thus, productivity growth in the economy as a whole is spurred by a mutual positive feedback among the sectors, and for this very reason is potentially self-reinforcing. But this also implies that the problem of growth cannot be solved by simply transferring labour from less productive agriculture to the more productive non-agricultural sector of the economy. As we can see, the sustained increase of per capita income, that is growth, requires continuous productivity growth in *both* the sectors.[22]

It ought not to be assumed that the role of agriculture in the process of growth is that of a passive recipient of a free gift in the form of a rising industrial productivity that transforms its productive potential. Rising agricultural productivity is usually the first cause of expansion of the market for non-agricultural goods and services.[23] This is a development of some significance in the growth of an economy. Since the time of Adam Smith we know that the division of labour is limited by the size of the market. The 'division' being referred to was famously pictured in the form of a disintegration of pin-making into many separate activities, the point of the breaking-up itself being that it would raise productivity in manufacturing. Thus, the market constituted by the expansion of agriculture extends the frontier of feasible reorganization of production in the manufacturing sector. As agriculture expands there arise support services such as banking, insurance, and transportation, aiding its further expansion. As these services are potentially inputs across economic activities, that is, they enjoy economies of scope, they are not without a role in the expansion of manufacturing.

The most important route by which agriculture contributes to expanding the market for industry is by providing progressively cheaper food. Cheaper food leaves consumers with greater real incomes to spend on industrial goods. This expands the market for manufactures and services, with its productivity-increasing consequences as described. The latter makes manufacturing products cheaper, thus further expanding the demand for them. Note that as in the sequence imagined the real price of food declines because of rising labour productivity it is fully compatible with agricultural producers becoming richer. Historically, this is precisely what has taken place in the industrialized West. Let us look at the phase of growth there referred to as 'the golden age of capitalism', so called because high sustained growth of per capita income combined with low inflation for almost a quarter century from after the Second World War till the early 1970s. In the context of our present concern, what is significant about this phase of growth is that it was a period when the growth of labour productivity in agriculture had outstripped its growth in manufacturing.[24] This is surprising in that it has been claimed that manufacturing is the engine of growth precisely because of its amenability to rapid increases in productivity, unlike agriculture. It still does not imply that agricultural productivity rose independently, but it does imply that the assumption that manufacturing is the economic activity most prone to productivity growth, maintained even by so incisive an observer of the industrialized capitalist economies as Kaldor[25], is not always correct. It also suggests that even late into the history of economic growth in a country, agriculture can play an important role. This possibility has been overlooked in the almost exclusive focus on the role of agriculture at the stage of initiation of growth in an economy.[26] At the level of economic policy in India, for instance, the role of agriculture has tended to be placed on the back burner as the first flush of success following the Green Revolution was interpreted as a sign that our food problem had been solved permanently, a premise that has been shown to be false.

The earliest explicit account of the role of food in the growth process is found in the Ricardian theory of rent. This is worth recounting as it offers a clear perspective on the central role of the price of food. David Ricardo's approach was infused by the premonition of a natural-resource constraint to economic progress that formed a central part of classical political economy starting with the Physiocrats of late eighteenth-century France. This stemmed from the belief that agricultural production was subject to diminishing returns. In Ricardo's work this was due to the perceived scarcity of fertile land. Writing at the time of the Industrial Revolution in England, Ricardo viewed economic growth as ever-rising industrial production. This would increase the demand for labour and raise the wage rate over the subsistence level, triggering via the Malthusian mechanism a rise in the population. The growth of population would in turn raise the cost of production of corn, as land of lower quality would now have to be brought into cultivation. This would raise the price of corn, with consequences for industrial production. There, as the subsistence wage was related to the price of corn, the 'wages fund'—which Ricardo treated as a form of capital—would have to be increased, implying a lower industrial profit rate. As the profit rate declines, the incentive for further investment in industrial production too declines. Eventually, rising price of food due to population growth would choke-off industrial investment altogether and growth would grind to a halt. This was the Classical 'stationary state'. Ricardo had a clear strategy to ward off the stationary state, which was to allow the import of food to contain the price rise. In the England of his time, he argued for a repeal of the Corn Laws, which were of the form of a tariff on food imports. Ricardo believed that these laws constricted the growth of manufacturing and thus growth of the British economy itself. It may be expected that as the original trade theorist Ricardo is unlikely to have lamented the decline of agriculture that cheaper imports would inevitably have caused, as this would be in keeping with the principle of comparative advantage.

The writings of the Classical economists make us more acutely aware of the fundamental role of agriculture in growth than anything written on the subject since. From Ricardo we can see that the rising price of food can bring growth in manufacturing to a halt, from Smith we realize that declining price of food actually expands the market for industry's product. The mistake policymakers in a hurry often make is to overlook that 'Industrialisation and modern economic growth can hardly be successful without healthy developments in the agricultural sector, which is so dominant in the early stage of development' (Hayami 2001: 85). The history of attempts by the former colonies to rapidly industrialize after they had gained independence following the Second World War is full of instances of the failure to transform their agricultures, which has left these economies permanently in the 'early stage of development'. In the context of our discussion, a backward agriculture delays the structural transformation of the economy, which the history of modern economic growth shows us, is essential to growth.

Some economists have conceived of the role of agriculture in economic development as historic in significance. They start by observing that at the early stages of development per capita income is low. At this point,

> Food being at the bottom of the hierarchy of commodities, it has a high income elasticity of demand at those income levels. Also, the productivity of labour in agriculture is low, so that the bulk of the labour force will be engaged in that sector. At the same time,

the price of food is also high, so that the non-agricultural sectors have to pay a high wage for their labour. During this phase, there is also a rapid growth of population. Therefore, agricultural production and the supply of food cannot rise much faster than the growth of population. Hence, the agricultural sector will be a constraint on the growth of other sectors, both on the demand side and on the supply side. But as development proceeds, there comes a time when the population growth slows down, the income elasticity of demand for food falls, the productivity of labour in agriculture rises, and more labour becomes available to the other sectors at lower wages. Then the agricultural sector is no longer a constraint on overall growth. To reach this stage is the historical mission of agriculture (Sundrum 1990: 98).

Countries may vary in the time it takes for their agricultures to fulfil their mission, so conceived, but fulfil it they must if the growth of their economies is to proceed unabated. Implicit in this mission is a declining price of food, the final destination of rising agricultural productivity. The growth of real wages and profits elsewhere in the economy depends upon this outcome.

The Pattern of Growth and Its Determinants: A Cross-country Investigation

As the relationship between growth and structural transformation has received so much attention, we study the evidence on this across the world's regions, including India. In Table 1.1 seventeen countries[27] have been arrayed according to region and income level. The sectoral composition of gross domestic product (GDP) in these economies is also presented. The pattern evident is that economies with a lower share of agriculture and a higher share of industry in their outputs are generally richer. The relation between the share of services and per capita income, however, is less clear cut.

To appreciate the second feature of the structural transformation of the economy historically associated with growth, namely, the changing distribution of the workforce across the sectors, we present in Table 1.2 data on this development for the same set of countries. Again, notice a definite pattern whereby the richer economies have a lower share of their workforce in agriculture, though, as before there are countries that do not fit into this pattern.

Next, from the data in the same table we identify a feature alluded to in the preceding discussion but not stressed enough in the literature on growth and development. That is, labour productivity in agriculture is very high in the rich countries. We even find this to be disproportionately so vis-à-vis the share of the workforce in agriculture. However, a check

Table 1.1 Structural Transformation with Growth: The Sectoral Composition of Output

Country	*GNP per capita (2004, in $)*	*Percentage share of GDP (2004)*		
		Agriculture	*Industry*	*Services*
Ethiopia	110	47	10	44
Nigeria	430	17	57	27
Kenya	480	27	17	56
Bangladesh	440	21	27	52
India	620	21	27	52
Pakistan	600	22	25	53
China	1500	13	46	41
Indonesia	1140	15	44	41
Thailand	2490	10	44	46
Korea Rep.	14,000	4	41	56
Peru	2360	10	30	60
Brazil	3000	10	40	50
Argentina	3576	10	36	54
UK	33,630	1	26	73
France	30,370	3	22	76
USA	41,440	1	22	77
Japan	37,050	1	31	68

Source: World Development Indicators, World Bank (2006).

is advisable on this finding. With labour productivity measured as value-added per worker, it can be unduly influenced by the relative price structure within agriculture. For example, agricultural labour productivity in economies producing high-value cash crops will show up as higher than that in economies producing the staples. To avoid this trap we present an alternative measure of agricultural productivity, namely, cereal yield measured in kilograms per hectare. Note that the relationship between per capita income and high agricultural productivity is more or less replicated in this case too, serving as a check on the relation between labour productivity in agriculture and a country's per capita income, which is what we are ultimately interested in. There appears to be no getting away from the feature that the rich economies have highly productive agricultures, however measured.

Table 1.2 Structural Transformation with Growth: The Role of Agriculture

Country	*GNP per capita (2004, in $)*	*Percentage share of agriculture in employment (1989–91)*	*Agricultural labour productivity (value added per worker in 2000, in $) (1992–4)*	*Cereals yield (kg per hectare) (1993–5)*
Ethiopia	110	–	123	1106
Nigeria	430	–	610	1165
Kenya	480	17.0	301	1711
Bangladesh	440	65.7	251	2572
India	620	68.7	362	2104
Pakistan	600	49.9	603	1946
China	1500	55.8	273	4581
Indonesia	1140	55.7	498	3875
Thailand	2490	63.2	481	2383
Korea Rep.	14,000	17.4	6257	5780
Peru	2360	1.1	1169	2745
Brazil	3000	23.0	1839	2384
Argentina	3576	0.3	7335	2821
UK	33,630	2.2	23,089	6618
France	30,370	6.4	24,724	6504
USA	41,440	2.9	22,868	4836
Japan	37,050	7.2	19,958	5627

Source: *World Development Indicators*, World Bank (2006).

Can it be averred, then, that there is a universal model of growth and development to which all economies must conform? We would think not. However, the empirical regularity of structural transformation, notably the shift out of agriculture of the workforce and its rising productivity, may be accepted as a stylized fact and thus deserving of consideration in an assessment of the future of growth in an economy. At a minimum, the empirical regularity does suggest an expected pattern of modern economic growth. The pattern itself is likely generated by certain 'transnational factors', in the sense of being intrinsic to growth and therefore applicable to all economies. Kuznets had recognized early that if there was no substantial transnational factor, there would be no common features of significance in the economic growth of nations and comparative study would be hardly warranted.

Chenery was to fine-tune the idea that 'universal' factors would lead us to expect uniform patterns of development while 'particular' factors and policy would account for divergences from a common path.[28] For Chenery, the universal factors were (i) common technology, (ii) similar human wants, (iii) access to the same markets for imports and exports, (iv) accumulation of capital as income increases, and (v) the increase in skills as income increases. While these transnational factors would lead us to expect a certain uniformity across countries in their long-run transformations, providing us with a framework for evaluating a country's economic prospects, it does not in any way imply that there is a single path which all economies must take. We know by now that factors making for diversity are strong. The histories of enclaves, the erstwhile socialist bloc, and the oil-rich Middle-Eastern economies show that a unique path is not inevitable. At the same time, for India—which is the object of our ultimate analysis—an economy of subcontinental proportions with growth represented in all the sectors for over a century, the Kuznets view holds promise as a guide to understanding the past and the future of growth there.

Finally, though not apparent in the work of Kuznets, it may be deduced from the history of the countries that industrialized successfully that a factor governing both the migration out of agricultural labour and its absorption into industry is education of the labour force. In the literature on development, the role of education has been stressed quite heavily over the past two decades or so. Perhaps the one most important reason for this is the realization that at the base of the quite spectacular rise of the economies of the Far East in the last quarter of the twentieth century lay a strong educational foundation. Significantly, these countries had invested heavily in education even at time when they were not rich.

It is not difficult to visualize a major role for education in modern economic growth once we recognize that structural transformation is integral to it. The transfer of labour out of agriculture and the associated growth in labour productivity cannot be imagined without a spreading of education deep and wide across the economy. Hereditary agricultural labourers, or even erstwhile farmers, cannot make the move without at least basic education, including the learned ability to learn continuously as the pace of technological progress quickens.[29] And industry cannot easily absorb once-rural labour without such an education. Skills after all can be imparted on the job, but we know from economic theory that an industrial firm has no incentive whatsoever to educate labour that may not remain with it. In the context, it is evident that the educational thrust must commence in the rural areas where the greater part of labour rests. It is not surprising that at the time of Kuznets' writing, this vital contribution of education to the structural transformation that accompanies growth was not emphasized. Kuznets was focusing primarily on the experience of the Western industrialized economies. By the 1950s there had existed in these economies, for close to a century, compulsory, and mostly publicly-provided, education. Therefore, the fact of basic education would very likely have been taken for granted and its provision requiring no special pleading. This could not credibly have been assumed for the India of the time, then among the poorest countries of the world in terms of per capita income.

So far in this chapter we have argued that the structural transformation that is a feature of the sustained increase in per capita income, referred to as growth, is enabled by dynamism in agriculture and the spread of education across the economy. A simple check on this argument would be to evaluate how in a cross-country sample agricultural performance and education measure up among the determinants of growth identified by economists.

In the vast literature on economic growth, several determinants have been proposed, so a choice is necessitated. We have selected four such variables for which cross-country data were available to us. In our view, these represent a balanced collection of determinants, comprising both those proposed from a theoretical perspective and those that have come to be accepted as a result of empirical study of a wide range of country experience. They also form a nice mix of macro- and microeconomic factors. The proposed determinants are the growth of investment, the rate of inflation, the rate of growth of per capita food production, and the level of education measured by the gross enrolment ratio for schooling. We compute the rank correlation coefficient between each of these variables and the rate of growth of per capita income (gross national product [GNP]) over the period 1965–96 for the thirteen developing countries in our original sample of seventeen in Table 1.1. Naturally, the original OECD (Organisation for Economic Co-operation and Development) countries on that list have been left out. The rank-correlation coefficients[30] are presented in Table 1.3.

Table 1.3 Search for the Determinants of Growth

	r_s
Investment	0.83
Inflation	–0.25
Educational attainment	0.35
Growth of food per capita	0.85

Notes: r_s is the Spearman rank-correlation coefficient; critical values, for n = 13, at the 0.05 level are +/- 0.554.

We first discuss the outcomes of the test of a relationship between growth and the macroeconomic variables. As expected, the rank correlation between growth and investment is very high. On the other hand, the relation between growth and inflation is low and not statistically significant. This is not entirely surprising even though the assertion that inflation is damaging of growth is widely encountered, and not only in the academic literature.[31] In fact, the observed correlation between inflation and growth for some countries at some stages is very likely a reduced-form relationship, with inflation the symptom of a deeper malaise that adversely affects both growth and price stability at the same time. More to the point, a coherent story of how inflation affects growth is yet to be told by those arguing for the priority of inflation control in the economic policy agenda. Though there are some clear costs of inflation, whether it affects investment and thus growth is linked to its distributional consequences, but the latter are excluded from the discourse on inflation in the mainstream of economics today. In the context of the repeated claim that inflation is a determinant of growth, the low rank correlation we find is striking.

We turn next to the determinants of growth that have emerged more from empirical investigations of growth than from economic theory. The rank correlation coefficient on education was found to be both low and not statistically significant. This is surprising given the attention that this variable has recently received in the literature on economic development. However, in an evaluation of this finding, two caveats ought to be put forward. First, we are here correlating the rank order of the countries in terms of the *level* of education with their rank order in terms of the *rate of change* of income. In all the other cases here we are relating rankings of rates of change. Second, the specific form of the indicator of education used should be borne in mind. In this case, it is the gross school enrolment ratio in 1965, the initial year of the period for which the growth in per capita income has been measured. It cannot be asserted that this is the exclusively valid measure of education. Arguably, it is a little too narrow as an indicator of the level of education in a country. We can think of other indicators, such as the number of engineers per 1,000 population, public expenditure on education, or perhaps we could have even chosen an index of the quality of education. The cross-section evidence from India, where the growth rate is currently higher in the states of the south and the west, which have higher education levels, and the extremely clear-cut econometric evidence on the relation between schooling and growth from a global sample of over a hundred countries reported by Barro (2001) would suggest discounting the low rank-correlation coefficient that emerged from our test here.[32] It may safely be assumed that the expansion of education will influence the future trajectory of growth in India, in particular the growth rate that it will be able to sustain.

Finally, we turn to the estimated relation between growth and the domestic production of food. Note that the rank correlation registered is not only the highest among the four determinants chosen here but also very high of itself. The importance of the growth of per capita output of food does not routinely enter discussions[33] on the drivers of growth, leave alone find a place in the modern theory of economic growth. However, our own discussion of the role of agriculture in the structural transformation of the economy that has been found to accompany growth must leave us unsurprised by the strength of this relationship that we have found from cross-country evidence. It strengthens the case for a Ricardian view of the determinants of growth. Though it runs the risk of appearing mundane in the context of elaborate discussions on the crucial importance to the future of India of reforms in the financial sector, lower tariffs, and a fully convertible currency, we treat this information as being of utmost importance in understanding economic growth in India in the past and in evaluating its prospects for the future.

Before concluding the present discussion, we present in Table 1.4 the cross-country data on education, food production, and growth in the last third of the twentieth century for the very countries that had constituted our sample for the rank-correlation tests.

First is the cross-country data on education. Allowing for the feature that the rate of growth of per capita income is inversely related to its initial level, we find that the region with the highest growth rates is the one where educational attainment was high to start with and its rate of expansion rapid, namely, East Asia. Apparently, however, expansion of

Table 1.4 Growth, Food, and Schooling: A Cross-country Comparison

Region/Country	*Average annual growth rate of per capita income (1965–96)*	*Average annual growth rate of food production per capita (1965–96)*	*School enrolment ratio*	
			1965	*1995*
Africa (Sub-Saharan)	−0.2	−0.3	23	50
Ethiopia	0.0	−1.1	7	22
Nigeria	0.1	0.3	19	63
Kenya	1.5	−0.6	29	67
South Asia	2.2	0.8	46	69
Bangladesh	1.0	−0.6	31	62
India	2.3	0.9	51	72
Pakistan	2.7	1.0	26	–
East Asia	5.5	1.3	63	88
China	6.7	2.7	67	94
Indonesia	4.6	2.0	42	82
Thailand	5.0	0.9	46	71
Korea Rep.	7.3	2.0	68	98
Latin America	1.1	0.7	60	84
Peru	−0.3	−0.2	62	92
Brazil	2.4	1.9	62	94
Argentina	−0.3	0.2	65	98
World	1.2	0.5	58	82

Source: Hayami (2001); see the original for the definition of variables and their sources.

education, unattended by other contributory factors is insufficient to spur growth as may be noticed from observing the record of the African economies.[34] Altogether, it is the comparison of South and East Asia that is most instructive, as the per capita income of these regions was similar in the mid-1960s, the starting point for the growth estimates in our study. First, note that in the mid-1960s Indonesia and Thailand had school enrolment ratios lower than India's. However, they made rapid strides in the next three decades. It is this expansion of education in the economies of the East that is so impressive. China and Korea, for instance, achieved higher absolute increases in school enrolment than India despite having already started at higher levels. It is significant, given that the data on education and growth refer to the same period, that this has been a phase of exceptionally fast growth in Korea. We also know that China's economic growth had begun to accelerate in the second half of this period, that is, the early 1980s. India's effort in the sphere of education is unimpressive even by comparison with that of Africa. While it has been suggested (see Hayami 2001: 47) that East Asia may have 'over-invested' in education, we have every reason to believe that India has historically underinvested. The data in Table 1.4 show that in 1995, school enrolment in India was more than 10 per cent below the global figure. Also, since 1965, India has expanded education at a rate marginally less than the world average. This information on the comparative educational level in India must be factored-in when evaluating her growth prospects so as not to succumb to the temptation of imagining that the liberalized trade and industrial policy regimes will automatically lead the economy to the global per capita income.

Finally, we turn to the cross-country evidence on the rate of growth of food production. Merely eyeballing the data is sufficient for us to see that a fairly close relationship exists between the growth of per capita income and the growth of per capita food production. We find Africa as a region where both the growth rates are relatively low. Once again, a comparison of the growth of food production across India and East Asia is illuminating. The average rate of growth of per capita food production for the latter region is almost 50 per cent higher than India's. East Asia's best performers in terms of per capita income growth recorded per capita growth rates for food production that exceeded the growth rate in India by over a 100 per cent! China bests India by a factor of three in this department and Korea does so by a factor of more than two. Oddly enough, this consideration seldom makes an appearance when India's prospects are compared to that of China. Admittedly, the precise mechanism by which the growth of food production enables a faster growth of the economy is not likely to be simple but it is unlikely that it would require rocket science to figure it out. By now we have a reasonable understanding of it, as outlined earlier in this chapter. Between the Smithian perspective of extending the market and the Ricardian one of maintaining an incentive to invest in the non-agricultural sectors, we comprehend sufficiently well the role of food production in the growth of an economy where the level of food availability is still relatively low.

This brief excursion into the cross-country historical experience must leave the reader with a sense of the centrality of agricultural progress and educational development to the sustained economic growth of a country.

Towards an Analytical Growth Narrative

This book is devoted to a study of the history and prospect of growth in India since 1950. However, the framework within which this is to be conducted remains to be stated. As we have seen at the beginning of this chapter, post-war growth theory offers a most impressive array of models, perhaps unrivalled for their precision and elegance by those in other branches of the discipline. Arguably though, they cannot serve as a sufficient framework for the empirical analysis of a concrete situation. For a start, they are far too pared down to serve as a guide to understanding the twists and turns of the economy. Let us take, for instance, the case of the Lucas version of endogenous growth theory.[35] It can certainly help us see what makes for the fundamental difference in growth rates achieved in India and the countries of East Asia, namely, human capital accumulation. However, as we can see right away, it cannot help when it comes to making sense of the mother-of-all turnarounds in this country, being the growth acceleration of the mid-twentieth century, or even the later history of repeated acceleration at shortening intervals, both outlined in the 'Introduction'. As for the idea of an endogenous cumulative change, though superior when it comes to explaining the subsequent trajectory of growth in India, it does not fare very much better when confronted with the initial quickening of the economy itself, as the first half of the twentieth century was without a growth dynamic. Altogether, then, for an explanation of growth in India since 1950, we would need a framework more capacious than that afforded by either of the representations of growth considered in this chapter. One that can accommodate sectoral distinctions such as agriculture versus industry, the possibility of aggregate demand failure, the role of non-market institutions, the implications of an open economy, and provide at least a modicum of political economy. No readymade version is available. However, more recently the 'analytical growth narrative' has emerged as a recognizable methodology for empirical growth studies.[36] This approach is adopted here.

An analytical growth narrative may be seen as a theoretically informed empirical analysis of growth in a country over a specified period. Being alive to economic theory, it avoids descending into simple-minded empiricism; being addressed to experience, it does not ascend into a purely theoretical orbit. These are not merely examples of hypothetical alternatives, but they describe the nature of some actually existing studies of economic growth. In any case, as it is my intention to avoid both these outcomes, the methodology of the analytical growth narrative recommends itself as one's best insurance. As a practice it stems from the belief that it would be incredible to assume that the primary factors causing growth of an economy are invariant to time period, initial conditions, or other aspects of a country's circumstances. Quite simply, it is unlikely that there are universal rules about what makes a country grow, rendering pre-fabricated models of growth practically useless when it comes to understanding growth in a particular country at a particular time.

As Rodrik, the economist most closely identified with this methodology, has stated in his introduction to a collection of country studies based on the methodology of the analytical growth narrative: '[T]hese narratives explore the respective roles of microeconomic and macroeconomic policies, institutions, political economy, and initial conditions in driving patterns of technological convergence and accumulation' (Rodrik 2003: 3). As for theory, it is not unduly privileged and must come under the scanner too. So, while theory is meant to guide the narrative, the project also envisages a reversal of roles. The value of the narrative method 'lies in drawing the connections between specific country experiences, on one side, and growth theory and cross-national empirics, on the other' and in enabling us to 'evaluate and extend our understanding of economic growth using the country narratives as a backdrop' (Ibid.: 9). As a method, the analytical growth narrative is less likely to lose its way, guided as it is by economic theory and being alert to the empirical reality that is to be explained. We now proceed towards an analytical growth narrative on India.

Notes

1. Abramovitz (1989) has traced it to the writings of John Stuart Mill in the early nineteenth century.

2. From a graphical perspective, with the production function in labour-intensive form, the former two together would account for the movement along the production function and the last the shift of the function itself.

3. This demonstration is based on Hulten (2000: 13).

4. Four decades later Fisher was to return to cautioning applied economists on the use of the aggregate production function while addressing questions in macroeconomics, a practice that has increased many-fold due to rising access to computing power. See Felipe and Fisher (2003).

5. When it is long-term growth that is being studied, we may safely assume that growth is always positive.

6. Note from equation (1.3) that the measured contribution of a factor to the growth of output is its share-weighted rate of growth.

7. Note that this was actually a prediction made by Krugman (1994). A decade, and an external payments crisis, later the tiger is still licking its stripes!

8. See Young (1995).

9. See Nelson (1998).

10. See, for instance, the country studies in Rodrik (2003).

11. See Barro (2001).

12. Specifically, '... in a technologically progressive or dynamic economy production management is a function requiring adaptation to change and ... the more educated a manager is the quicker will he be to introduce new techniques of production. Educated people make good innovators so that education speeds the process of technological diffusion' (Nelson and Phelps 1966: 70).

13. And its variation over time as seen in the figure in the 'Introduction'.

14. See Easterly and Levine (2000) and Helpman (2004).

15. A rarity among academics normally loathe to soil their hands in a trade!

16. 'But just what constitutes a large market? Not area or population alone, but buying power, the capacity to absorb a large annual output of goods. This trite observation, however, at once suggests another equally trite, namely, that capacity to buy depends upon capacity to produce. In an inclusive view, considering the market not as an outlet for the products of a particular industry, and therefore external to that industry, but as the outlet for goods in general, the size of the market is determined and defined by the volume of production' (Young 1928: 533).

It is in this sense that increasing returns was for Young a 'macro', or economy-wide, phenomenon. In fact, he took pains to clarify that he had in mind 'large' and not 'large- scale' production, presumably to distinguish his own idea from that of firm-level returns to scale (see Ibid.: 531).

17. Over five decades later Young's vision was to be incorporated into a formal model of growth by Romer (1986), which was the harbinger of the 'endogenous growth revolution' in macroeconomics.

18. Here development is an objective description and not a normative evaluation as, for instance, in the view of development as the expansion of freedoms conceived of by Sen (1999).

19. 'The epochal innovation that distinguishes the modern economic epoch is the extended application of science to problems of economic production' (Kuznets 1966: 9).

20. See the tables that follow.

21. See Hayami (2001).

22. See Crafts (1985) for a discussion of the importance of rising agricultural productivity in sustaining the early growth of England, the 'first industrial nation'. The economics of the Industrial Revolution have been a subject of reappraisal more recently, for which see the essays in Mokyr (1985).

23. See Dobb (1946).

24. See Bairoch (1997), who has referred to the resurgence as the 'third agricultural revolution', the first two having taken place in the middle of each of the two preceding centuries, respectively.

25. See Kaldor (1966).

26. For instance, in the empirical literature on growth in the West, it is the role of agriculture in the Industrial Revolution that is emphasized, while in the theoretical literature on economic development of the Third World, the role of agriculture has been confined to the stage of initiation of growth by the state. See Bairoch (1973) and Johnston and Mellor (1961), respectively.

27. The choice of countries conforms to a criterion proposed by Hayami (2001) for an international comparison. The idea is to represent the larger countries from all the geographical areas of the globe. Following this, it so happened, conveniently for us, that the countries chosen represented the entire range of per capita income.

28. For a survey of the literature on structural transformation with growth, see Syrquin (1988).

29. For instance, information technology can be thought of as both a cause and an effect of this quickening.

30. Data on investment and inflation were taken from Hayami (2001). Data on the remaining variables are from Table 1.4.

31. See *The Financial Times* (2008).

32. A positive, statistically significant, relation between the level of education and the 'level' of GNP in a sample only slightly larger than ours has been reported by Hayami (2001: 48).

33. See World Bank (2008), for instance. Headed by independent economists of the highest distinction and sub-titled *Strategies for Sustained Growth and Inclusive Development, The Growth Report* is perhaps the most important ideas document to have emerged from the Bank in at least a decade.

34. It must be borne in mind, though, that parts of Africa have witnessed prolonged civil war, a condition relatively absent from the other countries in our sample and a factor likely to have brought to naught any early educational advantage.

35. See Lucas (1988).

36. I am grateful to Anjan Mukherji for bringing this to my attention. See DeLong (2003) for an earlier analytical growth narrative on India.

2 A Moribund Economy Quickened, 1950–64*

The whole philosophy ... is to take advantage of every possible way of growth and not to do something which suits some doctrinaire theory or imagine we have grown because we have satisfied some text-book maxim of a hundred years ago.

—**Jawaharlal Nehru (1956)**

There exists an account of the recent history of economic growth in India that proceeds as follows. Following the end of colonialism, the Indian national leadership, fascinated by the Soviet view of economic development, adopted the path of a *dirigiste* inward-looking industrialization. The economy settled down to an anaemic rate of growth till 1991 when the economic policy regime was liberalized. Only then, finally, did the economy begin to show signs of an inherent dynamism, vindicating the critique of the economic policy followed in India for over four decades. We are about to embark on a study of economic growth in India which will resolve the veracity of such a reading. However, even a passing familiarity with history, as reflected by the time series of gross domestic product (GDP) graphed in the 'Introduction', is enough for us to

* Parts of this chapter were originally published as 'The Recovery of India: Economic Growth in the Nehru Era', *Economic and Political Weekly*, 10–17 November, 2007. A revised version of the same appeared as 'Visible Hand: Public Policy and Economic Growth in the Nehru Era', *Indian Economic Journal*, April–June, 2008.

be able to detect in it an inadequacy. For one, it underplays the dynamism of the economy in the early 1950s which had brought about the first sustained growth transition of the twentieth century in India. Second, it overlooks the fact of a *second wind*, so to speak, for the economy, in the form of a growth transition in the late 1970s. But not even recognition of these transitions can adequately account for the choice of periodization in this study. In particular, it can be asked: why have we chosen to treat the period 1950–64 as a distinct phase as far as growth is concerned?

The years 1950 to 1964 mark the period from the constitution of the Planning Commission to oversee planned economic development to the exit of Jawaharlal Nehru from the political stage. The decisive role of India's first and longest-serving prime minister suggests the label 'Nehru era' to this phase of Indian economic history. Nehru's substantial influence on his party, on the issue of economic policy at least, and the Congress Party's own domination of parliament gave a particular edge to politics as it affected the making of economic policy of this time. Economic policymaking of the era had certain integrity to it, the term being used here strictly in the descriptive sense. It is meant to connote a process of decision making that is relatively independent of economic vested interests and free of the narrow party-political considerations that have increasingly come to characterize India's Westminster-style system of governance. The distinctiveness of the Nehru era draws from the feature that almost never since has the political leadership of India enjoyed as much relative autonomy. This ensured some integrity at least to the choices made, even when it may not always have carried over as much to the implementation. That after Nehru, within the same overall framework of state-directedness, much of the intervention was aimed largely at maintaining the ruling dispensation's hold on power, provides a rationale for viewing the mid-1960s as the end of an era in India's history.

The year 1950 marks the beginning of any concerted approach to economic development by the state in independent India, no significant intervention towards the goal having taken place prior to this date. The delay is hardly surprising, as at least a couple of years from 1947 were spent by the political leadership in consolidating the Union of India, made vulnerable by the Partition and handicapped by the lack of experience of governance. In 1950 the Planning Commission, the body entrusted with the task of steering the economy, was formed. The First Five Year Plan was launched within a year. However, it may be said that this had not amounted to a coherent strategy for growth and development, having been no more than a collection of projects aimed mainly at agriculture and infrastructure. For India's political leadership, notably Jawarharlal Nehru, it was very likely only a dress rehearsal. Having convinced itself that both the nation's Independence and the people's well-being lay in industrialization, the leadership was ambitious. It did of course help that the initial interventions were mostly successful, instilling confidence and buying time for some serious thinking on a strategy for accelerated growth and the instruments for achieving it. It is a mark of the determination and capacity of the political leadership of the time that the latter had been more or less worked out even before the First Plan was to end in 1956. The Second Five Year Plan was the vehicle by which the strategy was launched. That strategy, which was to dominate thinking about the economy for the rest of the Nehru era, and the associated record of growth constitute the focus of this chapter.

Imagining Economic Growth: The Nehru–Mahalanobis Strategy and Its Critics

Though narrowly identified as the basis for the Second Five Year Plan, nothing is more emblematic of the economics of the Nehru era and representative of the means adopted to pursue its goals than what is referred to as the Mahalanobis Model. The best known version of the eponymous model had appeared in an essay on growth by Mahalanobis.[1] This was intended to provide the analytical foundation for the project of raising the level of income via industrialization, already deliberated upon in the National Planning Committee of the Congress, which was chaired by Nehru at the request of Subhash Chandra Bose in his capacity as the party president in 1938. For this reason, the larger vision that had encompassed the Model is often referred to as the Nehru–Mahalanobis Strategy. Its objective was to raise the level of income through rapid growth as this was considered the means to eliminating widespread poverty.

Mahalanobis had conceived of an economy with two sectors, producing capital and consumer goods, respectively. Being a model of a closed economy without government, their outputs would sum up to the gross national income. Within the Model, the capital good enters into the production of the consumer good and of itself, while the consumer good is not an input into production at all. In an interesting departure from the economic theory of the time, capital was not subjected to diminishing returns. This implies that a greater allocation of investment to the production of capital goods would leave the economy with a continuously rising stock of capital. With the capital good being the physical counterpart of investment, a higher allocation to capital goods production enables higher investment in the future. Assuming that all such feasible investment is undertaken, a higher level of investment is actualized. Now future-dated output is higher compared to the case where the share of capital goods in a given investment outlay is lower. The outcome is strongly related to the feature that the capital good is required in all lines of production while the consumer good is not. So, a higher share of capital goods in investment yields a higher rate of growth of the economy. Now the planner's problem is to arrive at the share of investment to be allocated to the capital-goods sector given the target level of income.

I have here provided a bare-bones description of the Model and its logic.[2] However, when trying to understand the economic policy of the 1950s, it is important to recognize that, even for its architect, the Model was meant only as a guide to a strategy for industrialization. Therefore, it is equally important to understand the practical aspects of the strategy as manifested in what in the language of the day was referred to as 'the plan frame'. But before moving on to an exposition of the strategy by Mahalanobis himself, it would help to be acquainted with the mathematical structure of the model.

Let Y_t = national income, C_t = consumption, and K_t = investment at time t; with Y_0, C_0, and K_0 the corresponding values at the initial period. λ_k and λ_c (with $\lambda_k+\lambda_c = 1$) are fractions of investment allocated to industries producing capital goods (K-sector) and consumer goods (C-sector), respectively. Let β_k = ratio of the increment of income to investment in industries producing investment goods and β_c = ratio of increment of income to investment in industries producing consumer goods, and β = the ratio of increment of income to investment for the economy as a whole, with $\beta = \lambda_k \beta_k + \lambda_c \beta_c$ necessarily. We also have $K_{t+1} - K_t = \lambda_k \beta_k K_t$ and $C_{t+1} - C_t = \lambda_c \beta_c K_t$. We then get $K_t = (1 + \lambda_k \beta_k)^t K_0$ and, finally,

$$Y_t = Y_0\left[1+\alpha_0\frac{\lambda_k\beta_k+\lambda_c\beta_c}{\lambda_k\beta_k}\{(1+\lambda_k\beta_k)^t-1\}\right]$$

giving national income in terms of the initial income Y_0, the initial rate of investment α_0 and the allocation parameters λ_k and λ_c (which are at the planner's choice), and the contingent coefficients β_k and β_c (which are determined by the pattern of investment and conditions of production).[3]

In the application of the Model to Indian planning, the critical choice was that of λ_k, the share of investment devoted to capital goods. How in the context this was arrived at is best described in the author's own words:

> We found from available data that β_k is usually much smaller than β_c (that is, the marginal increase of income per unit of investment is much less in basic industries producing capital goods than in industries producing consumer goods). This being so, the larger the value of λ_k, the smaller is the increase of income in the short run; but, after a critical period of several years, income begins to rise steeply. Using the initial rate of investment, $\alpha_0 = 7$ per cent, $\beta_k = 0.2$ and different plausible values of β_c we found that to attain a fairly rapid increase of income over, say about 30 years, it would be desirable that λ_k should have a value between 0.3 and 0.5. We adopted the value $\lambda_k = 1/3$, as we felt it would not be possible to go beyond this value under present conditions. (Mahalanobis 1955a: 28–9)

While aware that his model implied income 'steeply' rising beyond some critical stage, Mahalanobis had not dwelt on this aspect particularly. As seen from the aforementioned quote, he had only treated it as information relevant to the problem of the allocation of investment across sectors. However, it is of interest in a study of growth in India, such as this, that he had imagined a mechanism whereby growth accelerates in a planned economy. While conceding that some improvement in the productivity of investment would be feasible via an optimum utilization of resources at the given level of investment, he foresaw further increases following directly from the investment in capital goods production itself:

> The value of β would also depend on the rate of investment and on the stock of capital already accumulated. With a low rate of investment and a small stock of capital it would not be possible to utilize the resources in a complementary way to the fullest extent owing to indivisibilities in the scale of production. The higher the rate of investment and the greater the stock of available capital the greater is the possibility of making the fullest use of the resources mobilized in the plan. As already pointed out in a country (like USA) with a very high stock of capital it may become progressively easier to secure external economies and hence to have higher values of β. In India an important object of planning must be to increase the rate of investment and to build up quickly a large stock of capital which may, in its turn lead to an increase in the value of β.[4] (Mahalanobis 1955a: 46)

Both Mahalanobis' radical idea that the purpose of public investment was to raise the productivity of capital and the implication of his model that the growth rate would accelerate over time were to be quickly forgotten by both India's political managers and academic economists, respectively. We shall return to both these issues.

We now turn to a discursive review of the Nehru–Mahalanobis Strategy for growth as a means of entry to the criticism that it has received. At the heart of the Strategy was a fast-growing heavy-goods sector. What are these 'heavy' goods and what was their perceived relevance? They have been described as 'machine-building complexes with a large capacity for the manufacture of machinery to produce steel, chemicals, fertilizer, electricity, transport equipment, etc' (Mahalanobis, quoted in Joshi 1982: 28). The means to bring about a fast-growing heavy-goods sector was to invest disproportionately in these machine-building complexes. The significance of the heavy-goods sector itself stemmed from the premise that Indian industrialization was essentially constrained by the availability of capital goods and that since foreign exchange was limited, it paid to build them at home.[5] As we have seen from Mahalanobis' account of how the value of λ_k was chosen, it was believed that as the investment goods sector was characterized by a higher incremental capital–output ratio, the rate of growth that adheres to the Nehru–Mahalanobis Strategy would in the short-run be lower than that resulting from titling investment towards consumer goods production. However, the long-run rate of growth of the economy resulting from a shifting of the investment allocation towards heavy goods would be higher.[6] Whether this feature of the Model only emerged out of the simulation of his Model or was intuitively available to Mahalanobis is surely of interest; but either way, once revealed, it must have provided a strong justification for adopting the Nehru–Mahalanobis Strategy.

In a sense the underlying idea of the Model is no more than accounting. It estimates growth prospects based on the pattern of investment and chooses the allocation that yields the target rate of growth. It is not entirely value-free of course, in that by preferring a higher income in the future it implicitly adopts a lower social rate of discount than could have been the case. But its author was not unaware of the trade-off, and in the choice of λ_k had been guided—as we have seen—by a concern for not imposing 'too great a sacrifice of immediate benefits' given the low levels of consumption in India.

The Nehru–Mahalanobis Strategy, with planning in particular, has been particularly castigated for having been based on an ideological predilection.[7] This criticism begins to make sense only when one is told that the Model had been inspired by that of Feldman from the Soviet planning literature. Mahalanobis had stated[8] that he was not aware of this work at the time of formulation of his own Model. Presumably then, the criticism justifies itself by identifying any policy orientation influenced positively by the Soviet experience as ideological. However, in light of the quite spectacular expansion demonstrated by the former Soviet Union by the mid-1950s such a criticism can in turn be termed ideological, even if today, armed with knowledge of the collapse of the Soviet Union, we might aver that the model was not sustainable.

In the 1950s, however, newly independent countries with ambition could hardly have been faulted for aspiring to what the Soviets had achieved, namely, rapid industrialization and the consequent increase in income within a remarkably quick time.[9] It is not as if the entirely compromised politics of the Stalin regime, with the gulags and the ethnic genocide, were overlooked. Only that Nehru was clear that India would avoid them through democratic practice even at the cost of achieving a lower rate of growth. It was clear that neither forced collectivization as a route to raising the rate of growth of agriculture nor the suspension of democracy as a way of quelling dissent on the chosen strategy were conceivable to the Indian leadership. So a relevant criticism of the strategy would only be of its economic logic and what it leaves out rather than of its alleged provenance. Here the comment by Desai (2007) that Mahalanobis' Model has in it no unemployment, inflation, or balance of payments is far more to the point. But once again, it is important to separate out the Model from the strategy, and each of these issues was explicitly addressed by Mahalanobis in the drafting of the Second Five Year Plan.[10]

There was, however, a flaw in the logic of the Model that may have derived from trying to replicate the Soviet experience of rapid industrialization without the associated institutions. As more or less an accounting scheme, the Mahalanobis Model was exclusively a supply-side model. There was inadequate recognition of a likely demand constraint to capital accumulation subverting the growth process. A model based on the purely physical relationship between inputs and outputs may have made sense for the Soviet Union, the classical 'command economy' where investment can be decreed by planners and enforced by commissars, but not so in India with a ubiquitous private sector that invests only in response to growing profits or its anticipation. Here demand is a driving force. In the command economy, the surplus could be constantly re-invested irrespective of market signals, maintaining a more or less constant growth dynamic at least for some time. Or, from within the discourse on growth economics, the savings are invariably always invested, which since Keynes we recognize as a fiction for a market economy, which India mostly was even by then. The only constraint to a seemingly endless growth in a command economy would be a declining investible surplus, which could also arise for entirely non-economic reasons such as political disaffection. Something of this kind perhaps describes the decline and fall of the Soviet economy after about five decades of rapid growth. However, even as late as the 1960s, there was no inkling of any impending collapse. As far as the Nehru–Mahalanobis Strategy is concerned, however, we may reiterate that it is important to draw the distinction between the Model and the plan, and the plan did explicitly recognize the role of demand, as we will see shortly.

While the hubris that the state could direct investment indefinitely may occasionally have carried away the planners in the 1950s, the criticism often encountered that they failed to recognize the importance of agriculture is merely ill-informed judgement. It is important to understand this not so much as to rehabilitate the planners as to establish that they may not have succeeded to the extent they would have liked to. In the process, we may succeed in throwing some light on the situation in India today, when even into the twenty-first century the agricultural base of the economy is emerging as an area of concern. This indeed is the one of the main uses of history for the economist. But before I turn to the role envisaged for agriculture within the Nehru–Mahalanobis Strategy, I must consider what in the mind of some[11] had constituted an alternative vision for the development for India and, therefore, a challenge to the Mahalanobis Plan. This was the plan presented by C.N. Vakil and P.R. Brahmananda of the Bombay School. The centrepiece of the Vakil–Brahmananda Plan was a 'wage-goods sector'. We get an insight into what had gone on in the minds of these two economists when we appreciate the reason for their scepticism regarding the relevance of the Keynesian problematic[12] for India. As recaptured by Brahmananda more recently, Keynesian unemployment assumes excess capacity including 'stocks of wage goods and other circulating capital' while in India 'unemployment of labour exists because supply of wage goods to sustain labour as a cooperant factor with land and labour is inadequate' (see interview in Balasubramanyan 2001: 29). Note the self-consciously Classical terminology, for when Brahmananda is pressed to name the wage goods, he chooses 'corn and clothing'. He had gone on to list fourteen items, but we may rest with 'foodgrains and textiles'. Essentially for Vakil and Brahmananda, the multiplier mechanism cannot work in the absence of wage goods, and this led them to the proposition that employment cannot expand without wage goods: 'So you see, for these reasons, agricultural development becomes fundamental. It has to be accorded priority independent of whatever you posit for industry' (Ibid.). And again, an observation quite relevant for India fifty years later, 'The service and industry sectors cannot absorb more than a small proportion of the labour force. The service sector is important, but services can be expanded only with growing wage goods surpluses' (Ibid.).

So what is the proper appraisal of the Vakil–Brahmananda Plan? There can be no doubt that in focusing on unemployment they had honed in on a key reality of India in the 1950s.[13] Also, the centrality accorded to agriculture could not have been faulted. However, the authors of this plan appear to have underestimated the importance of capital goods for raising agricultural production. There is Brahmananda's suggestion (Balasubramanyan 2001) that these could have been imported in return for the wage goods; but if wage goods were scarce enough to limit the expansion of employment in the first place, it is not clear how easily a sufficient export surplus could have been generated. This question precedes any proclivity for 'export pessimism' among India's planners, the attitude that had allegedly led them to underestimate the role of the world market as a potential engine of Indian economic growth.

Next, for exports there is the question of competitiveness to be reckoned with. A much vaunted sterling balance had, of course, been built up during the Second World War when India had supplied the Allied effort in a virtual seller's world market. However, these goods—being minor armaments, clothing, and equipment—would no longer have been demanded to anything like the same extent after the War. As for the agricultural sector, the primary source of wage goods, it had been unable to supply even the domestic population adequately[14] during the first fifty years of the twentieth century. Moreover, there is also the question of the very availability of capital goods to be purchased from industrial economies either recovering or booming following the War. The moment in history is well captured by Chibber (2003: 147) when he states that:

> In the years after the war, capital goods in the form of plant and machinery were extremely scarce; not only did India not have any capital goods industry to speak of, but imports from the developed world were not on the near horizon, as European

powers embarked on the reconstruction of their own economies and because the United States did not regard South Asia as a pivotal region. The problem with plant and machinery was mirrored by the problems with raw materials and intermediate goods, especially since, after partition, much of the Indian cotton and raw jute was now in Pakistan. In both these cases, businesses constantly called for the assistance of the state in securing the requisite import of goods.

Far from being a tangential comment on the credibility of the Vakil–Brahmananda Plan, recognition of Indian export and import possibilities in the 1950s is suggestive of the prospects for an Indian economic development through trade based on comparative advantage. The notable absence in the wage-goods model is the economist's *deus ex machina*, the 'engine of growth'. It is evident in Brahmananda's assertion that 'If the system is expanding and you have a supply of food, people could stay in their homes and produce wage goods' (see interview in Balasubramanyan 2001). This agreeable picture begs the question of the source of demand for the expansion of the economy. With hindsight, we can see that the Vakil–Brahmananda model was Classical more than just in its chosen terminology, with employment determined in the labour market. There is no autonomous investment function, which would have implied that the demand for labour as a derived demand gets determined in the goods market—independent of its price—and, in the context of their framework, independent of whether there is an adequate supply of wage goods. Of course, prices could still rise in the absence of wage goods and this would hold back the multiplier mechanism. However, as the unemployed are surviving as it is, it is possible to exaggerate[15] the degree to which the expansion in output is curtailed from the supply side following the expansion in aggregate demand.

It is possible to espy a strange 'symmetry' between the Mahalanobis and the Vakil–Brahmananda models, with the former downplaying the importance of consumer goods and the latter downplaying the importance of capital goods in the growth process! In the Mahalanobis two-sector Model the absence of consumer goods *per se* cannot constrain output growth, which the subsequent history of the Indian economy makes suspect as an assumption. However, once the overall Nehru–Mahalanobis Strategy is taken into account, we find that the degree of its oversight of a crucial ingredient for growth of the Indian economy, namely, consumer goods, is arguably less than that of the underestimation of the importance of capital goods by Vakil and Brahmananda. At least, Mahalanobis saw industrialization as an input into agricultural growth and industrialization was to be promoted by public investment.[16] No serious scheme for transformation of the productive capability of the wage-goods sector appears in the Vakil–Brahmananda Plan in comparison. But it is with respect to the crucial role of demand in the sustained expansion of an economy that the Nehru–Mahalanobis Strategy appears to have been set to win. In a talk delivered over All India Radio on 11 September 1955, a date prior to the launching of the Second Five Year Plan, Mahalanobis had explained the logic of planning in India thus:

> The basic strategy is (now) clear. We create demand by a planned expansion of the basic industries and of the social sector, that is, health, education, etc. We meet the demand by a planned increase in the production of consumer goods as much as possible in the small and household industries, and the rest in factories. As both production and income increase, we divert a portion of the increase in income for new investments again in a planned manner to balance new demand by new production, and the process continues. At each stage, we must be careful that the right quantity of raw materials is available at the right time for production; and the right quantity of consumer goods is available at the right time to meet the demand. (Mahalanobis 1961: 52)

Of course, we can see the heroic assumptions of physical planning at work here—especially the implicit premise that it is possible to plan without full control of prices in a private enterprise economy—but at least on the drawing board Mahalanobis' plan had hung together a little better than anything else that was on offer[17] for India at that stage in its history. It had demonstrated an eye for the big picture.

Finally, as an aside, one might observe that critics of Indian economic policy in the 1950s who saw the Nehru–Mahalanobis Strategy as violative of economic freedoms due to its reliance on controls[18] could not have taken much comfort from the Vakil–Brahmananda Plan, as its authors had placed it squarely in the field of planning. Surely, once employment rather than output is targeted, it is difficult to conceive of reallocation of labour without envisaging forced migration, Brahmananda's vision of cottage industry notwithstanding. The use of force in shaping development was ruled out of court by Jawaharlal Nehru who held firmly to the belief that the only kind of economic progress worth having was that attained by consent.[19]

Returning to the question of agriculture, not only was Mahalanobis acutely aware of its role in the scheme of things but he had incorporated this awareness into his strategy if not so fully into his model. He had instantly recognized that in the 1950s Indian agricultural growth was severely constrained by the availability of the most basic kind of industrial inputs. Thus, agricultural progress was itself linked to industrialization, even though the extent could have been debated, that is, while brick and mortar were clearly essential it is certainly not true that aircraft and automobiles were. Nevertheless, the suggestion of a role for industrialization in launching the transformation of Indian agriculture is not so entirely far-fetched. At this juncture I quote from the late Raj Krishna, an economist who having placed himself at a distance from the establishment that had donned the Nehruvian mantle is unlikely to have been in thrall to it. Yet he had stated:

> To some extent, the kind of development which occurred in the Nehru and post-Nehru periods was inevitable. In a subcontinental economy with a very large market, abundant natural resources of every kind, and vast reserves of unskilled and skilled manpower, the building up of a strong and diversified capital-goods base was a historical necessity. If today we can boast of a large measure of self-reliance, it is because considerable capacity has been created in the metallurgical, mechanical, chemical, power and transport sectors. These sectors are basic precisely because they are equally indispensable for defence, for large-scale consumer goods production, for small-industry development and rural development. The technical linkages between agriculture and industry are such that even a 4 percent rate of growth in agriculture is not possible without a high rate of growth in industries which supply the input requirements of a growing agriculture in the form of cement, bricks, pipes, pumps, electric power generation and transmission equipment, agricultural implements, diesel oil, fertiliser, pesticides, roads, vehicles, etc. And a seven percent growth in industry is not possible without a high rate of agricultural growth, because nearly half the modern industrial sector either processes agricultural output or supplies agricultural inputs. (Krishna 1979: 59)

Notice that the links conceived of here between agriculture and industry in India at that early stage of development were both rudimentary and fundamental at the same time, and, for that very reason, recognition of it should have been central to any serious growth strategy. It is not credible to argue that the Nehru–Mahalanobis Strategy had ignored, by design or by default, these links. For instance, note:

> It was appreciated that, in India, surplus is the key to industrialization. It is not only essential to grow enough food and fibres for our own requirements but it is also necessary to produce a surplus in the form of either industrial or food crops. In India agriculture and manufacturing industries are completely interlocked. Economic progress depends on the advance of both. Advance of one step in agriculture would supply food and raw materials for advance of one step in manufacturing industries which again, in its turn, would speed up irrigation and increase the supply of fertilizers and pesticides and help in the promotion of scientific research, which would lead to further advances in agriculture. (Mahalanobis 1961: 95–6)

While raising the level of income is widely recognized as having been the main objective of planning in the Nehru era, Mahalanobis himself was additionally engaged with another one, a feature that is not widely known. This was to release India 'permanently' (Mahalanobis 1961: 74) from the foreign-exchange constraint. Indeed, in his view, this was the very objective of planning for industrialization. This feature is seldom recognized, but it needs to be. And when it is, we are given an internal criterion by which to judge the economic policy of the Nehru era. After all, autonomy was at the core of the Nehruvian vision of economic development, not to mention of post-colonial India, and nothing would epitomize this more than a strong balance of payments position. Indeed, if independent development was the objective, then this would never be achieved if India were strapped permanently to a balance of payments deficit. Having flagged this, I return to the more recognizable objective of the economic policy of the time, namely, the accelerated growth of income.

So a rapid increase in the level of income was the main objective of planning and this was to be brought about via greater investment in heavy industry. We have also seen that this was central to the plan for the transformation of Indian agriculture, a process that would require increased industrial inputs. But how was this to be financed? The planners were fully aware that the step-up in investment envisaged in the Second Five Year Plan was very substantial indeed. Indeed, in retrospect, they appear to have had a better sense of the role of public finance in a credible economic plan than is found in the public discourse on growth in India of the early twenty-first century when the 'policy regime' per se has been elevated to far too important a role.

The importance that was accorded to resource mobilization is apparent from two elements of the plan to raise the level of income. First, no major foreign assistance was envisaged. This was in keeping with the idea of an independent development, a project incompatible with excessive reliance on foreign aid or, even, foreign direct investment (FDI). Taking the Second Five Year Plan as a case, foreign assistance was put down to less than 5 per cent of total public expenditure in the proposed 'government budget' for 1956–7 to 1960–1, even as the investment rate was to be raised by over 50 per cent from 7 to 11 per cent of GDP. Of course, the actual achievement with respect to foreign savings had differed, as we shall soon have occasion to see. Second, as part of the same plan, the envisaged contribution of the public enterprises was significant, revealing the political leadership's expectation of their role in the economy, for instance, the item 'Additional Taxes and Loans & Profits from State Enterprises' along with the 'Contribution from the Railways' equalled 'Loans from the Public' and were over twice what was to be taken as foreign assistance.[20] I shall return to this central premise of public policy in the 1950s that the public sector was expected to contribute resources to the larger project of national development.

Thus far I have been concerned with trying to establish what the leadership of the Nehru era had in mind as the ends and means. We have a reasonably good picture already, but this gets crystallized when we turn to the speeches of Jawaharlal Nehru himself. Recall that Nehru was the Chairman of the Planning Commission and was closely involved with the planning process. These speeches are of interest to us today not only in revealing the arduous process of deliberation by which policy was formed but also in pointing out the surprisingly remarkable grasp that, despite being an active career politician, Nehru had on matters related to the economy.

The first of these, made in 1952, gives us two insights into the economic calculation of the political leadership. It reveals that the idea of industrialization as a goal to raise incomes was adopted even before the Mahalanobis Model, which had undergirded the Second Plan, was written down. Further, it conveys the full recognition prevalent among the planners of the importance of agricultural growth to the industrialization project. The extract follows:

> There is much talk of industrialisation. In the initial chapters of the Plan, certain figures pertaining to the amounts allotted to industry, agriculture, social services, transport, etc., are given. In this respect, industry does not seem to occupy as important a place as agriculture. If I remember correctly, a very large sum is to be spent on irrigation. We certainly attach importance to industry, but in the present context we attach far greater importance to agriculture and food and matters pertaining to agriculture. If our agricultural foundation is not strong then the industry we seek to build will not have a strong basis either. Apart from that, the situation in the country today is such that if our food front cracks up, everything else will crack up, too. Therefore we dare not weaken our food front. If our agriculture becomes strongly entrenched, as we hope it will, then it will be relatively easy for us to progress more rapidly on the industrial front, whereas if we concentrate only on industrial development and leave agriculture in a weak condition we shall ultimately be weakening industry. That is why primary attention has been given to agriculture and food and that, I think, is essential in a country like India at the present moment. (Nehru 1952)

This speech was made at a relatively early stage of the economic transformation that was being attempted.

Next I quote from two sets of speeches made almost at the end of Nehru's tenure as prime minister, indeed close to the end of his life. The first of these is really a politician's justification of the policies pursued by his government and reads as such, but it does convey a remarkably clear understanding of the inter-temporal distribution of gains that was central to the economic strategy that was being pursued. It also reflects a certain understanding of the uniqueness of India, not in a civilizational sense but in the sense of the challenges it faces given its economic backwardness and its democratic polity. The extracts follow:

> Planning has of course been done in other countries; but not through democratic processes. Other countries which are democratic have not accepted planning. But the combination of these two concepts is rather unique. ... The first thing we realised was that it was no good copying America or Russia or any other country. The problems of India are her own. We can learn from America or Russia, as certainly we should. But the economic problems of India are different. We learn from them, of course, as they have acquired great experience. We always realised that the fundamental factor was growth in agricultural production. Agriculture is basic to us because however much importance we attach to industry unless we have surplus from agriculture, we cannot progress in our economy. We cannot live on doles from other countries. We have always to choose between benefits accruing today, or tomorrow, or the day after. From the country's point of view, if we spend the money we now have for some petty immediate benefits, there will not be any permanent benefit. One has to find a healthy balance between the immediate benefits of today and the long-range benefits of tomorrow. All the money we have put in heavy industries is for tomorrow's benefit, though it brings in some benefit today also. It will take some years before this investment yields fruits. ... So, our strategy of economic development is essentially modernisation of agriculture and training of our rural masses in the use of new tools and new methods. At the same time, it seeks to lay the foundations of an industrial structure by building the basic or heavy industries, above all by producing electric power. Middle and small scale industries will inevitably come in their train. (Nehru 1963a)

A clearer articulation of the central issue in investment planning, namely, the choice of the long-run output-maximizing allocation of investment across activities would perhaps be hard to find.

The second set of speeches that I had referred to shows us a Nehru somewhat despondent regarding the extent of progress made on the agricultural front. He even suggests that agriculture has been neglected relative to its importance. The first extract is from a speech made to the chief ministers at the annual meeting of the National Development Council in 1963. It is as follows:

> Emergency was declared in the wake of Chinese invasion. ... Emergency does not merely mean raising soldiers or getting aircraft. It means production, production for defence specially. All other types of production, more particularly on the agricultural front, is equally necessary. ... We have done many things which are creditable to us. But the overall picture is not one of fast progress, specially in the agricultural domain.

> This is rather distressing because agriculture is the basis of all our development work. If we fail in agriculture, it does not matter what else we achieve—how many plants we put up—our economic development will not be complete. ... Agriculture is more important than industry for the simple reason that industry depends on agriculture. Industry, which is, no doubt, very important, will not progress unless agriculture is sound and stable and progressive. I find there is a passion in many areas of India for industrial plants. Well, all good luck to those who want them. Let them have it. People seem to think that an industrial plant solves all the problems of poverty, which it does not. It has a long-term effect on the economy, no doubt. And I have no doubt in my mind that the problem of poverty will not be solved in India except through industrial progress, industrial progress of the latest type. That is the truth. However, at the present moment, whichever way you start in India, you come back to agriculture. We dare not be slack about it, as we have been, I'm afraid, in many places. (Nehru 1963b)[21]

The final extract is from a speech delivered less than six months before Nehru's death:

> Though we all know that agriculture is essential and basic, it has been rather neglected. I say neglected in the sense that people hoped that crops will grow by themselves and not by much effort on our part. Now, greater attention is being paid to it and I hope this will bear results. There are all manner of things that go into agriculture. We have large irrigation schemes, but it takes a long time for us to take advantage of them fully. We first spent a lot of money and energy in building them. Between the two there has been a long gap. We should plan for their full utilisation in advance. (Nehru 1964)

As is often the case, political leaders can be a little too close in time to historical events to be able to evaluate them dispassionately. In retrospect, Nehru was proved to be unduly pessimistic. A growth transition in agriculture was to come within a year of the last of the speeches. An acceleration in agricultural growth rate took place in the mid-1960s, plausibly[22] even in 1964–5, the year of his death. Though he did not live to see its beneficial effects spread cross the Indian economy by stimulating other sectors, arguably, as set out in Chapter 3, this transition has at least partly to do with the policies implemented by his government.

I now turn to the record of economic growth in the India of the Nehru era.

THE GROWTH RECORD OF THE NEHRU ERA

We may use two sets of comparators to evaluate the growth performance of an economy. One is the record of preceding growth in the economy itself. The other is the contemporaneous growth of other economies similarly placed and the growth of leading economies over the long haul of their histories. We start therefore with a comparison of growth in the Nehru era with growth in the first half of the twentieth century, more precisely the period 1900–47, which marks the second half of the British Raj in India.

In Table 2.1 are arrayed growth rates over time of the three main sectors of the Indian economy. The layout of the Table enables us to see the economic performance of the Nehru era in century-wide perspective. In the first column are the data for the years 1900–47. In the second are the data on the same indicators for the rest of the twentieth century including the seventeen years of Jawaharlal Nehru's prime ministership. Finally, in the third column are presented the data for the period 1950–1 to 1964–5, the year of Nehru's death. Read together, the data convey two important points. First, not only does growth in the Nehru era amply exceed what was attained in the final half-century of colonial rule, but the quickening of the economy observed over the second half of the twentieth century may be seen to have been *already* achieved[23] in the Nehru era.

Table 2.1 Growth of GDP in the Twentieth Century

Sector	*1900–1 to 1946–7*	*1947–8 to 1999–2000*	*1950–1 to 1964–5*
Primary	0.4	2.5	2.6
Secondary	1.5	5.5	6.8
Tertiary	1.7	5.0	4.5
GDP	0.9	4.1	4.0
GDP per capita	0.1	1.9	1.9
Population	0.8	2.0	2.0

Source: Sivasubramonian (2000).
Notes: Growth is the average annual compound growth rate of GDP in 1948–9 prices; pre-1947 data are for 'undivided India' which includes the Indian states and Pakistan but excludes Burma.

Second, not only is there an acceleration of growth across all sectors but also the ranking of sectors by growth is reversed early with the commodity-producing sectors now growing faster than services which had been the fastest growing segment of the colonial economy. Following Kuznets's work on economic growth, high services growth in a low-income economy would be treated as a pathology. In a poor economy with a low level of consumption of even the most basic goods, a faster growth of the commodity-producing sectors would be considered desirable. The broad-based expansion of the economy during the Nehru era amounts to a transformation of the economy that is, perhaps, more likely to be readily recognized as such by economic historians.

To bring perspective to my argument, I refer[24] to a debate among economic historians on the significance of the Industrial Revolution, agreed to have taken place in Europe in the middle of the eighteenth century. In this context, Joel Mokyr (2005), a historian of technology, has observed that growth after the Industrial Revolution was not just higher but qualitatively different in at least three respects from what had gone before Mokyr. First, according to Mokyr, growth ceased to be a 'niche phenomenon'. Before 1750, it had been limited to relatively small areas or specific sectors. Second, while pre-1750 growth had seen 'institutional change in the widest sense', technological change, though not absent, was far too slow and localized compared to the role it was to play afterwards. Third, 'pre-modern' growth was vulnerable to setbacks and shocks both man-made and natural that made doubtful its sustainability. While it may not be entirely appropriate to transfer this description to the transformation of India during the Nehru era, as a certain amount of modern industry was already in place by 1947, the parallels are there to see. Though not all three of Mokyr's observations are evident from the data I have presented in Table 2.1, it would be agreed upon that the Nehru years witnessed growth spread across the economy, a technological advance was fostered, and, as we can now see, the rise in income has not only been sustained for over fifty years but the growth rate itself has actually been accelerating since.[25]

However, two of Mokyr's comments on the significance of the Industrial Revolution appear to have been tailor-made for the period that we are studying here. First, in response to the observation that the growth achieved in the early stage of the Revolution was not that much, he had responded that the change must not be seen as one of mere degree: 'There is a qualitative difference between an economy in which GDP per capita grows at 1.5 percent and one in which it grows at 0.2 percent' (Mokyr 2005: 286). While the parallel between the growth records for the period Mokyr speaks of and for the India of our period is—as is evident from Table 2.1—close indeed, it is his comment on the overall significance of the Industrial Revolution that is of greater import to us here. His evaluation is that 'It may have been slow, it may have been not all that industrial and even less revolutionary, it may not even have been wholly British, but it was the taproot of modern economic growth' (Mokyr 2005: 286). To seek parallels between the growth following the Industrial Revolution in Britain and the growth of India during the Nehru era may well prove to be a promising line of inquiry for a historian of the Indian economy.

However, I shall put to use Mokyr's characterization of the Industrial Revolution not to draw such a parallel but to highlight a difference between the two phases of the twentieth century in India under comparison here. While growth in the Nehru era was distinctly Indian, in that it was not dependent on either foreign trade or foreign aid, it certainly was 'not all that industrial'. Indeed the greatest expansion of the Indian economy of this period is not in industry at all. While the categories for which growth is recorded in Table 2.1 are somewhat broad, the data reveal that growth acceleration in the primary sector, largely comprising agriculture, had exceeded that of the secondary sector, more or less synonymous with industry. This has generally gone unrecognized, and I shall return to consider at length both the approach to agriculture and the record of its performance in these years. But for now, it is entirely worth recording Sivasubramonian's apposite assessment of the economic achievement of this period. He speaks of the economic recovery of the Nehru era as having been 'swift, smooth and remarkable' (Sivasubramonian 2000: 563).[26]

Before moving on, I might raise a point crucial to the comparison of growth over time. As the comparison has to be made at constant prices to be of any use, the choice of the base year for prices is crucial. I have used Sivasubramonian's estimates of GDP as they provide data at constant, that is, 1948–9, prices for the entire twentieth century. There are of course alternative estimates for the period 1900–47 and these give way to a very different insight into the period. For instance, Angus Maddison's estimates[27] of GDP growth, in 1938–9 prices, for this period show the average annual growth rate of per capita output virtually stagnating at 0.04 per cent per annum. This estimate would suggest a far more significant turnaround following the end of the colonial era in India.

I now turn to the second of the two standard comparators of the growth performance of an economy already alluded to, namely, the performance of other economies. Two sets of economies have been chosen here for comparison with India during the Nehru era. The first is a set of Asian economies. These were more or less at par with India in terms of per capita income in 1950. The second is a set of the world's best-performing economies of all time. In Table 2.2 are presented growth rates attained by these two groups of countries. Of the two sets of economies for which data are presented, a comparison of India's performance with that of the Asian economies is of greater interest for two reasons. First, the data are for the same period; second, as stated, in terms of per capita income,

Table 2.2 Economic Growth in India Compared

	1950–64	*1820–1992*
India	4.1	–
China	2.9	–
Korea	6.1	–
United States	–	3.6
United Kingdom	–	1.9
Japan	–	2.8

Source: Maddison (1995).
Note: Data are average annual growth rates.

Korea and China had economies that were more or less at par with India in 1950. A noteworthy finding emerges. From the work of DeLong (2003) we know that while India has grown faster than most of Africa during the last five decades, it has performed worse than East Asia. If Korea is taken as synonymous with East Asia, then this feature holds also for the period 1950–64. Korea's growth rate is 50 per cent higher than India's for this period. However, we find that India's growth rate is 25 per cent higher than that of China. This may be little known, but it is not entirely surprising. Actually, China was to pull ahead of India only a decade and a half after the Nehru era, in the late 1970s, following the reforms launched by Deng Xiao Ping. Possessed of this information we would be inclined to believe that admiration for Mao Zedong's China in certain circles in India during his lifetime must have been based more on his revolutionary potential than on the early economic achievements of China.[28] This is clear, for the revelations of the disastrous consequences of the Great Leap Forward—including an estimated 30 million deaths allegedly due to famine in the late 1950s—were received uncritically here. While this may well be expected of those ideologically committed to the Chinese path, one thing is clear from our comparison. In a comparison with China it now appears that, at least in terms of growth, Nehru had not left the Indian economy too far behind. The subsequent tearing away of China, reflected in the falling behind of India in the world's growth league tables, must therefore owe itself to causes other than his leadership.

No less revealing is a comparison of the growth in India during 1950–64 with long-term growth in the leading OECD (Organisation for Economic Co-operation and Development) economies. We find from Table 2.2 that the former had exceeded the latter, often substantially. It is now possible to place in perspective Raj Krishna's lament (see Krishna 1980: 28) that independent India's record of growth, over 1960 to 1977, placed it lower than ninety countries worldwide. Krishna had used *per capita* GDP as his measure. This succeeds in masking the degree of progress made in the Nehru era. An altogether unexpected consequence of the transformation of the economy had been a very significant rise (see Table 2.1) in the rate of growth of population. Now the measured rate of growth of per capita GDP is lowered.

Two observations are in order here. From Table 2.1 we can see that were the rate of growth of population to remain at the colonial rate, the rate of growth of per capita income during 1950–64 would have exceeded 3 per cent. This is more than twice[29] the rate of growth of per capita income of US and UK during 1820–1992, and exceeds that attained by Japan during the same period. Before I move on to my second observation I might remark that, actually, the counterfactual considered is quite absurd as the growth of population is very likely endogenous with respect to the growth of income. This leads me to the observation itself. The rise in the rate of growth of population per se serves as an indicator far more vivid of the extent and nature of the economic transformation achieved than any estimated rise in the rate of growth. Life expectancy at birth rose from 32 years in the 1940s to 37 years in the 1950s and to 43 years in the 1960s (Bhat 2001). Demographers (Ibid.) have put down the rise in the rate of growth of population in the period that we are studying to the increase in the fertility rate, itself due to the decline in the incidence of malaria and widowhood, presumably due to improving public health outreach. The fertility rate itself may be seen as an index of a population's perception of the future of an economy. Instances in world history that encourage such an interpretation range from the decline in fertility observed during the uncertain transition to a market economy in Russia in the 1990s to its rise in post-war United States, a time of high optimism of America's future as a society. The 1950s in India had witnessed the highest increase in the fertility rate among all decades since 1947.[30]

A methodological point needs to be made here, one that will serve as more than a mere justification for the method that I have pursued. Note that in Table 2.2 I have compared growth in India during the Nehru years with very long-term growth of the advanced OECD economies. Far from loading the outcome of the comparison in favour of the former, as may be assumed, this actually tilts the balance in the direction of the latter economies. For we know that long-term growth rate of the industrialized economies has accelerated[31] over the last couple of centuries. Therefore, the longer the time period we consider, the greater the likelihood of observing a higher growth rate for these economies when compared with a shorter series commencing from a time when their per capita income was the same as that of India's in, say, 1950. This observation has, in addition, the virtue of placing in perspective the achievement of the Nehru era. In the presence of increasing returns to scale, the observed growth cannot be dismissed as merely the arithmetic outcome of measuring a given increase against a 'low base'.[32] At best a statistical commentary, such an assessment misses the implication that from an *economic* standpoint a low base is actually a serious impediment to initiating growth in the presence of increasing returns to scale.[33] At the level of the firm, increasing returns to scale can arise from a variety of sources, the simplest to comprehend being large fixed costs due to the lumpiness of investment. This retards entry. As for increasing returns at the level of the economy, we have already encountered Allyn Young's conceptualization of the phenomenon in Chapter 1. Thus, the early initiation of sustained growth in the India of the 1950s after half a century of stagnation is non-trivial. Indeed, it was a substantial achievement. Interestingly, at the time, Nehru himself had demonstrated a clear idea of the magnitudes involved in the task of raising the rate of growth: 'We have aimed at 5 percent in this Plan, and five percent is going to be a hard job. We shall have to work very hard, because we have started at such low levels, with such low surpluses. India is almost at the lowest rung of the income ladder. Even China, I believe, is a little higher. So was Russia at the time of the Revolution' (Nehru 1956). The challenge that India was faced with as it aimed at faster growth in the 1950s had been sharply appraised by its leadership.

WHAT QUICKENED A MORIBUND ECONOMY

There remains no question about the fact of a dramatic quickening of the Indian economy since the initiation of planned economic development in the second half of the twentieth century. To quote a prominent economist of the time writing in 1965, 'The rate of economic growth that has been achieved in India since 1950–51 is 2 to 3 times as high as the rate recorded earlier under British administration. As a result the percentage increase in national income in the last thirteen years has been higher than the percentage increase realised in India over the entire preceding half century' (Raj 1965: 2). However, it remains to be established what brought about this transformation. Accounting for this transformation would also serve a constituency larger than those with a particular interest in the recent history of India. It would constitute one answer to the larger question, flagged in the 'Introduction' as generally of interest to economists, namely, 'How do economies grow?'[34]

To get a handle on the task that confronts us, we may start by eliminating the factors that clearly cannot be credited with the turnaround. Going by the conventional wisdom of today, trade would be a prime candidate for consideration as potentially crucial. For a sample of the view that openness is central to faster growth, consider this: 'Low or declining barriers to trade constitute a necessary condition for sustained rapid growth' (Panagariya 2005: 7). Trade clearly is a non-starter when it comes to explaining the growth acceleration of the 1950s, for the fifteen years from 1950 had witnessed a progressive closing of the trade regime. Of course, export promotion is not necessarily at odds with a regime of imports controls, especially in the 1950s when international surveillance was not of the order that we find today. So it would not be entirely absurd to imagine export-led growth even in a relatively protectionist regime. But this is clearly not a reasonable description of the Nehru era when the economy had faced severe balance of payments stress, a feature inconsistent with export-led growth. In fact, though Mahalanobis had been inspired by the vision of an India permanently freed from the balance of payments constraint, this was certainly not achieved even ten years after the launching of the Second Five Year Plan. Yet, from a methodological point of view, we would want to remind ourselves that a balance of payments surplus is not a recipe for faster growth. It is instructive in this context to note that India had ended its colonial period with positive sterling balances. Nevertheless, the period 1900–47 was one of the most stagnant phases in India's recorded history. To take a more contemporary example, in the second half of the twentieth century, Africa has remained one of the more open economic areas of the world (Castells 2000). However, this has not prevented it from remaining the most depressed.

Let us now consider another possibility among factors responsible for faster growth in India. That is the end of colonialism. Much of India had been a *de facto* colony for about two centuries prior to 1947. This meant that its economy had been subjugated to Britain's imperial interests, an arrangement likely to have stifled its potential. Though some economists today tend to overlook this,[35] it was recognized by Indian entrepreneurs of the time. In particular, the visionary engineer M. Visvesvaraya (1936) has written extensively of the obstructions by the colonial Government of

India that Indian industrialists had faced in their plans to invest in new projects and points to this as the reason for the failure of industrialization[36] in the Indian subcontinent. Visvesvaraya had listed four 'failings' of the colonial government. These were the refusal to publish the statistics that would reveal the dismal condition of India, the neglect of banking, the denial of tariff protection to Indian industry, and 'the grave deficiency which affects economic advance [which] is neglect of mass education'. Overall, Visvesvaraya paints a picture of the malign neglect of India's industrialization by the colonial state in comparison with the role of government in the West, particularly England itself. It is markedly at odds with the characterization by Morris (1992: 199) that 'there can be no doubt that in India during the century and a half of British rule the market was given its head. India was one of the great social experiments in letting self-interest and markets do virtually everything'. If Morris' characterization of British policy were true, the data in Table 2.1 would constitute a particularly damaging verdict on the capacity of markets on their own to promote economic development.

An apparently straightforward test of the Visvesvaraya hypothesis would be whether the tide turned after the end of colonialism with India's entrepreneurs, set free from the colonial yoke, leading the turnaround of the economy. However, this is a proposition not easy to test, as 'everything else' did not 'remain the same', violating *ceteris paribus*, the staple of economists. Principally, the post-colonial state had adopted a role which would have profound implications for private sector behaviour. On the one hand, it intervened in the economy by raising public investment, which is likely to have extended the market for the private sector's product. On the other hand, it also intervened by restraining private sector activity. Indeed, in the minds of some, this stifled the private sector at least as much as it had been stifled by the colonial Government of India. Be that as it may, granting that there was a change in the overall policy regime after 1947 makes it difficult to test the proposition of interest here. For instance, it would be difficult to deny that Indian entrepreneurship was stifled under the Raj even if the private sector is seen not to have led the revival after 1947. But we are not without clues whatsoever. We have seen that the revival of the Indian economy was broad based (see Table 2.1) while the sector that had allegedly been suppressed most, in order to further British industrial interests, during the colonial era was the manufacturing sector. So the end of the colonial suppression of India entrepreneurship cannot be credited as the sole factor responsible for the revival of the Indian economy, even though the end of colonialism was *sine qua non* for actualizing the political project of quickening India. The factors responsible for this must be traced to some more active agency. How then was the dramatic turnaround of India achieved? There can be no doubt that it was state-directed.[37] However, it yet remains for us to provide an account of the mechanism.

It can be argued that the quickening of the Indian economy followed from a coordinated public effort to spring the economy from the low-level equilibrium trap that had held it down for close to half a century.[38] To see how low levels of national income can result from coordination failure we need to first apprehend the idea of a complementarity between the economic actions of individual agents. This is best understood in the context of a firm considering making an investment. A central element in this decision problem is the firm's forecast of its future revenues. Now this productivity depends upon the future path of average capital accumulation by all firms in the economy. If our firm believes that this path will swiftly rise, it would predict a correspondingly high rate of growth of its own productivity because of the 'externality' involved. Where firms hold identical expectations, each firm will be more willing to invest, raising the rate of growth of its capital, and thus income in the economy. We see here that the decision to accumulate capital by one firm provides an incentive for others to undertake the same action. This is the externality referred to. Here it takes the specific form of a complementarity in that capital accumulation by one firm encourages capital accumulation by others.

It was Rosenstein-Rodan (1943), reflecting upon the question of the reconstruction of a war-torn Europe, who had identified the role of complementarities in precipitating a low-level equilibrium trap. He had proposed that a low level of income is the outcome of an economy-wide coordination failure, in which some investments do not occur simply because other complementary investments are not made and the latter are not forthcoming only because the former are missing. It is possible to comprehend this outcome from the decision problem of the firm that we had considered. At a very general plane, one firm's investment is the source of another firm's profits, making this second firm viable and providing it with the incentive to invest.

Coordination failure results as follows. Where no entrepreneur is large enough to invest in more than one line of activity, each entrepreneur would invest only if he/she were to believe that others would invest as well. Now we have two possible equilibria, one in which the region is devoid of any investment at all and another in which there is investment by all, expectations being uniform across firms. Either way, the outcome is a 'coordinated equilibrium' in that each firm's decision is based on its expectation of the behaviour of others, resulting in an outcome coordinated in this sense. In this account, a low-level equilibrium is a market failure. The implication of this type of reasoning is that a better outcome—with income high—is possible, but is not necessarily attained in an economy of free agents maximizing profits. Notice that whether or not such an outcome arises depends upon each agent's expectations of the actions of others. To the extent that the formation of expectations is driven by past history, a stagnant society could remain so whereas an already active one would remain active, even though there may be nothing intrinsically different between the two regions.

The idea of a coordination failure—whereby an economy is trapped in a 'bad' equilibrium when a more desirable one exists—is particularly compelling when it comes to a diverse economy with industries developed to a different degree, if only for the reason that now coordination across these many diverse industries would be required. Such diversity is likely to be appropriately descriptive of the Indian economy at Independence. If 'coordination failure' describes well the stagnant state of the Indian economy at that point in time, it is also easy to imagine the complexity of the task of achieving a coordinated expansion to a higher level of income in a large and diversified economy.

The early literature on development economics had proposed two solutions to the coordination problem. To understand them we need to take on board the concept of linkages. This concept springs from the view that the economy is an interlinked entity. Hirschman (1958) had conceived of backward and forward linkages. Forward linkages ease the supply conditions of a sector. Thus, the steel industry facilitates the development of the railways by making available a crucial input at a lower price. On the other hand, a backward linkage raises the demand for the product of a sector, as when the development of the steel industry historically raised the demand for coal. Forward linkages *push* the economy while backward linkages *pull* it, so to speak. This feature, that an economy is interlinked, provides the means to shift the economy out of a coordination failure that leaves it stranded at a low level of income. In 1943 Rosenstein-Rodan had proposed a programme of coordinated investment in several sectors meant to shock an economy out of its lethargy, so to speak. Such a policy has two requirements. The first is economic in that a very large investment outlay is needed to make a difference. In subsequent writing Rosenstein-Rodan (1963) was to refer to this critical minimum effort as a 'Big Push'. The second requirement is informational. The 'coordinator'—reasonably assumed to be the state alone—must have an idea of the proportions in which consumers spend their income on the different commodities, or we could end up having too much coal and too little soap, for instance. However, the existence of linkages between the sectors of an economy makes it possible to overcome both these potential handicaps. This takes us to the solution proposed by Hirschman.

Hirschman had implied that Rosenstein-Rodan's proposal of investing in the major sectors simultaneously was akin to promoting balanced growth in the economy. Instead we could envisage *unbalanced* growth, a situation where the initial investment is targeted on some specific sector(s). Indeed, the idea is to deliberately foster unbalanced growth by investing in certain leading sectors. With this, both forward and backward linkages are activated and the production response gets the whole economy moving. Exactly as does the Big Push, this strategy too shifts the economy onto the desirable equilibrium. However, it differs in that it makes use of the market, exploiting potential linkages, with the government presumably investing only in the leading sector. Note that this strategy is less vulnerable to the two requirements of the Big Push, for here both the scale of the public investment entailed and the informational requirement are likely to be less.

But where the government's investible resources are limited and not all sectors are equally endowed with linkages, the question of which sector to choose is not a trivial one. It is obvious that the sector(s) chosen must possess both numerous and strong links with the rest of the economy. However, it is a less obvious criterion that emerges as of interest, that of the intrinsic profitability of a sector. In the context, this is a treacherous concept as we had earlier introduced the idea of a complementarity by arguing that the profitability of an investment depends upon investments elsewhere in the economy. But let us overlook the circularity that this implies and persist with the idea of intrinsic profitability best captured by the American expression 'bang for the buck'. Once we have arrayed activities according to their intrinsic profitability, the investment priority of government would turn out to be the exact reverse of that of the private sector. That is, in the context, the government's priority would be to first invest in the least profitable sector because this is unlikely to be taken up by the private sector. Exactly as a chain is only as strong as its weakest link, '*the government maximises the chances of overcoming coordination failure by investing in the least profitable activity*, provided of course that such activities have linkages as well' (Ray 1998: 141; emphasis original). Now, adopting the least profitable sector for public investment is the strategic choice to be made.

This extended foray into the debates in early development economics was meant to provide a window on what was attempted in India in the Nehru era. We of course know that in a bid to quicken the economy, a programme of massive public investment was initiated with the onset of planning in 1951. However, it is of interest yet to understand how precisely this may have worked to bring about the dramatic rise in the rate of growth. Ray (1998: 142–3) has imaginatively suggested that the Mahalanobis Model was essentially a scheme for promoting unbalanced growth, with heavy industry as the leading sector. It is certainly true that heavy industry has substantial linkages with the rest of the economy—forward into agriculture and backward into consumer goods and services. Ray's view appears to be borne out by the data on the proposed sectoral allocation of investment in the Second Five Year Plan presented in Table 2.3. From there, we find that, in line with popular perception, 'industry' does get the largest share of the outlay. However, this is not overwhelmingly so. First, there are other sectors of the economy that come close to having been allocated a similar share. Second, and in any case, industry's share does not exceed even a third of the total outlay. Therefore, even as the share received by industry may count for its being singled out as the 'leading' sector, the suggestion of an 'unbalanced growth' having been pursued in India would appear inappropriate as a characterization of the Nehru–Mahalanobis Strategy.

Table 2.3 The Allocation of Public Investment in the Second Five Year Plan

Sector	*Outlay (Rs crore)*	*Share (%)*
Electricity	450	13.2
Industry	1000	29.4
Transport and communication	850	25.0
Agriculture and irrigation	750	22.1
Construction	250	7.4
Stocks	100	2.9

Source: Adapted from Mahalanobis (1955b).

Of course, in relative terms, industry was allocated much more than agriculture than is conveyed by the figures per se, for industry accounted for a much smaller share of GDP than agriculture in 1956. But what strikes one most after a gap of half a century is how balanced the proposed allocation of investment appears, given India's needs at that stage of its development. Also, the large allocation to industry must be seen in perspective. I repeat a point made by me earlier and one that I shall return to. This is that the planners had envisioned industrialization contributing directly to raising agricultural productivity and thus agricultural growth. Interestingly, from the point of view of the history of ideas, this would be case of recognizing forward linkages even before the appearance of Hirschman's article on the unbalanced growth. Nevertheless, though the Nehru–Mahalanobis Strategy, which had undergirded the industrialization drive of the Indian state, did have as its central element the heavy goods sector—thus bearing similarity with a strategy of unbalanced growth—I find it more plausible to see the quickening of the Indian economy as due to a Big Push driven by expanding public investment.[39] Not only was there a wide spreading of this investment across the economy, as seen in Table 2.3, but the economy had already quickened[40] before the launching of the Second Five Year Plan and all its sectors were to accelerate again, though at differing points, over the next three decades.

However, the most important reason for rejecting an unbalanced-growth type explanation for the acceleration of growth in India during the Nehru era is that the acceleration was very likely led by agriculture. This may be surmised by taking the information in Table 2.1 along with the additional information that agriculture constituted by far the largest share of the economy in the 1950s. Recall that a sector's contribution to the growth of the economy is its share-weighted growth rate. The full contribution to Indian economic development of the state-directed heavy-industry-drive was to come much later, and some suggest it continues to this day.[41] Be that as it may, the industrial sector did expand substantially (see Table 2.1) in the Nehru era. Its accelerated growth during this period along with that of the agricultural and services sectors reflects the movement along a broad front that is the hallmark of the Big Push strategy.

The argument that the expansion of the Indian economy in the post-colonial era may be seen as due to a state-directed drive such as a Big Push is properly verified by reference to the data on public investment. Data on

Table 2.4 Saving and Investment
(per cent of GDP)

Year	*Private corporate sector*			*Public sector*		
	S	*I*	*(S-I)*	*S*	*I*	*(S-I)*
1950–5	1.0	1.4	–0.4	1.7	3.1	–1.4
1960–5	1.7	3.6	–1.9	3.0	7.5	–4.4
1989–90	2.1	3.9	–1.8	1.7	10.7	–9.0

Source: *National Accounts Statistics*, New Delhi: Central Statistical Organisation (CSO).

saving and investment by the public and private sectors, respectively, are provided in Table 2.4.

All of it points to the plausibility of the explanation provided here. Several points may be noted. First and foremost, there is a very substantial expansion of public investment as a share of GDP. Note that such an expansion, exceeding two-and-a-half times the original figure by the end of the Nehru era, has not been matched in India for the next quarter century. Though not apparent from the highly aggregative data presented here, it is not only the magnitude of the expansion of public investment that is significant but also its direction. As in the Big Push, according to the Nehru–Mahalanobis Strategy, investment was to have flowed in all directions (see Table 2.3) simultaneously. Contrast this with the limited public spending outside of administration and the railways by the colonial government. Interestingly, there is an almost identical expansion of the private corporate sector during this period. This too is unmatched for the next twenty-five years.

Some comments would be appropriate here. The first concerns causality. Even though the expansion is contemporaneous, going by economic theory we would on balance imagine the public sector contributing to the expansion of private investment by expanding the market for its goods and at the same time supplying the capital goods necessary at a lower price. Forces making for greater public investment following from private investment are more difficult to imagine, reflected in the assumption of autonomous public spending in macroeconomic theory. Second, the degree of expansion of the private sector in the Nehru era is perhaps little known today and seldom recognized as a feature of the period. However, this record makes it a little difficult to sustain the argument that the policy regime was relentlessly hostile to it. Added to this is the fact that the expansion of the private sector was also very likely financed by the other sectors within the economy. Note that the saving–investment gap for the private corporate sector widened very substantially during this period. This implies that corporate investment was financed by the household sector, the external sector, and even by the public sector[42] itself. Therefore, it is not as if, even in the era of so-called 'high planning', the private sector had had to pull itself up by its bootstraps. Of course, this could not have neutralized any heavy-handedness of the bureaucracy in the implementation that may have stifled the growth of some firms and retarded private sector development to an extent.[43] However, judging by the expansion in investment, it would not be inappropriate to surmise that the private corporate sector as a whole appears not to have done too badly in the Nehru era.[44]

The role of the government in quickening the economy in the second half of the twentieth century is unmistakable. It was of course in keeping with the plan of the Indian state. However, the government's calculations had gone awry in the process on one count. This pertains to the role of external assistance in financing plan outlay in the public sector. As I have already pointed out, the proposed budget for the Second Five Year Plan had anticipated for foreign assistance a share of only 5 per cent. The outcome was to turn out to be far different. The shares of different sources in the financing of public sector outlay during the Nehru era (and slightly beyond, as we have included the entire Third Plan period) are to be found in Table 2.5. Note that the figure recorded for the Second Plan had exceeded by far the figure of 5 per cent intended. More significantly, the share of foreign assistance had risen steadily after the commencement of planning.

Table 2.5 Financing of the Public Sector Plan (in per cent)

	First Plan	*Second Plan*	*Third Plan*	*Seventh Plan*
Own resources	38.4	26.3	33.8	27.4
Domestic capital receipts	35.0	30.8	24.8	48.9
Net foreign inflow	9.6	22.5	28.2	8.7
Deficit financing	17.0	20.4	13.2	15.1
Total	100.0	100.0	100.0	100.0

Source: Bagchi and Nayak (1994).

The role of foreign assistance in financing the public expenditure, which in turn had stepped up the rate of growth in India, cannot be overlooked. Indeed, by the end of the Third Plan, it was a significant source at close to 30 per cent. This is mostly glossed over. However, three observations may be made relating to foreign assistance to India during the Nehru era. First, except for the Soviet Union, it is difficult to think of many other countries that have transformed their economies as rapidly without significant external financing. The United States had received British capital and Britain in its time had had its trade surplus with India, arguably some of it disguised plunder[45]. China had received aid from the USSR[46] and South Korea from the United States. So foreign assistance per se does not take away from India's achievement in transforming her economy quite rapidly and against significant odds. Second, by comparison with other developing countries attempting a similar transformation at that time, the amounts received by India were not large in relation to its size. For instance, at US$ 1.8—being the average for the years 1962 and 1963—the aid per capita received by India was a fifth of that received by South Korea and less that thirty times that received by Israel. In 1964–5, total aid—loans and grants—stood at 3.5 per cent of national income.[47] Finally, it is significant that, at least during the Nehru era, aid did not compromise India's objective of self-reliant industrialization. As Bhagwati and Desai (1970: 187) have observed: 'By and large the aid has gone towards "Industrial Development". This is in keeping with, and sharply underlines, the general Indian strategy of development as also the economic philosophies of the time which under-emphasised the *productive* significance of expenditure on education and other social services as also the role of agriculture.' Indeed, India's position appears to have been stronger than it is today when in somewhat frantically seeking FDI by showcasing its economic architecture it appears to have lost a sense of its priorities, the haste to usher in full capital account convertibility before the global financial crisis succeeded in erasing its charm being the most noticeable case in point.

Of course, more than any particular strength of India's, the availability of external funding for her economic plan in the 1950s had to do with the international politics of the time. The Nehru era had coincided with much of the Cold War and as a non-aligned country India had been sought after by the protagonists on both sides. While Soviet aid had come early and without strings, aid from the West and the multilateral loans under the aegis of this grouping predominated over loans from the Eastern Block, though these came at a higher rate of interest (Bhagwati and Desai 1970: Tables 10.1, 10.2, and 10.5). There is altogether little reason to believe that Indian economic policy had been influenced by excessive dependence on borrowing from any particular quarter. On the contrary, Kalecki (1976: 35) must surely have had India in mind when he compared the developing countries with intermediate regimes to 'the proverbial clever calves that suck two cows'.

Caricature of a Vision: Through a Glass, Darkly

In a final section of this chapter I address some lingering perceptions regarding the Nehru–Mahalanobis Strategy and the outcome of the policies that had been adopted as part of its implementation. Though these are often propagated by simplistic or, worse still, sentimental readings, I consider it important to do so as the allegation that we continue to pay for a misguided road map adopted in the 1950s is a serious one.

'The Neglect of Agriculture'

There are two ways in which a sector can be neglected. First, it could be ignored in the policy discourse itself, with insufficient attention devoted to its problems. Negligence could also take the form of insufficient resources being devoted to the desired expansion of a sector. I have already suggested in the course of the discussion so far that agriculture had received direct attention and considerable resources during the Nehru era. To widen the window, I first present the view on the matter of two economists of the time, and then return to provide a perspective of my own. V.K.R.V. Rao, a doyen of Indian economists, had had a ringside view of the Indian economy for about five decades starting in the 1940s. He has had the following to say:

> It has been alleged that the priorities assigned … in India's planned development have been based on a mistaken imitation of Soviet planning and that higher priority should have been given to agriculture and consumer industries instead of to capital goods industries. … The emphasis placed on capital goods industries was the result of an understandable desire to furnish the country with domestic supplies of the crucial inputs of economic growth so that the rate of growth could be much faster than if the country had to rely essentially on foreign aid for its requirements of capital and intermediate goods. Apart from this it is not correct to suggest that planning under Nehru did not give sufficient priority to agriculture. In fact, of the total investment undertaken during the first three Five-Year Plans … agriculture, including irrigation, accounted for Rs. 3, 446 crores, or 22.7 percent, while economic infra-structure, like transport and communications, and power, accounted for Rs. 5, 737 crores or 37.7 percent and social services for Rs. 2, 760 crores or 18.1 percent. Industry accounted

for only Rs. 2, 651 crores or 17.2 percent of investment in the public sector during the fifteen years covered by the three Plans. (Rao 1971: 72)[48]

Raj Krishna was an economist in a very different mould from V.K.R.V. Rao. Chicago-trained and, given the political climate of the time, cast as somewhat of a right winger, his writings show him to be a more acute observer of Indian economy history than many of his peers. Overall, Raj Krishna suggests that there may have been a mistake only in the proportions in which investment had flowed into different channels rather than 'in the choice of the plural strategy which had always characterized Indian planning'. On the specific issue that we are considering, he has stated:

Nehru, as indeed all planners, attached prime importance to agriculture. Nearly a fifth of the public sector Plan outlay has been consistently allocated to agricultural development. In addition, heavy investments were made in industries producing agricultural inputs and processing agricultural outputs. There was a massive increase in the flow of credit to the agricultural sector from Rs. 70 crores in 1950–51 to Rs. 2, 000 crores in 1975–6. Almost all agricultural inputs are subsidized; agricultural income is lightly taxed, and during the last thirteen years minimum prices, covering the full cost of production have been guaranteed for all major crops. This set of policies can hardly be described as embodying the neglect of agriculture. But the fact still remains that the allocations for agriculture (particularly irrigation, extension and fertilizer production) and for rural infrastructure and social services could and should have been higher. (Krishna 1979: 60)

The facts of the case, at least with respect to the allocation of resources, as presented by Rao and Krishna, must persuade all but the wilful disbeliever. Of course, it would be the case that in per capita terms the direct allocation to agriculture was certainly lower than that to industry as the rural population dwarfed every other cohort in the economy. But to rest with this awareness would be to adopt a myopic approach. To state somewhat differently a point already made, planned industrialization is not a rival to agricultural expansion, and Mahalanobis had realized the same, as we have observed. On the contrary, faster agricultural growth, it was diagnosed, needed more industrial inputs, whether fertilizer for nutrient replenishment, iron and steel for implements, or cement for irrigation conduits. Moreover, agricultural production was relatively free from controls in the Nehru era while private industry was subject to stringent policy controls, above all in the form of licensing. license raj

There is of course a different approach to assessing the belief that agriculture was neglected. This is to account for intent by outcome rather than pronouncement. Now, only the performance would count. We have already looked at the growth of agriculture in the Nehru era, though the information had been nested within the larger category of 'primary sector'. The data presented in Table 2.1 show unambiguously that the agricultural sector grew very impressively in this period, recording the highest growth acceleration among all sectors in making a dramatic recovery from the colonial era. This can hardly be seen to result from neglect, either benign or malign.[49] Indeed, the scale of this achievement and the role of political agency in the form of a determined and capable leadership are fully comprehended only when we study in some detail the state of Indian agriculture in 1947.

Though it is the de-industrialization of India under colonial rule that has received most attention from historians, it is the decimation of the countryside that is perhaps the leitmotif of the British Raj in India. For a century and a half, ending with the Bengal Famine of 1943, there had been some devastating famines, with one particular famine in Bengal under the administration of the East India Company in the eighteenth century believed to have wiped out a third of the population. These famines were directly related to the policies of extortionate taxation and forced commercialization of agriculture pursued by the Company. As historians have provided outstanding accounts and analyses of these events, I go directly to summarize the findings of George Blyn on the trend in output in the first half of the twentieth century. Blyn had divided the period 1891–1947 into ten overlapping ten-year slices which he termed 'reference decades'. He then estimated both the average annual rate of growth and the change in the rate of growth across these reference decades, for foodgrains and non-foodgrains separately. To help focus a little better on his findings, I have collected in Table 2.6 the estimates for foodgrains. This data presents us with an unedifying picture of Indian agriculture under the Raj.

First, the rate of growth of foodgrains as a whole is far lower than the rate of growth of population, implying declining availability per capita. The output of rice, the grain consumed by the largest number in India then (and even now), actually declined. His findings were summarized by Blyn as follows: 'In the most general measure of the change in rates over time, the trend in reference decade rates, all eight foodgrains showed retardation' (1966: 96). The record of non-foodgrains is better, with a far greater average growth rate in the aggregate. However, this reflects accurately the raison d'etre of the colonial project in India, which was the exploitation of natural resources and commandeering of the market

Table 2.6 Agricultural Growth in British India

Crop	*Average annual growth over ten reference decades*	*Change in the reference decade rates of growth*
Aggregate	0.11	–0.17
Rice	–0.09	–0.03
Wheat	0.84	–0.09
Jowar	0.05	–0.12
Gram	0.26	–0.34
Bajra	0.72	–0.11
Barley	0.02	–0.55
Maize	0.51	–0.17
Ragi	–0.37	–0.23
Population	0.67	0.11

Source: Blyn (1966: 96).

of the colony for the benefit of metropolitan industry. Indeed, the glacial progress of foodgrains production is directly related to this strategy, implemented partly through price incentives and partly by brute[50] force. It cannot come as a surprise that food supply for the native population experienced collateral damage.

The performance of the economy in the Nehru era must also be evaluated in light of the agricultural legacy of colonialism. To have contributed to two accelerations in the rate of growth of agriculture[51] within two decades of the end of colonial rule comes close to being spectacular and places in perspective the grievance that agriculture was ignored in comparison with the attention paid to industry within the Nehru–Mahalanobis Strategy. Indeed we need to recognize the reversal of the decay of agriculture in the first half of the twentieth century as one of the great achievements of independent India, and this was largely achieved in the Nehru era.[52] I submit this radically revised reading of the period.

'The Black Hole of Public Enterprise'

The second among perceptions of the policies of the Nehru era that I would like to flag pertains to the idea of a public sector. In India today there is an unmistakable frustration with the public sector. It is associated with a poor performance record, marked for its lack of innovation, disdained for its shirking of social responsibility, and perceived as parasitic on the public finances. On the last, an additional consideration from further left, beyond the political parties intermittently in power in some states, would be that it is financed disproportionately by the poor who are not even among its principal beneficiaries. Much of this is not off the mark as a description of the state of affairs. However, the belief among many that this outcome is intrinsic to the Nehruvian conception of the public sector is far from correct. In this section I undertake two tasks. I first establish the rationale for the setting up of the public sector in India. I then consider one indicator of its performance during the Nehru era.

I choose to retrieve the original idea of the public sector and its performance record during the Nehru period within the overall project of resource mobilization. This would not be considered unusual, I presume, for the hallmark of any successful developmental effort is the mobilization of resources. It is not necessary that the resources mobilized must be contained within the public sector. After all, private investment is an equally legitimate component of aggregate investment in an economy. However, in the context of Indian industrialization, launched in the 1950s, a large part of this mobilization would necessarily have had to be in the public sector as it was intended that the state would play the leading role here. For planning to be effective, there is required, if not a concentration of resources in its hands, a substantial financial capacity with the state.[53] Where an economy is at a low income level, this requirement is likely to be large, in turn requiring the productive surplus to come progressively into the public sector, thus enabling it to maintain a command over resources.[54] In this section, I first present views on resource mobilization and the role of the public sector enterprises within that overall objective of both the government and of independent economists then active. Subsequently, I study the evidence on both resource mobilization and the contribution of the public sector to it.

As the Second Five Year Plan constituted the single largest instance of resource mobilization during the Nehru era, the official documentation related to it is the best source of the government's view on the question of interest to us here. There, in the section on financing in the recommendations for the Plan we find:

> Large financial resources would be required for the Second Plan. A small portion would come from sterling balances or foreign loans and aid; and the bulk of the resources must be found from within the economy. The tax system would be directed to collect an increasing part of the growing national income in order to permit greater capital formation in the public sector and to finance an expansion of social services.

The public sector would be extended to industrial and commercial activities where necessary for raising resources for public purposes. (Mahalanobis 1955b: 73)

This is echoed in the Industrial Policy Resolution of 1956 which states that the public sector was expected to 'augment the revenues of the state and provide resources for further development in fresh fields' (cited in Krishna 1988: 9). We find that the original idea of the public sector was not welfarist. In particular, the objective of having a public sector at all was to raise resources for the public purpose. Of course, this is not inconsistent with a strong welfare orientation. The issue here, however, is the role envisaged for the public sector when planning for economic development was launched in India.

The need for a very significant resource mobilization and the role of the public sector in relation to that task was also recognized by the independent economists of the day. Emphasizing that 'the effort involved in this increase is considerable, and will strain the economy a very great deal', the economists empanelled by the Planning Commission to scrutinize the proposals for the Second Plan had spoken of

the great difficulty of increasing tax proceeds unless a fundamental revision in current concepts that underlie the tax system is accepted. One of these concepts relates to the exemption of essentials from the scope of an important part of commodity taxation. When so large a measure of effort is necessary to increase the proportion of tax revenues to national income, which has remained so obstinately static, one cannot escape the logic of the fact that the mass of consumption is by the mass of the people. Unless this bears a somewhat higher burden of taxation, no perceptible change in the stubborn ratio of public revenues to national income can be achieved. We wish to endorse in particular, the Recommendation of the Taxation Enquiry Commission to the effect that Article 286(3) of the Constitution may be amended to remove the present exemption of articles 'essential to the life of the community' from the scope of state sales taxation. Simultaneously, measures to secure a practical ceiling on incomes through a steepening of taxes on income and wealth, including estate duties, becomes an imperative necessity. *A revision of the price policy of important public enterprises with a view to obtaining a larger surplus as a contribution to the resources for economic development is similarly required.* Besides the general increase in rates of direct and indirect taxation that will be involved in the considerable stepping up of tax effort will be part of the challenge to administrative efficiency that the big development effort for putting through the next Plan entails. (Planning Commission 1955: 115; emphasis mine)

Apart from the replication of the views of the government on the role of the public sector, quoted earlier, two points may be noted. First, the independent economists had recognized the serious resource mobilization effort entailed in the project of industrialization. Second, note the complete absence of populism in the recommendation that in the short-run even the convention of excluding essentials from taxation may have to be put in abeyance. The unstated expectation from the public sector is also reflected in the proposed government budget for the Second Five Year Plan. There, as I have pointed out already, the profits from state enterprises along with 'additional taxes and loans' exceed the amount of foreign assistance allowed for, and when combined with the contribution from the railways, amounts to close to one-eighth of the total outlay.[55] Finally, it is illuminating in the context to read Mahalanobis:

> In the highly developed countries of the West, taxes on commodities are usually looked upon as 'regressive', as being a burden on the poor. Public enterprises are also expected to be run on a no-loss-no-profit basis. Fortunately, our outlook is changing and it is being realised that in an underdeveloped country like India excise and customs duties, purchase tax on commodities or a levy on services would be convenient and adaptable methods to raise resources. It is also agreed in principle that public enterprises should earn and contribute increasing returns for purposes of national development. (Mahalanobis 1961: 96–7)

One thing is clear from these records of the time. Unlike today, fiscal populism was not considered a credible option by the architects of economic policy in early independent India.

While we may by now have an idea of the original conception of the role of the public sector in India, we are yet to have a picture of its performance. First, it may be repeated that a surge in public investment had been achieved in the Nehru era, a fifteen-year record of expansion that has not been surpassed. Second, the share of public savings in total savings had risen[56] by the end of the period. Though the extent of this increase is not much greater than that of the private corporate sector, it is still noteworthy that the expansion of investment was accompanied by an expansion of public saving, as was intended. We have in this an index of the role of the public sector in resource mobilization. Of course, this is not an argument regarding the sufficiency of that mobilization. While still on the topic, I present evidence on the behaviour of public sector savings during the period that we are looking at here. In Table 2.7 are presented data on savings of the public and private sectors. The public sector has been classified further into the 'public authorities' (comprising government administration and departmental commercial enterprises) and the 'non-departmental enterprises' (comprising government companies and statutory corporations).

Table 2.7 Public and Corporate Sector Savings (in current Rs crore)

Year	*Public sector*	*Public authorities*	*Non-departmental enterprises*	*Corporate*
1950–1	168	159	9	89
1951–2	252	243	9	132
1952–3	145	129	16	60
1953–4	127	107	20	86
1954–5	151	126	25	114
1955–6	172	145	27	130
1956–7	231	193	38	151
1957–8	245	195	50	117
1958–9	227	170	57	136
1959–60	236	176	60	180
1960–1	425	362	63	276
1961–2	494	426	68	315
1962–3	566	480	86	338
1963–4	709	586	123	387
1964–5	817	679	138	381

Source: Adapted from *National Accounts Statistics 1950–51 to 1987–88*, New Delhi: CSO.

Note from the table that while the expansion of savings in the public sector as a whole is as it is faster than the expansion in savings of the private corporate sector, within the former the non-departmental enterprises turn in a vastly superior performance compared to all groups. Though the savings of the non-departmental enterprises have continued to improve steadily for the next twenty years or so, during no other phase is the quite spectacular growth in their savings during 1950–64 matched.[57]

Three caveats to our assessment need be introduced, however. First, the rise in aggregate profits of the public sector is not incompatible with instances of chronic loss-making by individual units. Second, the data cannot serve as a measure of profitability, for which purpose we would need to factor in the volume of capital invested. And finally, this is not to be taken as a mark of the efficiency of the public sector, as we are very likely dealing also with monopolies here.

Emerging from this discussion is a view of the public sector held by the leadership in the Nehru era that is entirely at odds with what is perceived by latter day academic commentators. Equally, among the next generation of India's political class it has not been sufficiently well recognized that the public sector was originally conceived of as an active agent of resource mobilization for development. This led to its reincarnation as a flaccid employment-granting welfarist agency after the exit of Nehru from the political scene. For that very reason while we might today view with shock and awe the extraordinary record of public sector savings highlighted in Table 2.7, it was very likely seen as *comme il faut* by Nehru himself! For instance, consider the following extract from a speech made on the occasion of the inauguration of the second Hindustan Machine Tools Factory at Bangalore in 1961:

> There is a certain uniqueness about this function and the factory. The uniqueness lies in the fact that this factory has been made out of the profits or the surplus of the older Hindustan Machine Tools factory and, rightly, therefore, it is called a gift to the nation by those who have been working in the old factory. This should be a matter of great satisfaction to all those who are concerned with the HMT factory. (Nehru 1961)[58]

However, though the record of the public enterprises during the time may have been seen as entirely appropriate, the data presented in Table 2.7 must challenge the accounts of some economists of today. Thus, referring to 'the losses made by public enterprises', Bhagwati (1998: 6–7) has stated: 'Capital-intensive white elephants in the public sector were supported on the basis of models that deduced that this choice of techniques would yield a higher savings rate and hence higher growth: a conclusion that would now sound laughable, had its consequences not been so tragic.' Presumably Professor Bhagwati had had in mind the performance of the public sector well beyond the end of the Nehru era. Nevertheless, in the face of so strident a commentary, it is worth repeating that during the Nehru era at least the savings of the public enterprises actually grew faster than that of the private corporate sector.

Neither the official approach to them nor the actual record of the public enterprises during these years suggest that the public sector was one of the wasteful legacies of the Nehru era. Their drift in that direction owes more to the political culture of a subsequent era when the public sector was turned into a vast machine for dispensing patronage and buying out the vested interests of the day. The evidence presented here also allows us to evaluate the assertion that *dirigisme* is recipe for a fiscal crisis of the state.[59] The growth of the central government's tax revenues, as share of GDP, in the fifteen years since 1950 had not been exceeded[60] since even by the year 2000. However, my aim here has been to argue that in its original *avatar* the public sector was a strategic intervention in the cause of growth, and that during the Nehru era it had delivered to an extent far greater than usually acknowledged.

'A Model that Could Never Have'

There exists a strong body of opinion that directly links the comparatively slower growth recorded in India over the long haul to the flawed Nehru–Mahalanobis Strategy. Though it has already been established here that the record of growth in the Nehru era is hardly disappointing, and we know that some of the narrative is meant as caricature,[61] this view needs to be addressed as it is often encountered. I shall consider criticisms from two angles, each representative of a view of what constituted the core of public policy in the Nehru era.

The first of the lines of criticism draws not so much on mainstream economics as on socio-political philosophy, and perhaps precisely for that reason is more widely held. This identifies state intervention as having stifled private enterprise. Add to this the construction of 'a loss-making public sector' and we have a strategy that far from mobilizing resources needed for development actually squandered them. The view is neatly summarized by Chibber (2003: 6) thus: 'India's mistake was its very turn toward development planning in the first place, an economic strategy that relied so centrally on state intervention in markets.'[62]

Of course, in some spaces of the economy the loss of economic freedom due to state intervention in the Nehru era was indeed real. But it is important to have a measure of its extent. Prominent among the controls and emblematic of the restriction of freedom of enterprise was industrial licensing. Instituted with a view to channelling resources according to plan priorities, industrial licensing did seriously limit the freedom to invest, including in capacity expansion, of the private sector. Moreover, even apart from defence and atomic energy—in which areas it is likely to have had little interest in investing—private investment was mostly excluded from the utilities and much of infrastructure. However, the area over which licensing had had an impact must be seen in perspective. It was confined almost entirely to manufacturing, leaving out of its purview about 80 per cent of the economy in the 1950s. Agriculture was a notable area of exclusion as it was the largest part of the economy. In addition to licensing there was reservation, with certain sectors—chosen mainly on grounds of their being 'traditional'—reserved for industrial units with capital investment less than a prescribed limit. In the language of a strand of development economics, such intervention was 'distortionary' in that it contributes to a deviation from the market outcome. However, in a perverse sense the same intervention may be read as expanding (or 'protecting', as one's perception may dictate) the economic freedom of the beneficiaries of the reservation who in its absence may have been competed out altogether. Nevertheless, the reservation policy had limited the freedoms of the private *corporate* sector. The policy of reserving certain segments of the manufacturing sector for small units would have had the obvious impact of not allowing for any potential economies of scale to be reaped in these sectors. Among its consequences, it has been alleged, has been the destruction of India's more automated cotton textile industry which now had to face competition from a handloom sector protected from competition by the reservation policy.

The perception of loss of economic freedom during the Nehru era is closely linked to the presence of controls in the India of the time. Further, whether by design or default, much of these controls gradually came to be referred to as 'socialism'. What is, however, interesting is that a large part of this structure had been instituted during the Second World War. Put in place by a colonial government guided not solely by the objective of protecting India but largely of ensuring that finance and resources flow in a direction compatible with maintaining the Allied war effort globally, these controls encompassed economic activity from foreign trade, to capital issue, prices, and even the internal movement of goods, notably grain. The origins and development of much of the controls in post-Independence India have been traced to the first half of the 1940s by Mohan and Aggarwal (1990). Even the urban bias of the public distribution system, an intervention associated with left-wing politics today, can be traced to the colonial government's desire to maintain the internal peace needed to continue the outward-oriented war effort.

Two instances clarify the precise relationship of these controls to the Nehru–Mahalanobis Strategy. First, the debate at the time of the launching of the Second Five Year Plan model was about the maintenance of the *war-time* controls and not the institution of a new set. Thus, it was that B.R. Shenoy's note of dissent[63] had actually argued for its rescinding. It is not known widely enough that there had been no proposal for a significant increase in controls as part of the Plan, perhaps because the powers with the government since the War left it with sufficient clout to control economic activity anyway. Import controls came to evolve in an ad hoc manner after a balance of payments crisis in 1957, itself precipitated by liberalization, interestingly of consumer goods imports[64]. Investment licensing, however, did figure prominently in the Industrial Policy Resolution of 1956, providing the legislative muscle for the actualization of planning for growth.

I conclude this discussion of the place and role of controls in the Nehru era with two observations. First, despite the allegedly debilitating impact of controls, the economy did recover from almost half a century of stagnation. Moreover, it was the manufacturing sector—the area of the economy most subject to controls—that had recorded the fastest growth, though not the highest degree of acceleration. Second, and this anticipates a theme in my overall conclusion on the nature and role of public policy in the Nehru era, there is a need to distinguish the economic policy of this period from what was yet to emerge. What we now recognize as the major distinguishing features of the policy regime of India since Independence were to come later. I have in mind the Monopolies and Restrictive Trade Practices (MRTP) Act and the restrictively amended Foreign Exchange Regulation Act (FERA), an astronomical marginal rate of taxation of income, the nationalization of banks, and the legislation[65] that tightened the 'labour laws'. These together provided a happy hunting ground, being a rich source of rent, for an increasingly unregulated bureaucracy. Most of this has been draconian in its impact and served little the cause of upliftment of India's poor, but it is worth recalling that all of these had come after the death of Nehru. Indeed, that it had followed that event so closely is itself indicative of the importance that was assigned to these forms of intervention in the Nehru–Mahalanobis Strategy.

Some handle is got on the question of the role of left-wing ideology *per se* in accounting for the presence of controls during the Nehru era by considering 'The Bombay Plan'. This plan for an overall development of the country proposed in 1944 by the leading industrialists of India bore an uncanny resemblance to what finally got adopted as official policy, including the emphasis on capital goods and the focus on the domestic economy. If anything, the Bombay Plan was far more tilted towards heavy industry than was the Mahalanobis Plan, but it is the approach to controls in the former that is unexpected given its origin among private entrepreneurs. It was stated: 'During this period, in order to prevent the inequitable distribution of the burden between different classes which this method of financing will involve, practically every aspect of economic life will have to be so vigorously controlled by government that individual liberty and freedom of enterprise will suffer a temporary eclipse' (All-India Manufacturer's Organisation 1944: 48).[66]

The second angle from which the Nehru–Mahalanobis Strategy is criticized focuses on what we would more readily recognize as an economic model by itself, rather than merely the loss of economic freedom contingent upon the adoption of a particular strategy of development. This critique is a little more fleshed out than the first and claims for itself an empirical validity, though I shall point out that a purely empirical approach can lead the argument to unexpected conclusions, including the validation of the choice of the very model in the first place. It proceeds by arguing that the model of import-substituting industrialization (ISI) that India had followed was unlikely to have done any better that it actually did in the long run, and that India's mistake was to have chosen this model over one of greater outward orientation, with a central role for trade. Even though the critique of ISI was that protection induced high-cost production, this by itself was not enough to disqualify such a model from the perspective of growth, for there is no particular reason to insist that growth will be necessarily slower within such a regime irrespective of the context. So reference was now made to historical experience, and this had gone as follows.

By the late 1970s the larger and more prominent developing economies that had adopted ISI had begun to appear stuck in a groove of slow growth. On the other hand, the economies of East Asia, namely Korea, Taiwan, Hong Kong, Singapore, had all arrived on the global stage as leading exporters and were also at the same time the fastest growing economies of the world. From this was born the idea of an export-led growth, and the ISI model was written off completely as a non-starter. Proceeding from the poor record of exports of some large countries, India included, that had promoted ISI, it was concluded that interventionism was responsible for the disappointing outcome. As I shall demonstrate, this conclusion was somewhat premature. Answers to two issues need to be sorted out first. These pertain to competitiveness and causality. While it is no more than a matter of accounting that fast-growing exports, treated as exogenous, will raise the rate of growth of an economy, it has been recognized that the causality between growth and exports is not always of the kind usually presumed by arguments for an export-led growth. For instance, where dynamic economies of scale are to be reaped, a faster economy-wide growth leads to faster productivity growth in all sectors and this enhances the international competitiveness of an economy's exports. Now the causality is directly from growth to exports and not from exports to growth. However, not all cases of international competitiveness can be attained thus, and for many of the far-eastern economies the domestic market was much too small to depend upon for faster growth to bring about a greater international competitiveness. Here competitiveness was developed, and the question remains how.

While protection is fundamental, the rationale being no more than the century-old 'infant industry' argument of Friedrich List, it is clear that it is far from sufficient to explain the attainment of this competitiveness. The work of Alice Amsden (2001) has helped us understand the specific interventions by the state that were entailed to achieve this in these other economies of the Far East which, unlike Japan in the inter-war years or China today, actually entered markets for fairly sophisticated manufactures, especially electronics. Combined with the work of Wade (1990), this has led to a 'significant re-thinking in development studies' (Chibber 2003) of the strategy of growth to be pursued by the underdeveloped economies of the world. Their work has conclusively established the role of ISI in general and intervention in particular as having laid the base of the East Asian success. No longer are we satisfied with hoary accounts of free trade, export-led growth, and merely 'market-friendly' governments that always conducted themselves at arm's length from private agents.

Bruce Scott (1997) has investigated the historical basis for the claim that the successful economies of the world had abjured intervention, or state directedness, and adhered to free trade. Scott has studied two historical episodes, one less often encountered in development economics today. The first episode is that of the East Asian experience and his comment is as follows:

> Taiwan and South Korea ... now have relatively free economies. In earlier decades, these countries did have some economic freedoms, notably in product markets. But both were authoritarian regimes with non-transparent controls aimed at simultaneously promoting exports and restricting foreign entry into their economies. The state-owned banking system in South Korea allowed the *chaebol* conglomerates to develop rapidly with little retained equity, much like the Japanese *keiretsu* in the early 1950s. South Korea's leaders chose to develop the economy by concentrating their efforts on a small number of large companies, which they protected by eliminating the market for corporate control. They also instituted a regime governing labour that all but eliminated workers' ability to bargain collectively, thereby ensuring that companies would have the lion's share of income with which to promote growth. Taiwan used purchasing policies of state-owned enterprises for similar purposes. Only in recent

years, as their economies achieved a high degree of success, have Taiwan's and South Korea's governments begun to relax their grip. (Scott 1997: 159)

Though other accounts of the East Asian experience, including of the associated role of government, abound,[67] I have dwelt on this one in particular for its clarity of expression.

But Scott's contribution to the debate on 'economic freedom' was yet to come, by taking on the argument in the context of the historical experience of the first industrial country, referred to in the context as Great Britain. Addressing the view that it had gained economic supremacy in the nineteenth century when it moved to a free-trade regime, he has argued:

But its rise took place mainly in the previous century, when in competition with France and the Netherlands, it relied on a protectionist policy of trade promotion and on forced mobilisation of resources. Great Britain dismantled its trade regime after it became the undisputed economic, financial, and industrial leader of the world, not before. Under its new, freer policies it began its relative economic decline and was slow to take advantage of the newer industries based on electrical and chemical engineering. For all its freedoms, it had performed below average for industrial countries for more than a century—and especially since World War II—as its incomes have fallen below those in most of the rest of Western Europe.

It is true that Great Britain began its initial rise to supremacy by freeing up its internal market, a step it took while other sizeable countries were divided into regions with their own trade barriers. The Great Britain of the 18th century had the largest domestic market in Europe even though its population was less than half of France's, and that market encouraged a great deal of economic innovation and resourcefulness. The United States followed the same pattern during its ascendance: it combined a free domestic market with sizeable tariff barriers until after World War II. Indeed all the leading industrial powers developed as protectionist regimes in the 19th century, whereas countries such as India and Portugal, following free trade regimes, found themselves stripped of industry. (Scott 1997: 159)[68]

However, it is Scott's observation on contemporary China that serves most to query the privileging of economic freedom as a driver of economic growth, and that has the greatest potential of sorting out ideological predilection from plain economics. Scott observes: 'With almost twenty consecutive years of growth exceeding 5 percent per capita per year, China already seems to be demonstrating that the lives of 1.2 billion people can be radically improved in an environment that sharply limits freedom' (Scott 1997: 159). In the context of the debate on the optimal model or 'ideal architecture' for growth, this example has an interesting implication. It shows that selecting the model that ought to have been chosen in the past using current growth rates as the criterion can be treacherous for those committed to a narrow vision of the growth process. For, if, on the basis of that country's current performance, China's economic model is to be adjudged as the right choice for development, it must follow that India's mistake was not in having adopted the Nehru–Mahalanobis Strategy but in not taking it far enough by investing more heavily in heavy industry and sealing itself off from the rest of the world in the early days.

Indeed, in some remarkably prescient writing done over three decades ago, at a time when China's rise to economic power status was yet to be imagined, Byres and Nolan (1976) had concluded that 'China has progressed towards industrialisation at a faster rate than India and appears to be poised for an even faster pace of industrial advance than India in the future'. The basis for their prognosis is:

> [T]he greater emphasis given by China to the development of 'key' industries places her in a better position for *future* economic development, since it has freed her to a greater extent than India from the foreign exchange constraint over the rate of investment and growth. China now appears to have a significantly greater capability than India to produce domestically the 'producer' goods that are the physical wherewithal of investment.[69]

Interestingly, in the context of the general distrust of planning as an unnecessary interference in the market mechanism, Byres and Nolan state that China's superior performance is due to the 'quality and effectiveness of planning' in that country compared with that attempted in India. It is possible to recognize their forecast as an instance of extraordinary economic intuition even as one may disagree outright with their assertion that China had attained what it had 'without the terrible cost in human suffering' that has characterized the Indian experience. Though weighing-up deprivations one against the other would be akin to comparing apples and oranges, one might yet argue that it is not credible to assert that the costs of political repression, and the alleged death by starvation following economic adventurism in China amount to less than that of the widespread hunger in India. Silence over apparent political repression cannot be excused even if it was at a time when the Chinese leadership had yet to start implementing the 'one child per couple' policy through third-trimester abortions, for accounts of the excesses of the Cultural Revolution had begun to filter through by the early 1970s.

What emerges from our discussion can be concisely summarized thus: while it can hardly be denied that markets are fundamental to sustained growth, it would be naïve to dismiss governments as dispensable to the outcome. Indeed, that would be a misreading of a by now richly documented history of economic growth in diverse historical settings and across centuries. Even without insisting that government is the driver of growth, experiences of economic growth and development show us that government is *an* economic driver in the sense that its actions can have directly productive consequences.

With so much historical evidence of success in countries pursuing ISI, it is difficult to walk away from it insisting that the choice of model *per se* explains India's relatively slow growth for about two decades from the mid-1960s. The answer must be sought in the domestic political economy, the balance of economic and political forces that determine economic outcomes, and the nature of the Indian state.[70] Following the work of Wade (1990) on Korea, we are able to see that what went wrong with ISI in India is that the government singularly failed to 'govern the market'. As for the 'heavy investment strategy', Jha (1980: 79) has persuasively argued that the reasons for its disappointing results over the long haul must be sought in political economy—'because the government chose to make it fail, and adopted policies which ensure that this would happen'— rather than economic model. In fact, this is the principal message that we get from a study of the Nehru era when, as I have shown here, economic performance was far from what it has been portrayed by critics of the Nehru–Mahalanobis Strategy.

Critique of a Strategy: The Missing Counterfactual

While the discussion so far in this section may have served to dispel the perception that public policy in the Nehru era had neglected the crucial role of agriculture or the savings potential of the public sector enterprises and that it was based on an economic model that stood no chance of success, there is one area that appears to have been neglected quite severely then. And that was primary education. Rare were interventions in the 1950s by Indian economists on the relevance of primary education, but there was a particularly insightful one by B.V. Krishnamurti,[71] an economist then with the Bombay School. In 1955, within months of the publication of the 'Recommendation for the Second Five-Year Plan' by the Planning Commission, Krishnamurti had written 'how absurdly low are the sums allotted for education in the Mahalanobis Plan', speaking of it as being lopsided, with little importance given to education and other social services, and calling for a reallocation to expenditure on this account from the outlay on heavy industries. More important are Krishnamurti's argument for greater expenditure on education and his explanation for why it was so low in the Plan. 'A concerted effort to educate the mass of the population, specially in the rural areas, would undoubtedly have far-reaching benefits of a cumulative expansionist character. This would greatly lighten the task of the government in bringing about rapid economic development.' Pointing to the government's lack of even-handedness in dealing with education in comparison with 'heavy industries or river valley projects' for which it was willing to adopt deficit financing, he speculates whether this has to do with the fact that 'being brought up in the traditions of mid-Victorian finance' it continues to 'apply the calculus of the private grocery merchant to a matter like education'.[72]

Interestingly, in all the counterfactual scenarios that are sketched for India, it is openness to trade that tends to get emphasized, the implicit suggestion being that the possibilities of trade were neglected. There may well be a point to this observation, at least surely for the period starting in the mid-1960s. However, the absence of primary education from these exercises of counterfactual analysis is striking. One cannot overlook the likelihood that the very face of India, not to mention the rate of growth of output via human-capital accumulation, may have been vastly different had more attention been paid to primary education at the very outset. As this study is also an evaluation of the contribution of Nehru to the growth and transformation of India, I am reminded of the comment made to me by a civil servant in Bangalore (now Bengaluru) that the man whose birthday is celebrated as Children's Day in India had actually managed to do very little for the very young. Cruel as it may sound, and appearing odd given Nehru's publicized[73] empathy with children, the verdict is certainly close for it is indeed correct that primary education ended up being severely neglected in the Nehru era.[74] It is of course technically true that, given the constitutional distribution of powers in India, education—being a 'State Subject'—was then at least partially a responsibility of the states, but this does not absolve the policymaker of the Nehru era of a grave error of judgement regarding the factors that drive growth, leave alone development. Of course, both policymakers and economists continued to neglect the continuing neglect of primary education in India till into the twenty-first century when suddenly India's disparity with the rest of the world on this count could no longer be ignored. We return to this topic in Chapter 4.

In our effort to try and understand where the Indian economic strategy may have foot-faulted, it is instructive to read Korean economists on country's progress. Thus, we have Kim (1995: 286):

> [W]hat distinguishes Korea from other developing countries is the way it has invested in human resources even before launching a drive to develop its economy. Had it not been for the formation of trained human resources in advance, Korea's economic development in the 1960s and 1970s would have been much retarded... What this implies is that investment in human resource development should precede industrialisation, as human resources cannot be trained overnight when needed.[75]

Contrast Korea's educational preparedness with India's at the beginning of its industrialization programme. Public expenditure on education, by the Centre and states combined, decomposed by level, is presented in Table 2.8. Note that while an awareness of the relevance of technical education for industrialization is reflected in the rising share allotted to this segment, the share of elementary education declines very sharply. So much so, the relative expenditure on schooling declines by the end of the Nehru era, despite a rising share of total expenditure going to secondary education. At the same time, the share of higher education almost doubled, this after technical education has been accounted for separately. Note also the negligible expenditure on adult education programmes given the stock of illiterates in the country in 1947. Altogether, it is difficult to avoid the conclusion that during the Nehru era higher and technical education were privileged over mass literacy and primary schooling. While a shift of expenditure towards higher and technical education may have been necessary for an industrializing economy, arguably in India the shift was implemented somewhat hastily. As a result, it has remained the country where public expenditure per student as a percentage of GDP per capita is most skewed in favour of higher education (see Table 4.18).

At the level of a history of ideas, it is difficult to square the neglect of the role of education among India's economists at a time when it was emerging as a part of the mainstream of the discipline. The idea that industrialization would require training the peasantry, and that the private sector is unlikely to be sufficiently interested in this task, was already in the work of Rosenstein-Rodan (1943), Schultz's essay on investment in man—which had in it the idea of 'capabilities'—had appeared in 1961, and by the mid-1960s academic collections of country experiences with education had begun to appear.[76] This seems not to have made much of an impact on the cohort of India's economists otherwise much attuned to the progress of Anglo-American economics. We may compare this with

Table 2.8 The Distribution of Public Expenditure on Education, 1951–66 (in per cent)

Sector	*First Plan (1951–6)*	*Second Plan (1956–61)*	*Third Plan (1961–6)*
Elementary	58	35	34
Secondary	5	19	18
Higher	8	18	15
Technical	14	18	21
Adult education	–	–	–
Others	15	10	12
Total	100	100	100

Source: *India 2009: A Reference Annual*, Publications Division, Ministry of Information and Broadcasting, New Delhi, 2009.
Note: Includes expenditure by the states and union territories.

the state of interest in education within the economics profession in late nineteenth century Russia, as recorded by Kahan (1965: 5):

> Finance Minister Vyshnegradskii's concern with the level of skill and education of the Russian industrial labor force in the 1880s both expressed and stimulated a concern for education as an economic investment of the society. His pronouncement was reflected in a large number of studies, both empirical and normative, or policy oriented. An early and probably representative example of the latter is an interesting collection of essays published in 1896 under the general title of *Economic Evaluation of Popular Education*. It contains contributions of I.I. Yanzhul', A.I. Chuprov and I.N. Yanzhul'. That by I.I. Yanzhul' (which is still of considerable historical interest) is based upon the assumption that various 'external' stimuli of economic growth (tariffs, subsidies, government regulations) are less effective than education and training. He invokes the authority of J.S. Mill, Thomas Brassey, and Alfred Marshall, and provides empirical data from American experience to argue that the level of productivity of labour in various countries is positively correlated with per capita expenditures on education and with rates of literacy. The general conclusion of the essays is summarised by the authors as follows: 'There are, of course, many factors impeding the development of the Russian economy, but the foremost among them is the general illiteracy which distinguishes our country from all other civilized countries ... an increase of labor productivity is the only means to erase poverty in Russia and the best policy to achieve it is through the spread of education and knowledge'.

Note the reference to the importance, when it comes to growth, of education relative to 'tariffs, subsidies and government regulations', the stuff of so much of the debate over growth in India over the past three decades! On the other hand, no comparable discourse on the role of education in economic development had taken place in India during the era of high planning, or since for that matter. Much of the energy of professional economists, it seems, got dissipated in skirmishes about the mathematical properties of the plan models.[77] In the midst of all this argument, however, a salvo for education appears to have been fired by Amartya Sen, who had queried the increased target for agricultural growth in the Fourth Plan on grounds of an inadequate spread of elementary education in rural India. A response from C.H. Hanumantha Rao had followed.[78] The immediate success of the Green Revolution that was to follow may suggest that Sen had been proved wrong, but this would be a hasty conclusion to draw if we were to take a longer and broader view of India's economic growth.

CONCLUSION: THE RECOVERY OF INDIA

There is an influential narrative on growth in India that goes like this: 'India's post-World War II economic history begins with a disastrous wrong turn by India's first prime minister, Jawaharlal Nehru, towards Fabian socialism, central planning, and an unbelievable quantity of bureaucratic red tape. This "licence raj" strangled the private sector … As a result, India stagnated until bold neo-liberal economic reforms triggered by the currency crisis of 1991' (DeLong 2003: 184).[79] Surely, the account of growth in early independent India presented in this chapter restores perspective to the recent economic history of this country. We have shown that, contrary to the above, actually, the very origins of growth in twentieth-century India can be traced to the early 1950s. The Nehru era witnessed the revival of a moribund economy and the igniting of a growth process that has remained undimmed for over five decades during which the rate of growth of the economy has hastened slowly. The repeated acceleration of the growth rate implies that the penchant for drawing a likeness between the policies of the Nehru era and the Soviet Union is misplaced, as growth in India has been sustained in a way that it was not in the former Soviet Union. Actually, India's growth rate has accelerated repeatedly, and this feature is not incompatible with the Nehru–Mahalanobis Strategy.[80]

Within the recovery engineered, I have flagged two specific achievements of the Nehru era that had a bearing on growth, namely, the quite spectacular transformation of agriculture as reflected in the acceleration of growth and the unprecedented mobilization of resources by the Indian state which enabled a hike in public investment. There may have been errors of commission, such as the spawning of an increasingly unregulated economic bureaucracy, and of omission, such as the gross neglect of schooling. But there have been four decades at least in which to correct these. To hold that this is due to a 'lock-in' (Chibber 2003) effect of the Nehruvian strategy and suggest that nothing could have been done to alter the situation is only to confirm that we have not understood the lessons of even our recent past.

Though I have not focused on the particular role of Jawaharlal Nehru in the formulation and implementation of the economic policy of his time, I have provided a window to his views on the economy including, to an extent, of their evolution. Arguably, no Indian leader at the helm of this country since has been as central to the navigation of its economy. The economic record of this time therefore serves as one indicator of the effectiveness of his role as independent India's first prime minister, a topic of perennial interest to so argumentative a people as us Indians.[81] Under Nehru, the Indian economy had been transformed from a colonial enclave to one with at least some of the prerequisites for sustained long-term growth, while at the same time maintaining an autonomy from the superpowers vying for influence on a newly independent subcontinent. The acceleration of the rate of growth of the economy achieved in the Nehru era may be considered as a marker of this transformation. I have provided both historical and comparative perspective on this variable and argued that the achievement was indeed quite remarkable in the context.

Further, the framework within which it had been achieved has a bearing on today's thinking on the ideal economic architecture for growth. Central to the latter is the construct of economic freedom defined as absence of restraint. Considered 'economics' since the implosion of the Soviet Union, this view is contradicted by the recent history of China where freedom, economic or political, is not a prominent feature of the landscape of a heaving economy.[82] While the situation in the Nehru era was a far cry from today's China, both in terms of economic and political freedoms, India's growth performance of that period, largely engineered by the state, is a serious challenge to the thinking on growth encapsulated in the Washington Consensus, a recipe for prosperity influential in the 1990s but no longer so.[83]

The historic role of the economic policies of the Nehru era needs to be better understood. For sheer prescience it would be difficult to best the contemporary evaluation by Nehru's alter ego in the charting of a uniquely Indian economic journey. For a statistician, likely to have been ever tempted by the calculus of probability, Mahalanobis's forecast, made in the late 1950s, is markedly free of confidence intervals! He had averred: 'One thing can be said with complete certainty. Jawaharlal Nehru has carried India into a new epoch. Whether there is a smooth transition or whether India has to pass through storms on her way to progress, it will be impossible to go back to a stagnant economy' (Mahalanobis 1961: 563). This prediction has acquitted itself. It must encourage us to view the recovery achieved by the policies pursued in the 1950s as a bridgehead to the higher growth rates that have followed. The shibboleth 'Hindu rate of growth' (see Panagariya 2005: 18) serves more to obscure than to illuminate the nature and significance of economic change in the Nehru era of India's history.

Notes

1. See Mahalanobis (1955a). Mahalanobis's non-technical papers on planning and economic development have been collected in Mahalanobis (1961). These taken together convey the evolution of his thinking, particularly on the topic of a growth model for India.

2. For authoritative and contrasting accounts, as they approach the Nehru–Mahalanobis Strategy from different angles, see Chakravarty (1988) and Srinivasan (1996).

3. See Mahalanobis (1955a).

4. It may be mentioned that while Mahalanobis may not have been entirely clear in his exposition always, this must surely count as a forerunner of the models of endogenous growth that came to fascinate the profession from the 1980s on. This is also pointed out by Srinivasan (1996).

5. The premise of a foreign exchange constraint has been severely criticized as amounting to no more than 'export pessimism'. We will have occasion to review this position shortly.

6. See 'Technical Note', Appendix to Section 4 of Mahalanobis (1955a).

7. For example, see Price (1967), and the interchange between Vasudevan (1968) and Price (1968) that had followed.

8. See Chakravarty (1988: 13). Interestingly, Mahalanobis had also stated (1955a: 24) that while the earliest version of his model of growth is similar to those by Harrod and Domar, he was not aware of them when he had formulated his own. We find that the Anglo-American lineage of the Mahalanobis Model tends to get overlooked in favour of the Soviet, presumably because recognizing it would take the sheen out of the criticism of its foreign origins. More recently it has been suggested by Ray (1998: 55) that Soviet planning was 'deeply influenced' by the Harrod–Domar model. With this we come full circle!

9. At that time, admiration for the Soviets was present in some unexpected circles globally. Thus, we find the following reference to its achievements in *The World Economic Survey, 1931–32* of the League of Nations at Geneva, quoted approvingly by M. Visvesvaraya (1936: 71): 'Russia is one of the chief prodigies of

the time. From extreme backwardness it has advanced at a stride to the forefront of mechanical development.'

10. See Mahalanobis (1955b). It is significant that Mahalanobis had also addressed health and education, though, arguably only in passing. We return to this issue at the end of this chapter.

11. See Desai (1998).

12. This had already been raised by Rao (1952). In any case, it is not clear that the Nehru–Mahalanobis Strategy should be equated with the Keynesian problematic to the extent that the latter was addressed to the short run in an economy with unemployed capital. On the other hand, the objective of the former was to build up the capital goods base in a country that was seen to be lacking in it.

13. But then the Nehru–Mahalanobis Strategy was actually motivated by the objective of eradicating it.

14. Evidence of this follows.

15. See the response to Rao (1952) by Raj (1954), and a conceptualization of how macroeconomic equilibrium is restored when aggregate demand expands in an India-type economy by the then remarkably young Bhagwati (1956).

16. Whatever may have been the structure of the Model, when it came to the strategy, Mahalanobis (1955a: 23) had recognized the 'paucity' of consumer goods as a 'limiting factor' on growth.

17. To be sure, there was also the Gandhian model of the self-sufficient village economy, but it had been explicitly rejected by Nehru himself even before Independence. And, in any case, it stood little chance of being adopted by the largely urban political leadership of post-colonial India.

18. See Shenoy (1955).

19. '[T]he price paid for rapid industrialisation has been terrific in some socialistic countries. I am certain that no country with any kind of parliamentary democracy can possibly pay it' (Nehru 1954).

20. See Mahalanobis (1955b: Table 8).

21. The speech is of interest also for the vehemence with which the problem is identified: 'agriculture is more important by itself than any chief minister'!

22. See Chapter 3 for an estimate of the date of the growth transition. While the Green Revolution is conventionally treated as having originated in the second half of the 1960s, it may be noted here that the rate of growth registered in 1964–5, the year of Nehru's death, was at nearly 12 per cent, the highest annual production increase in crop agriculture in a decade and a half (see Ministry of Agriculture 2003). However, this was to be followed by two years of drought.

23. Of course, as evident from the graph in the 'Introduction', finer partitions of the data points over the period 1950–2000 would yield a higher rate of growth of the economy from the late 1970s on. However, from the same graph we can see that the acceleration during the Nehru years outweighs by far the ones that were to follow.

24. I thank M. Suresh Babu for having drawn my attention to this literature.

25. This can be seen in the figure in the 'Introduction'. More formal evidence appears in Chapter 3.

26. This assessment is noticeably at odds with the customary assessment of the economic record of the Nehru era by economists. Historians, it appears, bring a greater objectivity to the study of the economy than economists, perhaps because they privilege economic theory less.

27. Reported by Sivasubramonian (2000: Table 6.3).

28. See Dhar (2003) and Guha (2007) for accounts of the reception of Mao in India during the Nehru era.

29. See Maddison (1995).

30. See Dyson (2008).

31. See Romer (1986).

32. An instance of this tendency may also be found in the reported comments on economic growth in India by Alan Greenspan. Having first castigated Nehru's 'Fabian socialism', Greenspan acknowledges the higher growth in recent years but plays down this acceleration as having been from 'off a low base'. See 'Give up Socialism: Greenspan', *The Times of India*, New Delhi, 24 September, 2007. Apart from its oracular nature, the observation displays an empirical oversight in that India had already grown at over 5 per cent per annum in the 1980s, which was the highest rate of growth outside of East Asia by then.

33. For a broader, historian's, account of the burden of the colonial legacy in India, see Chandra (1992).

34. See Scott (1997).

35. See, for instance, Lal (1999).

36. See also Bagchi (1972) for an economist's perspective on the period.

37. Indeed, this must be the obvious conclusion of those who claim that an excessively interventionist state pursuing the Nehru–Mahalanobis Strategy best characterizes the economic environment of early independent India.

38. In making my case I shall draw upon the exposition of this view of underdevelopment by Ray (1998).

39. For a suggestion along these lines, see Rao (2004).

40. See the figure in the 'Introduction'.

41. See Reddy (2006).

42. '[I]nvestment in industry in the private sector [was] largely assisted by financing institutions in the public sector, and by fiscal concessions and tax incentives provided by Government' (Rao 1971: 72).

43. It is equally significant but inadequately recognized that the bureaucratic approach is likely also to have lowered the productivity of public investment.

44. For a qualitative assessment of the gains to the private sector during the Nehru era, see Zachariah (2004).

45. See Habib (1973).

46. Somewhat uniquely in the form of trade credit for 'complete plant installations for machine-building industries' (see Raj 1967: 24).

47. Figures on aid reported here are from Bhagwati and Desai (1970: 181 and Table 10.3).

48. Note also from this account the substantial difference in the planned allocation of investment to industry for the Second Five Year Plan set out in Table

2.3 and the actual share of investment of this sector over the Nehru era. The latter, as recorded by Rao, turns out to be barely above half of Mahalanobis' preferred value of 0.3.

49. For a rejection as 'simplistic' of the claim of a neglect of agriculture under planning, see Srinivasan (1996).

50. 'Not a chest of indigo reached England without being stained with human blood' (British colonial civil servant quoted by Winchester and Winchester 2004: 56).

51. As raised already, even if the second acceleration is established to have occurred immediately after the death of Nehru, the Green Revolution ought not to be seen as episodic but the result of some years of preparation of the seed bed, so to speak, in terms of the spread of irrigation, the diffusion of best practices via an extension service, and preparatory measures such as field trials under the auspices of the public agricultural research system, Indian Council of Agricultural Research (ICAR), some of them commencing as early as the First Five Year Plan itself. The comment by 'AM' (1964: 1195), popularly believed to be Ashok Mitra, in a special issue of *The Economic Weekly* in July 1964 devoted to an assessment of the Nehru era—'[d]espite all the gains of the last seventeen years, in many respects we have to make up for the lost time of these very years, during which all of us have grown a little less romantic and during which our per capita availability of food has not gone up by a single grain'—is appropriately hortatory but wrong in its claim regarding the progress made in agriculture. The per capita net availability of grain had grown slowly but steadily over the Nehru era, despite the significant rise in the population growth rate. Of course, that the performance could have been better is unexceptionable, but two caveats are in order here. First, subsequent growth in availability of foodgrains in India has barely matched the record of this period. See *Economic Survey 2006–2007*, Table 1.17. Second, in the Nehru era, the relative price of agriculture having first declined remained depressed for most of the time—for which see Appendix Table 4.4 in Misra (2004)—while agricultural growth quickened. Apart from the fact that this would be considered the pre-eminent marker of a successful development strategy, it is the best imaginable evidence that the Nehru–Mahalanobis Strategy had, in practice at least, *encompassed* the Vakil–Brahmananda Plan which had predicated a wage-goods constraint binding Indian economic growth.

52. The agricultural turnaround achieved in the Nehru era, even when acknowledged in India, mostly receives the back-handed compliment that it was merely 'extensive growth', achieved via extension of the cultivable land frontier. This view is mistaken. Recent research on the Indian subcontinent originating in Japan shows that the 1950s in India witnessed the reversal of a trend decline in land yields , the latter being known to us since Blyn (1966). Further, among the decades of the twentieth century, the average annual growth of yield achieved in the 1950s is exceeded only in the 1980s. 'It is important to note that the reversal of land productivity occurred before the *breakthrough* of the "Green Revolution"' (see Kurosaki 2007: 18; emphasis original). Clearly, the author had had in mind the 'growth' of 'land productivity'.

53. Even when this is not acknowledged as such by professional economists, it is widely recognized within civil society. See the report on a debate in Kerala today in the Malayalam daily *Mathrubhoomi* (2007).

54. A strong public sector revenue base is required also in high-income economies with substantial welfare interventions, for instance, the economies of Western Europe.

55. See Mahalanobis (1955b: Table 8).

56. See Rao and Sen (1995).

57. See Table 3 in Rao and Sen (1995).

58. Interestingly, Nehru was not at all squeamish about acknowledging assistance from the West when he felt it appropriate to do so. For, the speech had continued: 'May I also refer to those who originally set up the plant here, the well-known Swiss firm of Oerlikons who laid the foundations? They built the first HMT plant and helped in training our people in the early stages, and their work has yielded this fine result.'

59. See 'Introduction' in Lal (1999).

60. See Ministry of Finance (2005).

61. See, for instance, the description 'model for going backwards' in Bhagwati (1998).

62. However, the author himself does not subscribe to this view.

63. See Shenoy (1955).

64. See Chibber (2003).

65. Of course the original legislation governing work and employment in the factories dates from the colonial era.

66. The context was that, having advocated deficit financing—'finance [is] only a camp follower'— to move the economy, the authors of the Plan anticipated a temporary inflation.

67. See in particular Chang (2003).

68. In the context, the following conclusion of Crafts (1996: 200) may also be noted: 'The British Industrial Revolution was accompanied by growing protectionism in product markets but continuing receptiveness to foreign ideas.' It pretty much stands on its head the conventional wisdom on UK in the eighteenth century that it was highly open to trade in goods and self-sufficient in technology when it was not passing it on to the rest of the world.

69. See Byres and Nolan (1976: 86) for this and all following references to their work.

70. Such explanations have been provided by Chibber (2003) and Kohli (2004), respectively.

71. See the entry under 'Krishnamurti' in Balasubramanyan (2001). I am indebted to Ramachandra Guha for bringing this little known critique to my attention. It is of some value to the economics profession in India, not only due to its perspicacity but also as some kind of record, that not all our members had pulled their punches during the great debates of their times!

72. All quotations are from 'Krishnamurti' in Balasubramanyan (2001).

73. See Crocker (2008). Nehru's defenders, however, are quick to point out

that he had little to do with the institutionalization of his birthday as Children's Day, not to mention 'the phoney appellation' *Chacha*! (see Sharada Prasad 1979: 8).

74. A historian's account of how this came to be despite Nehru's own intentions is to be found in Spear (1967). Spear proposes that it was the very body that was given the responsibility of implementing the plan, namely, the functionaries in government, who sabotaged it, as they were hostile to the project of social upliftment. Interestingly, a twenty-first century parallel has been suggested with regard to the implementation of the National Rural Employment Guarantee Scheme by Dreze (2009). For a perspective on the state of educational provision in India beyond the Nehru era, we may turn to Romila Thapar (2009): '[M]any of us feel that the foundation of primary and secondary schools has still to be established and nurtured. I suspect that nothing is done about the foundation because political parties fear an educated electorate that can ask questions. It would then not be swayed by mass meetings and would make vote-banks irrelevant. The moment people ask questions and relate the present to the past and have a project for the future, it becomes a different electorate. I don't think it is just an oversight that governments and politicians pay so little attention to education.' Clearly, even Nehru's influence on matters that could not be settled in Delhi was limited. This was the age of the satraps, who called the shots in the states.

75. For an econometric investigation that confirms the role of education in the long-run development of Japan, see Self and Grabowski (2003).

76. See, in particular, Anderson and Bowman (1965).

77. An instance of this is Komiya's observation that the Mahalanobis solution was 'inefficient', cited in support of their critique by Bhagwati and Desai (1970: 237). The East Asians, on the other hand, were very likely blessed by the fact that they did not base their growth strategy on any explicitly advertised model, as a result of which they spent less time quarrelling over it! It is of interest to note Mahalanobis' own view of the purpose of his modelling efforts: 'I do not think that the models have any permanent value of their own. I have used them as scaffolding to be dismantled as soon as their purpose has been served' (1955a: 6).

78. The references are in Rao (1964). I am indebted to Professor Rao for bringing this exchange to my attention.

79. However, the author does not himself subscribe to this view.

80. Recall from the discussion in the section 'Imagining Economic Growth: The Nehru–Mahalanobis Strategy and Its Critics' that Mahalanobis' model did predict income rising steeply in the long run.

81. Interestingly though, most assessments tend to underplay Nehru's pre-occupation with the economy, privileging instead his role in fostering a parliamentary democracy within the country and shaping a just order globally. This is so even of the sympathetic accounts to be found in Gopal (1975, 1979, 1984) and, more recently, Malhotra (2007).

82. See Huang (2008).

83. See Rodrik (2006).

3 Second Wind, 1965–91

...every increase of wealth tends in many ways to make a greater increase more easy than before.

—**Alfred Marshall (1890)**

Though for the purist focused on the policy regime nothing much changed in India as the government pressed on with an 'interventionist framework of policy' (see Srinivasan 2005: 2–3) till the economic reforms of 1991, arguably, the end of the Nehru era did alter the economic environment in the country.[1] Unanticipated exogenous shocks, ranging from war to drought, followed quite closely the exit of India's first prime minister from the stage. There was also uncertainty deriving from the question of political succession. These developments were to impact strongly on an as yet far from mature economy. The process of policymaking became less consultative and its implementation resolutely top–down.[2] This mirrored an authoritarian turn in politics that peaked in the mid-1970s. The Congress Party itself was progressively captured by Indira Gandhi, and inner-party debate stifled even before it could raise its head. This was not without collateral damage for the economy. The years of Mrs Gandhi's consolidation of power, from 1966 to around 1970, were grim for those areas of the economy where the government's presence was significant either as producer, regulator, or fiscal arbiter.

While it may appear odd in a period that is described as witnessing a turn towards authoritarianism in politics, this was a time when the leadership was, by comparison to the Nehru era, less securely in command and hence less independent of vested interests in the polity. The principal actors were the emerging surplus farmers, the industrial capitalists, organized labour in the public sector, and the central-government bureaucracy. Having adopted a left-wing image for herself, Indira Gandhi initially distanced herself from the industrial capitalists, though she was soon to discover that she could hardly ignore them if she was interested in growth. Be that as it may, the net effect of the loss of relative autonomy by the political leadership was that economic policy now lost its integrity. It could no longer be entirely independent of the demands of the politics of survival in a democracy. In the public eye, policy would no longer be viewed as guided by a long-term vision. On the other hand, policymaking was seen as taking on a narrowly partisan hue and, very likely with greater derision, devoid of the capacity to foresee the very consequences of the interventions made. With hindsight, the apparent lack of concern for consequences is not too surprising, for at least some of the policy was driven solely by the objective of retaining political power. This was in marked contrast to the Nehru era, when the aim of the leadership was to come to power precisely to improve the living conditions of the people of India.

Though apart from Indira Gandhi three other prime ministers had presided over the economy during this period, this need not lead us to temper the characterization of this period as one when the Indian state had to come to terms with a reduced autonomy while at the same time persisting with an interventionist economic policy. Governing India was far more of a challenge by now as the leadership no longer enjoyed the legitimacy that came out of having delivered political independence after a long, protracted, and highly visible anti-colonial struggle, a legitimacy that had been gratefully bestowed upon the first generation of India's leaders. There were by now new political parties on the scene and also stronger economic interests to contend with. Governing India would now mean forging alliances and buying support, often from sections with starkly opposing ideologies. The economy, and growth in particular, began to experience collateral damage. The premise of politics had come a long way from what it had been in the 1950s, allowing Nehru to state in Parliament:

> May I say here while I am for the public sector growing, I do not understand or appreciate the condemnation of the private sector? … We talk about nationalisation as if it was some kind of a magic remedy to every ill. I believe that ultimately all the principal means of production will be owned by the nation, but I just do not see why I should do something today which will hamper my progress, my increasing production, simply to satisfy some theoretical urge. (Nehru 1956)

These thoughts turned out to be prophetic as, following his departure, economic policy—with nationalization in particular—came to be increasingly justified on ideological grounds until political competition was, finally, to make the practice unsustainable within barely a decade.

The shift to a more interventionist economic policy regime after Nehru has been identified as ideological, actually even acquiring the taint 'Nehruvian socialism' among its detractors, though measures such as nationalization and the extreme discretionary use of the regulatory apparatus had played next to no role in the economic policy of the Nehru era.[3] Part confused thinking and part the intellectual counterpart of sleight of hand, the characterization of multiplying controls as 'Nehruvian' needs to be deconstructed. Applying to the case of India a mode of analysis long used by political scientists, Hankla (2006) has proposed that the economic policies of Indira Gandhi, especially over the period 1969–74, had little to do with ideological imperatives as much as with extending the sources of state patronage, with a view to weakening the political opposition and fetching fresh political support.

The underlying idea is that in democracies, interventions beyond those stemming from the coherent programme of political parties are driven by the imperative of ensuring survival, especially in the presence of 'unstable electoral linkages'. Hankla has argued that both social change and the split within the old Congress Party had left the emerging party of Indira Gandhi with tenuous electoral linkages, creating an altogether new and uncertain political environment. State control of the trade regime, industrial regulation, the allocation of credit, and the mandated sharing of national resources were all now leveraged to sustain the project of staying in power. The timing of the interventions, closely following the Congress split of 1969, and their demonstrably discretionary nature lend some credence to his argument.[4]

Given the concerns of this study, the egregious feature of the quarter century or so that we have hived-off for discussion here is that despite its turbulent politics and the resulting disjointedness in economic policy, it had contained a transition[5] to a higher growth rate. Moreover, as will be shown in some detail later, it was spread across the sectors, leaving the aggregate growth rate of the economy permanently higher. An explanation of this growth transition at a time when the overall policy regime appears not to have changed significantly and the economy received unfavourable exogenous shocks is the main challenge for an economist addressing the history of this period.[6]

1965–91: A Time Capsule

Viewed from almost every angle, 1965–91 must count as the most troubled quarter century in India's history after 1947. Events had unfurled along two parallel tracks. The first reflects the changing nature of politics in India, of which the centrepiece was the determined rise to power of Indira Gandhi and the opposition this had evoked. The other is the sequence of exogenous events ranging from wars to drought and oil-price shocks, some of which were to have a lasting effect on the future of India via their impact on the balance of payments, at that stage the Achilles heel of its economy.

Though brought up in close proximity to power, Indira Gandhi was not an obvious successor to Jawaharlal Nehru as the prime minister that she was to become shortly after his demise. She did, however, find a berth in the cabinet of Lal Bahadur Shastri who succeeded Nehru. Early on she was to mark herself out as independent-minded, bold, and donning a mantle more pan-Indian than most of her colleagues. A glint of this was in evidence when during the violent protests staged there against the imposition of Hindi as the sole official language of the Government of India, she was to fly to Madras (now Chennai) as the representative of the Cabinet, to both take stock of events and to assure the Dravidian peoples of southern India that their concerns would be taken care of. The political capital generated by this journey was substantial.[7]

It was the untimely death in office of Shastri that was to give Indira Gandhi an unexpected opportunity to seize power. Though not the obvious choice, as candidates of far greater experience as Congress workers, chief ministers of states, and Central cabinet ministers were willing and eager, Indira Gandhi was nevertheless catapulted to the position of prime minister under the eponymous 'Kamaraj Plan'.

Finally prime minister of India, Indira Gandhi discovered that her hold on power was yet tenuous, as the traditions of the Congress Party required her to adhere to party discipline and accede to the convention of being consultative on matters of policy. She could hardly count on the full backing of the old guard of the Congress as her rise to the position of prime minister was via the special purpose vehicle, so to speak, of the Kamaraj Plan. Predictably, this was to breed resentment among those who considered themselves natural claimants by far to the position. Indira Gandhi's response to the predicament in which she found herself was remarkable for its sheer audacity. She split vertically the nearly one-century-old Party, based on the claim that she alone represented the true spirit and original programme of the Congress, a programme committed to the betterment of the lives of the ordinary people of India. By contrast, her rivals in the erstwhile Party were painted as sympathizers with, even if not actually representatives of, the landlords, big business, and feudal privileges of the former royalty of India. To ensure a stable parliamentary position for her new-formed party, she was to align herself with the Left, notably the Communist Party of India (CPI), the Soviet-leaning among the two main left-wing groups in Parliament.

How these political developments enter the narrative on growth in India is that they were to have a direct bearing on the evolution of economic policy, at least for long enough to have had an impact.[8] As political power had come to Indira Gandhi as a result of a manoeuvre that portrayed her rivals as representatives of the right, her own programme had to be recognizably more left-wing in a comparison. A slew of interventionist economic legislations and promulgations were to follow from the late 1960s into the second half of the 1970s when she was dramatically voted out of office for suspending civil liberties. It was only in what turned out to be her last term in office commencing January 1980, having spent a period in the political wilderness, that Indira Gandhi chose to temper her extreme economic policies by some mild moves towards liberalization.

Prominent among the left-wing interventions were the nationalization of fourteen major banks and the legislation of the Monopolies and Restrictive Trade Practices Act (MRTP) in 1969, the abolition of the princely privy purse in 1971, the nationalization of coal in 1972, and the amendment of the Foreign Exchange Regulation Act (FERA) in 1973. Other interventions, less symbolically radical but, some of them at least, wider in their impact were the nationalization of the Indian Copper Corporation in 1972 and of general insurance and the wheat trade in 1973. The last was just as quickly rescinded though, as it turned out to be a wholesale failure. Along the way there was recourse to vertiginous income-tax rates, price control, and 'no exit' clauses for industry. All of this was enacted with 'Garibi Hatao!' audible, as it were, in the background. Finally, 'Socialism' was interred in the Constitution, ironically at a time when civil liberties had been abrogated by fiat during the Emergency. Generically, the interventions were overwhelmingly in the nature of controls and clearly of little use whatsoever as a means of eradicating poverty in the absence of growth, as per capita income was far too low for income redistribution to make any difference. Under the circumstances, there was not much redistribution that was even attempted anyway. The politics of it all is discernible from the feature common to all these interventions that they were projected as targeting some economic interest inimical to the advancement of the left-wing programme of the Indira Gandhi–led Congress Party, itself aimed at the welfare of the people of India. 'Garibi Hatao!' having first emerged as merely an election slogan now came to stay, as if echoing the rationale of all economic policy interventions of the government.

Two aspects of these policy interventions may be noted. First, when not aimed at the form of ownership, they were mainly in the nature of controls. Second, while they were justified in terms of their likely long-term impact, their immediate consequences for growth were far less clear cut. Perhaps the political mileage that these gestures appearing to soak the rich were expected to yield was considered sufficiently valuable *per se*. This marks the biggest political shift in practice of economic policy-making from the Nehru era when the thrust had been resolutely on growth, almost to the neglect of redistribution. Planning as it had been practised thus far was to become the biggest casualty.[9] Ad hoc interventions meant that it became progressively difficult to keep policies aligned and the economy moving resolutely towards a predetermined goal. In some spheres of the economy, the adverse consequence for growth was almost immediate.

The overwhelming consequence of the proliferation of controls that was witnessed in this period was to restrict economic liberty. This came to be viewed, by both the government and its opponents, as 'socialism'. Positive freedoms which enhance human capabilities, an aspect of development that Amartya Sen has done much to popularize, and which arguably are more congruent with socialism howsoever imagined, had little to do with it all. With hindsight, at any rate, we can see that such freedoms are not likely to be advanced via the proliferation of controls. On the other hand, prima facie there is a case for believing that overzealous application of controls that restrict entrepreneurial freedom may curtail growth and with it employment, being the only route to poverty eradication in the absence of strong social protection as in the economies of Western Europe.

Though in the rest of this chapter we continue to focus on an explanation of the growth transition that took place, we shall also be seeking to answer two questions that emerge from this account. First, 'How did the leftward shift of economic policy after the Nehru era affect growth in India?' Second, in the history of this period, 'Do we find economic mechanisms that ensure that once growth has taken root in an economy, it takes on a life of its own that is impervious to random interventions?' The answers to these two sets of questions have a bearing on some central issues in the economics of growth apart from being of interest within a study of growth in India as this one.

The course of events that I have briefly reviewed here had a subtle but definite impact on the nature of governance. With its relative autonomy compromised, the political leadership was no longer able to withstand pressure from particular interests. I have already referred to a weakening of planning which requires adherence to pre-set targets, especially of investment, and the maintenance of a balance between activities. Next, political considerations began to enter inexorably into the making of economic decisions, particularly decisions regarding location, expansion, and employment[10] in public sector units. The practice of the state taking over loss-making units in the private sector with a view to safeguarding employment also appeared.[11] A large part of such takeover was of cotton textile mills. This is particularly ironic as some of the private sector mills were very likely driven to sickness due to the government's own policy of reserving handloom production for small-scale units and favouring them with fiscal concessions. This had the consequence of making the larger power loom mills uncompetitive, first domestically and then *ipso facto* globally. Reservation of items for exclusive manufacture in the small-scale industry (SSI) sector was statutorily provided for in the Industries (Development and Regulation) Act, 1951, a milestone of the Nehru era. However, the practice of taking over the large private mills that had become unviable is of later vintage and came to be extended to jute and engineering too. Today it is difficult to imagine that a government can be so casual about the consequence of the continuation of its policies for the health of so long-standing an Indian industry such as textiles, not to mention the locking up of bank credit from the by-now nationalized banking sector that industrial sickness results in.

As planning lost its edge and a bloated public sector lost its capacity to invest—both developments being due to politics—the government lost some control over the economy, a control that it had wielded quite closely for nearly a decade and a half from the early 1950s. The Indian state was now set never to regain its once iconic status, even though its presence as a restraining force in the economy was to increase. In its new avatar it was to be powerful, overbearing, and capable of snuffing out enterprise. In an uncannily anthropomorphic display of vengefulness, the state attempted to compensate for its lost resource-mobilizing power, and the capacity to steer that this gave it, by resorting to a strategy of command and control. This appears to be the only meaningful way to see the unleashing of a plethora of controls that followed the death of Nehru, a move with debilitating consequences and one that the country has found difficult to shake off. It heralded a period during which the economy would be 'over-regulated but under-governed',[12] a time when the political leadership would remain politically unchallenged over the consequences of its economic policies. The growth transition that emerged out of this morass is surprising, especially if one were to see only the market-repressing interventions of the time.

A final comment on the viewing of the period 1965–91 as self-contained may now be made. Two sets of arguments may be brought to account for adopting such a periodization in our study. First, 1965 and 1991 were years of crises that affected the subsequent course of the Indian economy. The drought of 1965 was followed immediately by a balance of payments crisis, and in July 1991 India was to once again face a severe balance of payments crisis. In the interregnum, the policy regime in India turned more interventionist than it had been in the Nehru era. The trade regime was closed progressively and industrial regulation made more stringent. While some[13] argue that there was an incipient liberalization from the 1970s on, others[14] have remained sceptical of this claim, pointing to instances of further restriction of economic freedom in that very decade. What would meet all-round agreement, however, is that the sharpest break in the economic environment in India, after the adoption of planned development as state policy in 1950, occurred in 1991 when a substantial liberalization of the trade and industrial policy regime occurred. Thus, 1991 is an obvious choice as the end of the era of planning, broadly described. However, we have here argued that 1965 ought to be considered the beginning of a distinct phase as it marks the emergence of a new politics following the death of Nehru, getting reflected in the economic policies though not the overall policy regime. It could not have been without implication for the pace of economic growth. This style of politics, centred around a leader, was to go out after 1991, when in any case the adoption of an avowedly liberal policy environment made ad hoc interventions more difficult to rationalize. From the perspective of governance of the economy, then, the period 1965–91 emerges as a valid division in India's post-Independence economic history.

It was pointed out at the beginning of this section that events during 1965–91 had unfurled along two parallel tracks. Of these, the first was the evolution of governance which increasingly took an authoritarian turn, lasting for a while, with consequences for economic policy. The second is the successive exogenous shocks that the economy was subjected to. These had nothing to do with the political developments but surely affected both the course of the economy and the evolution of policy itself. The first among these shocks was drought in two years successive years, namely, 1965–6 and 1966–7, when agricultural output remained severely depressed. Even during this very episode, the country had faced a war with Pakistan in 1965, and then another in 1971. The latter was followed by the two oil-price shocks of 1973 and 1979. The drought of the mid-1960s exacerbated a chronic shortage of foreign exchange. The second oil shock fast led up to balance of payments stress with India having to go in for the largest ever borrowing by a member country from the International Monetary Fund (IMF) in 1980. It is difficult to conceive of any other period of equivalent duration in the recent history of India when the economy was buffeted by so many diverse external shocks.

Concurrently, there developed internally a crisis of governability with Indira Gandhi in the eye of the storm. This reached a crescendo in 1974–5 when Jayaprakash Narayan unleashed his movement for social transformation which he called 'Sampoorna Kraanthi' or 'Total Revolution'. This, however, was largely confined to the northern states of Bihar and Uttar Pradesh. More visible nationally was the strike by the railway employees led by the mercurial George Fernandes at around the same time. However, both had posed a serious challenge to her legitimacy. Indira Gandhi's means of overcoming these challenges was the imposition of an Emergency which, with the suspension of civil liberties, gave the executive unbridled powers. This was costly not only to her but also to the polity as it paved the way to unaccountable governance even of the economy, a feature by and large absent from the Nehru era. What is of significance, given the theme of this study, however, is that growth was not only not arrested but in some sectors actually accelerated amidst the negative shocks and the political disarray.

The Trajectory of Growth, 1965–91

We now identify the trajectory of growth during the years 1965–91. Actually this is less simple a task than may be assumed as there is a methodological issue involved. For any economy, the tempo of growth may be expected to be non-uniform over time, that is, the growth rate varies. Now the task of picking out the phases over which growth quickens or slows is credibly undertaken only when the researcher's priors are not allowed to intervene in the process. We adopt the econometrics of estimating and testing for multiple structural breaks in a time series wherein this criterion is internalized.[15] The advantage of this methodology may be described briefly. In studies of growth in India, researchers[16] have identified significant changes in economic policy and tested for whether an anticipated growth shift has followed from the date of implementation of the new policy. This is flawed in that, even in instances when the method turns in a statistically significant structural break, it precludes the discovery of a break having occurred earlier.[17]

Our approach, on the other hand, is outright empiricist by design. Here, growth regimes are estimated rather than identified on the basis of exogenous information, such as the date of initiation of a policy change or the timing of a supply shock. This immunizes the methodology to a researcher's priors regarding the timing of growth shifts and their likely causes. Our econometric procedure is the one developed by Bai and Perron (1998, 2003). While this is described in detail in the Appendix, a clarification needs to be issued at this stage itself. It is that though the approach does ensure that the researcher's priors do not infiltrate his/her method, in that the breakpoints are actually estimated from the data, some criteria for the identification of growth regimes have to be imposed. Among these is the minimum length of the interval between breakpoints, implying that judgement cannot be dispensed with altogether. Following the recommendation in Bai and Perron (2004) we have chosen this interval to be eight years.[18]

This study itself is concerned with growth in India since 1950. The maximum time series available at the time of the initiation of this study has been assembled, giving us a sample of over fifty observations extending up to the year 2003–4. For the econometric exercise in this chapter, the GDP (gross domestic product) data from the Central Statistical Organisation's (CSO) *National Accounts Statistics* is in 1993–4 prices. This series was considered more appropriate than others as the period of our study in this chapter is 1965–91. In the next chapter, where we study growth after 1991, we work with the GDP series in 1999–2000 prices and extending for a little longer.[19] Results in both cases are presented in the Appendix.

The growth rates across the phases of growth identified according to the procedure just referred to are presented in Table 3.1. As the estimated break-dates and the associated confidence intervals are likely to be of interest mainly to the specialist, they have been relegated to Table A4.1 of the Appendix.[20] Further, though the procedure has been applied to the data at a more disaggregated level, the growth rates presented in Table 3.1 are confined to those for the main sectors of the economy, with the results at the more disaggregate level made available in Table A4.2 of the Appendix. Finally, as a time series for the combined services sector GDP at constant prices is not published by the CSO, when it came to this sector, the econometric procedure had to be applied to the components separately. Accordingly, the growth rate for services alone appears by sub-sector in Table 3.1.

We now analyse the results of our procedure. First, crucially, growth of both aggregate GDP and every sector show acceleration at some stage during 1965–91. This is significant. Note that, statistically, the aggregate growth rate of an economy would display acceleration even with the sector-wise growth rates constant so long as the sectors are growing at different rates and the fast growing sector(s) inevitably come(s) to assume(s) a larger share of total output. So, it needs to be stressed that our estimates unambiguously imply a growth transition actually having taken place in the Indian economy during the period 1965–91. The economy-wide transition, measured by GDP growth, occurs at the end of the 1970s.[21] The precise date indicated by our procedure is 1979–80. However, it would serve our purpose to label the date as *circa* 1980.

A second feature of growth during this period may be noted. It is that the sectors accelerate at different points in time. For manufacturing, actually, there is first a deceleration in the mid-1960s before the recovery to an all-time high rate of growth in the early 1980s. The four main sub-sectors within services: trade, hotels, and restaurants; transport, storage, and communication; financing, insurance, real estate, and business services; and community and personal services—being mainly public administration and defence—all show at least one acceleration during 1965–91. None of these groups within services turn in a deceleration. Agriculture shows an acceleration in the mid-1960s. This, termed the Green Revolution, is of course widely known. Our estimates show that the acceleration has been maintained ever since.[22]

The rest of this chapter is devoted to explaining the sectoral growth trajectories established here with a view to explaining the growth transition in the economy itself. As stated, the challenge for the economist is to account for the transition during a period when the economic environment appears to have turned less than benign towards private enterprise in the manner described earlier. However, some implications of our econometric results for any attempted explanation of the growth transition itself may be noted right away. Above all, from Table 3.1, the growth transition in the economy occurs before the acceleration of manufacturing growth. This makes it difficult to sustain the argument that the trajectory of the Indian economy was in this period tied to the fortunes of manufacturing, which in turn was set by the trade and industrial policy regime. The explanatory power of a manufacturing resurgence having driven the growth transition in the economy is thus circumscribed. The disconnect between the growth of the economy and that of manufacturing has been stressed to such an extent here only to flag the misguided tendency of so much of the writing of the 1970s and 1980s

Table 3.1 Growth across Phases and by Sector, 1950–1 to 2003–4

Sector	*Period 1*	*Period 2*	*Period 3*	*Period 4*
GDP	3.34 [1950/1–1978/9]	5.20 [1979/80–2003/4]		
Agriculture	1.73 [1950/1–1964/5]	2.78 [1965/6–2003/4]		
Manufacturing	6.27 [1950/1–1965/6]	4.26 [1966/7–1982/3]	6.76 [1983/4–1994/5]	6.07 [1995/6–2003/4]
Trade, hotels, and restaurants	5.79 [1950/1–1962/3]	3.80 [1963/4–1971/2]	5.12 [1972/3–1994/5]	8.40 [1995/6–2003/4]
Transport, storage, and communication	6.12 [1950/1–1961/2]	5.50 [1962/3–1973/4]	5.55 [1974/5–1993/4]	9.21 [1994/5–2003/4]
Financing, insurance, real estate, and business services	3.06 [1950/1–1966/7]	3.44 [1967/8–1979/80]	8.88 [1979/80–1992/3]	8.00 [1993/4–2003/4]
Community and personal services	4.20 [1950/1–1961/2]	4.46 [1962/3–1976/7]	5.95 [1977/8–1992/3]	6.86 [1993/4–2003/4]

Notes: Average annual growth rate over the period reported in brackets.
All the estimated growth rates are significant at the 1 per cent level.

to conflate manufacturing with the economy.[23] However, the absence of a correlation between the accelerated growth of the economy and that of manufacturing only complicates the matter for the economist seeking an explanation of the former. Clues are available though. First, there is the obvious one that an impulse from outside of manufacturing will now have to be sought. Second, as the growth transition *circa* 1980 had occurred at a time when there was no significant change of the policy regime, the growth process very likely had an underlying dynamic that was relatively autonomous of the highly visible left-wing policy interventions that had targeted manufacturing.

Growth Viewed by Sector

It may appear that in a study of aggregate growth dynamics, knowledge of the sectoral growth experience has no particular value. However, I hope to demonstrate that an analysis of growth sector-wise is indispensable to understanding of the growth transition that occurred during 1965–91. Often we find that in aggregated accounts, though bearing the imprimatur of economic theory, the story of the economy-wide growth transition is not always consistent with the sectoral growth pattern. Indeed, for the period 1965–91, the estimates in Table 3.1 categorically imply that the project of providing such an overarching account, that is, a story based on a single causal factor, would be a non-starter due to opposite trends among the sectoral growth rates at least for some time. Accordingly, I proceed to an account of growth sector by sector. My final objective, however, remains an account of the economy-wide growth acceleration dated by us as having occurred *circa* 1980.

An Agricultural Transformation

Our econometric excursion had pointed to a break in the agricultural growth rate in the mid-1960s, showing an acceleration from then on. It is particularly significant in that the trend growth rate has remained higher for over four decades by now. A noticeable lowering of successive annual growth rates since the second half of the 1990s has not yet turned into a statistically significant deceleration.[24] However, statistics alone do not succeed in conveying the momentousness of the transformation represented by this acceleration. For the first time in the twentieth century, the rate of growth of production of foodgrains in India exceeded the rate of growth of the population. Popularly referred to as the Green Revolution, this development radically altered the long-term prospects of the economy. Once viewed as a basket case—the unspoken premise of the international discourse in the 1960s—India was by now more or less self-sufficient in food, a transformation that was to alter perceptions of the country globally. The change in perception must also have been encouraged by the demonstration that India could, when it finally came to it, get its act together. In the eyes of the Western establishment India had remained not only an 'area of darkness' but also one of anarchy, so wasteful of the splendid institutions bestowed upon it by that torch-bearer of progress, the British Empire. Now, within two decades of the departure of the great and the good, the erstwhile colony had shown itself to possess the mettle to engineer two agricultural transformations in relatively quick succession, first in the Nehru era and now once again within a decade and a half after the first. In the context, international perception needs concern us only thus far, however. More important is to appreciate the significance of the transformation for the growth of the wider economy and to understand the drivers of the said Revolution itself.

While the rapid growth of agriculture, especially during the first half of the 1950s, had already intimated the increase in the living standards that was attainable, the results of the population census of 1961 were to suggest that these expectations may not be realized after all. Unexpectedly, along with Independence had come about a rise in the rate of growth of population. From the reports of the decennial censuses we know that a decline in the death rate took place. While some of this would be directly related to the changed economic environment—the end of shortages, the steady increase in income howsoever small, and the spread of public health outreach—the sheer immediacy of the acceleration in population growth suggest that other factors may be at work. Among them was probably a wave of optimism that had washed over the subcontinent as colonial rule had ended. Whatever the precise reason, the rise in the rate of growth of population was entirely unexpected. It had the effect of offsetting the potential gain in per capita availability of food brought about by the acceleration in agricultural growth.

By the early 1960s the rise in the growth rate of population had entered the radar of the policymakers and the need to accelerate food production was firmly on the political agenda. This was reflected in Nehru's speeches to Parliament, quoted in Chapter 2. However, Nehru's gathering pessimism appears to have got the better of him. In 1964, the year of his death, was registered an increase in agricultural production exceeding 10 per cent, the second largest annual increase in the decade that had just passed and one that has seldom been surpassed since. Also, by that year the index of agricultural production[25] had registered a level 60 per cent higher than in 1950–1. This could not but have been the cumulative effect of the policies pursued during his tenure as prime minister. These range from the expansion of irrigation, the consolidation of landholdings to eliminate the parcelization of land, agrarian reform (however limited), the Community Development Programme for rural regeneration combined with a national agricultural extension service, and the general sense of urgency communicated by the Grow-More-Food Campaign aimed at achieving self-sufficiency. The last had included Central assistance to the states to improve land quality and purchase fertilizer, and, notably, reward-based competition across the country for raising yields. But disaster in the form of drought was to strike the very next year after the bumper harvest. In the crop-year 1965–6, foodgrains' output was to decline by 20 per cent. This was followed by another poor crop in 1966–7, when production rose but marginally. For two consecutive years then, output remained depressed by close to a fifth of what it was in 1964–5.

While the negative supply shock was not insignificant, it would not have been as severe in impact were it not for the conditions in which India found herself. Not even the low domestic food stocks need have posed a problem had India not also faced a severe shortage of foreign exchange at the same time. This ruled out imports from the world market. Negotiations for a balance-of-payments adjustment loan from the IMF turned out to be protracted and conditionality laden, revealing to India her weak hand. A border war with Pakistan in August–September 1965 had left the West, especially the United States, bound to Pakistan by the defence treaty Central Treaty Organization (CENTO), reluctant to come to India's aid. Finally, perhaps convinced of the implications for its democratic credentials of withholding assistance at the time of a humanitarian crisis, American food aid finally came. But it came literally by the shipload, a design that was allegedly intended by Lyndon Johnson to 'keep India on a short leash'. India had been publicly humiliated for her independent foreign policy. No further illumination of the truth was needed that political independence was hollow if it was not accompanied by economic wherewithal, especially of food.

Though Indira Gandhi was not always democratic when she was at home, her publicly displayed authoritarianism was trumped by a fierce hidden patriotism. Stung to the last by the demonstration of American hauteur, she was now determined to energize a fairly extensive national agricultural research and extension system towards the goal of raising the rate of growth of production of food in India. The subsequent developments that succeeded in turning around the rate of growth of food production in India have been termed the Green Revolution. While good enough as a description of the outcome, the term reveals little of its origins. Above all, the perception is encouraged that the permanent increase in the rate of growth of production was brought about by a costless infusion of technology and, more so, that it was produced quite instantaneously. Such a view underplays the role of resources, especially public resources, in the transformation of Indian agriculture in the 1960s. I shall address this issue at some length, but first the technological aspect.

Central to the new technology of agricultural production that succeeded in raising the rate of growth was the new seed. Initially confined to the wheat crop, these were capable of generating more grain per stalk, hence 'high-yielding varieties' (HYV). The miracle seed's capability was somewhat limited on its own though. It was prone to pestilence, more vulnerable to drought conditions, and more demanding in terms of nutrient intake. This meant that its adoption was dependent on the use of pesticide, the assured provision of water, and the enhanced application of fertilizer. The flipside of this was that if the new seed was used without the requisite doses of these inputs, there was the risk that the yield would be even less than that from using the traditional variety. The implication was that the cultivation of an HYV crop was relatively more input intensive. That the adoption of the new seed was profitable despite the increased cost of production, due to the complementary inputs, may of course be surmised from the evidence of its quick adoption in parts of the country where the economic environment was conducive to its use. Here, assured irrigation was very likely the most important consideration to the farmer.

Two aspects of the Green Revolution are worthy of note, and one of some relevance to the future of India in the twenty-first century regardless of what the policy regime may be. The first is the international nature of the research programme that generated the new seed. The principal international agricultural research stations were based in Mexico for wheat and the Philippines for rice. The research funding was part public, from the Western democracies, and partly from the major global philanthropies such as the Rockefeller and Ford Foundations. There was also some Soviet aid to India, a feature not so well known.[26] So we find that the Green Revolution cannot be viewed as cent per cent Indian in all its aspects, assuming for a moment that we would even want to do so. International contribution to India's growth and development via this agricultural transformation was considerable. It cautions us against the tendency to view international economic relations in terms of resource flows alone. There was also the flow of ideas, which include new ways of doing things, what we often call 'organization',[27] not to mention the technology itself. Be that as it may, the permanent increase in the rate of growth of food production in India was the outcome of a truly international research effort, ironically made at the height of the Cold War. In conclusion, it would not be advisable to view the Green Revolution in India as *episodic*, so to speak.

Though the food crisis of the mid-1960s and the political humiliation that had followed may have been the beacon on the hill that had illuminated the only way forward, the sustained rise in the rate of growth of food production that occurred in the 1960s is properly seen as the culmination of efforts that had been initiated in the Nehru era. I have earlier recapitulated briefly what these efforts were. The food shortages are very likely to have only provided a renewed urgency. In this context, the following observations of M.S. Swaminathan, the agricultural scientist most closely associated with the Green Revolution in India, are of interest. Referring to Prime Minister Lal Bahadur Shastri, Swaminathan (2007) said:

> During his brief period as Prime Minister, he sowed the seeds of the Green Revolution. He spent several hours with us in April 1965 on our wheat fields and then approved the import of a substantial quantity of seeds of the semi-dwarf varieties from Mexico, which had undergone rigorous testing on our farms for several years. Consequently our farmers were able to increase the production during 1964–68 by a quantity higher than that achieved during the preceding 4,000 years.

This actually suggests that the idea of a technological transformation of Indian agriculture, and the necessary inputs, was with the governing elite for some time and was not merely a panicked response to the drought of the mid-1960s, much as the latter must have pointed to gravity of the food situation and the need to address it with alacrity. The seed bed, so to speak, was clearly under preparation well before the actual acceleration of output growth in the mid-1960s and international cooperation was vital to this effort.[28] An aspect of the Green Revolution of relevance to understanding long-term economic growth in India, already referred to in passing, is taken up next.

While the miracle seed is emblematic of the Green Revolution, it is worth reflecting upon the question whether the transformation constituted merely a transfer of technology from the international sphere without any significant transfer of resources to agriculture from within our own borders. In the context, a question of interest would be 'What was the role of resources?'. To answer this, we may study public capital formation in the agricultural sector. Data on public capital formation in agriculture and, in contrast, industry for the period 1960–80 are presented in Table 3.2. There it is clearly noticeable that while public capital formation as a whole declined in the economy in the mid-1960s, its subsequent history varied across its sectors. After a one-shot decline in real terms in the mid-1960s, public capital formation in agriculture grew at a faster rate till the late 1970s. This record is markedly different from that in industry.

Table 3.2 Public Investment in Agriculture, 1960–80

Year	*Agriculture*	*Industry*	*Total*	*Ratio*	*Share*
1960–1	211	420	1826	0.50	0.12
1961–2	210	314	1797	0.67	0.12
1962–3	240	363	2181	0.66	0.11
1963–4	246	406	2421	0.61	0.10
1964–5	278	484	2665	0.57	0.10
1965–6	301	645	2846	0.47	0.11
1966–7	270	689	2574	0.39	0.10
1967–8	270	590	2635	0.46	0.10
1968–9	310	509	2397	0.61	0.13
1969–70	311	463	2373	0.67	0.13
1970–1	329	436	2773	0.75	0.12
1971–2	349	522	2957	0.67	0.12
1972–3	419	593	3135	0.71	0.13
1973–4	416	807	3738	0.52	0.11
1974–5	358	889	3517	0.40	0.10
1975–6	408	822	4433	0.50	0.09
1976–7	561	1035	4920	0.54	0.11
1977–8	644	932	4184	0.69	0.15
1978–9	683	1016	5012	0.67	0.14
1979–80	690	1224	5301	0.56	0.13

Source: 'Transactions of the Public Sector 1960–61 to 1979–80', Central Statistical Organisation (CSO), 1983.

Notes: Investment figures are in Rs crore at 1970–1 prices. 'Ratio' is public investment in agriculture to public investment in manufacturing. 'Share' is public investment in agriculture to total public investment in the economy.

As we find from the data in the table, though public capital formation in industry continued to rise beyond the date by when it had peaked in agriculture in 1965–6, when its decline commenced in 1967–8 it was both precipitous and sustained for much longer. On the other hand, public capital formation in agriculture remained depressed only for a very short while, recovering almost instantly and progressing steadily all the way up to 1980. These trends are visible in the graph in Figure 3.1.

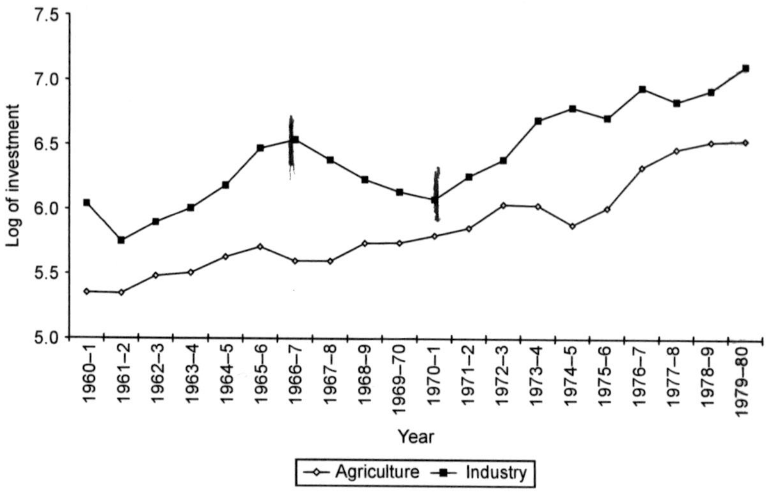

Figure 3.1 Public Investment, 1960–80

While the cause of the decline in public capital formation in these two sectors and in the aggregate in the mid-1960s is a matter of interest, it need not detain us here. The point is that very soon after, contemporaneous with the acceleration in agricultural production, there has also taken place a substantial rise in public capital formation in this sector. That this reflects a strategic shift in policy may be surmised from the fact[29] that the share of agriculture in total capital formation in the public sector is on average higher for fifteen years after 1965–6. However, this shift is mild. What comes across far more strongly, though, is the reversal from the mid-1960s of the steady decline through the Third Plan (1961–6) in the ratio of public capital formation in agriculture to that in industry. A fairly marked upward shift is evident for the next fifteen years, even though it has fluctuated, often sharply.[30] Taken together, these two developments point to a policy of an increased support to agricultural production. It seems reasonable to conclude that besides the infusion of technology, the Green

Revolution was enabled by a public-investment strategy that had targeted the agricultural sector. Therefore, the agricultural growth acceleration we call the Green Revolution was made possible and sustained by more than just a technological fix. This has tended to be overlooked.[31]

Further there is a message in this for what is feasible in India today, and not only in the sphere of agriculture, when there is tendency to assume that the market can bring about the necessary transformations so long as the incentive structure, reflected by the relative prices, is got right. India's Green Revolution suggests that resource flows are central to growth transformations.

Public capital formation in agriculture is of course only the visible aspect of public resource flow into the sector. It is important to note that since the mid-1960s the government has operated a fairly complex and extensive system of interventions, though mainly in the grain markets. From theory and empirical evidence[32] we have reason to believe that government intervention has had the effect of buoying up the market price. Publicly held stocks purchased at an 'incentive price' engineer a resource transfer to agriculture as the market price, it may reasonably be expected, would be lower in the absence of this intervention. Further, since the nationalization of banks in 1969, 'directed credit' has opened up an input channel non-existent hitherto. Not all sections of farmers may have gained equally from this facility, but this flow of credit to agriculture very likely ensured working capital to at least the better-off sections of the farmers. An interpretation of the politics of the Green Revolution is that nationalism prevailed over radicalism, in that in a determined bid to make India self-sufficient in food, the erstwhile emphasis on measures such as land reform was unabashedly traded for one on growth.[33] To see this is insightful, alright. However, while a policy of encouraging private producers may appear conservative from a political point of view, the development was itself radical in its approach to the role of government in the economy. Intervention was widespread, ranging from the shift in the public investment strategy to the regulation of the output, input, and the credit markets.[34] Significantly, it was to be the last initiative of this range and magnitude by the state in India which has had a direct impact on the growth of the economy.

Cyclical Growth in Manufacturing

It is the trajectory of industrial growth during 1965–91 that comes closest to the general perception of an indifferent economic performance in this period. Our estimates, reported in Table 3.1, show the growth rate of manufacturing decelerating from 1966–7 and remaining depressed till 1982–3. From the next year on, it accelerated to an all-time high rate of progress which was maintained for more than a decade.[35] Despite this history, it is mainly the prolonged phase of substantially lower average growth of manufacturing industry since the mid-1960s that tends to dominate typical characterizations of the period 1965–91. However, even when acknowledging this phase, it is important to emphasize that we are here speaking of a *slowing* of growth. Industrial performance during this period has been presented as 'stagnation'.[36] As pointed out by Raj (1984), this is incorrect even though there may have been years of a decline in production, mainly in the 1960s. After all, the trend growth rate of over 4 per cent registered during 1966–83 does not answer to the description of stagnation. Taking into account the full range of growth experience, the appropriate characterization of industrial growth during 1965–91 can only be that it was cyclical, with significant swings of the growth rate in either direction. This is clearly observed in Table 3.1.

The subsequent acceleration of industrial growth during 1965–91 has been attributed to the liberalization of the trade and industrial policy regime in the second half of this period.[37] A detached viewer may espy in this a tendency to claim a potency in the past for influences that are strong today, that is, of allowing knowledge of an economy thriving in a liberal investment climate after 1991 to encourage the claim that liberalizing reform alone could have led to an acceleration of the rate of growth of manufacturing in the past—in the second half of 1965–91. It is significant that in the 1970s when the possibility of liberal economic reforms in India was not yet imagined, economists[38] had explained the trajectory of industrial growth largely in terms of movements in public investment and agricultural growth. Actually, these remain explanations that have merit for much of the period that we are looking at now, namely, 1965–91. Before returning to demonstrate this, however, we first devote attention to the evolution of industrial policy with a view to evaluating its contribution to the cyclical pattern of industrial growth in this phase of India's economic history.

The Random Walk of Industrial Policy, 1965–91

The government's approach to industrial policy over the period under consideration has been appraised by Marathe (1986: 135) as follows: 'The enunciation of government policies was relatively strong on statement of goals or objectives, much weaker on the elaboration of operating strategies and there was, virtually, no regular mechanism for the appraisal of policy.'[39] In general, reviews that were undertaken were not followed up by significant changes to policy or even to the mechanisms aimed at achieving the stated objectives of policy. Therefore, the much publicized reviews of industrial policy during this time, namely, the *Hazari Report on Industrial Licencing* of 1967, the *Dutt Inquiry Committee Report on Industrial Licencing Policy*, also of 1967, and the *Ramakrishna Study Group on Industrial Regulations and Procedures* of 1978 did not lead to much change, which Marathe (1986: 35–6) has accounted for as follows:

> [T]he elaborate structure of regulation and controls—industrial licensing, import controls, price and distribution controls, foreign exchange regulations, controls over induction of foreign capital or technology and FERA/MRTP approvals, etc.—had a dynamics of its own. This system, interacting with the social and political milieu of the country tended to create a powerful lobby of bureaucrats, politicians and industrialists, each having a vested interest in avoiding any major modification of the prevailing system. This is reflected in the policies enunciated and in the unwillingness to act on the advice of recommendations contained in the Plan Documents or reports of various committees including Parliamentary Committees.

So, as may be expected for a heterogeneous democracy with a thriving market economy and experiencing growth, which India was by the mid-1960s, we find that political economy is vital to our understanding of the impact of a policy regime. Further, we must recognize that its impact evolves as implementation itself sets off a continuous interaction between the government and private agents. Some validation of Marathe's view that the larger houses were very likely able to work the system if not always to their advantage, at least to ensure a mitigation of stringency in the application of the rules under the law, may be found in the evidence that the total assets controlled by the large industrial houses continued to grow after the MRTP legislation.[40] For an account of how the interaction between implementation and agent response can steer the regime away from its original intent, we may turn to the observations of S. Bhoothalingam, a senior ICS man involved in economic policymaking in the early years after Independence:

> In the process of determining the number and capacity of new units required to achieve a plan target, the judgement of the Government and Planners on questions such as the size, the nature of the equipment, the process and sometimes even the actual physical location of a unit often prevailed over the judgement of the entrepreneur concerned. The well-intentioned desire to spread new capacity equitably among different regions, combined with the need to do so without the risk of creating 'excess capacity' often led to limitations on the size and technical character of new enterprises which hampered

efficient functioning and growth. The limitations, in turn, led some entrepreneurs to seek dubious ways of getting over or around them. These, in turn, attracted counter-measures by way of more interference and policing than was ever intended. (quoted in Marathe 1986: 87–8)

Note here the suggestion of some unintended consequences of the licensing policy arising out of a repeated interaction between the government machinery and private agents. In hindsight, while it need not surprise us that this possibility was unimagined when the policy was originally conceived, it is indeed surprising that its emergence was not addressed in the many reviews of industrial licensing. In any case, these observations by the government's own representatives reveal that the 'change-proofness' of the policy regime and the disregard for the original intent of a legislation by the implementing agency have little to do with the absence of a technical proficiency in governance or of modern methods of administration. It goes back to the absence of political will, itself determined by the configuration of interests that bear upon a particular situation. We now turn to the evolution of industrial policy during 1965–91.

There are three identifiable landmarks in the evolution of industrial policy after 1965 prior to the acceleration of industrial growth in the early 1980s that is indicated by our statistical analysis. These are the Industrial Policy Statement of 1973 and the innovations that followed during 1975–6, both having been ushered in at a time when Indira Gandhi's left-wing economic policy stance was as its most angular; the Policy Statement of 1977 that had come early in the brief tenure of the Janata Party; and the Policy Statement of 1980 that was issued when Indira Gandhi returned to office. Studying these may be expected to enhance our ability to judge whether changes in the policy and regulatory regimes may have influenced the trajectory of industrial growth in this period.

1973 By the 1970s awareness was spreading that the economic development that had taken place was not yielding the results hoped for. A frontal attack on poverty was the stated objective of the Fifth Five Year Plan that was launched in 1974–5. Accordingly, the industrial licensing policy was reviewed for fit. The objective of the Statement of 1973 was 'to update the industrial licensing policy in order to reflect the approach to the Fifth Plan and taking into account the legal and institutional arrangements that are now available for the effective control of the concentration of economic power' (quoted in Marathe 1986: 94).[41]

It is not clear how this could ever have had more of an impact than an extension of the purview of the MRTP Act, which had been designed to counteract concentration.

Moreover, though the stated purpose of the policy was to provide 'greater certainty in the investment climate', it aimed quite narrowly to stimulate growth in the industries of relevance to the objectives of the Fifth Plan. All this was a far cry from liberating private investment, though the Statement indicated that a move in the direction of streamlining licensing and associated procedures was in the offing so that private investment would be facilitated. As a follow-up, the government now undertook an examination of the extant procedures with respect to letters of intent, industrial licensing, foreign collaboration approvals, capital-goods-import clearance, and approvals under the MRTP Act. With a view to expediting clearances, a Secretariat for Industrial Approvals (SIA) was announced in October 1973, the streamlining of procedures for clearance to be effective with respect to applications made after 1 November.

1975–6 During 1975–6 a number of steps were taken to liberalize licensing. These were freedom to diversify within the same group of scheduled industries, recognition of additional capacity as a result of modernization, allowance of the maximum utilization of installed capacity even if it meant exceeding what was licensed production, and the de-licensing of certain industries. Marathe's (1986) assessment is that the consequences of such streamlining and liberalization were not as expected. For instance, while the SIA was an important organizational innovation, the period immediately following actually witnessed a rise in the percentage of rejected applications. By 1981 the majority was rejected, and it has been suggested that this was the bureaucracy's show of resistance to the policy of a time-bound processing of applications! Marathe is of the view that the impact of the various licensing-policy liberalizations in this phase could not have been more than limited as approval was never made automatic and the detail was in the caveats. For instance, while in October 1975 substantial expansion and manufacture of new articles was exempt from licensing for twenty-four industries, this de-licensing was subject to the condition that no imports or foreign collaborations were involved. The liberalization did not extend to goods reserved for the small sector, and were of course inapplicable to undertakings which were under the MRTP Act. The whole approach appears to have been hobbled by half-heartedness and hesitancy.

While taking note of the efforts being made to streamline licensing procedures, it is important not to lose track of some of the changes that were coming into effect, which would impinge upon production. In 1976, perhaps the most stringent of the restrictions governing industrial production policies was enacted. Owners of private industrial units now had to seek the permission of the state government before closing down an industrial unit.[42] This stiffened the already existing barrier to exit and could only have been a further disincentive to entry. The best way to comprehend its effect is to imagine the impact on inward migration of the lack of guaranteed emigration from a country. A political economy view would suggest that this law, passed during the Emergency, was Indira Gandhi's overture to both organized labour in employment and to the Communist Party of India who were aligned with her in the Lok Sabha.

The keyword here is 'labour in employment', as restrictions on exit can be potentially damaging of the interests of the currently unemployed or future generations of labour. Exit restrictions on firms can dampen private investment and thus, via the derived demand for labour, the generation of employment. Alternatively, we may comprehend exit restrictions for firms as part of a strategy of governance that addresses exclusively the interests of the organized in society. Note that the unemployed are not organized and future entrants into the labour market perhaps do not even exist as yet. Evidently, either the hubris spawned by the extraordinary powers at her command under Emergency provisions or the sheer compulsions of staying in power had left Indira Gandhi with no incentive to reflect upon the long-term consequences for the Indian economy of some of her actions.

1977 In 1977, for the first time in India, there was a non-Congress government in office. It was a disparate group ranging from the socialists to former members of the Swatantra, a party committed to a market economy, as its name suggests. There was also the Lok Dal led by Charan Singh, which was committed to peasant farming and, as if in an afterthought, to decentralized village industries. As expected, given the 'power shift' represented by the rise of the Janata Party, the new government was highly critical of the policies pursued in the past to which it attributed the inadequate growth of per capita income, the slow growth of industrial production, and the distortion of industrial prices. In listing the inadequacies of the working of the Industrial Policy Resolution 1956, the Industrial Policy Statement of 1977—laid in Parliament by George

Fernandes, by now the minister for industry—marked a departure from the norm of political practice in India. Direct indictment of past polices had till then not figured in the government's declarations, and for reasons not far to seek. India had till then been ruled by a single party and serious criticism of past policies would be tantamount to acknowledging a long-term failure or, worse still, a misguidance.

As far as the strategy of growth was concerned, the Industrial Policy Statement of 1977 pointed to the existence of an interactive mutual feedback between agriculture and industry. In particular, it recognized that power, fertilizers, pesticides, steel, and cement were as important for agricultural growth as for the industrial growth. Interestingly, this argument is entirely consonant with the vision underlying the Nehru–Mahalanobis Strategy wherein agriculture and industry were complementary and not seen as rivalling one another, a vision that the Janata Party was seeking to distance itself from. The specific policies in the Statement, intended as a showcasing of the philosophy of the party, were as follows.

1. A 'tiny' sector: In a firm bid to change the erstwhile emphasis of industrial policy which had, reportedly, been on large industries, 'neglecting cottage industries and relegating small industries to a minor role' (quoted in Marathe 1986: 104), the list of industries reserved for the small-scale sector was significantly expanded. Further, a 'tiny' sector, with investment in machinery and equipment up to Rs 1,00,000 and located in towns with a population of less than 50,000 was identified for promotion. District Industries Centres were to be set up to provide support to this move to spread industrial production across the country. This was meant to shift the locus of decision-making to the district headquarters away from the capital of the states, not to mention of the country itself. To this extent, it was a departure from the Industrial Policy Resolution of 1956 which had willy-nilly encouraged concentration of power at the Centre.

2. Large business houses and the public sector: The Statement claimed, and correctly, that past policies had not succeeded in restraining the growth of Indian industry's large houses. More astutely, it pointed out that this growth has been disproportionate to the size of their internally generated resources, being largely based on funds borrowed from the nationalized banks and the public financial institutions. This was to be reversed. Viewing the public sector as 'a countervailing power' to the private, the Statement recorded the government's intention of expanding the role of the public sector, interestingly, in 'contributing to

decentralised production' by making available its expertise in technology and management to small-scale and cottage industry sectors.

3. Foreign trade: Given the improved foreign exchange position and the progress of industrialization, it was considered timely to initiate a selective dispensation with import quotas and quantitative restrictions, protection being maintained via tariffs. Second, compulsory export obligation merely for ensuring the foreign exchange balance of an industrial project was no longer to be insisted upon.

4. Foreign investment: On the issue of foreign investment, the Statement signalled the intention of adhering strictly to the provision of the FERA. Under FERA, foreign equity holding was to be diluted. However, an innovation in this area was that after the dilution was completed, companies with non-resident investment not exceeding 40 per cent were to be treated on par with Indian companies, except in cases specifically notified, and their future expansion guided by the same principles as those applicable to Indian companies. This eliminated a perceived lack of clarity in the policy stance towards foreign investment.

Overall, there appears to have been achieved some finessing of the industrial policy regime under the Janata government. The changes themselves, however, were all in the sphere of policy and not in the operation of the regulatory mechanism, which some economists have seen as the more serious issue.[43] In this connection, note Marathe's (1986: 112) observation: 'It has to be recognised, however, that the brief Janata interlude did not find it necessary (or possible) to make any radical change in the operation of the complex system of regulation and control which had evolved over a period of nearly twenty-five years.'

1980 In January 1980, Indira Gandhi was returned to the office of prime minister. It has been suggested that she had returned chastened[44] by an ignominious defeat in 1977. Surely she must have had an opportunity to reflect upon the consequences of her past economic policies. In any case, within about six months of her return to office, an industrial policy statement was issued. The preamble to this was political, exceeding in this respect the stridency of even the Janata Party's Statement of 1977. First, it indicted the Party by name, alleging that in its thirty-three-month rule it had 'choked off' the channels of growth in the economy.[45] Further, 'The runway of the economy has been damaged by the last two governments and the entire process of development was put in reverse gear.'[46] The Statement then went on to claim that new thrusts were needed to establish a dynamic industrial economy as indicated in the election manifesto of the Congress Party. With hindsight, some of these claims must now strike us as either based on ignorance or mere political grand-standing given that the economy had accelerated precisely around then! Some burrowing in the data suggests a government grasping the opportunity provided by a negative growth in 1979–80 of both the industrial sector and the overall economy to wound the political opposition. Actually, the two years of rule by the Janata Party were years of very high industrial growth.[47] It seems when governments decide to change course they can even resort to dissimulation at the cost of exposing themselves!

Interestingly, in spirit the Industrial Policy Statement of 1980 was the very opposite of the Statement of 1977. It contained no major policy shifts, despite the rhetoric it had managed to whip-up for itself, but did effect some regulatory changes.[48] These were:

1. Automatic expansion of capacity at the rate of 5 per cent per year up to a maximum of 25 per cent over the five-year period of 1980–5.

2. Established capacity in nineteen selected industries and fifteen other industries was regularized.

3. In the case of small-scale and ancillary-producing units, the limit of Rs 10 lakh and Rs 15 lakh, respectively, fixed for exemption from licensing was enhanced to Rs 20 lakh and Rs 25 lakh, respectively.

Marathe's observations on the Statement are of interest. He has stated:

> Measures adopted in pursuance of the Industrial Policy Statement of 1980 once again revealed that even when a greater degree of freedom for the industrial system was deemed to be necessary and desirable there was tremendous reluctance for this enhanced freedom to be determined by the market forces or to use the other instruments of control in the hands of government, for example, taxes, tariffs, lending policies of nationalised banks or development institutions, etc. The emphasis was still on easing of regulations which continued to be administered by the Central Government; and the main concern of the administrative machinery responsible for the regulatory framework was to ensure that the investment decisions were not allowed to be influenced by the market forces except within the narrow limits of the administrative liberalisation. (Marathe 1986: 130)

Our own assessment of the Statement of 1980 varies somewhat from that of Marathe. He overlooks the likely impact of measures other than those which are strictly liberalizing in the sense of giving greater role for market forces. Arguably, an administered relaxation of limits such as those listed earlier may be as significant depending upon the objective to be served. For instance, the allowance of a time-bound but automatic capacity expansion over a period constitutes a staggered but definite easing of a supply constraint. When it comes to production or investment, its impact may be as important as that of complete de-licensing depending upon the level of demand. Marathe's valuable account of the evolution of industrial policy during this period is at times overshadowed by a tendency to underestimate any measure short of copybook liberalization. The predictive power of such an approach must necessarily be weaker compared to a less rigid but surely more astute one that evaluates a change in policy in terms of its likely impact on supply and demand.

The role of changes in the regulatory regime for industry is now addressed along with that of the other factors that may have contributed to the cyclical growth of industry during 1965–91.

The Cyclical Growth of Manufacturing Explained

The estimates presented in Table 3.1 show a slowing of manufacturing growth from 1966–7 and an acceleration from 1983–4. Our explanation of this proceeds as follows. At the outset, we can reject the role of agriculture in determining the trend growth in industry during this period as the former shows a sustained contemporaneous acceleration from 1965–6. By implication, agricultural growth could not have been the binding constraint on manufacturing during this period. We believe that two factors are responsible for the pattern of industrial growth during 1965–91—the changing trajectory of public investment and a varying stringency in the implementation of the legal provisions of the trade and industrial policy regimes.

Public investment in industry, a category a little broader than manufacturing, exhibits a cyclical pattern for about a decade from the mid-1960s, as may be seen from the data presented in Table 3.2. Note that, having risen steadily throughout the period of the Third Plan (1961–6), it collapses abjectly in the year 1967–8. At its trough in 1970–1, it is less than two-thirds of the level in 1967–8, which it took till 1973–4 to clear. The data are graphed in Figure 3.1. In a digression, we might mention that perhaps not all of the decline in public sector investment in industry need have resulted from financial constraints, even though public saving declined at this time. An element of strategic choice in the matter is suggested by the observed shift in the investment outlay towards agriculture, already highlighted by us. In the event of changed allocation, a decline of public investment in industry would very likely have resulted even with public savings steady. It is of course a different matter that public sector savings too show a cyclical pattern, a decline commencing 1964–5 and lasting for close to decade.[49]

Be that as it may, the depression of public capital formation in industry for six years from the mid-1960s is likely to have impacted manufacturing growth from the directions of both supply and of demand. Public sector output in the form of infrastructure and capital goods was central to private production in the manufacturing sector. In the mid-1960s the role of the public sector as supplier of capital and intermediate goods was far more significant than it had been earlier or has ever been since. Therefore, dependence upon the public sector of the private sector is likely to have been considerable. This would not be surprising as the capital goods that the public sector produced had been assigned a strategic role in the Nehru–Mahalanobis Strategy which had been adhered to quite closely in the allocation of plan investment till the mid-1960s at least. Public investment also impacts industrial activity from the demand side, directly as a source of demand for capital and intermediate goods outputs of the private sector and indirectly via the generation of demand for its consumer products from wages and salaries paid out in the process of public production. Thus, supply and demand effects are likely to have ensured that the decline in public investment, lasting for a decade, would have led to slower growth of manufacturing production in both the public and private sectors of the industrial economy. Further, via the accelerator, this may be expected to have acted as a dampener on private corporate investment.

While there exists econometric evidence[50] on the direct relationship between public and private investment in India, clear evidence of it can be had from the data in Table 2.5 in Chapter 2 which shows the picture during the period 1950–65, the period just preceding the one we are discussing here. 'Crowding in' appears to best characterize this relationship. To enable judgement on the role of public investment in determining the trajectory of industrial growth during 1965–90, time series on gross capital formation by type of institution are presented in Table 3.3. Note that unlike the data in Table 3.2, here it is economy-wide capital formation that is being considered, not only that in the industrial sector. However, the figure for the 'private corporate sector' may safely be assumed to refer almost exclusively to investment in manufacturing, for at least during the period under consideration corporate activity was thus confined. For econometric evidence of the role of public investment in the determination of industrial production over the period 1950–80, see Balakrishnan (1991).

Table 3.3 Gross Domestic Capital Formation by Type of Institution

Year	*Public*	*Private Sector*		*Total*
		Corporate	*Household*	
1960–1	8.7	4.0	5.9	18.6
1961–2	8.1	5.0	5.4	18.5
1962–3	9.4	3.4	6.5	19.4
1963–4	9.9	5.0	5.0	19.9
1964–5	10.1	4.5	5.8	20.4
1965–6	11.4	3.5	7.6	22.5
1966–7	9.6	2.7	10.3	22.6
1967–8	9.3	3.2	9.0	21.5
1968–9	8.2	2.8	9.3	20.3
1969–70	7.5	2.1	11.1	20.8
1970–1	8.2	2.9	9.2	20.3
1971–2	8.8	3.1	9.4	21.3
1972–3	9.4	3.3	8.5	21.1
1973–4	9.2	3.1	8.2	20.5
1974–5	8.8	4.2	8.8	21.8
1975–6	10.5	2.9	7.8	21.2
1976–7	11.4	1.7	9.1	22.2
1977–8	9.6	2.8	10.0	22.4
1978–9	10.3	2.3	10.5	23.2
1979–80	11.0	2.8	9.6	23.4
1980–1	9.4	2.7	8.7	20.9
1981–2	10.8	5.8	7.4	24.0
1982–3	11.3	5.7	10.9	28.0
1983–4	10.3	3.4	7.2	21.0
1984–5	10.9	4.3	7.3	22.5
1985–6	10.3	5.0	7.3	22.6
1986–7	11.0	5.0	6.9	22.8
1987–8	9.6	3.5	9.2	22.4
1988–9	9.4	3.8	10.2	23.4
1989–90	9.2	3.9	9.7	22.8
1990–1	9.0	4.0	10.2	23.2

Source: Author's calculation from *National Accounts Statistics* data presented in Economic and Political Weekly Research Foundation (2006).
Notes: Rate of gross capital formation is the ratio of investment to output at constant (1993–4) prices. Double deflation was adopted.

Among the early observers of economic growth in the mid-1960s was Jha (1980). For Jha, the year 1966–7 marks a decisive turning point when a 'healthy, if modest' economic growth turned into a prolonged economic decline and 'the cut in public investment was only the beginning of the slide backwards' (Jha 1980: 67). While in his account the author appears to conflate the economy with manufacturing industry, his exposition of how public investment impacted on manufacturing output is persuasive. It is pointed out that as the public sector provided the bulk of the demand for the output of private industry, with a decline in public investment, profitability in the private sector was struck a blow and excess capacity emerged. As a temporary disincentive now emerged for private investment, it lowered the demand for capital goods produced in the public sector. As an indicator consider the following: 'The total sales of machine tools in the country declined from Rs. 54.16 crores in 1965–66 to Rs. 5.42 crores in 1970–71, the second year of the Fourth Plan' (Jha 1980: 67). As the public sector's investment was at least partly dependent upon its operating surplus, its investment outlays were to shrink further, thus completing the cycle.

Take the case of the government-owned Hindustan Machine Tools. It went from a comfortable surplus in 1965–6 to heavy deficit (Jha 1980: 67) in 1967–8. This is significant as we know that in the very recent past it had actually financed its own expansion.[51] No longer able to fund the plan, the government announced a Plan Holiday which lasted for the period 1966–9 during which the annual average investment outlay was less than in 1965–6. Excess capacity was to proliferate in manufacturing for the next five years and even leading manufacturing firms were to go into liquidation.[52] The plausibility of a public investment–driven decline in industrial growth from the mid-1960s is reflected in the composition of industrial production at this time. While the average annual rate of growth for 'All Industries' had only declined, indicating a slowing of production increase, the counterpart figure for 'Machinery and Equipment Manufacturing Industries' was actually negative during 1965–71. No other industry group turned in lower output, though the growth rate declined in all cases.

As evident for the data in Table 3.3, after almost a decade of decline commencing 1966–7, public investment begins to rise from the mid-1970s to levels comparable with those achieved in the mid-1960s. From then on it remained buoyant till the end of the period that we are concerned with in this chapter—the year 1991. To run ahead a little, this is a vital clue to the growth process in India in the last quarter of the twentieth century. But to return to the explanation of cyclical growth in manufacturing industry, which is what concerns us here, this reversal of the slide in public investment may be expected to have contributed—via the classic interaction of the multiplier and the accelerator—cumulatively to faster growth and greater private investment, raising the rate of growth of manufacturing. Though there is only the barest notice given of a rise in private investment from the mid-1970s, it is there alright; and from the very beginning of the 1980s, private investment demonstrates an upward shift that, unlike public investment, was not reversed. With hindsight, we may presume to remark that the cusp of the late 1970s–early 1980s was a watershed in the private investors' perceptions of the future of the Indian economy. The point, however, is that the private sector's perception may be expected to have taken a view of the factors affecting its prospects wider than just the policy regime, for the latter had not changed significantly at all. A buoyancy of demand, provided by steadily higher public investment, very likely was on its radar too.

As a check on our argument which grants a role to fluctuating public investment in accounting for the cyclical growth of manufacturing, we turn to the results of some structural-break tests, applied this time to capital formation in the economy.[53] The variable chosen is the rate of change of capital formation rather than the investment rate, the progress of which we have already scrutinized in Table 3.3. In the presence of exogenous shocks to output, changes in the investment rate, being the ratio of investment to output, may be biased as an indicator of swings in planned investment. Now the rate of change of capital formation would serve as a better measure of the pace of autonomous investment in the economy.

The rate of growth of capital formation by institution, in phases implied by the structural break tests, is reported in Table 3.4. The estimates indicate that the argument made earlier is robust with respect to the index of investment, that is, whether we use the investment rate or the rate of growth of capital formation. We find that the rate of expansion of public investment falls precipitously in the mid-1960s and rises again in the mid-1970s, to be so maintained for a decade. Private corporate investment was to slow down exactly at the same time but shows a quickening only well after public investment does. From this record, we may conclude that public investment emerges as a candidate among factors responsible for the cyclical growth of manufacturing. The timing of the breaks suggests

Table 3.4 The Pace of Capital Formation

	Phase 1	*Phase 2*	*Phase 3*	*Phase 4*	*Phase 5*
Total	2.96 [1950/1–1963/4]	1.94 [1964/5–1977/8]	2.65 [1978/9–2003/4]		
Public	5.93 [1950/1–1956/7]	3.45 [1957/8–1964/5]	0.52 [1965/6–1974/5]	3.41 [1975/6–1984/5]	0.78 [1985/6–2003/4]
Corporate	4.21 [1950/1–1963/4]	0.21* [1964/5–1978/9]	5.89 [1979/80–1986/7]	6.15 [1987/8–1994/5]	1.49* [1995/6–2003/4]
Household	1.24* [1950/1–1963/4]	2.34 [1964/5–1978/9]	4.96 [1986/7–1993/4]	2.86 [1994/5–2003/4]	

Notes: Average annual growth rate of gross capital formation (in 1993–4 prices). Period is in brackets. * denotes not statistically significant.

that private corporate investment was more of a follower during the period of our study. As stated in Chapter 2, while it would be hazardous to assert cause and effect here, macroeconomic theory and the trajectories of the two variables point to public investment being the independent one, at least in the 1970s. This would lead us to view the cyclical growth of public investment as a factor of primary importance in the cyclical growth of industrial production. In the more recent writings on the economy, it has not received the attention that it deserves on this score, with researchers privileging a discourse that relies overly on the impact of a changing policy regime on private investment.[54]

Before leaving off our discussion of public investment we observe that unlike in the period 1950–64, subsequently public and private investments show low synchronicity on an annual basis, with public investment exhibiting greater cyclicality. However, while the relationship may have weakened, it did not vanish altogether. From Table 3.4 we find private investment collapsing less than public investment in the mid-1960s but beginning to rise as the latter turns around, as stated, very slowly initially but at the same time quite definitely, as time would show. While proposing the importance of public investment as a determinant of industrial growth during the greater part of 1965–91, it needs be noted that economic relationships in general need not remain the same across time and policy regimes. This appears to apply equally to that between public and private investments. By the second half of the 1980s, private investment appears to have come into its own and has remained less dependent upon the rate of public investment for its progress. As a result, manufacturing production itself has grown quite rapidly in the 1990s despite the decline in public investment. This takes me to the second of the factors responsible for the cyclical growth of manufacturing during 1965–91, namely, developments on the trade and industrial policy fronts.

In the main, the trade and industrial policy regimes remained largely unchanged during 1965–91, at least by comparison with what was initiated in July 1991. Indeed it is this feature that led us to the treatment of the period as relatively self-contained. However, within the same overarching regime of import restriction and industrial licensing, a more or less stringent implementation of the policy may be imagined and it is precisely in these terms that phases can be discerned even during the period 1965–91. We have reason to believe that a changed approach to the implementation of economic policy occurs broadly in the middle of this period.

Following the crises of food availability and the balance of payments in the mid-1960s, referred to at the beginning of this chapter, a more stringent implementation of the regulatory mechanism for both trade and industry came into being. This is also likely to have been enabled by the political vacuum that emerged following the exit of Nehru. Now, the general lack of accountability[55] that characterized the functioning of the regulatory machinery at the best of times was compounded by the bureaucracy being left with a free hand. It is only the disincentive of being checked and reprimanded by the elected politician if found to have erred that keeps the bureaucracy from assuming an upper hand. Nehru had been ever alert to the bureaucratic tendency to amass power to delay, stall, and scuttle at will. The unparalled legitimacy bestowed upon him by history, one that even vaulted over the electoral victories he had led the Congress Party to, ensured that the bureaucracy dared not assume an independence during Nehru's leadership of India. Personal experience of the colonial machinery of government, still more or less intact after Indian Independence, had left Nehru contemptuous of the self-importance of the upper echelons of the bureaucracy and raging at the insolence of the lower. Nor did he shrink from expressing publicly his views on the role of the bureaucracy in a democracy.[56]

Indira Gandhi, on the other hand, could hardly maintain this Olympian aloofness, leave alone assume political disdain. Her rise to power was slow and far from steady and her grip on it far from strong, as may be gauged by the fact that she had to declare Emergency to hold on to it even after almost a decade in office. In general, weaker leaders depend upon the support of visibly organized groups, even if they constitute a minority in society. Her far weaker position compared to that of Nehru led her to actively seek the isolated support of groups as diverse as organized labour to please the Left in Parliament, the minorities to ensure electoral majority, and the bureaucracy to implement her will. This left the bureaucracy largely unregulated and thus impervious to the legitimate aspirations of the citizenry. Added to this was the fresh entry into the political scene of a strident left-wing rhetoric which identified socialism mostly with controls on industry rather than provision of public goods by government. The bureaucracy was now established in a way that it had not been since the end of the colonial era when the executive had functioned without any checks and balances.[57]

Even as a regulatory machinery meant less for enabling growth than that of furthering 'social objectives', such as the control of monopoly, had re-emerged with extra vigour, a new set of controls was clamped upon economic activity. Those that affected manufacturing were the MRTP Act, amendment of FERA, a vertiginous income tax rate,[58] and a plethora of price and distribution controls. For about a decade from the second half of the 1960s the economic climate could not have been congenial to the private investor.[59] This is also the period when the deceleration in industrial growth was at its most pronounced.[60] It took till the early 1980s for the investment climate to alter favourably. While professional economists have maintained ascepticism, interestingly, industry spokesmen view the policy since the 1970s as being progressively liberalizing.[61] My own reading of the industrial policy statements since 1973 is that they signalled a government's willingness to review existing arrangements, thus acknowledging that they may even be responsible for the less than satisfactory industrial performance. Finally, as observed, the Statement of 1980 did liberalize, within the overall structure of licensing, the expansion of capacity. While the magnitudes were not very large, the move was clearly pro-growth. Strikingly, as evident from Tables 3.3 and 3.4, the response of private corporate investment was immediate.

Meanwhile, changes were taking place in the trade policy regime. Interestingly, unlike the stop–go theatricality of the efforts to liberalize industrial policy, once trade policy began to be eased it proceeded only in one direction, that of liberalization. This shift commenced in the mid-1970s. However, as we are looking at the period 1965–91 as a whole we ought to start at the beginning. Note that our ultimate objective is to explain the cyclicality of industrial growth which straddles close to two decades from the mid-1960s. The question is whether there was a role for trade policy at all.

After the Nehru era, trade policy became more restrictive, leading to the characterization of the economic policy shift as 'turning inward'.[62] The single impetus for this was the balance-of-payments crisis of the mid-1960s which had driven India into the clutches of the IMF. As compliance with conditions for a prospective loan, in June 1966 the rupee was devalued by over 50 per cent. Further, some import liberalization and trimming of export subsidies were initiated. Note that this is the classic package of reforms prescribed for a balance-of-payments-constrained economy by the IMF. By 1968, however, when it was found that the aid had not materialized to the extent agreed upon in return for these reform measures, a domestic political reaction to the liberalization was, predictably, aroused. The incipient import liberalization was largely reversed and the regime of trade controls tightened. An amendment of FERA mainly aimed at foreign direct investment in India was to follow, though much later in 1973. For close to a decade from the mid-1960s the now tightened foreign trade and payments regime remained unchanged. It is clear that India's economic relations with the West were influenced by this episode, and it is therefore worthwhile dwelling on it briefly.

The current account had deteriorated greatly in 1964–5 and India had to resort to historically high drawings from the IMF. The droughts of 1965–6 and 1966–7 raised the import bill,[63] worsening further the current account as exports, being largely agricultural, were adversely affected too. Net aid flow, being gross aid less total debt servicing, increased marginally in 1965–6 but declined substantially[64] in 1966–7 to a level lower than it was at in 1964–5. The rupee was devalued by 57.5 per cent on 6 June 1966. Import liberalization followed, premised on greater foreign aid. In July 1966 the government published a 'Supplement to the Economic Survey 1965–66' where a justification was provided that devaluation was a long-term solution to the balance-of-payments problem. No such justification of the accompanying import liberalization—simplification of procedure and reduction of tariff—was given. However, it was made explicit in that document that the consequent rise in imports was to be 'financed by aid' (see p. 15). As stated, the aid did not materialize. Net aid actually declined in 1966–7, while India's drawings from the IMF increased. External debt servicing increased steadily for the next five years.[65] India's commercial policy now lapsed into a more restrictive mode shaped by a sense of vulnerability and disappointment.

The first trade policy review after this episode took a decade coming. In 1976 imports on OGL (Open General Licence) List were reactivated. The OGL allowed for imports without a licence. When the OGL reappeared, it had seventy capital goods on it. This list was gradually extended. To get an idea of the pace and depth of import liberalization, by April 1987 the list contained 1,007 items. It has been argued by Sen (2007) that the effect of liberalized capital goods imports was to lower the relative price of capital goods, by itself believed to favourably impact domestic capital formation. This suggests a strategic approach to the trade policy changes. Further, from the mid-1970s a depreciation of the real exchange rate is also noticeable. Whether this was intended is difficult to establish. However, it is noteworthy that exports expanded rapidly in the second half of the 1970s.[66]

Looking back at this period, the impression is formed that at least some of India's trade policy was evolving in tune with its fortunes, that is, both the tightening and the relaxation over the decade and a half from the mid-1960s can be seen to be correlated with the fluctuating health of the balance of payments. We have already referred to the dire straits in which India had found herself over 1965–7. Equally, from the mid-1970s India's balance of payments improved dramatically, largely due to remittances from the Arabian Gulf region where Indian labour had migrated following the oil boom there. It seems pragmatism rather than ideology, as it has been too easily assumed by some commentators, guided India's trade policy during the period 1965–91.

Returning to the task of accounting for the cyclical growth of industry, we find that during 1965–91 there was a shifting stance towards the external sector. After a very brief episode of liberalization to satisfy loan conditionality in the mid-1960s, there was a reversal in the late 1960s and then a gradual liberalization from the mid-1970s. The most vigorous phase of external liberalization during 1965–91 was to come in the second half of the 1980s when during the prime ministership of Rajiv Gandhi there was an unconcealed attempt to open up to the rest of the world. While this was a period of fast industrial growth, the opening up itself cannot account for the acceleration of manufacturing growth that had already occurred in the early 1980s. The successive tightening and relaxation of industrial regulation already recorded here and a similar pattern in the government's approach to import restriction may reasonably be taken to have contributed to the cyclical growth of industry during 1965–91. This is in addition to the cyclicality of public investment, arguably a close determinant of output growth in manufacturing during this period. This was set to change in the 1990s. Perhaps for this reason, in recent accounts of industrial revival in the 1980s the role of public investment tends mostly to get ignored.[67]

It must strike the reader that we have barely mentioned the role of agricultural growth in determining the growth of manufacturing during 1965–91. Recall that this was based on the divergent trends (see Table 3.1) in these sectors for about a decade and a half since the mid-1960s, which implies that agriculture could not have been the binding constraint on manufacturing growth during this phase. However, the buoyancy of agricultural growth for twenty-five years since 1965 could not but have helped sustain the industrial acceleration that finally occurred in the early 1980s. We return to this theme later in this chapter.

Services: The Dark Horse of Indian Economic Growth

Continuing with our study of growth by sector, we finally reach the growth of services. In the National Accounts for India, data on GDP in services can be grouped into four categories:

1. Trade, hotels, and restaurants
2. Transport, storage, and communication
3. Finance, insurance, real estate, and business services
4. Community and personal services

The estimates presented in Table 3.1 show that all four groups began to grow faster during the period 1965–91 and that too before the economy-wide acceleration represented by the trajectory of GDP growth. The timing of the acceleration in the growth rate of the service industries in the economy during this period is a feature that has gone relatively unnoticed in discussions of the growth transition until recently. Growth of services has of course been flagged as having been dominant since 1991 but not earlier.[68] As discussed at the beginning of this chapter, part of the reason for this is the limitation of the very methodology of break-date estimation followed.[69] Presuming that the timing of the break is 1991, the tendency is to focus on the period after then. Moreover, empirical studies of growth—and not just for India—have mostly been based on economy-wide GDP. There can be no doubt that it is the combination of our using the methodology of estimating multiple breaks simultaneously—leaving no room for the researcher's priors—and working with data at a lower level of aggregation that alerts us to the buoyancy of services growth over a much longer period of recent Indian economic history than usually allowed for. As will be apparent, this finding of an acceleration of services growth in the 1970s has a direct bearing on the search for a data-congruent explanation of the growth transition during 1965–91.

Though growth of all the four groups within services had accelerated, even though at different rates, during 1965–91 they mostly registered growth rates slower than those attained by manufacturing after 1982–3. In any case, we were yet to return to the history of the colonial era when services were the fastest growing activity in the economy. One inference from the full set of results presented in Table 3.1 is that services growth appears to be relatively independent of the growth of manufacturing. Significantly, we find that the former had accelerated while the growth of manufacturing had decelerated in the mid-1960s and remained depressed for the next decade and a half. The representation of the growth of services as an outcome of the 'disintegration' of manufacturing production[70] due to what we now recognize as 'outsourcing' is therefore not relevant for this phase. Equally, assessments of the growth of services over the past three decades that point to the Indian experience—characterized[71] by 'too high' a share of services in relation to per capita income—being out of synch with the global norm can learn from a journey into India's past. As had been pointed out in Chapter 2, the tertiary sector was the fastest growing in the economy during the first half of the twentieth century, even though per capita income growth was almost static. This suggests that the 'cross-country regression', which implicitly assumes that a single model of growth applies to all the countries in the sample,[72] is an unreliable method for understanding services growth in India. It would be expected that the growth of services, unlike that of goods, is related as much to interaction between economic geography—including the pattern of settlement—population growth, and even cultural practices as it is to the level of income. In our view, three factors have the potential to explain the observed acceleration of services growth in India during our period, and the role of each is now considered.

A purely economic factor that can account for the fast growth of services in an environment of low per capita income growth is the rise of inequality. Growing income inequality can rob per capita income of its explanatory power in the context. Now the gainers from a growth process demand a wider range of services than may be predicted from the contemporaneous growth in per capita income. The most obvious examples are private expenditure on health and education, entertainment, and hotels and restaurants. Interestingly, the last, in the form of privately owned five-star hotels and up-scale eating establishments, had begun to make an appearance in India by the first half of the 1970s, a time when left-wing rhetoric by the political leadership was particularly shrill. The proposition that at least some of the rapid growth of services during 1965–91 is related to rising income inequality is difficult to test due to absence of time series on summary measures of income distribution during that period.

However, we may point to two developments which suggest that those at the upper end of the income distribution may actually have benefited disproportionately from some of the policies of the period to have been left relatively better off. First, we know that more restrictive trade and industrial polices contribute to a higher mark-up.[73] Corporate profits would have risen as a result. Second, the introduction of an incentive-based procurement price along with a faster growth of agricultural output from the mid-1960s is likely to have made a considerable difference to the incomes of the surplus farmers. In the presence of high and/or rising inequality, a low economy-wide per capita income *per se* has little informational content for the understanding of spending patterns. The inordinate growth of services in India in the period we are studying, or even throughout the twentieth century, may well have been driven in part by high and rising inequality.

A second reason for the acceleration of services growth in this period could have been a faster growth of employment in government. If this were so, we would be misguided to seek for an explanation in terms of the income elasticity of demand for services, as is conventional, or even to entertain a role for income inequality. The expansion of services would be now purely driven by other factors. In fact, growing employment in government would now account for the fast growth of services at a time when per capita income has not grown so fast. To check for this possibility we turn again to the estimates presented in Table 3.1. Note that while the acceleration in the growth of 'community and personal services' is fairly large, when we study this growth by components of the group we find that growth of 'public administration and defence' actually decelerates, even though only towards the end of the period, in the second half of the 1980s. Surprisingly, the growth of income on this account had slowed down once even earlier, in the early 1960s. Thus, contrary to suggestion, it is not as if services growth has accelerated because government services have expanded, income generation in this area having perforce to be measured by wages and salaries.[74] From Table A4.1 of the Appendix, we find that 'public administration and defence' were on a declining trend close to thirty-five years, finally reversing this record quite sharply in the mid-1990s, interestingly, at a time when the government had pledged to disengage itself from the economy.

The third factor that we consider as likely to have influenced the faster growth of services in India is the impact of the regulatory environment on the supply side of the economy. As we have argued when explaining the cyclical growth of manufacturing over 1965–91, while the policy regime did not change much in India after 1965, the economic environment for business did. It has been proposed here that the regulatory machinery very likely turned more stringent as part of the generally left-wing posture of the time and possibly was even encouraged by the political leadership to occasionally bare its fangs. We have anecdotal evidence of the special attentions of the Income Tax Department towards unbending bureaucrats and opposition politicians, of labour inspectors towards manufacturers, and the Enforcement Directorate and Economic Offences Wing towards much of private economic activity!

As the Indian state got more authoritarian under Indira Gandhi, its organs gained commensurately in the unaccountable exercise of power. It is possible to imagine a tacit political compact whereby the bureaucracy was left increasingly unregulated in its relations with business in return for its allegiance to the powers that be. It may further be surmised that the effect of this was that the economic environment in this period turned business-unfriendly. The brunt of this would have been borne by investors of the manufacturing sector as it was the almost exclusive target of regulation in the economy. Certainly, by default at least, services were regulated less, if at all. The licensing and labour laws, including the exit clause, applied to them far less due to their smaller size in relation to the average unit in manufacturing industry. Furthermore, as they were largely non-traded goods and attracted even less foreign investment, neither FERA nor the trade policy restrictions impinged upon the potential investor in this sector. While technically subject to taxation of profits, the absence of clear guidelines on the taxation of income from services and in the context of an overworked administration focused obsessively on the likelihood of an accretion of monopoly power in manufacturing industry meant that the long arm of the law was more or less limp by the time it reached the service industries, if at all.[75] It is not inconceivable that the smaller entrepreneur, without the deep pockets or the stomach to work the thicket of the regulatory jungle was induced to head for the services sector.

The flip-side of all this was that for the large investor with the muscle built from long years of experience and financial clout to deal with an increasingly tightening regulatory apparatus, hanging on in an industry made good sense as licensing was, by default at least, geared towards generating a winner-takes-all outcome. This view of the rapid rise of services in the period 1965–91 is inspired partly by Prem Shankar Jha's (1980) argument that the controls of the period, which led to shortages, created an incentive to enter trade rather than manufacturing. Apart from the fact that it is difficult to test, as unaccounted income cannot be directly measured, manufacturing had continued to grow throughout this period, even though at a slower rate, thus weakening the argument itself. However, suitably modified, Jha's hypothesis has some relevance in the search for valid explanations of the accelerated growth of services from the 1970s. Only, Jha, who had studied mainly the 1970s, had seen fast growth of services as part of the pathology of slow growth in India. Now, with hindsight, we find that services have been more closely aligned with the accelerating growth in this country than any other sector.

The Growth Transition *circa* 1980

We have thus far identified, analysed, and explained the sectoral growth trajectories. This material forms the building blocks for our own explanation of the growth transition over 1965–91. However, before turning to this task two important contributions to this topic are discussed.

Narratives Wanting

An important intervention in the discourse on growth in India had come from the American economist Bradford DeLong. In so highly globalized a profession as economics, actually, his national origins must surprise us less than the fact that he had never before published anything on India, thus affirming the wisdom that newcomers often bring a fresh perspective to a problem. We have already referred to DeLong's work in Chapter 2. DeLong pointed out that while 'conventional wisdom' had it that close to three and a half decades since Indian Independence were wasted due to a turn to 'Fabian socialism' by Jawaharlal Nehru and the economy began to grow faster only after the Rao–Singh reforms initiated in 1991, 'the aggregate growth data tells us that the acceleration of economic growth began earlier, in the early or mid-1980s, long before the exchange crisis of 1991 and the shift of the government of Narasimha Rao and Manmohan Singh toward neo-liberal economic reforms' (DeLong 2003: 186).

While DeLong did not state the method by which he dated the break, he presented a graph in which it could be seen that for every year after 1980 the actual level of per capita GDP is higher than the level predicted by a trend line fitted for 1962–80. Conscious of having to account for an acceleration that precedes the initiation of major reforms in the economy in 1991, he argued that the policy changes in the mid-and late-1980s under the last governments of the 'Nehru dynasty' were sufficient to start the acceleration of growth, minor as these reforms may appear in retrospect. DeLong honed in on the policy changes initiated by the government of Rajiv Gandhi, a young reforming prime minister swept to power by a landslide electoral victory. DeLong's take on the moment conveys the impression of the dawning of a new age in Indian politics. With 415 out of 545 seats in Lok Sabha, this government clearly had the necessary majority. But perhaps more importantly, the prime minister himself was fresh in political life with his own circle of advisers and his own priorities, which meant that his government had the relative autonomy to be a strongly reforming executive. The reform programme of the government is neatly summarized as being 'focused on (a) encouraging capital imports and commodity exports, (b) a modest degree of industrial deregulation, and (c) a modest degree of tax system rationalisation' (DeLong 2003: 196–7). Thus, a certain degree of liberalization was initiated early in the ministry's tenure.

DeLong's article was the first academic[76] study to place the growth impact of the 1991 reforms in longer-term perspective. However, he had less convincingly linked his explanation for the acceleration to the Rajiv Gandhi reforms that commenced in 1985 while dating the acceleration to 1980. Nevertheless, after DeLong's intervention the myth of the overriding significance of 1991 for long-term economic growth in India was broken, and it was open season for the dating of the growth transition and explaining it. Above all, DeLong introduced a whole new style to the study of the Indian economy, the 'analytical growth narrative', a combination of data analysis, political economy, and growth theory.

Within the genre of the analytical growth narrative, a paper by Rodrik and Subramanian (2005) followed that of DeLong. It took as its aim the explanation of the growth transition already dated by DeLong at 1980. Their method of dating is not only more transparent but also uses the then state-of-the-art methodology of Bai and Perron (1998, 2003). They date the transition to 1979–80, which corresponds exactly to our own finding, reported in Table 3.1. There are two building blocks to the Rodrik and Subramanian account. First they adopt the results of a study by Bosworth and Collins (2003) which, within the framework of growth accounting, demonstrated that total factor productivity (TFP) growth in the Indian economy accelerated from 1980. This led them to take the explanation of this productivity 'surge' from 1980 as the main task in an explanation of the growth transition that they detect. The growth transition itself is termed a 'mystery' as it bucks the belief that only a switch to a more liberal policy regime can bring about an acceleration of the growth rate, while in their view no such switch is evident close to the time of the transition.

Rodrik and Subramanian relate the faster growth of productivity to changes that coincide with the return of Indira Gandhi to power in January 1980. It is argued that, wiser after her apprenticeship in the political wilderness and in a bid to widen her political base, she decided to woo the very industrial capitalists towards whom she had been extremely hostile in the past. Such moves as were allegedly made[77] are termed 'pro business' rather than 'liberalization' for they were only aimed at improving the position of the incumbents rather than extending the field of competition. This is in line with their political economy explanation of the change in the economic environment in terms of Indira Gandhi's political agenda of consolidating power. The crux of their thesis is that what had occurred following the return of Indira Gandhi was purely an attitudinal shift, prominent being 'the suspension of the national government's hostility to the private sector ... something that left little paper trail but had an important impact on investors' psychology' (Rodrik and Subramanian 2005: 195–6).

While the novelty of the Rodrik–Subramanian account needs to be acknowledged, it does not rest easy with a 'surge' in productivity growth that distinguishes this phase of Indian economic history from what the authors term 'Hindu growth'—with its disappointingly slow movement—that preceded it. Economic theory does not readily yield an explanation of how a mere attitudinal shift on the part of the government can lead to faster growth of productivity. A favourable impact on investor psychology may of course be expected to lead to a rise in the investment rate *a la* 'animal spirits'. A quickening of productivity growth is however altogether another matter. It is implausible to assume that firms await a nod and a wink from the policymaker—the authors speak of Indira Gandhi 'currying favour' with the larger business houses—to extract more output than they currently do from given inputs. Indeed, when an increase in productivity is recorded, it implies that the firm was not an efficient producer to start with. Of course, even though this goes against the premise of both Chicago microeconomics—which asserts that every profit opportunity would be exhausted—and Marx's characterization of capitalists as beset by a 'boundless thirst for surplus value', a firm away from the frontier is not necessarily a contradiction. What is less than credible though is that the move towards the frontier is 'pay back' for less 'attitude' on the part of government! As there is no change in policy, not even Austrian competition—involving rivalry that leads to a competitive cost reduction, and thus faster productivity growth—can be invoked.

The second weakness of the Rodrik–Subramanian account of an economy-wide transition is their almost exclusive focus on the manufacturing sector. By their own admission, manufacturing accounted for 'about 16 percent' of the GDP between 1986 and 1992. It may safely be assumed that it was even less around 1980, when the transition was taking place. To maintain that a faster productivity growth in organized manufacturing, accounting for so small a share of the total output of the economy, drove the economy-wide growth transition is implausible for the high value of multiplier that this implies. This is so even if a clear mechanism were to be provided by the authors. In the absence of evidence of both such high-valued multipliers and a plausible economic mechanism based on spillovers from the manufacturing to the other sectors of the economy driving the transition, we are left with a claim which amounts to the tail of manufacturing wagging the dog of the economy. Evidence the authors have provided, showing that states politically aligned with the central government of Indira Gandhi turned in faster manufacturing growth, may count as evidence of a positive attitudinal shift driving output but does not constitute evidence of it driving productivity growth in manufacturing, leave alone as evidence of a surge in manufacturing growth—however engineered—having driven the economy-wide growth transition. It is of course conceivable that states aligned with Mrs Gandhi, or actually led by the Congress Party, received central governmental fiscal largesse which drove their manufacturing growth. However, Rodrik and Subramanian close off this option as an explanation by insisting on a mere 'attitudinal shift'.

Third, even if we accept[78] the Bosworth–Collins estimate of faster productivity growth for the economy, we would yet need evidence of faster productivity growth in manufacturing. It may be useful to survey the independently published evidence on the growth of productivity in manufacturing around the date of transition. We now know that estimates of accelerated TFP growth since 1980 are conditional on the use of a particular methodology of estimating value added, namely, the single-deflation method. As this is well known, and not wanting to overly emphasize the outcome of a debate in which the present author has been a protagonist,[79] this is not dwelt upon. Rodrik and Subramanian scrupulously acknowledge that the claim of faster of growth of TFP in Indian manufacturing during the 1980s has been 'challenged' but continue to maintain the very hypothesis.

Criticisms aside, the Rodrik–Subramanian study is important for having extended in an imaginative way the 'analytical growth narrative' approach introduced into the study of contemporary Indian economic history by DeLong. As a political economy account of industrial revival in India, it is with considerable merit. Private corporate investment accelerated soon after the re-appearance in 1980 of Indira Gandhi onto the political stage (see Table 3.3). This is consistent with the hypothesis of an animal-spirits-driven industrial revival. Also, it has the advantage of not relying on a 'productivity surge', the reasons for which Rodrik and Subramanian fail to establish. Nevertheless, even sticking to this route, it would be misleading to overlook the evolving change in the quantitative control regime on trade initiated in the latter half of the 1970s and the time-bound expansion of capacity allowed for in the Industrial Policy Statement of 1980, both discussed earlier in this chapter. The 'paper trail', it seems, can be detected if only one chooses to look for it. Moreover, the role of public investment could not have been negligible. From Table 3.3, note that public investment had been on an upswing for five years by the time private corporate investment shifts up around 1980 and had remained buoyant for the next five. Yet, all of this can only account for the acceleration of manufacturing growth, while we are actually addressing an economy-wide transition.

Despite the high standard of explanation that they set for themselves by placing centrestage an explanation of the 'productivity surge', Rodrik and Subramanian may have set themselves off along the wrong road altogether. Granting TFP growth an independent and causal role in the growth process—that is, viewing TFP growth as a driver of output growth—is tantamount to treating growth accounting as an exercise in explanation. This is untenable as, in the presence of fixed factors and increasing returns to scale, we cannot rule out that the evidence of faster rate of growth of estimated TFP is merely due to a faster rate of growth itself. Now setting yourself the target of explaining the faster growth of productivity, as Rodrik and Subramanian do, while appearing to be setting your standards of argumentation high, may yet be the wrong road to take. In empirical studies, especially of the US economy, the Solow residual has been marked as being pro-cyclical, suggesting its lack of independence vis-à-vis the rate of growth of the economy.[80] Moreover, as argued in Chapter 1, critical thought needs be given to the foundations of growth accounting, which yields estimates of TFP, as an exercise. Specifically, it is premised on the existence of an aggregate production function. The comments of Fisher are important here. First, 'The conditions for the existence of aggregate production functions, at least when widely diverse industries are included, seem very very strong.' Next, in an observation of direct relevance to the context: 'Just because it is possible to use aggregate production functions for statements about long-run growth and change it is important to be careful about the foundation for such statements' (Fisher 1969: 576). As the results of growth accounting can be misleading, explanations reliant on them are to that extent to be discounted.

A Transition De-mystified: Growth Viewed Bottom–Up

The explanation of the growth transition *circa* 1980 to be provided here is based on the preceding analysis of sectoral growth trends. This is intentional to the extent that it stems from the recognition that an aggregated approach, based on a one-good model and driven by a single exogenous factor, would be inadequate to the task. Principally, we now have the awareness that after the Nehru era, while growth in all sectors had accelerated, sectoral growth trends have at times veered in opposite directions. The most egregious of these divergences is the acceleration in agricultural growth from the mid-1960s accompanied by a deceleration in manufacturing growth that had lasted for a considerable period. This history of a divergent growth among the sectors suggests that most growth-theoretic approaches, due to their parsimony, would be of limited utility in the context.[81] Equally limited would be explanations that focus on the progress of a single variable such as the savings rate or grand narratives based on a single overarching theme such as the policy regime evolving towards greater openness.[82] In fact, alerting us to the weakness of such accounts is perhaps the most important lesson from our study of the sectoral growth pattern during 1965–91. The advantage of an approach to the transition based on the explanation of growth by sector is that it would be one that is built bottom up, implying firmer foundations, not to mention a wider perspective. As a consequence of the disaggregated approach, the precise dating of the transition loses the centrality, or even relevance, that it assumes in purely macroeconomic accounts. Of course, that GDP growth accelerated circa 1980 is incontrovertible and any account of the transition would have to be compatible with this timing.

Our study of sectoral growth trends provides us the following qualitative inputs. First, a significant impetus to the growth transition during 1965–91 is likely to have come from the transformation of Indian agriculture after 1965. Our structural break tests reveal a permanent increase in the rate of growth of this sector at a time when it constituted about half the economy in terms of share of GDP. Next we also have a negative input, in the sense that we are shown where not to look for the answer. This is that we can see that manufacturing could not have influenced the growth transition very significantly, except to have delayed it perhaps, as it accelerates only in the early 1980s after the economy-wide growth rate has already shifted. As a corollary, the view that India turned as the trade and industrial policy regime became more liberal has little or no purchase. However, as argued earlier, some liberalization of trade policy since the mid-1970s and easing of industrial regulation in 1980 may well have had a role in reviving the rate of growth of manufacturing itself. The revival of public investment too very likely had a role here. Finally, and most crucial to accounting for the timing of the transition, all four groups among services accelerate in the 1970s, with two of them accelerating in the second half of that decade. The leads us to the judgement that the faster growth of services accounts for the *timing* of the growth transition which we have dated to circa 1980.

A lead arising out of our study of sectoral growth trends and their proximate causes is the likely special role of agriculture in the growth transition during 1965–91. The *steady* deceleration of public investment growth from the second half of the 1960s to the mid-1970s suggests that for close to a decade, agriculture—as the more autonomous among the sectors—had had to bear on its own the task of buoying up demand in the economy. This was apart from its role as supplier of food and raw materials. Of course, as we have pointed out, even as public investment collapsed from the mid-1960s, agriculture had received a slightly larger

Table 3.5 Inter-sectoral Growth Relations, 1953–81

	Dependent variable		
	Δp_t	Δs_t	Δt_t
Constant	0.18	− 0.03	0.02
	(1.44)	(− 2.47)	(3.10)
Δp_t		0.05	0.07
		(0.42)	(1.99)*
Δs_t	− 0.01		0.13
	(− 0.01)		(1.37)
Δt_t	− 3.20	1.86	
	(− 1.00)	(5.40)*	
Δp_{t-1}	− 0.54		
	(− 5.27)*		
Δs_{t-1}		0.09	
		(1.08)	
Δt_{t-1}			0.40*
			(2.34)
Instruments	$\Delta p_{t-1,} \Delta s_{t-1,} \Delta t_{t-1}$	$\Delta p_{t-1,} \Delta s_{t-1,} \Delta t_{t-1,}$ rainfall	$\Delta p_{t-1,} \Delta s_{t-1,} \Delta t_{t-1,}$ rainfall
Hansen's J: χ^2 (1)	0.00	1.19	0.36

Notes: *p*, *s*, and *t* are the outputs of the primary, secondary, and tertiary sectors, respectively. All variables are in logs. *z*-values are in parentheses. Hansen's J-statistic reports the test of over-identification of all instruments. *indicates significance at 5 per cent level. Estimates are efficient for arbitrary heteroskedasticity and autocorrelation; statistics robust to heteroskedasticity and autocorrelation. Number of observations is 29.

share of the total. This was very likely a strategic move, as argued in our account of the agricultural transformation. Faster agricultural growth, maintained for at least three decades, provided the growth of demand that enabled faster services growth. At least during the first half of 1965–91 manufacturing growth showed itself to be impervious to the demand-enhancing impact of this agricultural transformation, apparently, being more closely linked to public investment.

When the record of public investment presented in Table 3.4 is read along with the information on sectoral growth rates in Table 3.1, the following account suggests itself. From around the mid-1970s, when public investment revived, manufacturing began a slow recovery, finally accelerating[83] in the early 1980s following a permanent rise in the corporate investment rate in 1981–2. A less rigorous application of the regulatory regime following the recognition that over-regulation, if not outright hostility to manufacturing, may have damaged the cause of growth in the past may also have contributed to the revival of manufacturing along with the mild liberalization of industrial policy in 1980 discussed earlier. Once the binding constraint of public investment was relaxed, faster agricultural growth may be expected to have aided manufacturing growth. The 1980s were a period of exceptionally high agricultural growth. Though not picked up by our test procedure for structural breaks, which may have set too stringent a criterion for the identification of an acceleration,[84] in a plain comparison of growth rates across the economy, it is agriculture, among all three sectors, that shows the most acceleration in the 1980s when compared to the 1970s.[85] Thus, very likely, agriculture continued to sustain higher growth in the economy even after the growth transition itself.

Adherents of the view that the changing policy regime—invariably interpreted as 'liberalization'—fully accounts for the growth transition of 1980 overlook the likely roles of both the revival of public investment and the lasting impact of the Green Revolution. While in our view they are central to it, the content and timing of their roles are clearly distinct. Our break tests for public investment had revealed that it shifted up in the mid-1970s, granting to it an immediacy as a driver, especially of industrial growth. On the other hand, the role of agriculture is likely to have been long drawn out but pervasive.

The explanation of the transition offered here may appear to have remained silent on the matter of savings in the economy. Of course, as may be expected, not all accounts of growth in India remain so. For instance, in a recent study Basu and Maertens (2007) have proposed that the growth of savings may be counted as a factor in the increase in the growth rate during the very period considered by us here. While the savings rate is by no means irrelevant, it would be inadvisable to grant it an independent role, as it is very likely endogenous with respect to the growth of income.

However, where investment is self-financed, savings can act as a constraint. Now savings would emerge as an important factor and, accordingly, the improvement in the public savings rate from the mid-1970s[86] very likely enabled the improvement in the public investment rate with consequences for growth, as outlined here. However, it is our judgement that the agricultural transformation of the mid-1960s trumps all other factors when it comes to an explanation of the transition.

Finally, a methodological point. Retrospectively, the role played by agriculture in the growth transition of this period, and the commencement of the sector's transformation in the mid-1960s, validates our identification of 1965 as the beginning of a new phase of economic growth in India.

An Econometric Check on the Argument

As a test of our argument that the growth transition of the late 1970s was driven by the agricultural transformation that began in the mid-1960s, we undertake an econometric investigation of inter-sectoral growth relations in the economy. For this purpose, we have recombined the GDP data according to the standard classification 'primary', 'secondary', and 'tertiary' as this makes the exercise more manageable and its results more easily interpretable.[87] The estimates are presented in Table 3.5. The regressions are the parsimonious representation of an original specification in which output growth in each sector was regressed on the current and lagged values of output growth in the other sectors and its own lagged values. When OLS was applied, the current-dated variables were statistically significant in the majority of cases (except in the regression for growth of the primary sector). For the sake of uniformity, the final specification was re-estimated by two-step GMM, as simultaneity may reasonably be expected when current-dated variables are included. It is these estimates that have been presented in the Table. The sample period is 1953–81, so chosen to satisfy the criterion that we have a reasonable number of observations in the years leading up to *circa* 1980, the date of the growth transition.

From the regressions, the following may be inferred about inter-sectoral growth relations. First, primary sector growth displays a certain autonomy, with neither the secondary nor tertiary sectors entering into its determination. Second, only the growth of the primary sector enters the growth of the tertiary. Third, only the growth of the tertiary sector enters the growth of the secondary. Finally, secondary sector growth does not enter into growth of the other two sectors of the economy. Our results imply a recursive structure, with the growth impulse running from agriculture ('primary') to services ('tertiary') and from there to industry ('secondary'). However, services growth appears also to be self-propelling to an extent, as the regression estimates reveal an autoregressive structure for growth of the tertiary sector. Together, these regressions lead us to conclude that secondary sector growth has not driven growth of either the agricultural or tertiary sectors during the period under consideration. By extension, manufacturing, being a very large component of the secondary sector, could not have influenced the growth shifts in the Indian economy even indirectly. Above all, the finding of a recursive structure to inter-sectoral growth relations in this period, combined with the estimated dates of the sectoral growth accelerations, points to the leading role of agriculture in the growth transition that took place in the late 1970s.

Conclusion: When the Economy Foxed the Pandith

This study is unconventional in its approach to growth in India in hiving off the period 1965–91 for separate study.[88] The rationale for the periodization adopted here was twofold. Both 1965 and 1991 were years of an external payments crisis. In 1965 a balance of payments crisis was accompanied by a severe drought. On both occasions, the external crises brought about changes in public policy that were to have an impact on the course of Indian economic development. In the quarter century in between, both trade and industrial policies initially turned more restrictive to become somewhat more enabling later. In the eyes of one set of critics of long-term economic policy in India, this would count as its most 'inward looking' and 'dirigiste' phase since 1947, which was to finally end with a full-blown external and internal liberalization in 1991. However, this is the phase when the economy experienced a *second wind*, as it were, and the growth rate accelerated. The precise timing is intriguing to those who tend to approach the economy with the premise that growth acceleration is dependent upon liberalizing reform. The second half of the 1970s was not a particularly liberal time in India. It had witnessed a stiffening of labour laws, the highly symbolic forced exit of Coca Cola and IBM, and increased reservation for the small sector. These interventions had all taken the economy away from greater competition. For this reason alone, the period that we have analysed in this chapter provides the most fertile ground for understanding the drivers of economic growth in India. At a certain level of abstraction, 1965–91 was a stretch of its history when the policy regime—taken to mean the trade and industrial policies in place—had remained more or less unchanged but growth transited to a higher plane. It needs to be emphasized that the transition extended to all the sectors of the economy, even though growth in manufacturing had followed the quickening of the economy. When these elements relevant to the transition are overlooked, we are invariably left with only partial accounts.

It has been suggested that this transition is a 'mystery'[89] as no 'paper trail' or publicly announced change in policy is evident immediately prior to the recorded date of transition. However, the observed transition of the late 1970s is mysterious only if you insist upon a 'paper trail', that is, that the economy can accelerate only if the policy regime changes, that too only in the direction of becoming more liberal. But economic growth is a disequilibrium process which continuously unleashes supply–demand imbalances that can lead to acceleration of growth intensively via increasing returns and extensively by enlarging the market. I have discussed such a representation of growth in Chapter 1. Accelerating growth via increasing returns is also envisaged in the work of Romer (1986). Thus, growth begets growth, unless the process is wrecked by an exogenous shock. The context of Romer's work is relevant too. Romer was trying to model the accelerating per capita growth rate of the economies of the West. When dealing with evidence of a similar history of growth in India, it pays to recall that the economies of the West did not experience any major swings in their policy regime. They had remained market economies throughout, though more or less open to foreign trade depending upon their stage of development. This makes it imperative to provide an account of growth stemming from within the economy rather than rely on exogenous policy shocks.

While Romer's work is of considerable theoretical import, there is no agreement among economists on an appropriate test of its predictions. The spillovers that it envisages are difficult enough to identify in theory even without trying to measure them.[90] We had therefore relied on a more directly verifiable explanation of the acceleration of growth during 1965–91, as presented earlier in this chapter. The acceleration of the economy-wide GDP had been traced to the transformation of the supply-side of the economy, specifically the raising of yield growth in agriculture. No liberalizing reforms had facilitated this transformation. Actually, it was initiated by the state, which had first engineered a Green Revolution. Our econometric investigation of inter-sectoral growth relations confirmed a model with the growth impulse running from agriculture to the rest of the economy. This recursive structure is faithfully reflected in the sequence of sectoral growth transitions.

While it is difficult to espy a role for liberalizing reforms quickening the economy during 1965–91, the manner in which the policy regime had been worked, as it were, is likely to have had a bearing on the trajectory of economic growth during the period. Both industrial regulation and trade controls had undergone a successive tightening and relaxation since the mid-1960s. Import controls were eased from the mid-1970s and capacity controls from 1980. The supply-response in the manufacturing sector, in the shape of a step up in private corporate investment, was as expected and almost immediate. The one lesson from this period is that incentives matter and the private economy is sensitive to the investment climate. Both political uncertainty, which can lower investment, and just plain hostility to the private sector expressed through the rhetoric of political mobilization are likely to have slowed growth for at least a decade from the mid-1960s despite the buoyancy of demand gained from faster agricultural growth.

Where some liberalizing reform did take place was in the external sector where from the mid-1970s quotas were converted into tariffs. It has been shown by Rodrik and Subramanian (2005) that this move coincided with rising tariff rates and therefore constituted a rise in the effective rate of protection. They have argued that this, being 'pro business' and not 'pro market', cannot then be counted as 'liberalization'. While this is a valuable insight from political economy, it does not take away from the fact that a removal of quotas eases trade restrictions. The point of remarking upon this is to show that it would be wrong to insist that no reform took place prior to the acceleration of manufacturing growth. It is altogether a different matter, however, to concur with the suggestion that trade reform alone contributed to the latter. By the mid-1970s the other sectors of the economy had already accelerated, and our econometric evidence suggests that this must have impacted upon manufacturing growth via demand linkages. Also, the supportive role of public investment cannot be overlooked. What can be ruled out of court, however, is that it is the reforms targeting the manufacturing sector that drove the economy-wide acceleration. Arguments that amidst widespread distortions, that is, deviations from market outcomes reflected in prices, even minor corrections can have major effects on *growth*[91] are without theoretical foundation, even when they may be Pareto-improving in the *level* of output.

Further, it pays to remember that in 1980 the manufacturing sector could not have accounted for much more than 15 per cent of the economy. Registered manufacturing, the interests of which alone are represented by industry groups whom Indira Gandhi apparently began to court from 1980, had accounted for much less. The historical role of liberalization of trade and industrial policies in relation to the economy-wide transition during 1965–91 comes close to 'leaving the stable door open after the horse has bolted'. Claims of its centrality are very likely exaggerated. Finally, the relatively weak linkages—backward and forward—of secondary sector growth during the period under consideration revealed by our econometric exercise, imply that the suggestion that economy-wide growth accelerated as Indira Gandhi became more 'pro-business'[92] does not work either.

Four points emerge from our study of growth in India during 1965–91. First, the growth transition had caught most economists unawares.[93] This has led Nayyar (2006) to term the transition 'growth by stealth'. Some of the inability to discern the transition as it was occurring must come from the academic economist's adherence to the idea that growth is exclusively determined by the policy regime without reference to the changing balance between the forces of supply and demand. This predilection ignores the possibility of a truly endogenous growth acceleration via 'learning by doing' or a declining cost of inputs due to increasing returns,[94] both plausible developments in an economy that had by then experienced a quarter century of growth. Equally relevant is the absence then, and even now, of a tradition of regard for vigorous empirical research within the profession in India.[95] Second, the acceleration of growth in India in the late 1970s is entirely in line with the prediction of the Mahalanobis Model. This was that growth would accelerate, that is, income would rise 'sharply', as the availability of capital goods would progressively increase in the future due to the heavy-goods-biased investment strategy, assuming as in the model, that all available capital goods would be re-invested. This apart, after a decade-long stagnation, the investment rate had grown steadily with the launching of the Fifth Five Year Plan in 1974–5. The increase was particularly sharp during this plan period. It is surprising that this development has been mostly missed in accounts of the growth transition.

Third, it is worth pointing out that excessive stress on the necessity of liberalizing reform to understand accelerated growth in all situations, that is, whatever the history, may be misplaced. Certainly the growth transition of this period places in perspective the role of the *policy regime*. To understand growth it may be more important to keep track of the shifting balance between the supply and demand factors. For instance, the surge in demand across the economy stimulated by the Green Revolution and growing public investment was missed by economists fixated on the policy stance towards manufacturing industry. Fourth, by the second half of the 1970s, political competition had finally arrived in India.[96] After the Janata interregnum, the Congress Party was guided by the realization that it was no longer politically invincible. Delivering on the economic front was now crucial for political survival. While this was also to herald an era of rampant subsidies, mostly politically inspired, growth came to occupy a central place on the government's agenda.[97] The results suggest that vigorous democracy can be good for growth.

Finally, for over half the period of 1965–91, which has been our focus in this chapter, political life in India had been dominated by Indira Gandhi. Given the fascination with the role of this politician in the career of this country, the economist cannot evade the question of the consequences of her leadership. Political scientists have proposed that despite some damaging interventions at the micro level, on balance, she left behind an economy stronger in macroeconomic terms than the one she had inherited.[98] This is a balanced view. At the same time, it may be asked whether we can say something specifically on the matter of growth based on our conclusions so far? Surely we can say that Indira Gandhi's main contribution was to give full-fledged political support to the project of raising agricultural production, a largely technocratic exercise. However, her tenure, including the time out of office, had spanned eighteen years. This is a significant length of time to nurture an economy, and in any case the far more difficult task of reviving a moribund economy had been accomplished in the Nehru era. Moreover, the evidence on growth gathered here suggests that despite the stability that was finally brought to the economy, the deceleration of manufacturing growth since the mid-1960s—itself related to the hostility shown towards private investment and the politicized governance of the public enterprises—may have delayed a potential growth acceleration by at least a decade.

NOTES

1. See Dhar (2003).

2. Contrast this with: 'Prime Minister Nehru has emphasised the need for associating public opinion in the formulation of the Second Five Year Plan: "When once you want their intelligent support, let it be in the thinking as well as in the final conclusion, and when the implementation comes about." Winding up the general discussion on the draft of the plan at the meeting of the National Development Council in New Delhi on May 7, he said, "I want the public to realise that I attach the greatest importance to them"' (*The Hindu*, 9 May 1955). Permission to reproduce this passage from *The Hindu* is gratefully acknowledged.

3. This is aptly captured by Desai (2007: 40): 'Today when people criticise the Nehruvian model, little do they know that it began with the daughter, and not the

man himself.' See also the distinction 'Nehru versus Nehruites' drawn by Dhar (2003), a close economic adviser of the successor regime.

4. Bhargava (1987) has argued that the basic strategy that Indira Gandhi had followed was a continuation of the Congress philosophy but that her policies were more closely related 'to her own political interests' (p. 195), shifting from 'populist' to 'pragmatic' (p. 206) over time.

5. See figure in the 'Introduction'.

6. The fact of a worsened economic environment referred to earlier only deepens the puzzle.

7. Most of south India was to remain loyal to Indira Gandhi for the rest of her political career, notably by enabling her return to political life by electing her to Parliament after she lost the elections in 1977 following the two-year Emergency declared by her. Suggestively, from the constituency of Chikkamagalur, Kannada for 'the home of the younger daughter [in law]'!

8. As for a longer-term one, we know from the idea of 'path dependence' that seemingly innocuous short-run dynamics of an economy can affect the long-run equilibrium of the system (see Arthur 1989).

9. Economists in government at that juncture later describe the exit of Nehru as marking 'the end of steadfast political commitment to planning' (see Guhan and Shroff 1986: viii).

10. An example is the pressure, hitherto non-existent, to give consideration to the native in recruitment to public sector units in Bangalore (now Bengaluru), a city with a particularly high concentration of public sector units and, equally significantly, a large non-native working-class population. See Subramanian (2008). Half a century later this remains the main plank of the Shiv Sena in Mumbai. For an indication of how similar pressures were dealt with earlier, note the interchange between Nehru and Bisnuram Medhi, the chief minister of Assam, on the demand that oil from Assam be refined within the state rather than be sent to the public-sector refinery at Barauni, Bihar (see Nehru 1957).

11. See: 'Another noteworthy feature of the functioning of Public Sector during this period has been the taking over of a number of industrially sick units from private sector with a view to protect the employees from unemployment. The number of employees working in enterprises which have been taken over by the government now constitute around 48 percent of the total number of employees working in Central Public enterprises' (Ministry of Finance 1981).

12. See Singh (2004).

13. See Nayar (2006).

14. See Marathe (1986).

15. The methodology was first implemented, for a shorter time series, in Balakrishnan and Parameswaran (2007).

16. See, for instance, Virmani (2006).

17. See Hansen (2001) for a discussion of the pitfalls of such an approach.

18. The basis for our choice, discussed along with the econometric procedure in the Appendix, is statistical. However, it does appear reasonable that in a sample of over fifty years, which we have here, a growth regime must last for at least eight years to be counted as one.

19. For a statement by the CSO on the procedure underlying the compilation of a long-term, constant-price GDP series for India, see Central Statistical Organisation (CSO 2007).

20. It may be remarked upon here, though, that the confidence interval for our point estimate of the break-dates is mostly very narrow, and by far more so when compared to that reported in some other studies of structural breaks in the Indian GDP data, to be referred to later.

21. The first study to establish structural breaks in the growth process in India is that of Wallack (2003). Interestingly while Wallack's result for GDP is very close to ours—that is, showing acceleration in the late 1970s—her results on the sub-sectors differ.

22. However, note that, as with all the results presented in Table 3.1, this finding could be sensitive to the interval allowed for between switches in the growth regime. While, due to this concern, we have performed sensitivity tests with the aggregate GDP series, we refrained from doing so with the disaggregated—that is, sectoral—data as it could open up a Pandora's Box (!) without significantly advancing our project of understanding long-term growth in India. At the same time, it may be repeated that the choice of an eight-year interval does not appear unreasonable when studying growth over a half a century. The results of testing for a sensitivity of the results obtained for aggregate GDP to the size of interval chosen are discussed in the section 'The Trajectory of Growth, 1965–91' of Chapter 4.

23. See, for instance, Krishna (1988).

24. See the discussion to follow in the section 'The Pace and Nature of Growth since 1991' of Chapter 4.

25. See Ministry of Food and Agriculture (1967).

26. For which see Sivaraman (1991: 297).

27. An example in the context would be the Japanese system of transplanting the seedling in paddy cultivation.

28. From the memoirs of the civil servant who oversaw the government's agricultural programme we have it that: 'The IARI was carrying out trials for the international wheat testing programme. Dr. Swaminathan noticed several dwarf wheat types in the nursery which he thought had potential for introduction in India for higher wheat yields. In May 1962 he advised Dr. Pal to invite Dr. Borlaug to India to help us in the matter. Dr. Pal sent the invitation through the Rockefeller Foundation in November 1962 and Dr. Borlaug landed in India in March 1963. After touring our wheat research stations and discussing with wheat breeders, he went back and sent a large assortment of wheat material to IARI for research trials in India. The material arrived in the middle of November 1963 and was immediately sown in several stations, under the close supervision of our prominent wheat breeders' (Sivaraman 1991: 305). Benjamin Peary Pal was the head of the Indian Agricultural Research Institute (IARI).

29. See column 6 of Table 3.2. Note that public investment takes place over a much greater part of the economy than agriculture and industry, which accounts for the levels registered for agriculture's share.

30. There are two sharply rising phases, commencing in 1966–7 and 1974–5, respectively.

31. An exception is the following observation by Raj (1982: 28): 'In the latter half of the 1960s [when] it was thought essential to cut the investment allocations of capital goods industries in order to make available more resources for investment in agriculture.'

32. See Dantwala (1967) and Balakrishnan (1991).

33. See Sengupta (2008).

34. For a historian's view, see Roy (2007).

35. Note from Table 3.1, though, that even this accelerated growth performance of manufacturing exceeded only marginally its performance over 1950–65. At the same time, our exercise cannot capture the very high growth of manufacturing for five years since 2003–4 (see *Economic Survey 2007–08*) as our sample ends with that year. This issue is taken up in the next chapter.

36. See Ahluwalia (1985).

37. See Panagariya (2005).

38. See Raj (1976) and Srinivasan and Narayana (1977).

39. The author had by then spent close to quarter of a century advising the government.

40. See Marathe (1986: 15–16). For evidence of the rising share of the large houses in 'total sales' in an industry, see Bardhan (1984: Table 15).

41. The original source is 'Industrial Policy—Government Decisions', Press Note of the Government of India, 2 February 1973.

42. The details are as follows: The Industrial Disputes Act was amended so that firms employing more than 300 workers needed permission from the respective state government to close down operations. The limit hitherto had been 1,000 workers. The Act was amended again in 1982 when the bar was lowered further to 100.

43. See Sundriyal (1996).

44. See Rodrik and Subramanian (2005).

45. This constitutes crucial and rare evidence that growth rather than redistribution had now begun to claim a larger part of the Indira Gandhi government's agenda.

46. The references here are to the Lok Dal headed by Charan Singh and the Janata Party that had preceded it. All entries in quotation marks are from Marathe (1986). Source cited by Marathe is Ministry of Industry (1982).

47. See Annexe Table 1.4 'Annual Growth Rates of Real GDP by Industry of Origin', *Economic Survey 2007–08*.

48. In theory the distinction between *policy* and *regulatory* change may not appear so sharp, but seems to be a useful one to make in the context of the economic environment in India during the period we are concerned with in this chapter.

49. See Economic and Political Weekly Research Foundation (2004: Table 6).

50. See Pradhan et al. (1990).

51. See Chapter 2.

52. See Jha (1980) for specific cases.

53. The results, based on the method of Bai and Perron presented earlier in this chapter, were generously made available to me by Prabhakaran Nair. They have by now appeared in Nair (2009).

54. See, in particular, Panagariya (2005).

55. Decisions of the bureaucracy on applications for a licence to produce or import are beyond challenge in the civil courts of law. The power of 'delegated legislation', whereby the bureaucracy is allowed to draft rules on behalf of Parliament and implement them as its sees fit, effectively leaves it unaccountable. On this see Sundriyal (1996).

56. The general administration of the country is a theme that appears repeatedly in his speeches. See *Speeches of Jawaharlal Nehru*, various volumes (New Delhi: Publications Division, Ministry of Information and Broadcasting, Government of India).

57. See Chatterjee (1979) for the characterization of governance in colonial India as 'built around intricate rules and procedures enshrining unfettered executive power'.

58. In the early 1970s the marginal rate of taxation in the highest tax bracket was raised to 97.5 per cent which, when combined with the then current rate of wealth tax of 5 per cent, implied a disincentive to income-generation beyond a point. See Rao and Rao (2006: 68) for details and a discussion of the evolution of India's tax regime.

59. Today it would be difficult to imagine that this was rationalized on political grounds. Thwarting the private sector's actions after it had been given the licence to enter into production was also far from the economic philosophy of the Nehru era.

60. See Raj (1976).

61. See Marathe (1986) and Sundriyal (1996), respectively.

62. See Panagariya (2005). The review of trade policy changes that follows draws on the account given there.

63. Not surprisingly, as cereals amounted to 25 per cent of the import bill, for which see *Economic Survey 1966–67*.

64. See Table 10 in *Economic Survey 1967–68*.

65. See *Economic Survey 1970–71*.

66. See Table 6.8 in *Economic Survey 1981–82*.

67. As pointed out by Nayyar (2006).

68. See Gordon and Gupta (2004) and Rakshit (2007).

69. See, for instance, Virmani (2006).

70. See Bhagwati (1994).

71. See Kochar et al. (2006).

72. Being the methodology that had in the first place led to the characterization of the Indian case as peculiar.

73. This would be consistent with the observation reported that the large business houses increased their share of sales in this period.

74. A rapid increase in employment in government—'sinecures'—has been emphasized by Jha (1980).

75. Recall that this was before the age of information technology and the surveillance that it enables.

76. In July 2001, on the occasion of the tenth anniversary of the reforms of 1991, I had, writing in the newspapers, wagered that the acceleration in the 1990s is unlikely to have exceeded that in the 1980s, implying that a growth transition had preceded the reforms. See Balakrishnan (2001).

77. None is listed.

78. And there is sufficient reason to be sceptical of a procedure that constrains factor shares to be the same across all countries in a global sample. See Durlauf (2003) on this aspect of the Bosworth–Collins estimates.

79. See Balakrishnan and Pushpangadan (2001).

80. See Gordon (2004), in particular chapter 8.

81. This applies equally to the models of exogenous and endogenous growth by Solow and Romer, respectively.

82. See Mohan (2008) and Bhagwati (1998), respectively, for examples of this genre.

83. In all of this, an aspect that has not got the attention that it deserves is the generally improved performance of the public sector in the 1980s extending from the profitability of public enterprises to efficiency in the infrastructure sectors, for which see Nagaraj (1991). This would have been a factor enabling the maintenance of high public investment and may be expected to have contributed to the revival of manufacturing in more ways than one.

84. Particularly, the requirement of an interval of eight years between breaks.

85. Sectoral growth rates across decades may be viewed in Acharya (2002).

86. See Economic and Political Weekly Research Foundation (2004: Tables 6a and 6b).

87. This is achieved by combining into a weighted average the growth rates of each of the sub-sectors within these three groups. For a clear description of what each of these sectors contain, the reader may refer to Table AI.1 of the Appendices.

88. It is not unique in adopting this periodization, however. See Joshi and Little (1994).

89. See Rodrik and Subramanian (2005).

90. I am indebted to Aditya Bhattacharjea for this insight.

91. See Panagariya (2005) and Rodrik and Subramanian (2005).

92. See, for instance, Kohli (2006a).

93. For a sample, see the prognosis for growth in the contemporary writings by Chakravarty (1979) and Lal (1979). K.N. Raj, alone among his fellow economists, had at the time observed: 'One cannot [therefore] be certain whether the latter half of the seventies has made a difference to the long-run growth rate of the economy or it still remains at 3.5 percent per annum. It seems highly probable however that a process of acceleration has got initiated during this period' (1979: 12).

94. See Arrow (1962) and Young (1928), respectively.

95. By contrast, note the prescience of a Daniel Thorner who had very early in its history signalled the Green Revolution on the basis of field visits across north India in January 1965. His account of the reception of this news by the profession in India is of relevance in the present context: 'It would be an understatement to say that some of my economist friends and colleagues received my presentation with skepticism. … At the heart of these profound reservations was the fact that my emphasis on the emergence of capitalist agriculture ran counter to one of the most deeply rooted convictions of India's urban intellectuals …: [that] barring a thorough-going social revolution, India's countryside was doomed to remain a bottomless pit of stagnant misery. In a number of cases this conviction is so firmly held that no data, analysis, or argument can shake it' (Thorner 1976: 2). Significantly perhaps, Thorner was neither Indian nor, by his own definition, a 'trained economist'.

96. Recognized by Lal (1979).

97. Evident in the Industrial Policy Statement of 1980, quoted earlier.

98. See Bhargava (1987). On the impact of the myriad micro-level interventions unleashed, the following characterization by Chandra et al. (2000: 359) is worth noting: 'The controls, restrictions, interventions … were paradoxically often resorted to in the name of introducing "socialist" principles and equity but ended up building a distorted, backward capitalism'. See also the distinction 'Nehru versus Nehruites' made in Dhar (2003) referring to the tendency to justify subsequent actions in terms of their origin in the policies of early independent India.

4 Getting up to Speed after 1991

India needs to grow at the rate of at least 10 percent per annum to get rid of chronic poverty, ignorance and disease which still afflict millions of our people.

—Manmohan Singh, Debate on the Confidence Motion, Lok Sabha, 22 July 2008

In the public eye, 1991 marks a watershed in the evolution of the economic policy regime in India after the 1950s. Academic economists, on the other hand, have debated whether the origins of the post-1991 regime reach back into the 1980s or, for some, even into the 1970s.[1] A nuanced view on this issue, however, would be that though some of the policy changes of 1991 were initiated in the previous decades, a systemic change of the policy regime occurred only in July of that year. This change was a demonstrated move towards the integration of the Indian economy with the rest of the world. Within this, there was also to be greater freedom for private enterprise effected through deregulation of product markets. While it is possible to see the economics of the regime change for what it is, the politics of it is less easily deciphered. Both are considered here, before moving on to the main issues deliberated upon in this chapter, namely, the pace and nature of growth since 1991 and the prospects of its acceleration to levels aspired to by India's policymakers.

The Economics and Politics of Regime Change

Going by the policy statements of the Government of India at the time and the contents of the then Finance Minister Manmohan Singh's celebrated budget speech of July 1991, the guiding principle of policy at that juncture was the integration of India's economy with that of the rest of the world. At the same time, the world over, globalization was being advocated by reference to the implosion of the Former Soviet Union (FSU). The latter event itself was interpreted as evidence of the unsustainability of the autarkic Soviet economic model upon which India had allegedly based her own. Everything, according to those who held this view, pointed to the imperative of granting freer play to the market. It is important to flag the casual reasoning involved in arriving at this conclusion. First, while the sustainability of the Soviet economic model was being projected as an event foretold, the collapse of the FSU had come entirely unexpectedly to the economists. Its roots had very likely lain as much in Gorbachev's policy of *glasnost* or openness (a radical regime shift in the sphere of politics) as in *perestroika* (or the restructuring of the economy).[2] This had first cut at the foundations of single-party rule by the communists and the vice-like grip of the bureaucracy, later spreading to dislodge the more than half century of ethnic Russian hegemony over the 'union' of nationalities. The unravelling of the FSU as a political entity had followed, and with it came the disintegration of the entire socialist bloc of Eastern Europe. With hindsight, a potential application of the 'domino theory', albeit in an entirely different corner of the world, had remained unimagined for over seven decades.

A recognition of politics as the most proximate cause of the collapse of the FSU does not for a moment reinstate the economy of the FSU as dynamic, but it does help us see that forces making for the disintegration of the European socialist world were largely political, and its timing almost entirely determined by them. It is not irrelevant here to note that China had, for at least three decades by then, adhered to a highly *dirigiste* model of import-substituting industrialization, initially yielding a growth rate not much higher than that of India's.[3] The argument advanced here that political liberalization may have been the more important factor in the disintegration of the FSU is strengthened by reference to the experience of China, where the move to a largely capitalist economic model has been underpinned by a severely repressive political regime, which alone contains the political disaffection due to growing inequality of income and regional imbalance.

The second reason why the justification of a regime change in India based on the Soviet experience would be inappropriate is that in 1991 it was quite far from having been a Soviet-style economy ever. Apart from the total absence of the coercive allocation of labour, perhaps the most significant marker of communism, even in 1991, over 80 per cent of gross domestic product (GDP) in India was generated in a barely regulated private sector, something entirely alien to the FSU. Organized manufacturing alone had been tightly regulated indeed but it had comprised a highly developed private sector and constituted less than a fifth of the economy. By 1991 the Indian corporate sector was also highly organized politically and boasting of a lobby with increasing access to the political class. However, in the approach to foreign trade, there was a strong resemblance between the Soviet and Indian economies. Here, import quotas were widespread, and when they were absent, there were tariffs which were among the highest in the world. So it can be said that India, as did the FSU, had attempted to industrialize via across-the-board import-substituting industrialization, no matter that some trade liberalization had been initiated from the mid-1970s, as we saw in Chapter 3.

However, the broad similarity of economic strategy would by itself hardly qualify India as a Soviet clone for, as we have seen in Chapter 2, much of East Asia too had pursued what has been termed import-substituting industrialization. But something a little more than mere economic strategy was in the balance when the policy regime had been chosen to start with by India's political leadership in the 1950s. Foreign capital had not just been discouraged but it had over time been more or less expunged from the economy by design. It was this closedness to foreign capital, also in forms not envisaged in the 1950s, that was to change in 1991. This was the truly radical shift accomplished by the reforms of that year. There is every indication that it was deliberate and intended to be irreversible. In any case, it is a move that has held for close two decades by now and shows no sign of waning.

Within the overarching objective of integrating India with the rest of the world, specific changes to the policy regime were undertaken. For the sake of convenience, these may be grouped under the rubrics 'internal' and 'external', even as we realize that their elements may not always be independent of one another. The principal changes in the former group were the scrapping of investment licensing and amendment of the Monopolies and Restrictive Trade Practices Act of 1969 that regulated the 'large industrial houses'. The most visible features of the *policyscape* for at least a quarter of a century, their evolution was of considerable symbolic value.

As for the changes with respect to India's interface with the rest of the world, the second of our two rubrics, three may be noted. First, the tariff rate was reduced across the board, clearly intended to lower protection enjoyed by Indian industry. Second, after an early devaluation of the rupee, it was left to float as far as transactions on current account were concerned. This amounted to allowing a greater role for market forces in the determination of trade flows. In the context, it could also have been rationalized as necessary when quantitative restrictions on import were being rescinded. Finally, a simplification of procedures for inward foreign direct and portfolio investment was announced. As a signal of the intention to integrate the country with the global economy, this remained unsurpassed. These changes to the external policy regime for the economy were unilateral.

Other changes were to come into effect in the mid-1990s following India's accession to the World Trade Organization (WTO) rules. This was part of a simultaneous move by member countries to a set of rules agreed upon multilaterally. Prominent elements of this new set were a commitment to phase out quotas, legislate a new patent regime granting recognition to product patents, hitherto non-existent in India, and recognize trade in services. Though these were not ceded unilaterally and came with reciprocal rights—particularly of market access—for India, the move was viewed with deep concern by some vocal sections of its polity. Arguably, however, the trade and industrial policy reforms of 1991 constituted a greater shock to the economy and were in this sense the more potent of the changes.

The expression 'liberalization, privatization, globalization'—'LPG' for short—has been used to describe the shift in the policy regime initiated in 1991. But this is misleading and it would be pertinent to demonstrate why.[4] Liberalization, in the form of the trade and industrial policy changes recounted here, was in the forefront of the economic reforms alright, but of privatization there has been very little. Evidently the politics of the public sector run far deeper than the differentiated agendas of India's political parties, as we can infer from the fact that alliances of both the right and the left have governed Indian since. The relationship to the public sector of India's political class appears to be independent of ideology, the reluctance to privatize reflecting an unwillingness to let go of a significant lever of power. That privatization had featured so prominently at all in the policy announcements of governments in the early 1990s only to be dropped as soon as the crisis of 1991 had passed and the economy had stabilized, has encouraged speculation on the role of some external agency in its inclusion in the agenda for reform.

Finally we come to globalization, the extent of which tends to get exaggerated. User-specificity is a hazard often encountered in the parleying of this term, and not just in India. One might ask if globalization is the adoption of supra-national standards in economic arrangements within a country or whether it refers to the unrestrained cross-border movement of goods, services, and factors. We can see that either way far too much by way of globalization is attributed to the reforms of 1991. For a surplus labour economy such as India, true globalization should encompass the possibility of labour emigration. This is restricted by immigration controls in the rest of the world, especially among the labour-scarce economies of the Organisation for Economic Co-operation and Development (OECD) which would count as the obvious destination. On the other hand, the barriers to the adoption of certain kinds of global standards are largely internal. Take, for instance, the norm of global standards in the education and health status of the population. For a large economy with considerable administrative reach and growing government revenues, which is India, these are not unattainable any longer. However, no move in this direction has been made as part of the reforms of 1991. The reforms themselves were almost entirely of the nature of a liberalization and had not initially addressed the issues of either human development or social protection.[5] India lags behind much of the world on almost every indicator of human capital and welfare provision. Therefore, while the share of trade in India's GDP has risen, the extent of globalization, defined more broadly, that has taken place is limited. The one notable move in that direction is that after a gap of four decades or so India has now once again become exposed to the global flow of financial capital for the first time since 1947.

Another feature of the reforms of 1991 may now be noted. The liberalization that has occurred has taken place mostly in the sphere of the central government's policy. In the case of foreign trade, Central legislation would be sufficient to qualify as the final stage of policymaking, but this cannot be said of the industrial policy. This is so because in India foreign trade is a 'Central subject' and trade policy within the powers of the central government. Not so the industrial policy. Here state governments retain substantial powers and a Central legislation does not yet remove the binding constraint on industrial investment. So while the Industrial Policy Statement of 1991 may have scrapped industrial licensing, fresh proposals for industrial investment continue to be dependent upon the state governments for clearances. In practice, some states have turned out to be more attentive to such proposals than others. That this is so is partly revealed by the growing divergence of industrial performance among the states.[6] Yet, the scrapping of industrial licensing, once a serious barrier to even a demonstrably profitable capacity expansion, is a significant event marking the end of an era as far as the policy regime is concerned. Returning to the question of how the reforms of 1991 and after are to be characterized, we might say that we have had liberalizing trade and industrial policy reforms. 'LPG' is not a particularly helpful account of the recent evolution of the economic policy regime in India.

As may be imagined, the politics of the regime change is less sure ground for the economist than is the economics. Judging from their writings, however, it does not appear fully mapped territory for the political scientists either.[7] The main axis of contestation, an expression favoured by one of them,[8] is whether the economic reforms' package of 1991 was only an egregious event in a sequence of market reforms that had been experimented with earlier by the domestic leadership or whether it was an imposition by the global multilateral agencies, notably the International Monetary Fund (IMF). Political scientists bring along an element much needed for a fuller understanding of the regime change, rendering their perspective invaluable. However, while they may be united by their interest in the origins of the reforms, the issue of the factors underlying the regime change has not been resolved by them similarly. Among the most recent accounts is that of Sengupta (2008: 36) who rejects the portrayal of the reforms 'as the outcome of a linear, cumulative process of learning'[9] among the country's policy elites, preferring instead an account of 1991 as a 'political event'. What is so political about it for her is the defeat of the old paradigm by the Washington Consensus, a view of economic policy discussed in the 'Introduction' to this book. In this defeat, a significant role is said to have been played by professional economists in the Indian government who subscribed strongly to the worldview that was emerging as dominant globally. Despite a self-conscious effort to provide a political explanation of the reforms, Sengupta's approach lacks a political economy, being without a role for the domestic political parties, global institutions, and historical events.[10] En route to our providing an account that encompasses these, it is instructive to note the views of two other political scientists.

Pedersen (2000) ascribes an important role in the regime change to an emerging economic class whose interests diverged from those of the class that had mostly dominated the private industrial sector of India for almost three decades. Neither mercantilist in outlook nor anxious in its dealings with the West, this class is said to have had less at stake in the old model and much at stake in the adoption of an open trade and industrial policy regime. This class was constituted by the owners and managers of the emerging industrial groups of India. These industries were professionally run, marked by absence of family influence, and different in their geography, being less concentrated in the west and the east. Southern Indian engineering firms with an interest in the global market were a large constituent. The managers of these industries had links with the global managerial elite and viewed themselves as differently positioned vis-à-vis the West by comparison with the first generation of Indian industrialists after Independence. Pedersen sees this group, which coalesced into the Confederation of Indian Industries, as having been a strong lobby for the kind of reforms which were undertaken in 1991.

Among political analysts, as he describes himself, Kohli's work on the politics of reform is the most grounded, scanning first the policyscape of the 1980s to provide a longer view of the regime change of 1991. While he recognizes the role of the newly emerged industry associations, Kohli (2006b) is most insightful when he links the change to the collapse of the Soviet Union. We have already encountered here the self-serving interpretation of the collapse of the Soviet Union as symbolizing the end of a paradigm in economics. However, Kohli is referring to something more palpable. This is the strong economic links the Indian economy had enjoyed with the FSU for almost four decades. A central feature of this was the rupee trade which had enabled India to buy oil and defence equipment without having to pay foreign exchange, a trade facilitated by the export of tea, textiles, and raw materials. The ending of this possibility, not to mention the market constituted by the Eastern European economic block COMECON, was with grave implications for the Indian economy. Kohli points to the recognition among India's elites that henceforth defence equipment would have to be sourced from the United States. And, more importantly, that a move in that direction would require the opening up of the Indian economy to American capital and goods, as the other developing countries have known all too well all along.

To this important insight we might add the following. With the collapse of the FSU, India would have had to export more to an open global market to earn the necessary foreign exchange. And rather like the historically observed relationship between markets and prosperity, it could not but have been apparent to any unbiased observer at that moment that it would be virtually impossible to be a successful exporter while remaining behind protective barriers. The latter has less to do with the element of reciprocity expected in trade, having instead everything to do with an exporter needing access to globally competitive technology and capital goods which in the first instance can only be imported. Of course, for India in particular, there was all along also the imperative to export to make up the foreign exchange needed to purchase oil and gold. We may add that adjustment in the form of a reduction of oil dependence was politically inconceivable, in that the Indian state is far too populist to restrict consumption.

Having surveyed the views of political analysts, we may now sift through them with reference to the history of the Indian economy. As may be seen from the discussion in the preceding chapter, where we had provided an explanation of the growth transition *circa* 1980, some form of incipient reform of the trade and industrial policy regime had begun in the mid-1970s. This had continued in dribs and drabs right through till the middle of Rajiv Gandhi's tenure as prime minister, which had lasted till 1989. The intervening two years before 1991 had seen two governments, led by V.P. Singh and Chandrashekar, respectively, which devoted little attention to economic matters as they were more concerned with political survival.

However, except for the Rajiv Gandhi era, the liberalizing reforms were also mostly accompanied by enhanced restrictions, approximating 'two steps forward, one step back', as it were. For instance, Mrs Gandhi's mildly liberalizing initiatives in the mid-1970s and the early 1980s were accompanied by a tightening of labour laws. Earlier, the Janata Party, led by the politically conservative Morarji Desai, had signalled its intention to liberalize licensing and external commercial policy by appointing the Alexander Committee on Import–Export Policies and Procedures in 1977. However, it granted further concessions to small industry and actively discouraged foreign direct investment, as may be seen in the highly publicized forced exit of Coca Cola and IBM. As for the Rajiv Gandhi era, it has been pointed out[11] that tariffs actually rose during this period, thus neutralizing the removal of some import quotas.

However, Rajiv Gandhi's role cannot be sufficiently captured by indicators of the restrictiveness of the trade regime. His tenure was on balance a period of reform. The young prime minister had positioned himself as one who was not afraid of initiating change, without of course rejecting the past in India's economic development. The radical rhetoric talked by Indira Gandhi and walked by George Fernandes in his brief tenure as the minister for industries in the Janata government was by now a thing of the past. There was a strong sense of using state-of-the-art technology to transform India. Also, without in any way dismantling the public sector, Rajiv Gandhi had provided room for the private. This was most noticeable with respect to information technology and telecommunications. The by now innocuous 'STD booth' was at the moment of its first appearance symbolic of the private sector having been allowed to scale the ramparts of a public sector monopoly. Given that after the Nehru era privileging of the public sector had become a marker of politics, this was a portent. Further, it could not have been missed by the political class that the move had a widely distributed welfare effect with not insignificant political payoffs.

The fact of plentiful evidence of a liberalizing change to the policy regime for over a decade before 1991 is not to deny that the reforms package of 1991 may have been strongly influenced by the IMF. Indeed, it is there for all to see. However, the influence was very likely more so in the macroeconomic reforms. The lowering of tariffs, reduction of the budget deficit, restriction of credit and devaluation—all bear the hallmark of the Fund's standard stabilization package for a balance-of-payments–constrained economy. That the reduction in the fiscal deficit must clearly have been influenced by the IMF is also suggested by the sharp cuts initiated in the early years of the 1990s to be followed by a slipping of targets soon as the Programme with the Fund had wound down. Public savings promptly turned negligible in the second half of the 1990s.[12] It is unlikely though that the Industrial Policy Statement of 1991 abolishing licensing would have been solely at the behest of the Fund, and, even if it was, the reform of licensing had (as we have seen in the previous chapter) been contemplated in Indian government circles for over two decades by then.

In conclusion, it is not particularly difficult to isolate the elements of the regime change imposed by the external agencies as the price of balance-of-payments support from that adopted quite willingly by the Indian political leadership, even if at the behest of the former. The balance of payments crisis had left India with little alternative but to travel, cap in hand, to Washington. This gave the Fund–World Bank combine the perfect opportunity to impose its view of the ideal economic architecture on the last major country that had for long resisted its writ. In fact, an opportunity had been missed in 1981 when India had been granted the largest ever loan made by the IMF to a member country, only for her to refuse the last tranche of the $5 billion assistance, as the economy had both recovered quickly from the impact of the second oil-shock and ingeniously tapped the non-resident Indians for foreign exchange support. The end of communism in the FSU and the wooing of the West by China had left India isolated as a practitioner of extensive restrictions on international trade and capital flows. It should not come as a surprise that the IMF had weighed-in with its trademark conditionalities, intending that this should change for ever. However, at least as far an internal liberalization was concerned, this was only the culmination of what had been attempted for very long and was therefore likely in keeping with the agenda of Congress government of Narasimha Rao.

The progress of the reforms, both macroeconomic and structural, provides an insight into the role of external agencies relative to that of the domestic liberalizing forces. It would be a fair summary to say that next to none of the structural reforms, whether of the 'external' or 'internal' type according to our earlier classification, has been reversed. On the other hand, the principal macroeconomic reform of permanently reducing the budget deficit, an important element of the IMF package, has more or less been abandoned since the end of the IMF programme in the mid-1990s. The Fiscal Responsibility and Budgetary Management (FRBM) Act of 2002 has had a shaky start, largely because the political class in India is aware of the restrictions that it places on its functioning, particularly the buying of political allegiance via budgetary subsidy while retaining a low tax rate. Clearly budgetary rectitude had been imposed from without in 1991. On the other hand, the structural reforms, in evidence at least since the 1980s, were very likely perceived by the political class as potentially contributing to growth and, therefore, beneficial to their political futures, even if some sectional interests are hurt in the process. In any case, the role of a domestic force in at least sustaining the structural reforms is evident. However, it is more difficult to place the proposed privatization of the public sector enterprises in perspective. The IMF actually refuses to acknowledge the accrual of revenues from privatization as legitimate input into fiscal correction.

The liberalizing reforms of 1991 stand out in marked contrast to the liberalization episode of 1966 when, faced with a balance-of-payments crisis, India had gone to the IMF. As recounted in the preceding chapter, then a sharp devaluation and some liberalizing reforms were implemented in return for promised balance-of-payments support. When this did not materialize, Indira Gandhi, outplayed by the international powers-that-be and goaded by domestic public opinion, had simply reversed the reforms. On the other hand, in India since 1991, we have thus far only had strongly liberalizing governments of all hues at the Centre, each advancing India's continuing integration with the rest of the world. Clearly, something has altered significantly in the sphere of politics, and the work of political scientists reviewed here helps us understand that change.

THE PACE AND NATURE OF GROWTH SINCE 1991

Given the theme of this book, the one question that must dominate all others when we are on the topic of the outcome of the reforms initiated in 1991 is whether the growth rate has accelerated. In India today this is no longer a matter of interest peculiar to an academic investigation. Growth has now fully entered the vocabulary of the discourse on governance in India, with political parties vying with one another to produce better performance.[13] Moreover, in 1991 the principal argument for reforms was that they are necessary for accelerating growth.[14]

In the econometric procedure of Bai and Perron (1998, 2003) encountered earlier in this book, we have the means to answer the question of interest. In fact, it would appear that we have even had a preview of the answer in Chapter 3 itself. There the said procedure had been applied to the time series on GDP for a little over fifty years from 1950, and the growth rates across phases thus identified were presented in Table 3.1. Recall that no evidence of a change in the rate of growth of aggregate GDP after 1991 was evident. However, in that exercise the break-dates had been identified from data—GDP in 1993–4 prices—extending only up to the year 2003–4. So the exercise was repeated using the current GDP series—in 1999–2000 prices—extending up to 2005–6. An acceleration is now observed from the year 1991–2 onwards and an annual average growth rate of 5.9 per cent observed. The estimated break-dates and the growth rates across phases thus derived are presented in Tables A4.3 and A4.4, respectively, of the Appendix.

Three points may be made regarding the pace of growth since 1991. First, when we approach the evidence by a route less formal than the econometric methodology followed so far, we recognize that the economy has entered a phase of high growth from 2003–4. From that year on for five years the economy has averaged a growth rate of over 8 per cent per annum.[15] The reason for this acceleration having been missed by our formal procedure is the minimum length of a growth phase having been set at eight years.[16] Our confidence in the procedure itself is restored, however, when we find that with this interval halved—that is, reduced to four years—2001–2 emerged as a breakpoint indicating the onset of faster growth from the following year.[17] To provide perspective on the pace of growth since 1991, the trend rate of GDP growth by decade from 1950 up to 2000 and annual growth rates from 2001–2 up to 2009 are presented in Table 4.1. Note from this that but for the high growth phase from 2003–4, the period after 1991 does not appear markedly superior to the 1980s. The growth acceleration following the reforms of 1991 took some time coming.

Second, granting that since 1991 the Indian economy has transited to a higher growth path, the average annual rate of growth of 5.9 per cent attained over 1991–2 to 2005–6 is yet lower than the Planning Commission's target of 8 per cent set to be achieved in the Tenth Plan (2002–7), leave alone the close to double-digit East Asian growth rates aspired for by the end of the Eleventh Plan (2007–12).[18] When, by including provisional estimates of GDP, the data is extended up to 2008–9, a much higher trend growth rate of 7.5 per cent per annum is registered, but this yet remains below target.

Table 4.1 The Growth Rate of the Indian Economy: A Long View

Period	*Growth Rate*
1951–2 to 1960–1	3.8
1961–2 to 1970–1	3.5
1971–2 to 1980–1	3.6
1981–2 to 1990–1	5.2
1991–2 to 2000–1	6.1
2001–2	5.8
2002–3	3.8
2003–4	8.5
2004–5	7.5
2005–6	9.5
2006–7	9.7
2007–8	9.0
2008–9	6.7

Sources: Decadal trend growth rates are the author's estimates; annual growth rates are from *Economic Survey 2008–9*.
Note: Figures for 2007–8 and 2008–9 are provisional.

Third, before finally exiting the econometric procedure that we have worked with in identifying growth regimes in India since 1950, we applied the Bai–Perron methodology to identify the breakpoint when only a single break is allowed for over the period 1950–2006. A positive break was discovered in the year 1984–5, implying a growth transition from 1985–6. Statistically, the discovery is intuitive, as 1984–5 is approximately midway between the two break-dates, that is, 1978–9 and 1990–1, when the estimation is left unconstrained.[19] More substantially, it places in perspective the role of the liberalizing reforms of 1991, that is, from the point of view of growth in India, the policy regime change of 1991 was not the defining moment. This finding is in line with that of DeLong (2003) and Rodrik and Subramanian (2005).

Having studied the pace of growth, we may turn to the nature of growth since 1991. The estimated contributions[20] of the three main sectors of the economy to the growth transitions of 1979–80 and 1991–2 are presented in Table 4.2. This allows for a comparison of the sectoral composition of the two growth transitions since 1950. It enables the identification of a change, if any, in the character of growth and also the site of the impact of the reforms of 1991, that is, when it is evident. Before proceeding though, it is important to bear in mind that this decomposition of the change in the growth rate by sector measures only the contribution directly attributable to each. However, the sectors possibly interact. Therefore, a high contribution does not imply an independent role. In fact, we can see from the inter-sectoral growth regressions in Table 3.5 of Chapter 3 that services growth was driven by agricultural growth over the first transition occurring in the late 1970s. These regressions had been run for the sample period 1953–81. Subsequently run regressions on data for the period 1978–2004 showed that inter-sectoral relations had changed by the time we come to the second transition, that of 1991. Principally, service sector growth now emerges as independent of agricultural performance, while continuing to be independent of manufacturing.[21] This relative independence of the growth of services since 1991 can be inferred by observing the pattern of growth across the sectors in Table A4.4 of the Appendix. In particular, three out of the four sub-sectors within services accelerate in the 1990s while agricultural growth remains unchanged.

The first impression that we get from the information in Table 4.2 is of the similarity between the last two growth transitions in India, in that it is the tertiary sector which has contributed overwhelmingly to the change in the growth rate each time. However, to stop at this pattern would be to

Table 4.2 Sector-wise Contribution to the Growth Transitions

		Transition of 1979–80	*Transition of 1991–2*
I	Primary Sector	–20.5	–30.3
1.1	Agriculture	–23.8	–25.8
1.2	Forestry and logging	–9.9	2.6
1.3	Fishing	0.6	–0.1
2	Mining and quarrying	12.5	–6.9
II	Secondary Sector	17.9	26.1
3	Manufacturing	14.1	16.4
3.1	Registered	24.5	7.8
3.2	Unregistered	–10.4	8.6
4	Electricity, gas, and water supply	7.8	–0.5
5	Construction	–4.0	10.1
III	Tertiary sector	102.6	104.2
6	Trade, hotels, and restaurants	12.6	35.5
6.1	Trade	11.4	31.7
6.2	Hotels and restaurants	1.2	3.8
7	Transport, storage, and communication	13.2	36.1
7.1	Railways	–0.1	–0.6
7.2	Transport by other means	11.0	8.6
7.3	Storage	–0.1	–0.1
7.4	Communication	2.4	28.2
8	Financing, insurance, real estate, and business services	45.2	25.0
8.1	Banking and insurance	18.3	19.0
8.2	Real estate, ownership of dwellings, and business services	26.9	6.0
9	Community and personal services	31.6	7.7
9.1	Public administration and defence	16.5	–3.4
9.2	Other services	15.1	11.1
	GDP	100.0	100.0

Notes: Contribution to the change in the growth rate across a transition is measured in percentages; for the transition of 1979–80 the change in the growth rate considered is the difference between the average annual rate for the periods 1950–1 to 1978–9 and 1979–80 to 1990–1, while for that of 1991–2 it is the difference for the periods 1979–80 to 1990–1 and 1991–2 to 2005–6. The GDP data is in 1999–2000 prices.

miss out on the quite dramatic shift between the transitions in the relative contributions of the four main groups within services. We find that the contribution of each of 'trade, hotels, and restaurants' and 'transport, storage, and communication' has increased very substantially while that of the other two—'finance, insurance, real estate, and business services' and 'community and personal services'—has declined. While the first development must come as a surprise considering that apart from 'communication' the reforms had not particularly addressed these sectors, the second must settle conclusively the idea that services growth was driven by the growth of wages and salaries in public administration. This second development assumes significance in the context of assertions of the role of public sector pay hikes whenever the overwhelming contribution of the tertiary sector to growth is highlighted, and not only for the 1990s.[22] However, the role of reforms may be clearly seen in the rise in the contribution of 'Communication'. At 28.2 per cent it exceeds the contribution made by the entire secondary sector of the economy, and is four times that of registered manufacturing. Clearly we are here observing the effect of liberalization of private entry into telephony, especially of mobile telecommunications.

If it is agreed that much of the liberalization had targeted India's manufacturing sector via the trade and industrial policy reforms of 1991, the result of this in terms of their impact on GDP growth of the sector is not impressive. The contribution of registered manufacturing has not only declined but it is also below that of unregistered manufacturing. In the case of the latter, a negative contribution has been converted into a positive one—amounting to a swing of 19 percentage points—across the two transitions. Whether the reforms have encouraged outsourcing—whereby some of the output which would have historically been produced in registered manufacturing has been shifted to the unregistered manufacturing—is a question that assumes relevance now but is impossible to settle with the information at hand. Finally, while yet on the role of the reforms, the component at the two-digit level which makes the largest contribution to the acceleration of growth is 'trade', a feature difficult to square with the policy thrust of increasing competition in the product markets. Altogether, one cannot escape the conclusion that, in terms of its sectoral composition at least, the growth transition of 1991–2 is more or less a replica of the transition of 1979–80, suggesting something more than just the role of liberalizing reforms here. With services growth displaying a somewhat independent momentum, the process of circular and cumulative causation considered in Chapter 1 could be a factor in the steady rise of this sector for over three decades, and consequently in the repeated acceleration of the economy itself.[23]

Delayed Transformation: A Structural Perspective on Economic Growth in India

Our investigation of growth in India since 1991 has so far proceeded by implicitly privileging the reforms initiated in that year as its likely determinant. Though by now more or less *de riguer* in studies of recent Indian economic growth, from a theoretical point of view, this approach is *ad hoc*. Indeed it is without any theoretical underpinning. While fully aware of this lacuna, we had adopted the approach in order to maintain a certain comparability for our study, but now the time has come to change tack.

In Chapter 1 we had demonstrated the usefulness of the approach to studying economic growth pioneered by Kuznets. Apart from the recognizable features of the narrative, we saw that this approach has considerable predictive power. Recall that the main contours of the transformation that accompanies long-term growth were identified as a rising share of industry in output and a declining share of agriculture in the labour force. A minor contribution of our own towards an understanding of this process had been to emphasize the role of a continuously rising agricultural productivity which results in progressively cheaper food. Assuming that the global history of growth is relevant for understanding the Indian case, we view the recent experience in this country within a Kuznets-type framework. The evolution of the sectoral composition of output and the distribution of the workforce in India since 1950 are presented[24] in Table 4.3.

From that data, the following features suggest themselves. First, the progress of structural transformation in India has been slower than we

Table 4.3 Structure and Change in the Indian Economy since 1950

Year	*Distribution of output (%)*			*Distribution of workforce (%)*		
	Agriculture	*Industry*	*Services*	*Agriculture*	*Industry*	*Services*
1951	58.9	13.5	28.1	72.4	10.2	17.4
1961	53.3	17.3	29.7	73.7	10.6	16.0
1971	46.9	20.3	33.0	71.8	11.0	17.2
1981	41.7	21.9	36.4	66.5	14.2	19.3
1991	34.1	23.9	42.0	67.5	11.9	20.5
2001	27.5	24.6	47.9	57.5	16.7	25.9

Source: Workforce figures are author's estimates from the Census of India, Registrar General and Census Commissioner, India, various issues; output—GDP—figures are from the *National Accounts Statistics*, Central Statistical Organisation, various issues.

would expect to have taken place over half a century, at least in some areas. After an initial expansion of industry, as a share of the economy, it is services that have progressed the fastest. The share of industry has barely grown in the ten years since 1991. This is striking as the economic reforms, when they have not been macroeconomic, have mostly addressed the industrial sector. The feature has not been reflected upon sufficiently in evaluations of the reforms. The low share of manufacturing in India, specifically in relation to the economy of China, has been flagged of course.[25] However, explanations of this feature have been fewer, and proposals of how to bring about the transformation even less. It has been asserted[26] that the low share of manufacturing is an inheritance from the *dirigiste* policy regime in place in India till 1991. This cannot be dismissed, of course. Accounting for the cyclical growth of manufacturing since the mid-1960s, in Chapter 3, we had ourselves proposed that the *regimen* governing production in industry has historically been more stringent than for services. However, the discussion in Chapter 1 has opened up for us another possibility in the context. We also need to consider whether the market for manufacturing has grown as fast as it could have. Consider, as one form of evidence, the evolution of food prices. The real price of food in India from 1993 is presented in Table 4.4.

Note that in over one and half decades the real price of food has not budged; if at all, it has actually risen slightly. For perspective, consider the US experience where since the Second World War the real price of foodgrains has declined by approximately 75 per cent.[27] In India, where on average over 50 per cent of the household expenditure budget is spent on food,[28] its rigid price can act as a dampener on the expansion of the market for mass consumption goods in the first instance. An indication of the level of the price of food in relation to incomes in India today is obtained from a global comparison of the share of food in household final consumption expenditure. In Table 4.5 is provided data on this share for the countries that we have been tracking from Chapter 1. Once again, missing countries speak of the absence of data from the same source. It is particularly unfortunate that none of the Latin American countries in our sample could be represented for this reason. As the countries have been arranged in ascending order of per capita income, we are able to verify the nature of the relationship between national (per capita) income and the share of food in household expenditure. We can see that the implied rank correlation is almost *perfectly* inverse. The richer countries spend commensurately less on food, which encourages their

Table 4.4 The Price of Food after 1991

Year	*Food*	*All Commodities*	*Real Price*
1993–4	100	100	100
1994–5	113	113	100
1995–6	122	122	100
1996–7	137	127	108
1997–8	141	133	106
1998–9	159	141	113
1999–2000	165	145	114
2000–1	170	156	109
2001–2	176	161	109
2002–3	179	167	107
2003–4	181	176	103
2004–5	186	187	99
2005–6	195	196	99
2006–7	210	206	102
2007–8	222	216	103
2008–9	240	234	103

Source: Author's calculation from *Economic Survey 2008–09*.
Note: Index numbers base 1993–4 = 100. Real price is the index of the wholesale price of 'Food Articles' relative to that for 'All Commodities'.

economies to expand in other directions, thus raising overall income.[29] This evidence vindicates the emphasis here on the central role of the price of food in the growth of economies with low levels of per capita income. It points to the type of structural change that the Indian economy must undergo to industrialize further and indicates the distance that needs to be traversed.

The assertion that faster growth of the Indian economy requires that the share of manufacturing increases, though relevant, begs the question of how this is to be achieved. The observation of the fixity of the real price of food and the high share of expenditure on food in the consumption basket is relevant in the context. The composition of output reflects the composition of final demand in an economy. Some light is cast on the puzzling Indian case when we see from Table 1.1 of Chapter 1 that India is not unique in South Asia where the three largest economies share an almost identical composition of output. That we are on the right track here in emphasizing the role of agricultural productivity in stimulating industrial expansion is also indicated by the feature that these economies

Table 4.5 The Share of Food in Household Expenditure

	GNP per capita (US$)	*Share of food* (%)
United States	41,440	7.0
Japan	37,050	14.3
United Kingdom	33,630	9.0
France	30,370	14.4
Korea	14,000	15.4
Thailand	2490	26.7
India	620	39.0
Kenya	480	45.8

Source: Income data is from Table 1.1; share is author's calculation from United Nations' country national income statistics, available at http://www.data.un.org.
Notes: GNP per capita is for 2004, and so are the shares' data except for the US, Japan, and India for which it corresponds to 2003. Share of food is calculated as expenditure on food and non-alcoholic beverages as percentage of household final consumption expenditure.

also share the lowest agricultural productivity outside of Africa.[30] The surprisingly high share of services alongside low per capita income appears as a 'South-Asian syndrome', and a comparative study of the economies of this region vis-à-vis those outside could be one route to understanding the Indian case better. This feature suggests that the role of the trade and industrial policy regime in determining the composition of growth in the subcontinent could be exaggerated somewhat, for India and Pakistan have followed dissimilar economic policies since Independence. As we had occasion to see in Chapter 2, the tertiary sector was the fastest growing in the last fifty years of the colonial period in India. Therefore, there is a history to the pattern of growth observed more recently in India. However, a conclusion emerging out of the discussion in this section would be that the role of agricultural labour productivity, in particular of the price of food, appears to have been overlooked in the vision of the future encapsulated in the economic reforms initiated in 1991. The future of industry in India may be dependent on more than just a fully liberalized trade-policy regime.

We next look at the distribution of the workforce over time presented in Table 4.3. After having displayed only minor variation for four decades since 1951—some of it contrary to expectation, such as the decline in the share of manufacturing in the 1980s—the transformation has accelerated along expected lines since 1991. However, the picture for 2001 yet shows a very high share of the workforce in agriculture by international standards.

Over the last fifty years, the shift in the labour force out of agriculture has been slow. If a comparative global perspective over the long haul is a guide to the factors governing growth in the poor countries, the prospects for growth in India are linked to the ability of policy to engineer a shift of the greater part of the agricultural labour force to the non-agricultural sector, in the first instance to industry. As elaborated upon already, in the migration out of the sector of both labour and economic activity, agriculture has a significant role. Agricultural labour productivity must rise and food must get cheaper. As more productive labour will have to be compensated better, producer profits can be maintained, leave alone increased, only if the yield of land is raised. Thus, a dynamic agriculture is the first requirement for a sustained expansion of the economy.

Going by its history, we have reason to believe that if the said structural transformation does not take place, growth will be stymied, or unevenly distributed across the sectors of an economy. Structural transformation and growth share a symbiotic relationship. Sustained economic growth in India depends upon the speed of transformation, the main feature of which is the shifting of labour out of agriculture. The share of agriculture in the labour force here is among the highest in the world. From our knowledge of the experience of the richer countries, addressed in Chapter 1, we would be led to believe that the prospects for shifting it out of agriculture into the rest of the economy hinge closely on the level of education. Recall that education was seen as influencing this shift in two ways. First, among those who remain in agriculture, it determines that the necessary growth of productivity occurs.[31] Second, for those who are potential migrants, it enhances their employability.[32] In India where the rural labour force is poorly educated even when it is not illiterate, the prospects for the structural transformation of the economy are circumscribed to that extent. The spread of education now emerges as an additional factor determining the trajectory of economic growth in India in the future.

Foundations for Accelerated Growth in India

The record of growth since 1991 suggests that the argument often encountered that 'more reforms' alone stand between India and a double-digit growth rate is simple-minded. If by this is meant greater liberalization alone, we can say with some confidence that the remedy is unequal to the task of further accelerating growth, even though there may well be scope for deregulation that enhances welfare in some areas of the economy. On the other hand, our own study in Chapter 1 of the cross-country historical experience with growth is quite illuminative of what is required by way of preconditions for an acceleration of the growth rate.

We had gathered from the data presented there that economies that have grown fastest in recent decades had higher investment, faster agricultural growth, and stronger educational foundations. The type of reforms initiated in 1991 may have contributed to raising the investment rate in the private sector but the decline in public investment has meant that for at least a decade after the reforms were initiated, the aggregate investment rate in India has not risen sharply enough to accelerate growth, an increase in both rates being evident only from the year 2003–4.[33] Even if the higher rate of investment is here to stay, it is yet some way below that in China.[34]

The other variable that had emerged as a strong determinant of growth in our cross-country historical survey was the growth of per capita production of food. In India the production of food has barely kept up with population growth since 1991. Finally there is education. Though our statistical exercise in Chapter 1 had not revealed a statistically significant association between growth and education for cross-country data, it would be naïve to ignore the comparatively much higher educational attainment in the richer countries of the world. The reforms of 1991 had little by way of a design for a quantum improvement in this area, though a decade later funding by the World Bank has enabled the central government to spend more on primary education via the Sarva Shiksha Abhiyan programme. Then in 2009 an ambitious plan for the expansion of higher education was unveiled. The rest of this chapter is devoted to an investigation of the constraints on faster agricultural growth and the state of educational preparedness for faster growth in India today.

The Agriculture Quotient

The pattern of growth that the Indian economy has experienced since the reforms has received wide attention within the profession in India. Of particular concern has been the slowing of agriculture at a time when the rest of the economy is growing at unprecedented rates.[35] Manufacturing output, when taken as bellwether for the policy stance since 1991, has even registered double-digit growth in some recent years. Growth of the services economy has been less spectacular but more steady over a longer period. The slow growth of agriculture has been explicitly noted in the 'Approach Paper to the Eleventh Plan',[36] and accelerating the rate of growth of agricultural production seen as central to a more inclusive growth, if not growth per se.[37]

With a view to understanding the constraints on accelerating the growth of Indian agriculture, we study developments there since 1991. The objective is to establish the movement during this period of the factors that have received recognition among economists as determinants of agricultural growth in India, with a view to identifying the causes of the indifferent growth of this sector. We are interested in separating out the influence of the changed policy regime since 1991 from other causes which we term 'structural', in the sense of their relative independence from the economic policy regime. Of course, it can yet provide only a 'macroscopic', as in sector-wide, perspective. Moreover, as we are aware, Indian agriculture comprises major differences between crops and across regions. However, we have retained the approach as we believe that a sectoral perspective is precisely what is needed when identifying a growth strategy for the economy.[38] Also, studying the recent history of agricultural growth is a means to understanding what the economic reforms launched in 1991 can achieve by way of bringing about the transformation of a sector that maybe expected to remain central to sustained growth.

Agriculture and the Economic Reforms

As a slowing of agricultural expansion is being encountered at a time when the economic policy regime has been undergoing reform, it has been suggested by some that this slowing is due to the reforms themselves. Even before proceeding to the empirical investigation that constitutes the main part of our study, we engage with this view.

Strictly, there is nothing intrinsic to the policy of liberalization of an economy in the form of trade and industrial policy reforms that must be damaging of agriculture. Even as we develop this argument, it must be pointed out that we are here speaking of a *slowing* of growth. No major segment within agriculture has shown evidence of a steady contraction, the tell-tale sign of damage caused, *ceteris paribus*, by changing policy. On the contrary, some segments such as cotton and horticulture have expanded rapidly despite having been directly in the path of the reform process.

A strand of development economics with a long and influential tradition has actually held[39] that the external liberalization of a developing economy would actually be beneficial to agriculture. According to this view, developing economies that have historically pursued import-substituting industrialization, as India had done, inherently discriminated against their agricultural sector. First, across-the-board protection of industry, without commensurate protection of agriculture, is believed to shift the terms of trade against agriculture, thus lowering the incentive for production. Second, protection of an uncompetitive industrial sector results in an overvalued exchange rate, as the balance-of-payments deficit in manufactures is now kept artificially low. This renders an intrinsically competitive agricultural sector uncompetitive, stunting its growth. From such a perspective, the liberalization of industrial imports is believed to advance the cause of both agricultural production and exports. The first is to be brought about by correction of the historical bias against agriculture by a restoration of the terms of trade. The second takes place as the exchange rate depreciates once the balance of payments for industry moves 'naturally' into deficit following the removal of protection to industry. The latter mechanism is reinforced if, as is often the case, the trade and industrial policy reforms are combined with macroeconomic stabilization. Now, any tendency of the exchange rate to depreciate automatically as a result of import liberalization for manufactures is reinforced by the devaluation that occurs as part of the standard package of macroeconomic stabilization in the presence of a balance-of-payments deficit. This is believed to act as an incentive for agricultural exports.[40]

Implicit in the argument of Little et al. (1970), however, is the premise that not only does the less developed country's (LDC) comparative advantage lie in agriculture and that is it optimal to stick with this, but above all that LDC agriculture is globally competitive. The latter would be necessary to ensure that trade liberalization will not affect it adversely. On the other hand, the theory sees such liberalization as positively beneficial, for exchange rate correction is expected to increase exports of LDC agriculture. We might mention that the last cannot be so easily assumed, as seen from the history that in some years in the 1990s the price of Indian wheat was higher than the world price. World prices themselves are often low due to the subsidization of their agricultures by the developed countries, especially the European Union. This feature is not internalized sufficiently in latter-day expositions of the view of Little et al.

It will be immediately recognized that the reforms initiated by the Government of India in 1991 fall entirely within the prototype described earlier. Structural adjustment had driven liberalization of the trade and industrial policy regime while the macroeconomic stabilization package involved a real depreciation of the rupee. Going by the arguments of the strand of development economics we have just reviewed, the economic reforms could only have benefited agriculture via enhanced incentives for production and export. Apart from the internally driven reforms in India in the early 1990s, the decade was to witness a further change in the economic environment. This was the accession of India to the WTO rules in 1995. The main implication of this was further trade liberalization, only of a kind that may be thought of as more aggressive in that it envisaged the ultimate elimination of quantitative controls. However, from a theoretical standpoint, the accession was no more than a further movement along the course of trade reform set unilaterally in 1991. Therefore, going by the argument of Little et al. exposited earlier, the WTO accession may be considered as potentially doubly beneficial to agriculture. First, if industry was historically the more protected among the sectors, agriculture's terms of trade may be expected to improve further upon across-the-board import liberalization. Second, harbouring the assumption of the inherent competitiveness of developing country agricultures, agricultural exports from India would now be expected to rise as developed country markets, hitherto inaccessible due to protection, would be opened up to it.

We have here examined the relationship of agricultural growth with the type of reforms India had experienced since 1991 only to suggest that to focus a priori on the reforms as the likely cause of observed agricultural slowing could be misleading. However, we must not overlook the possibility that the theoretical arguments for their enabling role aside, the reforms as implemented since 1991—including some associated policy changes—may not have been altogether benign towards agriculture. We shall return to this issue at an appropriate stage in the discussion.

Agricultural Performance since 1991

We focus exclusively on crop agriculture. It is of course conceivable that horticulture, animal husbandry, fisheries, and forestry, being the other components of the sector, may assume an increasingly important role in the future but we ignore this possibility here. As the facts related to the growth of crop agriculture since 1991 are by now fairly well known, having also received the attention of the government in the form of the Approach Paper to the Eleventh Plan, we present only such data as necessary to highlight the problem we address here and advance the analysis we undertake.

In Table 4.6 are presented data on half a century of growth in area, production, and yield in Indian agriculture. We have adopted the standard classification 'foodgrains' and 'other crops'. The fifty-year-long span enables a longer view and places the growth since 1991 in a comparative perspective. Data have been presented for three phases. The first, in order of appearance in the table, covers the first fifteen years since 1950, the second period covers close to three and a half decades since the Green Revolution, and the third accounts for the period from 1990s up to the year 2009. Ignoring changes in area which, as may be expected, show almost universal slackening if not shrinkage, we focus on production and yield.

Table 4.6 Agricultural Growth since 1991 in Perspective

	1949–50 to 1964–5			*1967–8 to 2002–3*			*1991–2 to 2008–9*		
Crop	A	P	Y	A	P	Y	A	P	Y
Foodgrains	1.4	2.8	1.4	−0.1	2.4	2.1	−0.1	1.3	1.6
Others	2.4	3.7	0.9	1.3	3.1	1.6	0.7	2.0	1.3
All crops	1.6	3.2	1.2	0.3	2.7	1.9	0.1	1.5	1.7

Source: Figures for the period 1991–2 to 2008–9 are estimated trend growth rates; the rest are 'compound annual growth rates' from *Agricultural Statistics at a Glance* (2003), Ministry of Agriculture.
Notes: A is area, P is production, and Y is yield.

Taking the growth of production first, we find that even close to four decades since the Green Revolution there is no permanent increase in the rate of growth. Armed with the information for the period after 1991, we can surmise that it is its slowing from that date which depresses the rate of growth for 1967–2003. Coming to yield, we may surmise that output growth during this period would have been lower still if yield growth had not accelerated as the growth in area was arrested almost completely. The impressive growth in yield was, of course, the true significance of the Green Revolution. Indeed, the rise in the rate of growth of yield over that during 1949–65 is as high as 50 per cent in some instances. However, yield growth slackened since 1991. To sum up then, there is an across-the-board slowing of area, output, and yield growth since 1991 for each of the two main groups in Indian crop agriculture. The period since 1991 now emerges as a kind of watershed when growth in Indian agriculture, resurgent from the mid-1960s, was arrested.

Concerns of livelihood in agriculture and food consumption elsewhere in the economy arise naturally from the record of agricultural growth since 1991. It also poses a challenge to professional economists to explain an outcome that is contrary to the prediction of the influential economic theory outlined earlier. With a view to an explanation, we proceed to an investigation of the factors that are likely to have determined agricultural growth since 1991, classifying these as 'price' and 'non-price'.

Relative-price movement In seeking an explanation of slow growth we start out by looking at price movements. We do so not because we believe that relative prices have an overarching importance, but to address the claim encountered that price shifts account for the slowing of agricultural growth since 1991. Given yields, relative prices form only one element in the set of incentives faced by the producer.[41] In Table 4.7 are presented indices of prices received and paid out by farmers and the corresponding set of relative prices. The first is the conventional barter terms of trade. The other is the ratio of 'prices paid out' to 'prices received' or an index of input–output prices. Actually, this is only a version of the barter terms of trade itself, with the difference that the latter is arguably a more finely weighted index.

Somewhat unexpectedly for us, the terms of trade and the input–output price ratio show dissimilar movement over the fifteen years since 1990–1, the year immediately prior to the initiation of reforms. On average, the terms of trade are higher for the period after, having displayed a move clearly favourable to agriculture till around the mid-1990s and a reversal after that. On the other hand, the input–output price ratio has moved to agriculture's disadvantage. It is, however, important to recognize this exercise for what it is. We are here comparing the average for a fifteen-year period with a single data point, namely, the figure for 1990–1. Also, both indices have shown a cyclical behaviour that is obscured by taking averages.

We could as well treat the data in yet another way. First, a statistical analysis revealed that while there is no trend to the barter terms of trade since 1991, there is a very mildly negative one, indicating a worsening for agricultural producers, in the case of the input–price ratio. Eyeballing the data suggests that this is due to a shift occurring from 2000. Second, if we are to take a longer view of the movement in agriculture's relative prices, we find that the 1990s are not an exception to the trend improvement in

Table 4.7 The Evolution of Farm Relative Prices

Year	*Index of prices paid*	*Index of prices received*	*Input–output price ratio*	*Agriculture's terms of trade*
1981–2	88.5	54.9	1.61	88.7
1982–3	91.1	60.3	1.51	91.4
1983–4	91.0	64.2	1.42	91.6
1984–5	92.3	68.0	1.36	93.9
1985–6	94.3	70.4	1.34	93.6
1986–7	98.7	76.7	1.29	95.7
1987–8	102.3	86.0	1.19	97.4
1988–9	96.9	90.3	1.07	98.3
1989–90	99.2	97.5	1.02	99.4
1990–1	104.0	112.3	0.93	101.9
1991–2	119.4	130.6	0.91	105.6
1992–3	139.5	138.7	1.01	103.9
1993–4	152.9	151.4	1.01	103.6
1994–5	166.1	171.1	0.97	106.6
1995–6	174.2	182.9	0.95	105.3
1996–7	181.5	190.6	0.95	103.1
1997–8	192.0	205.9	0.93	105.6
1998–9	197.1	220.8	0.89	105.2
1999–2000	203.9	219.8	0.93	102.7
2000–1	230.4	225.0	1.02	100.9
2001–2	236.4	235.3	1.00	102.6
2002–3	253.2	247.9	1.02	103.6
2003–4	259.1	251.2	1.03	101.0
2004–5	272.1	260.1	1.05	100.7

Source: *Report of the Commission for Agricultural Costs and Prices*, April 2007.
Notes: 'Prices paid' are for intermediate purchases which may be treated as variable inputs other than labour; index numbers are based on the triennium ending 1990–1 = 100.

farm relative prices commencing at least as far back as 1980. In the case of the input–output ratio, the improvement by the end of the 1990s is of the order of over 40 per cent. Even after the worsening since 2000, the input–output price ratio has improved by over 35 per cent in the quarter century leading up to 2005. The terms of trade show only a modest improvement over the long run, but are decidedly more favourable to agriculture after the reforms than before. Our analysis thus far suggests that while the prediction that agriculture's terms of trade will improve after trade liberalization is borne out, the predicted impact of this on agricultural growth has not materialized.

We conclude this section with two observations. First, the longer-term history of Indian agriculture reveals no unidirectional link between growth and relative prices. Indeed, there have been phases, such as in the 1950s, when production grew rapidly in the presence of declining terms of trade.[42] This is not surprising, for we know that in the determination of profit a contemporaneous change in the yield can neutralize a change in the relative price. Second, we also know from the history of Indian agriculture that shifts in the terms of trade have reversed themselves[43] in the past, so excessive focus on the relative price over a particular phase may not be appropriate to the long view. Indeed, this seems to have happened already. Between the years 2005–6 and 2008–9 the wholesale price index of both 'primary articles' and 'food articles' increased by more than the general price level.[44]

The Role of Import Liberalization There exists a strong body of opinion in India that the trajectory of agricultural growth since 1991 is largely determined by increased integration with the world economy often termed 'globalization'. In particular it is held that import penetration following India's accession to WTO norms is the main route by which trade has affected domestic production adversely. Though when considering the impact of global integration on domestic agriculture we must consider 'net' trade or both exports and imports, we shall here focus exclusively on imports in order to address the view that import liberalization is responsible for agricultural slowing in the 1990s.

Imports enhance supplies, and for agricultural commodities—the prices of which are determined by supply and demand—may be expected to lower the price relative to the one obtained in the counterfactual equilibrium. In the case of manufactures, the prices of which may be expected to be set by firms with market power, no actual increase in imports is necessary for a lower price following the integration. Mark-ups are inversely related to potential competition and the very integration of segmented markets is sufficient to lead to declining mark-ups and thus prices in the hitherto protected market. Not so for agricultural commodities, for which imports are *sine qua non* for lower prices, as they are ultimately determined by the supply–demand balance. However, as with the price of manufactures, we would expect only a one-shot decline in the price following the integration, unless the integration itself is staggered.

Before investigating the extent of import penetration in Indian agriculture since 1991, we take yet another look at the behaviour of prices of individual crops as prima facie evidence for the putative role of import liberalization. Of course, we have a certain idea of the evolution of prices already, but this is from data at a highly aggregated level and some further disaggregation may be warranted in the context. Thus motivated, we have estimated the trend in the real producer price for a set of prominent crops taken individually. The results are presented in Box 4.1. Against each crop, both the direction of movement and the statistical significance at the 5 per cent level of the estimated trend are indicated.

Box 4.1 Trend in Real Farm Prices for Selected Crops, 1994–2005

Rice	Negative/Not Significant
Wheat	Negative/Not Significant
Pulses	Positive/Significant
Cotton	Negative/Significant
Tea	Positive/Significant
Rubber	Negative/Not Significant

The exercise points to the following. Statistically, there is a negative trend in price for the cotton crop. The prices of pulses and tea show a positive trend. A summary account of price movement since 1991—perhaps more pertinently in the context, 'since the advent of the WTO'—is that for the majority of a selection of Indian crops there is no statistically significant worsening of their real price since the onset of the reforms, at least up to the year 2005.

Though the route by which imports have an impact on domestic production is via prices, and having studied the evolution of some important agricultural prices we observe no significant worsening across the board, we now investigate the extent of import penetration over the same period. From the list of crops for which the trend in prices was examined, we have dropped rubber, as its relative price has risen steadily since 2000, and added sugar to our list. Data on the ratio of imports to production is presented in Table 4.8. Note that for most crops this ratio has been low historically and is low now too. Pulses show a consistently high level of this ratio in the later years while the relative price of this crop has remained steady throughout and has even risen in phases since the late 1990s. Indeed the case of pulses demonstrates the fallacy of the proposition that high imports are always to be interpreted as a worsening of the position for domestic producers.

Table 4.8 Imports to Production Ratio for Selected Commodities (in per cent)

Year	*Pulses*	*Wheat*	*Rice*	*Other cereals*	*Sugar*	*Cotton*	*Tea*
1990–1	5.6	0.1	0.1	0.0	0.1	–	–
1991–2	2.6	–	0.0	0.0	0.0	–	–
1992–3	3.0	2.4	0.1	0.0	0.0	7.1	–
1993–4	4.7	0.4	0.1	0.0	0.0	0.2	5.0
1994–5	3.9	0.0	0.0	0.0	–	4.0	–
1995–6	4.0	0.0	0.0	0.0	1.0	3.2	–
1996–7	4.6	0.9	–	0.0	0.0	0.1	–
1997–8	7.8	2.2	0.0	0.0	2.7	0.5	–
1998–9	3.8	2.5	0.0	0.0	5.8	2.7	0.0
1999–2000	1.9	1.8	0.0	0.7	6.5	12.1	0.6
2000–1	3.2	0.0	0.0	0.1	0.2	13.1	1.3
2001–2	16.6	0.0	0.0	0.0	0.1	22.8	1.2
2002–3	17.6	–	0.0	0.0	0.2	16.0	2.8
2003–4	11.6	0.0	0.0	0.0	0.5	10.8	1.2
2004–5	10.2	–	–	0.0	7.2	6.9	3.6
2005–6	12.0	–	–	0.1	2.9	3.1	2.0

Sources: Balakrishnan et al. (2008); calculated from *Agriculture Statistics at a Glance*, various issues, Ministry of Agriculture.
Note: '–' denotes not reported/not imported/negligible.

Indeed imports may be expected to flood in precisely as domestic prices rise due to a supply–demand imbalance. Of course, we would expect the equilibrium market price to be lower now than it would have been in the absence of imports. But this is a far cry from asserting that imports always cause distress for domestic producers. For two crops, namely tea and cotton, the import ratio has for about five years starting 2000 been higher than the average since 1990. In the case of cotton, there was a surge about that time, but one that has equally dramatically subsided. The latest figures available show that for both crops the ratio is by now far lower than the highest figures recorded before accession to WTO. Except for pulses the ratio of imports to production is by now very low for Indian agriculture in general.

Given the attention it has received, we would like to dwell a little longer on the case of cotton.[45] This is a crop for which the relative price has shown a statistically significant decline. The import ratio has also declined, having stood at a historical high of 22.8 in 2001–2. This apparently contradictory pattern can be reconciled once we take into account the over 100 per cent expansion[46] of cotton production domestically since 2000. A likely scenario is that the expansion in production lowered the relative price and crowded out imports. Such a steady expansion in output in the face of a declining relative price suggests that cotton production is a profitable venture[47] and the story of distress related to cotton production is not uniform across the country. It suggests, more generally, that it would be wrong to always draw a direct line from prices to the profitability of production. No doubt, incentives are central but prices are, apparently from this experience, only one element in the determination of profitability.

From this study of the evidence of price behaviour and imports we do not see much ground for granting the latter a significant role in determining the trajectory of agricultural growth since 1991. However, integration with the world economy has a potential consequence that can be damaging independently of import penetration. One aspect of the new environment, it had been predicted, would be an increased[48] volatility of prices. Increased volatility can adversely affect producers, especially if they are smallholders. To address this issue we present in Table 4.9 the coefficient of variation in prices for some major crops in the Indian and global markets.

Two conclusions may be drawn from an inspection of the coefficient of variation. First, for the overwhelming majority of crops, price volatility in India is substantially lower than in the global market, implying that

Table 4.9 Coefficient of Variation of the Real Price of Selected Commodities (in per cent)

Crop/Commodity	*India*		*World*	
	1998–2002	*2003–7*	*1998–2002*	*2003–7*
Overall food	2.9	2.3	16.5	17.8
Rice	6.6	4.3	34.5	11.1
Wheat	6.0	4.6	16.9	17.4
Edible oil	15.2	7.6	39.9	24.8
Sugar	8.5	9.3	17.0	21.4
Tea	23.5	9.0	21.0	23.3
Cotton	13.2	14.7	24.2	33.2
Rubber	8.1	20.4	17.9	10.9

Sources: Balakrishnan et al. (2008); authors' calculation from the IMF's world price series, available at http://www.imf.org/external/np/res/commod/index.asp and wholesale price statistics for India.

Note: Real price is the price of the commodity relative to the general price level.

the integration is less than full. The latter in any case is also implied by the figures for import-production ratios presented by us earlier. Second, comparing data across periods for India and the world separately, we find volatility reduced for most crops in the Indian market but not so in the global, implying that as the world market has got more volatile, the Indian one has become less so. However, there is a clear divergence within the Indian market between food and non-food crops. While the price of food crops, including edible oils and sugar, has become less volatile, the majority of the non-food crops show increased price volatility, though the degree is worthy of comment only in the case of rubber. Altogether, an increased volatility of prices is not a feature of the environment faced by India's farmers since 1994 at least.

We conclude this section with the following observations. The profile of relative prices over the fifteen years since 1991 indicates too mild a shift, if at all, for us to consider relative-price movements as central to understanding the slowing of agricultural growth since 1991. The role of import liberalization in determining this movement appears to be marginal too, except perhaps for some crops in some periods. Prices are only one element in the producer's calculation. Yield can play the role of mitigating negative price movements. And yield has continued to grow in the 1990s, though at a slower pace (see Table 4.6). Price movements have received a great deal of attention of late, but we believe that an excessive focus could be misleading when it comes to a serious study both of the factors that have determined growth in the past and of the prospects for growth in the future, as price movements are also reversible, as we have found here. We now turn to a study of non-price factors in the determination of agricultural growth, largely via yield, since 1991.

Non-price Factors

Non-price factors governing agricultural growth may be seen as belonging to two categories, namely, those that are part of the longer-term evolution of production conditions in Indian agriculture and those that are related to public policy. Among the former, we consider the size of farm holdings and among the latter capital formation and the knowledge base.

Shrinking Farm Size A persistent trend in Indian agriculture is the shrinking size of the average farm. This is a long-term trend and unless addressed can have permanently adverse consequences for growth of the sector. To illustrate, in Table 4.10a we have presented data on the size distribution of operational holdings.

Table 4.10a The Size Distribution of Operational Land Holdings (in per cent)

Holding category	*1960–1*	*1970–1*	*1981–2*	*1991–2*	*2002–3*
Marginal (less than 1 hectare)	39.1	45.8	56.0	62.8	69.8
Small (1–2 hectares)	22.6	22.4	19.3	17.8	16.1
Semi–medium (2–4 hectares)	19.8	17.7	14.2	12.0	9.0
Medium (4–10 hectares)	14.0	11.1	8.6	6.1	4.3
Large (10 hectares and above)	4.5	3.1	1.9	1.3	0.8
All categories	100.0	100.0	100.0	100.0	100.0

Source: *Some Aspects of Operational Land Holdings in India 2002–03*, NSS Report No. 492.
Note: Entry for 2002–3 is the average of figures for the kharif and rabi crops.

Table 4.10b The Distribution of Operated Area by Holding Size (in per cent)

Holding category	*1960–1*	*1970–1*	*1981–2*	*1991–2*	*2002–3*
Marginal (less than 1 hectare)	6.9	9.2	11.5	15.6	22.2
Small (1–2 hectares)	12.3	14.8	16.6	18.7	20.6
Semi–medium (2–4 hectares)	20.7	22.6	23.6	24.1	22.4
Medium (4–10 hectares)	31.2	30.5	30.1	26.4	22.7
Large (10 hectares and above)	29.0	23.0	18.2	15.2	12.1
All categories	100.0	100.0	100.0	100.0	100.0

Source: *Some Aspects of Operational Land Holdings in India 2002–03*, NSS Report No. 492.
Note: Entry for 2002–3 is the average of figures for the kharif and rabi crops.

Note the significant increase in the share of holdings in the smallest category, and a definite decline in the share of holdings of larger size. Thus, by now the majority of India's farms are in the category referred to as 'marginal'. At the same time, as the smaller farms have come to predominate, due to the fixity of land, they have come to account for the greater part of the area operated. As an indication, note from Table 4.10b that while in 1960–1 marginal farms accounted for well below a tenth of area operated, in 2002–3 they made up only a little less that a fourth of it. Or, viewed top down, while in 1960–1 over 60 per cent of the cultivated area was operated by farms exceeding 4 acres, by 2000–1 the figure is barely 25 per cent.

Together these tendencies amount to a downscaling of production in the sense of cultivation taking place on progressively smaller farm units. This is likely to have had consequences unforeseen in textbook microeconomic theory implicitly addressed to the Western experience. Thus, while standard econometric exercises turn in evidence of constant returns to scale for Indian agriculture, implying that the downscaling that we observe is of no consequence for productivity, some scepticism regarding the implication is advisable as it does not allow for the varying form of labour organization across farm size in India.

Allowing for this possibility, we note from Sen and Bhatia (2004) that as farm size is reduced, members of the family are driven to look outside the farm to supplement their income, resulting in a possible neglect of production management, thus slowing growth. The authors have demonstrated the plausibility of such a scenario by computing for each state the minimum holding size required to maintain a family of five above the poverty line. They find that at least half the Indian states have average holdings below the minimum thus defined. Equally, the states revealed by Sen and Bhatia's estimates as the more dynamic, defined by a rate of growth of agriculture higher than the average, mostly have holdings on average greater than the minimum required.

The shrinking farm size with its consequence for agricultural growth has generally gone unrecognized in recent discussions of the latter. However, it may well be one of the factors that underlie the much reported finding from the National Sample Survey[49] that close to 40 per cent of Indian farmers report that farming is not profitable. In this context, the prospect of an acceleration in the agricultural growth rate, targeted in the Eleventh Plan, is dim unless an intervention addressing this issue takes place.

We draw two conclusions from the evidence on shrinking farm size. First, there is reason to believe that smaller holding size makes it more difficult for the majority of Indian farmers to access new technology and adopt more efficient forms of farm production organization as their capacity to leverage credit is reduced. While these are relatively less capital-intensive actions, their pay-off could be large in relation to the investment. Such investment in land improvement is very likely inconceivable for the largest number of Indian farmers today due to their meagre asset base. The slower growth of yield since 1991 may be, at least to an extent, related to this aspect. Second, an improvement of farm relative prices can do little to stem agricultural decline when structural factors governing production, such as farm size, turn adverse irreversibly.

Alongside the shrinking farm size should be acknowledged the developing environmental stress reported for the agricultural sector. This stress is difficult to record at the all-India level using official statistics, but its existence is obvious from field studies and media reportage. Two aspects of this are depletion of soil nutrients and a declining water table. This contributes directly to potential yield loss that can be compensated, if at all, only via greater expenditure which increases cost of production. It is clear that smaller farms strapped for credit cannot handle the ecological decline by themselves. This is an identifiable consequence of shrinking farm size. Its implication is that the proportional impact on production costs of a given increase in the fixed input is distributed unequally across farms. Smaller farms just cannot be expected to initiate much change. A diminishing economic size of farm and gathering environmental stress constitute a pincer movement that impinges upon the future of agriculture in India. This needs to be addressed directly and lies entirely beyond what can be expected from a liberalization of the policy regime.

We conclude this section with a brief comment on the role of policy vis-à-vis the specific constraints on growth identified here. Actually, economic policy may have contributed indirectly to some aspects of environmental degradation in the agricultural sector. First, the pattern of subsidization of fertilizer production has skewed fertilizer use in the direction of urea, very likely impacting the nutrient balance in the soil. Free or even unlimited subsidization of electricity has meant the depletion of ground water. The depletion of ground water is a negative externality which has no market solution. Concerted action is required as with most environmental issues, and the government is the obvious choice as the coordinator required in such situations.

Next, while the developing environmental stress has received some attention, possible responses to the consequence of shrinking farm size have received much less, if at all. Survey responses indicating low incentive for farming combined with evidence of the average holding size falling below the minimum required in the majority of Indian states imply that economic policy must turn to encouraging an active lease market. Current laws, dating back to some original land reform legislation, may actually be a hindrance to this. For instance, in some states tenancy is not officially recognized. This could hold back output expansion. Originally intended as a blow on the excesses of landlordism implicit in the zamindari system, its premises may not be valid today when the lessors are as likely to be marginal farmers, distinguished from the lessees only by their capacity for cultivation using family labour. It is worth noting that in contemporary China, where property rights in land are not absolute and households possess only lease rights on the land that they cultivate, they are yet permitted to transfer these rights.[50] A consequence of a land-lease market would almost certainly be an increase in the concentration of area operated, but this should be weighed up against its demonstrated advantages rather than being unconditionally opposed.

Capital Formation Capital formation in Indian agriculture is undertaken by both government and the private sector. However, there is an economic distinction between these two cases. Almost all of the public investment is in the nature of a public good, that is, it is non-excludable, and for that reason unlikely to be undertaken by the private sector. Including rural roads, drainage systems, and irrigation networks, public investment is a vital input into agricultural production. Recognition of its importance had made it central to planning for agricultural growth in the past.[51] That private capital formation is important too can be surmised from the very fact that it is undertaken by profit-oriented agents. In this section we review the record of investment since 1991 with a view to understanding its likely impact on the lacklustre growth of agricultural production observed for this period. Data on capital formation by sector is presented in Table 4.11. Aggregate capita formation appears to collapse with the initiation of reforms, remaining depressed throughout the 1990s. Of course, too much ought not to be read into the decline in 1991–2 as it is magnified by an increase in 1990–1 that far exceeds the trend value for that year. Nevertheless, capital formation finally rises above the level of 1990–1 only in 1999–2000, leaving the 1990s as a period of low investment in agriculture. We may expect it to have affected the rate of growth of output. Aggregate capital formation has recorded a strong revival more recently.

The figure for aggregate capital formation, however, masks a difference between the private and public sectors. The history of public capital

Table 4.11 Gross Capital Formation in Agriculture (Rs crore, 1999–2000 prices)

Year	*Total*	*Public*	*Private*
1980–1	27,450	12,521	14,929
1981–2	23,231	12,078	11,153
1982–3	24,924	11,928	12,996
1983–4	26,159	11,944	14,215
1984–5	23,929	11,562	12,367
1985–6	22,855	10,509	12,346
1986–7	22,187	9,848	12,339
1987–8	26,893	10,193	16,700
1988–9	24,023	9,488	14,535
1989–90	23,897	7,968	15,929
1990–1	35,573	7,882	27,691
1991–2	22,338	6,998	15,340
1992–3	28,469	7,333	21,136
1993–4	25,556	8,096	17,460
1994–5	24,377	8,949	15,428
1995–6	24,585	8,731	15,854
1996–7	26,697	8,373	18,324
1997–8	28,650	6,872	21,778
1998–9	28,366	6,926	21,440
1999–2000	43,473	7,716	35,757
2000–1	38,735	7,155	31,580
2001–2	47,043	8,746	38,297
2002–3	46,823	7,962	38,861
2003–4	45,132	9,374	35,758
2004–5	48,576	10,267	38,309

Source: *National Accounts Statistics* (2007).

formation in the 1990s is a continuation of a discernible trend going back at least to 1980–1. The level in 2004–5 is yet close to 20 per cent less than the level in 1980–1. The behaviour of private capital formation is more volatile, collapsing with the onset of the reforms as public capital formation did and remaining depressed during the first half of the 1990s.

However, unlike public capital formation it begins to rise from the mid-1990s, only to stagnate from around the year 2000. Nevertheless, there is a doubling of capital formation in the private sector over the decade from the mid-1990s, and it is difficult to square this with a perception of a widespread distress in the agricultural sector. Of course, we may expect a variation across crops, regions, and even farm households, a diversity that is obscured in the aggregation. That is, the observed surge in private investment may be confined to some areas.

However, the slowing of the rate of growth of output at a time of accelerating private investment requires explanation. We put forth two tentative ones. First, the impact of capital formation, private as much as public, is likely to be staggered into the future, as infrastructure projects in agriculture are of longer gestation than elsewhere in the economy. Second, the impact of the depressed state of public capital formation may not have been fully offset by the rising capital formation in the private sector from the mid-1990s as private and public capital very likely contribute differently to the production process. Public capital is more in the nature of public goods that are unlikely to be provided by the private sector and the economic role of which cannot be replaced by private capital formation. When we recognize that large irrigation projects and road networks are of the main type of capital formation in the public sector, this argument takes on greater force. Of relevance then is the fact that public investment in 2004–5 was yet below its level in 1980–1. The data on public investment in Table 4.11 has been graphed in Figure 4.1.

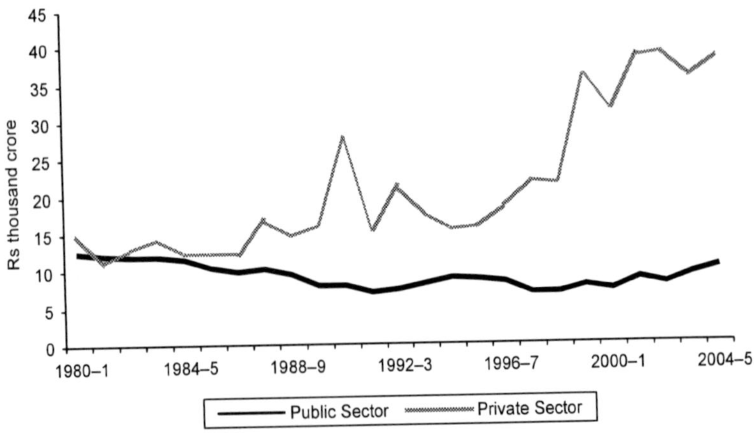

Figure 4.1 Capital Formation in Agriculture since 1980

Viewing together the evidence on private investment and the growth of agriculture, we have reason to believe that the strategy implicitly pursued since 1991 has been inadequate to the task of promoting growth.[52]

We have thus far been looking at expenditure on the capital account. This is not the same as evidence on asset accumulation of which we may attempt a direct enumeration. For this we choose to look at the expansion of area irrigated during the 1990s. For agricultural production, irrigation is arguably the most important[53] input after seed, and the most important element of public capital formation. Before reviewing the data we might mention that 'area under irrigation' very likely measures only the potential reach of an irrigation facility. How close to the potential is actual delivery we cannot infer from this measure. However, it is the only one that we have for water made available via irrigation.

Table 4.12a The Expansion of Irrigation (percentage area irrigated)

Crop/Year	*1970–1*	*1980–1*	*1990–1*	*2000–1*
Cereals	27.6	34.1	41.0	49.6
Pulses	8.8	9.0	10.5	12.3
Foodgrains	24.1	29.7	35.1	43.1
Oilseeds	7.4	14.5	22.9	22.5
Cotton	17.3	27.3	32.9	32.6
Sugarcane	72.4	81.3	86.9	91.3

Source: Economic Survey 2006–07.

Note from the data in Table 4.12a that the rate of growth of irrigated area for all the main crop categories has slowed in the 1990s. For oilseeds and cotton the area has actually declined. This information must be seen in light of the already very low levels of irrigated area in India by international standards. In the mid-1990s, the percentage area irrigated in India was less than in Bangladesh and Nepal, lower than in China, and less than half that in Japan and Korea.[54] Lower yield in Indian agriculture relative to East Asia is not so surprising any more, and the fact of agricultural-yield stagnation in India despite a holding size that is larger on average than in China[55] falls into place. Rice yields in India are exactly half that in Japan, also an economy of smallholder agriculture.

While the slow expansion of irrigation is a serious cause for concern given the low coverage, we have reason to believe that public expenditure may not be the crucial factor governing this lack of movement. In Table

4.12b are presented data on expenditure on irrigation (and flood control, an intervention of almost equal importance to Indian agriculture). Here we find that this expenditure has actually exploded since the 1990s. Clearly now the reasons for the slowing of an already slow rate of expansion of irrigated area must be sought elsewhere. Researchers[56] on irrigation and water usage speak of three deficiencies in the area of public provision of irrigation—deficiency at each of the levels of planning, implementation, and management. This diagnosis points squarely to the role of governance.

Effective governance requires institutional reform and needs to be addressed explicitly if efficiency in the use of the resource most valuable to agriculture after land is to be increased. Inefficient use of water under the current arrangements in irrigation management is said to lead to environmental degradation via water logging and induced salinity. The ultimate objective of this study and the nature of our own expertise preclude our elaborating upon the argument. Our intention is to draw attention to the fact that governance may be as important a factor as resources in the context of extending the frontier of irrigation in Indian agriculture. However, given the near-zero correlation between expansion

Table 4.12b Public Expenditure on Irrigation and Flood Control (Rs crore)

Period	*Nominal expenditure*	*Real expenditure in (1993–4 prices)*
Third Plan (1961–6)	664.7	7,402.0
Annual Plans (1966–9)	471.0	3,699.0
Fourth Plan (1969–74)	1,354.1	8,484.3
Fifth Plan (1974–9)	3,876.5	15,095.4
Annual Plan (1979–80)	1,287.9	4,127.9
Sixth Plan (1980–5)	10,929.9	25,717.4
Seventh Plan 1985–90)	16,589.9	28,349.1
Annual Plans (1990–2)	8,206.0	10,413.7
Eighth Plan (1992–7)	31,398.9	28,353.7
Ninth Plan (1997–2002)	63,009.5	42,817.0
Tenth Plan (2002–7)	103,315.0	55,450.3

Source: Data from *Economic Survey 2006–07.*
Notes: Figure for Tenth Plan is the plan outlay; nominal value of expenditure has been deflated by the wholesale price index at 1993–4 prices.

in area irrigated and expenditure on the same, implied when the information in Tables 4.12a and 4.12b is considered together, we argue for an urgent review of usage of funds allotted to this sector.[57] Public funds have alternative uses, and as we demonstrate below, some areas of agriculture are severely under-funded.

This review of capital formation in agriculture and of the expenditure on irrigation offers us one clue while trying to identify the factors responsible for the slowdown of agricultural growth since 1991. The fact of the recent explosion of spending on irrigation and the history of decline of public investment over a full quarter century suggests that it would be wrong to attribute, as is done, slow growth to the deliberate withdrawal of the state as a policy initiated in 1991, or to see it as the collateral damage of the fiscal correction associated with macroeconomic reforms. Note from Table 4.11 that public investment had begun to decline in the 1980s, actually a time of fiscal profligacy reflected in a ballooning deficit. Altogether, as far as capital formation is concerned, we find evidence of long-term tendencies predating the launching of reforms that are likely to have worked to depress agricultural growth.

The Knowledge Base We now address an issue that has only recently come into the public discourse on agricultural growth in India despite its ever-present relevance, namely, 'research and extension'. Agricultural economists have long pointed to the importance of research and extension to the acceleration of agricultural growth.[58] Our objective here is to provide an indication of how research and extension may have progressed since 1991 as data on these are even more scarce in the public domain than the recognition of their importance.

Rudimentary economics suggests that long-term growth of output in a land-scarce economy can come about only via rising productivity of land. Acreage expansion is more or less infeasible. Though double-cropping can be made possible via irrigation, we have seen that the expansion of irrigation has been very slow of late in India. Acreage actually appears to be at a standstill (see Table 4.6) since 1990. Yield growth has slowed too, compounding the challenge of bringing about faster output expansion. While yield growth in any context requires technological progress, effected via innovation, in India today this imperative is unlikely to be confined to better plant variety, as in the 1960s when the growth acceleration was engineered mostly via the use of high-yielding varieties of seed. It is clear that the production conditions today are vastly different. Three features characterize the present: first, we have had a long phase of stagnant public capital formation implying that the necessary public infrastructure is very likely lacking; second, compared to the 1960s, producers confront a more or less open trade regime and, as a result, face far greater international competition; third, and directly prioritizing the accelerated production of knowledge, the natural resource base is shrinking due to declining farm size and environmental degradation.

Technological progress in the future must encompass the imperatives arising out of these three developments. Now the need for knowledge-based inputs is very likely set to increase substantially, as producers are increasingly driven to get more out of a limited resource base. With smaller farms accounting for the greater part of the operated area, the need for a publicly funded and managed knowledge production and dissemination system is indispensable. Small farmers lack the capital to generate, or often even to purchase, the relevant knowledge inputs when they may be made available. Of course, India possesses a not insubstantial public research and extension network, the former being largely centred around the Indian Council for Agricultural Research. Researchers[59] who have studied the functioning of this network are critical of what it can achieve under its present form of organization. They also point out that such attempts to improve the effectiveness of public sector research and extension have focused too closely on their components, losing sight of the big picture of what needs to be done to put in place preconditions for innovation. As an example of how agricultural production today is held back by chronic constraints attributable to a fragile and diminishing resource base and the role of a public support system in addressing the challenge, consider this:

> Efforts to improve the resource base are channeled especially through the rehabilitation of micro watersheds. Such rehabilitation reduces soil and water runoff, improves percolation, increases the availability of fodder and water for irrigation, and so results in the introduction of new crops and varieties. Farmers are unlikely to be familiar with technologies that will enable them to take full advantage of the possibilities. Research and extension services can play a major role in providing these from outside. The uptake of farm-level technology could also be better enhanced through improved provision of the genetic resources used by farmers. (Farrington et al. 1998: Section 1.4)

While the case of irrigation expansion is exemplary in communicating to us that today governance is at least as important as funding in the transformation of Indian agriculture, our investigation suggests that the public funding of research and extension expenditure has not kept pace with the increasing need for such support. We now turn to the evidence on this aspect.

In Table 4.13a is presented data on the growth of public expenditure on research and extension, at constant prices, decade-wise for four decades up to 2005. In each of the main components of knowledge production and dissemination, namely, 'research and education' and 'extension and training', growth has slowed since 1990. In the case of extension services, the slowdown is particularly sharp. It is interesting to note that for this category the growth of expenditure was highest by far in the 1960s, the time of the last acceleration in the agricultural growth rate, suggesting that extension is a crucial component of an enabling policy. The rate of growth of real expenditure on extension services has declined threefold since 1990.

Table 4.13a Growth of Real Public Expenditure on Research and Extension

Year	*Research and education*	*Extension and training*
1960s	6.5	10.7
1970s	9.5	–0.1
1980s	6.3	7.0
1990–2005	4.8	2.0

Sources: Balakrishnan et al. (2008); figures for 1990–2005 are the authors' estimates from 'Finance Accounts', Government of India, and the rest are from Pal and Singh (1997).

Notes: Growth rates per annum; figure for 'extension and training' in the 1980s is for the period 1980–94.

An indication of the sufficiency of expenditure on the production and dissemination of knowledge is given by the ratio of this expenditure to agricultural output. This data is presented in Table 4.13b. Note that currently public expenditure on research and extension together—being the sum of the two columns in the table—stands at well below 1 per cent of GDP in agriculture. Though it has risen somewhat steadily over the past four decades, the post-2000 figure is above trend largely due to the slowing of output growth.[60] While only a technical appraisal can provide a norm for such expenditure, at less than 1 per cent it is well below international standards. As cited in Pal and Singh (1997), the figure for research expenditure as share of GDP for the agricultural sector was 2.4 for the developed countries in the year 1991. By comparison, spending

Table 4.13b Public Expenditure on Research and Extension as Percentage of Agricultural GDP

Year	*Research and education*	*Extension and training*
1960–2	0.21	0.09
1970–2	0.23	0.14
1980–2	0.39	0.11
1989–91	0.41	0.16
1992–4	0.40	0.15
1995–7	0.38	0.14
1998–2000	0.44	0.15
2001–3	0.52	0.13
2004–6	0.52	0.13

Sources: Balakrishnan et al. (2008); figures from 1992 onwards are the authors' estimates from 'Finance Accounts', Government of India, and the rest from Pal and Singh (1997).

in India is woefully[61] inadequate. A benchmark is also provided by the targeted spending on education of 6 per cent of GDP in the Eleventh Plan.[62] Finally, from Table 4.13b note that unlike spending on 'research and education' within agriculture, the spending on 'extension and training' has declined steadily since 1991. The estimated figure for the growth of spending on both 'research' and 'extension', especially the latter, is very likely being propped up by the unusually high increase in 2005–6 (see Table 4.13c).

It is clear that public support for expanding the knowledge base for agriculture is shrinking since 1991, precisely when, for reasons stated by us, the need for it is rising. As it would be useful to ascertain whether this is due to a generally tightening financial position of a government committed to expenditure curtailment, we look at the evolution of the share of 'research and extension'[63] in the total revenue expenditure of the Centre and the states. This data is presented in Table 4.13c. Note that for almost two decades by now, this figure has hovered around 0.5 per cent or less. This speaks of choice rather than contingency having determined the magnitude. While no absolute standard exists, the figure for spending on research and extension does appear very low. For perspective, if expenditure on agriculture is 20 per cent of total revenue expenditure, at 0.5 per cent the spending on research and extension would amount to 2.5 per cent of the former. Or, compare the figure of 0.5 per cent with the target for public spending on education set at 20 per cent of total spending

Table 4.13c Public Expenditure on Research and Extension (Rs crore)

Year	*Research and education*	*Extension and training*	*2 + 3 as percentage of total revenue spending*
1	2	3	4
1987–8	411	156	0.51
1988–9	477	191	0.52
1989–90	566	225	0.53
1990–1	697	254	0.54
1991–2	772	275	0.52
1992–3	836	307	0.50
1993–4	957	352	0.50
1994–5	1,091	410	0.49
1995–6	1,204	451	0.48
1996–7	1,327	476	0.46
1997–8	1,505	559	0.44
1998–9	1,887	714	0.50
1999–2000	2,356	691	0.51
2000–1	2,564	603	0.50
2001–2	2,520	648	0.46
2002–3	2,680	613	0.45
2003–4	2,838	660	0.43
2004–5	3,057	685	0.44
2005–6	3,509	905	0.45

Source: Balakrishnan et al. (2008); authors' calculation from 'Finance Accounts', Government of India.
Note: Figures are for Centre and states combined.

in the Eleventh Plan. Though the already miniscule rate of spending on research and extension has contracted by over 15 per cent since 1990 to a level less than the figure for the early 1970s, our judgement is that the low outlay on 'research and extension' has less to do with the reforms than reflecting a structural feature of the policy vis-à-vis agriculture in India. Clearly, we have not invested sufficiently in the production of knowledge for agriculture.

The set of three exercises undertaken here with the data on public expenditure on research and extension points to the shrinkage of an already meagre outlay. While expenditure on a service cannot reflect the quality of the output, especially of knowledge-based inputs, it remains the only indicator of the availability of the service itself. The shrinkage is occurring at a time of turbulence in the economic environment and a developing fragility of the bio-physical, when the need for publicly provided support services to production is greater. This is a matter of concern and compounds the existing challenge faced by the national innovation system for India's agriculture. In the discourse on the factors underlying the growth of agriculture since the initiation of the economic reforms in 1991, it has received less attention than it deserves.

A strong conclusion emerging from this investigation of the factors underlying agricultural growth since 1991 is that reliance on the policy regime to bring about the faster growth aimed at in the Eleventh Plan is likely to be inadequate. We find that along with trade and industrial policy reforms there has occurred a rise in agriculture's terms of trade, as predicted by Little et al. (1970). This, however, has not raised the rate of growth of yield. In fact, see in Table 4.6 that yield growth has slowed since 1991. That greater integration with the rest of the world cannot by itself bring about a growth transition in agriculture can by now be asserted with some confidence. Nor is there much evidence that liberalization per se will bring about an expansion of agricultural exports. The barriers to the expansion of agricultural exports from India are more than just the nature of the foreign trade and exchange rate regimes. The global commodity markets are highly distorted due to subsidy in the EU, US, and Japan. Equally, as pointed out with respect to wheat, market intervention via procurement in India may have ended up leaving some of its products uncompetitive. These two instances—the slowing of yield growth despite an improvement in agriculture's terms of trade and disappointing export growth despite trade liberalization—suggest that something more than just a liberal policy regime, the proclaimed destination of the 'economic reforms' in India, is needed to raise the average annual rate of growth of agriculture to the 4 per cent aimed at in the Eleventh Plan.

The approach of Little et al. (1970) to agricultural transformation ultimately rests on correcting the disincentive to agriculture under a regime of import-substituting industrialization. The *deus ex machina* there are agriculture's terms of trade. Traditionally in the political sphere in India, the demand for better prices has been associated with the right wing as it was seen as exclusively favouring 'surplus farmers'. In India today, however, the demand for higher farm prices comes mainly from the left. Either way, apart from the severely damaging impact of higher prices for poor consumers, the precise role of prices in the much needed agricultural transformation needs to be better understood. A valuable perspective on this has been provided by Timmer (1988: 302):

> Agricultural output can increase along a given supply curve or with a shift in the supply curve to the right. The scope for increasing output along a fixed supply curve by continuing to raise prices is extremely limited in fully commercial and technically advanced farming systems; nearly all long-term growth in crop and livestock production comes from investment that expands capacity and from technical change that increases output–input ratios. The importance of prices for transforming agriculture is not in triggering the short-run response of farmers, although this is sometimes quite dramatic in situations where severe distortions are eliminated, but in conditioning the investment climate and expectations of all decision-makers in the rural economy about the future profitability of activities in the sector. Positive expectations lead to rapid investment in technical change when it is available.

Our findings point in a definite direction with respect to what is needed for another much needed agricultural transformation in India, the last having occurred over four decades ago. Agricultural production in India has been affected by a downscaling due to shrinking farm size and slowing expansion of public capital, particularly irrigation. Add to this our awareness of severe environmental stress in the form of land degradation and water shortage and we should be concluding that the material conditions faced by producers require greater attention than economic incentives. We have also pointed to the importance of governance in the effective functioning of India's irrigation networks. The pre-requirement for an assault on unfavourable material conditions is an imaginative and enabling research and extension system. It is not obvious that India possesses one any longer. Here, apart from the poor governance, we find that public expenditure has historically been low by international standards and has been growing at an even slower rate since 1991.

Overcoming the drag imposed by the material conditions of production in Indian agriculture is a challenge and would require a hands-on approach. To persist with detached top–down approaches such as a shift in the policy regime towards greater integration with the rest of the world is to overlook entirely the question of the production conditions. It seems that in Indian agriculture we have reaped what the policymaker has sown.[64] For at least a quarter of a century since 1947, an effort was made to address the material conditions in Indian agriculture. The earliest concerted approach was the Intensive Agricultural District Programme, which peaked in the 1960s and laid the seed bed of the Green Revolution that followed.[65] However, these remarkable early successes appear to have made us complacent. We can no longer afford to remain so.

I now turn to the second of the two foundations of high long-term growth identified earlier in this study, namely, education.

Educational Preparedness for Growth

India in a Global Comparison

The role of education in growth and the importance of spreading it widely across society has already been raised in Chapters 1 and 2. I now return to this issue in the context of an evaluation of the prospects for accelerated growth in India today. The aim is to investigate whether, going by the experience of the developed countries of the world, India is in a state of sufficient educational preparedness. Some historical material is evoked as the present in India cannot be evaluated without understanding how we got here in the first place.

In assessing the educational preparedness for growth in a country, we can do no better than start with the figures for literacy. To place India in an international comparison, in Table 4.14 is gathered data on adult literacy by major regions of the world, including separately for India, in the early part of the present century. Find that India has the lowest literacy rate of all the regions in the world except Sub-Saharan Africa and West Asia. It is about a fourth lower than the world average and a full third lower than the figure for East Asia, a region whose long-term growth rate is alluded to aspirationally by India's policymakers. It is hard to explain away India's low literacy rate as a consequence of low income

Table 4.14 Adult Literacy Worldwide

Region	*Literacy rate*
World	82
Arab States	70
Central and Eastern Europe	97
Central Asia	99
East Asia and the Pacific	92
Latin America and the Caribbean	90
North America and Western Europe	99
South and West Asia	59
Sub-Saharan Africa	61
India	61

Source: *Global Education Digest 2006*, UNESCO.
Note: Adult is defined as 15 years and above; data is for the period 2000–4.

as there exist economies in Sub-Saharan Africa which have comparable literacy levels with far lower per capita incomes.[66] This finding points to the lack of a collective commitment to eliminate mass illiteracy in India, and its consequences have been significant. As observed, even in the early 1970s, by educationist the late J.P. Naik (1975: 5–6):

[T]hroughout the post-Independence period we have been spending less than one percent of the total educational expenditure on adult literacy classes and making only about half a million people literate every year. Adult education proper, which can be given with or without formal literacy, was not even attempted. The results have been disastrous. Literacy has increased from about fourteen percent in 1947 to only twenty nine percent in 1971 or roughly about five-eighths percent a year when population has been increasing at more than two percent per year! We have, therefore, more illiterates in our midst today than we had in 1947: and we still have the dubious distinction of harbouring more than half the illiterate population of the world.

The neglect of illiteracy is marked in relation to the low cost of making an adult literate. Naik had estimated that at the time of his writing, in 1974, this cost would have amounted to no more than Rs 30–40, leading him to comment that 'it would be difficult to conceive of so economical a method of social transformation' (Ibid.: 5).

Taking a broader view of educational attainment than mere literacy, we may look at the distribution of the Indian population in 2004–5 according to level of education, presented in Table 4.15.

The low level of educational attainment in India stares at the reader from the data in the table. A summary statistic would give further shape to the picture we see. Assuming a distribution of the population between

Table 4.15 Distribution of Persons by Level of Schooling (per 1,000)

	Illiterate	*Primary school*	*Middle school*	*Secondary school and above*
Rural				
Male	364	361	140	134
Female	550	293	89	67
Total	455	328	115	102
Urban				
Male	195	300	160	345
Female	307	294	144	255
Total	248	297	152	302

Source: *Employment and Unemployment Situation in India, 2004–05*, NSS Report No. 515.

rural and urban India according to the ratio 70:30, we would find that over 70 per cent of the population of India in 2004–5 has had no more than primary schooling. That is when it is not illiterate.

We can imagine two aspects of commitment to a societal issue, namely, a commitment to provide resources for a cause and a commitment to ensure results from the intervention. As we will see, these are not the same and the absence of either can derail the prospect of attaining the underlying goal common to both these aspects; in this case, the effective education of a population. The process by which resources committed are effectively used to attain the objective of the provision may be termed governance. It is intuitive that providing resources is not the same as securing the goal. Between the provision and the outcome lies governance.[67] In a brief evaluation of how much commitment there has been towards education on both these counts, I first turn to the question of the provision made for education in India in terms of public expenditure. Two indicators are chosen, namely, total public expenditure on education as a share of national income and the former as a share of all public expenditure. The data is presented in Tables 4.16 and 4.17, respectively.

Table 4.16 Public Expenditure on Education as Percentage of National Income

	1970	*1980*	*1990*	*2000*
Ethiopia	1.8	3.3	4.9	4.8
Kenya	5.0	6.8	6.7	6.4
Bangladesh	1.4	1.5	2.0	2.5
India	2.8	2.8	4.0	4.1
Pakistan	1.7	2.0	2.6	1.8
Thailand	3.5	3.4	3.6	5.0
Korea Republic	3.6	3.7	4.2	3.8
Peru	3.8	3.1	3.8	3.3
Brazil	2.7	3.6	4.6	3.8
Argentina	3.3	2.7	1.1	4.6
UK	5.3	5.6	5.4	5.3
France	4.9	5.0	5.8	5.8
USA	6.6	6.7	5.3	4.8
Japan	3.9	5.8	4.7	3.5

Sources: United Nations: *Statistical Yearbook*, various issues; and UNESCO: *Global Education Digest*, various issues.
Notes: For the minority of cases where data was unavailable for the first year of a decade, data for the closest year, where possible within the decade itself, has been entered.

An attempt has been made to retain the same set of countries included in the discussion of structural transformation with growth in Chapter 1.[68] Where some countries are missing from the tables, it may be read that data for all the countries was not available from the same source.

From Table 4.17 we find that though public expenditure on education has increased in India since the 1990s, historically, India has spent less than most countries in our sample. To be precise, India has spent less than almost every one in every region, including Sub-Saharan Africa. Only the other two countries of South Asia in the sample have spent less, pointing to the presence of a factor common to all countries in this region that has not been erased by their partition along religious lines. While public spending on education in India has increased since 1990, it continues to be lower than in most of the economies of Sub-Saharan Africa and the OECD.

Now turning to a second of the two indicators of the first aspect of commitment to education, namely, provision, we find from Table 4.17 that the share of education in total public expenditure in India has

Table 4.17 Expenditure on Education as Percentage of All Public Expenditure

	1970	*1980*	*1990*	*2000*
Ethiopia	12.9	10.4	9.4	13.8
Kenya	17.6	18.1	16.1	22.5
Bangladesh	13.6	7.8	10.3	15.7
India	10.7	10.0	10.9	12.7
Pakistan	4.2	5.0	–	7.8
Thailand	17.3	20.6	20.0	28.3
Korea Republic	21.4	–	14.8	17.4
Peru	18.8	15.2	–	–
Brazil	10.6	–	–	10.4
Argentina	16.0	15.1	10.9	13.6
UK	14.1	13.9	11.2	11.5
France	–	–	10.4	11.4
USA	19.4	–	12.3	15.5
Japan	20.4	19.6	16.5	10.5

Sources: United Nations: *Statistical Yearbook*, various issues; and UNESCO: *Global Education Digest*, various issues.

Notes: For the minority of cases where data was unavailable for the first year of a decade, data for the closest year, where possible within the decade itself, has been entered; '–' indicates not available in the source.

mostly been lower than in all the countries in the sample outside South Asia.

Once again, an increase in the share of education is evident for India in 2000. However, as most of the countries raised their relative spending on education, the increase does not alter India's ranking on this score. Interestingly, the gap between India and the economies of Sub-Saharan Africa has only widened. As a continuous time series could not be put together for China, a long-term comparison of the Indian experience with that of China was not possible. However, it is clear that the share of public expenditure devoted to education in the East and South-East Asian states represented in our sample has outstripped that in India very substantially. What the cross-country evidence on both the indicators of public expenditure on education presented here enables us to see is that if we were to find lower levels of educational attainment in India than elsewhere, it should not surprise us. There has been relatively less public provision for education here to start with than almost anywhere else in the world.

Table 4.18 Public Expenditure per Student as Percentage of GDP per Capita

	Primary	*Secondary*	*Tertiary*	*Pupil–teacher ratio*	*Adult literacy rate*
Kenya	24.7	23.8	27.7	29	74
Bangladesh	8.3	13.4	42.5	56	–
India	13.7	23.0	85.8	40	61
Thailand	15.9	13.0	31.1	21	93
Korea Rep.	17.2	16.9	7.4	32	100
Peru	6.4	8.7	14.0	10	88
Brazil	11.2	11.1	50.7	26	89
Argentina	10.9	14.9	13.1	22	97
UK	16.3	15.4	28.8	19	100
France	17.8	28.6	29.3	19	100
USA	21.6	24.9	25.9	15	100
Japan	22.1	21.6	17.1	21	99

Source: UNESCO: *Global Education Digest*, various issues.
Notes: Pupil–teacher ratio is for primary schools in the year 1999–2000. Adult literacy is the average over 2000–4. Expenditure figures are for the financial year 2001–2 for India, Bangladesh, Brazil, and Korea, and 2003–4 for the rest.

A picture linking the level of educational preparedness to the degree of commitment the project has received in India emerges clearly from the data presented by us. However, before moving on to study the second aspect of commitment that we had flagged, namely, the commitment to ensure results, we look at the 'type' of provisioning that has occurred. Aggregate expenditure data, such as we have looked at so far, can hide the distribution of the provisioning across levels of education. 'How even-handed has been the expenditure allocation?' is the question of interest here, and data on one indicator of this is presented in Table 4.18 for India and the set of economies that we have been tracking thus far. The specific measure adopted is 'public expenditure per student as a percentage of GDP per capita'.

The attraction of this measure is that it is normalized for the level of per capita income in a country, rendering it a measure of both the adequacy of provision and the capacity to spend at the same time.

A comparison of this measure across countries shows a skewness of public expenditure towards higher education in India that is far greater than elsewhere in the world. The comparative degree of skewness is actually quite staggering. Spending on higher education exceeds that on primary education by a factor of six in India. For the OECD countries in the sample, the highest factor of excess is only one and a half times. In Japan, spending is actually skewed towards primary education. The degree of bias in India has not been recognized. It may also be noted that as the figures are for the early twenty-first century, it cannot be argued that the skewness evident in India reflects the early expenditure on building up a virtually absent, and vitally needed, higher education sector. In any case, with adult literacy in 1947 at less than 15 per cent and infrastructure for primary education at a nascent stage, primary education deserved to have been seen as a priority. The data presented also allows us to compare with the rest of the world the absolute spending across levels of education in India. Note for instance that in absolute terms, that is, in relation to per capita income, India spends less per student in primary school than the OECD, East Asia, and the one African country in our sample (Kenya).[69]

The figures in Table 4.18 well reflect the priorities adopted by India's planners and politicians for close to five decades, and its consequences are there for us to see today. Note from the same table that, as a result, the average literacy level in India lags behind that in some countries of Sub-Saharan Africa; of all the countries represented, only Bangladesh has a pupil–teacher ratio that is worse than India's. In this book, as we are ultimately concerned with growth and considering that India is a democracy, we can gather how this neglect of primary education is likely to have impacted productivity growth in the economic sphere and effective participation in the political. In a democracy, participation is a crucial determinant of the type of policies adopted. Public expenditure can be divided into those that strengthen the foundations of the economy and those that satisfy special interests. All indications are that in India it is political economy rather than the incapacity to spend, stemming from a low income level, that better accounts for the observed pattern of public spending on education in India.

I now turn to an evaluation of the public commitment to education in India in terms of its second aspect, namely, the securing of the objective of intervention. This is done by studying some basic outcome indicators. In Table 4.19 are indicators of outcomes at the primary school level in India so arranged as to also cast some light on the progress being made towards gender balance, for which see the data presented in the last three of its columns.

Table 4.19 Outcome Indicators for Primary Schooling in India

Year	*Gross enrolment ratio*	*Dropout rate*	*Pupil–teacher ratio*	*Girls per 100 boys*	*Females per 100 male teachers*	*Absolute male–female literacy gap*
1950–1	42.6	–	24	39	20	18.3
1960–1	62.4	64.9	36	48	21	25.1
1970–1	78.6	67.0	39	60	27	24.0
1980–1	80.5	58.7	38	63	33	26.6
1990–1	100.1	42.6	43	71	41	24.8
2004–5	107.8	29.0	46	88	64	20.0

Source: 'Selected Educational Statistics 2004–05', New Delhi: MHRD, 2007.

There can be no doubt that over the second half of the twentieth century there has been considerable progress in the extension of primary schooling in India. The Gross Enrolment Ratio[70] has by now exceeded the optimum level and the drop-out rate has fallen very substantially. However, the drop-out rate remains significant. Where a failure is noticeable is in the pupil–teacher ratio having worsened secularly since 1950. This is consistent with the data in Table 4.18 that the ratio is high in India today by international standards.

We turn next to the data on gender balance. On this account, there certainly has taken place an impressive improvement within the school. However, at the societal level, the literacy gap between the sexes has worsened after 1950. This harks back to the point already made that no serious effort to liquidate illiteracy has been made in India. We may now infer that within this general pathology, the literacy of women who never enrolled in school did not receive sufficient attention. So when we look outside the school, we find that there is also a gender bias embedded within the generally lackadaisical approach to adult education in the country. However, when it comes to the subordinate educational status of women reflected in the worsening literacy gap between the sexes, clearly something more than throwing money at the problem is needed. Over three decades ago, J.P Naik (1975) had pointed out that the expansion and improvement of education in India would require the mobilization of the community for radical structural changes in society. For a start it would require that an overture be made to social groups that have historically neglected the education of their womenfolk. Given the observed relationship not only between women's education and reduction in fertility but also between educated mothers and the learning capacity of children, the neglect of women's literacy may be expected to have cost India dearly in terms of the quality of its human capital. Only an expansion of female literacy will enable India to break out of this cycle.

While I have termed the indicators scrutinized in Table 4.19 as 'outcome' indicators, it may be argued that they yet represent the quantity rather than the quality of education. Globally, research on education over the past fifteen years or so has undergone a major shift. This has been prompted by the recognition that quantitative indicators, important as they are, are not sufficient as indices of educational attainment. Research has shifted to the quality of education.[71] It is by now accepted that for early education to be worthwhile to both individual and society, it must equip its recipient with cognitive skills. Since around the mid-1990s, there have become available the results of uniform tests administered internationally that show wide differences across countries in the acquisition of these skills (Hanushek and Wosmann 2007). We can see from this data that the number of years of schooling, hitherto the accepted measure of educational attainment, does not effectively serve as a measure of acquired skills. In the cross-country comparisons, the measure of cognitive skills is taken to be represented by scores attained in tests of mathematics, science, and writing ability. While this suggests that we are yet no further than proficiency in the '3 Rs' as the measure of learning and ability, it is a fact that the approach to the evaluation of educational attainment has undergone a shift. The likely greater relevance of the quality of education, over its quantity, to growth is signalled by cross-country regressions in which test scores dominate years of schooling when entered in the same regression.[72] Science scores were found to have a particularly strong positive relation with growth.

Even as we would be advised to accept the implication of the radically new approach to the role of education in growth represented by the recognition of the primacy of quality, we can proceed only haltingly when it comes to an assessment of the situation in India. Beyond remarking upon the step-motherly treatment that has been meted out to primary education in the public policy historically, the task of evaluation is made difficult by the absence of any nation-wide data on learning in schools. Since 1970, India has not participated in standardized international tests of ability, currently the best known among which are the Programme for International Student Assessment (PISA) and Trends in International Mathematics and Science Study (TIMSS). Also, for a country where government agencies gather data on a wide variety of socio-economic variables, including in education, learning indicators are noticeably absent. While there is a move to measure educational development in the country, the outcome indicators still capture only attributes such as school infrastructure and teacher training, important as these are.[73]

In the absence of test scores for India from either PISA or TIMMS, the closest available are reports on learning published by the non-governmental organization (NGO) Pratham. In the context of the programme Sarva Shiksha Abhiyan aiming at universal elementary education in the country by 2010, Pratham currently conducts tests of learning in India's schools at regular intervals. Its Annual State of Education Report (ASER) is among the very few sources of information on learning within the Indian educational system. Some test results from ASER 2004–5 are reproduced in Table 4.20. These pertain to rural India, but as close to 70 per cent of the Indian population is rural, this was considered not wholly inappropriate.

Note that rather than being test scores, these are measures of learning across the student population based on specified abilities in reading and in arithmetic, but for that very reason more directly informative than scores. As the results are easily interpretable, I do not dwell upon them. A qualitative summary would be that a significant proportion of students in

Table 4.20 Learning in the Schools of Rural India

	Reading: % children who cannot read		*Arithmetic: % children who cannot do sums*	
	Level 1	*Level 2*	*Subtraction or Division*	*Division*
Govt: Classes II–V	43.9	65.3	49.7	77.9
Pvt.: Classes II–V	32.1	52.4	38.1	66.9
Govt: Classes VI–VIII	9.3	22.2	17.0	40.0
Pvt.: Classes VI–VIII	6.7	16.8	14.6	33.4

Source: *Annual Status of Education Report 2005—Rural*, Mumbai: Pratham Resource Center, 2005.

Notes: 'Level 1' and 'Level 2' refer to Class I and Class II material, respectively; Subtraction involved two-digit subtraction with borrowing and division required a 3-digit number to be divided by a single digit.

middle school—the cohort of ages 11 to 14—are not able to read material prescribed for the lower primary classes, that is, for those in the age group 5–7 years. Notice that the same picture of unpreparedness extends to arithmetic, with only the proportions varying. This confirms the argument of academic researchers that the number of years of schooling cannot adequately capture the extent of learning. Further, as the data is available separately for private and government schools and we find, interestingly, that learning is far from ideal in the former, the students there outperform the ones in government schools. This helps place the phenomenon of 'endogenous privatization', the flight of users from the government sector, generally. It is not as if the private sector is providing high quality *per se*, it is merely higher than what is available in the public. When this insight is combined with the information in ASER (2005) that 75.1 of the children aged 6 to 14 years in rural India are enrolled in government schools, we can see that from the point of view of attaining acceptable standards there is no alternative to addressing the problem of learning within the structure of the public school system of India.

The low level of learning imparted by much of the Indian school system opens up another approach to the low level of enrolment in India taken to be a proxy for the advance of education, that is, the latter may well be a reflection of the slow growth of demand rather than low commitment to provide schooling on the part of government. The role of demand has begun to get the attention that it deserves only relatively recently from education researchers. Considerations on the demand side have been gathered thus by Pritchett (2004: 177):

The choices made by parents and children about children are based on objectives, constraints and information. Since the vast majority of those not receiving education are children from poor households, it has to be acknowledged that their choices are difficult ones that trade off additional spending on necessities and additional help and labour from children in needed tasks versus more spending on and time devoted to education today. Their choices are also based on the information they have about the benefits to education generally: the abilities, aptitudes and preferences of their children, the quality of the available schooling options.

In general, among researchers, four factors have been identified as likely determinants of the demand for schooling—the quality of education, the income of the household, the rate of return to the education, and the cost of schooling.

This brief foray into the role of demand in the expansion of schooling gives us two very general insights which help us understand the Indian experience better. They are the following. First, given the direct impact of household income on schooling, government actions that improve living standards are almost certainly a necessary element in any plan to raise the level of educational attainment. Quite simply, higher household income means that children can be spared from income-earning activities and sent to school, the opportunity cost of which is the foregone income. Second, consideration of the returns to education suggests that the reason for low enrolment—including dropout at later stages of schooling—in many parts of the world is the low returns to education due to the very low levels of learning imparted there. These two insights help us see the Indian experience in a way that it has not been seen, that is, the low educational attainment, captured particularly sharply by the data in Table 4.15, may also be a reflection of the low demand for education due to its perceived poor quality and, therefore, the low returns that may be expected from an additional year's schooling.

To conclude, learning taken as an indicator of quality is clearly a matter of concern in schooling in India. Though we have been able to study only the most basic indicators of the extent of learning, we can see right away that even well-intended schemes such as Sarva Shiksha Abhiyan by focusing on enrolment reflect a continuation of the quantitative approach, which we now know will not suffice. While acknowledging that it is first necessary to get the child to school, India now needs to closely follow the global shift to a focus on quality. National audit by independent reviewers is particularly needed in higher education towards which, we have shown, public expenditure in India is highly skewed. As money is fungible and has alternative uses, in this case in the primary education sector, we would want to know what has been the contribution of this bias in the public spending. Even the rudimentary data on learning that we have been able to muster for primary education points to very low levels of educational attainment. In our understanding of the public sphere in India, this reflects the low commitment to schooling. Though we have no recent data for India from standardized international tests for school children, data from ASER (2005) does give us an idea of how India would fare in an international comparison of learning. The implication of this for sustained high growth, which above all relies on quality human input, is self-evident. Surely, from the point of view of education, India appears poorly prepared for the highest globally attained growth rates that its political leadership aspires to, not to mention the inclusive growth which is the government's objective as stated in the Approach to the Eleventh Plan.

Table 4.21 Public and Private Expenditure on Education (as percentage of GDP in 2001–2)

	Public			*Private*		
	Primary	*Secondary*	*Tertiary*	*Primary*	*Secondary*	*Tertiary*
France	1.7	2.7	0.9	Negligible	0.2	0.2
UK	1.8	2.5	0.8	0.1	0.4	0.3
US	2.3	2.0	1.2	0.3	0.2	1.5
India	1.5	1.7	0.8	0.1	0.1	Negligible

Source: *Global Education Digest 2004*, Paris: UNESCO.

Given the despair with the state of education in India, it is not surprising at all that public opinion is extremely sceptical of the role of government in this sphere. But how right would it be for us to rest upon this perception when considering options for India? For an indication, we may study the international record on the provision of education. Table 4.21 presents data on the expenditure on education by the public and private sectors in the leading OECD countries. Note that spending by government comes close to vector-dominance over spending by the private sector across all the three levels of education for all the OECD economies in our sample, except the United States where private expenditure on tertiary education exceeds that by the public sector, though only marginally.[74] It is very likely from a sense of its being a merit good, and in recognition of the externalities generated by the spread of education, that the pattern of spending in the world's richest countries today reveals a preponderance of spending by government. Given this picture, the insistence that the expansion of education in India must necessarily be led by the private sector is based neither on the international record nor an understanding of the economic aspects of the provision of education. A balanced approach would be to no longer restrict regulated private entry while concentrating on an overhaul of the government sector, including the regulatory structure itself.[75]

Resources, Governance, and the Revival of Education

After a shift in both attention and resources towards primary schooling, mainly channelled via Sarva Shiksha Abhiyan launched in 2001, by the end of the decade the focus of the government appears to have swung back to higher education.[76] It had become clear that the dwindling resource base of the Indian university system is unable to cope with the student numbers. This can be handled either by reducing the growth in numbers or by better provisioning. Actually, a combination of these methods may be best. Given the need to raise resources, the populist option of leaving fees unchanged for long periods even as there is inflation in the rest of the system, is destructive of the future of education as it undermines the resource base. Indeed, even apart from matching inflation, to reduce the regressive nature of the higher-education subsidies, a substantial hike in fees may be absolutely necessary. Higher subsidy for university education availed of by the middle class implies, given total public expenditure on education, less spending on the school-going poor. The government finally appears to have decided to deal with this thorny problem by infusing fresh funds into the system. However, while resources are undoubtedly part of the story, they are not the sole ingredient for improvement. In this final section we turn to a consideration of the issues involved.

It is clear that there is an issue of governance involved if the Indian university system is to match global standards of instruction and research. While exceptions exist, India's universities have more or less degenerated into degree-awarding bureaucracies. It is not clear how much learning takes place there. Though student apathy is widespread, it would be reasonable to assume that at least some part of it is a symptom and not a cause of the deterioration of the system. After all, it must be accepted as axiomatic that the onus of providing inspiration lies not with the student but with the teacher. While teacher motivation is abysmally low, we must not rush into translating this into a case of failed agency in all cases, at least not fully. It is by now widely accepted via our knowledge of organizational behaviour and social psychology that agents adapt to the conditions in their workplace. In the language of contemporary economics then, teacher performance is *endogenous* and needs to be explained even before it is simply assumed, or merely lamented. Rigidly regulated and bureaucratized work environments leave teachers in India with little freedom, sapping self-esteem. In the context, a recent proposal[77] for performance evaluation of university academics which involves the assignment of quantitative targets without reference to quality is likely to yield poor results with respect to content and delivery. Putting in place incentive schemes and enforcement mechanisms that will provide superior delivery of the subject matter, improve learning capability, and ensure objective assessment of this learning, I term 'governance' in the context of education. Nathan Rosenberg (2000), who has studied the history of technology, argues that what makes American universities world leaders is that they are responsive to the emerging needs of students, the market, and of society. Surely effective governance of educational institutions has a role in ensuring such responsiveness, and India's hopes of becoming a 'knowledge power' are dim unless this is first recognized.

If it is conceded that improved governance is at least as important as more resources in any drive to improve the functioning of the education system in India, it has implications for the success of the plan to raise the level of spending on education to 6 per cent of the GDP.[78] It is clear that increasing spending without serious changes to delivery and monitoring cannot bring about the necessary improvement in the quality of education. As resources have alternative uses, we need to guard against the proverbial 'throwing good money after bad'. In the face of such a reading of the situation, it would appear romantic to suggest that there is a substantial role for the state in education in India. My persistence with such a position, however, is based partly on what economic theory tells us and partly on the present history of education in India itself. The argument from economic theory is that in the presence of externalities, the good concerned will be undersupplied by a profit-oriented private sector. The historical evidence from India that the existence of a private sector in education has not ensured the elimination of illiteracy or the raising of educational standards across the board either at school or in higher education can be understood, at least partly, in light of this prediction of economic theory. Independently of such a reading of the evidence, the evidence per se tells us something of how much more we may reasonably expect of the private sector. For instance, as the level of affluence of the middle classes rises, as it is bound to, private provision of high quality schooling may well be expected. A swift response of the private sector to the need for engineering graduates as an input into the information technology (IT) sector was already evident in the 1990s, though perhaps more in the southern states. About three decades ago, a similar wave was evident in respect of medical education in India. However, what distinguishes the current phase is the generally acceptable quality of engineering education, while the quality of education in some of the private medical colleges of south India has been judged by their national accreditation body to be disturbingly low.

In the focused provision of medical and engineering education by the private sector, the play of the profit motive is clearly evident. It implies that subjects that we may consider as having a high worth as knowledge but less of a market value such as the arts, the humanities, and the social sciences are less likely to be offered by the private sector in India.[79] However, while any disappointment at the thought that future generations of Indians may not be reading Virginia Woolf after all may rightly be dismissed as 'mediated by culture', the disturbing thought that the children of India may be left to languish in poor quality schooling if the state remains idle, cannot be so easily put out of mind. It bears repeating that the role expected of the state in Indian education goes far beyond the throwing of money at the problem. First, it must initiate vigorous reform of India's vast network of government institutions now seriously underperforming. This is a direct role for the state. Here we may borrow from some of the thinking that has already gone into a review of the government machinery as pertaining to the economy. In particular, bureaucratic procedures in the running of our public institutions that contribute neither to equity nor to excellence, but only generate stasis, must be junked forthwith. Second, the Indian state needs to act as a regulator of a private sector that, despite a long presence in education, is fast expanding without any concern for either equity or excellence. This may be an indirect role for the state, but it remains equally important.

While yet on the role of the state we may flag the importance of an audit agency for education in India. Though valuable independent assessments, such as PROBE[80] and ASER exist, we require a statutory body constituted by independent persons—including ones selected globally—to periodically review the functioning of the Indian educational system. These reviews must be widely publicized and the reports made available to the public. Given the guiding role of the profit motive and of vested interests—note my early observation that 'private' is a broad category encompassing interests ranging from the corporate to the religious—it is clear that a private sector has little incentive to reform itself along socially desirable lines. In an electoral democracy, at least the rotating government can be forced to reform their agenda, even when the permanent functionaries of the state have no incentive to do so. This recognition must tilt our focus, at least marginally, in the direction of drastically reforming the existing public institutions in the sphere of education and towards the task of setting up independent public bodies to regulate the private ones. No agency other than the state bears legitimacy for this task.

I conclude this section with a return to the global discourse among economists on education. As commented upon in Chapter 2, surprisingly for a set of workers so closely glued to global currents in their discipline, global research on the importance of education for growth has taken a while impressing India's economists.[81] This research shows that developing countries fare poorly as far as educational attainment is concerned.[82] For a start, the quantity of schooling is low. In South Asia, along with Central America and South and East Africa, less than 50 per cent of a cohort complete Class V. The globally determined development policy of the multilateral institutions has responded to the low levels of educational attainment in these poorest parts of the world with schemes for expanding school enrolment. It is undoubtedly the case that in these regions there is a long way to go to reach global benchmarks set to levels attained in the industrialized countries. However, research on education has more recently unearthed what is perhaps a far greater challenge. This challenge is that of quality, being shorthand for the extent of learning that takes place in school, usually understood as 'literacy in the cognitive skills' proxied by scientific knowledge and mathematical ability. It has been demonstrated that the gap between the rich and the poor countries in terms of the quality of education *exceeds* that in terms of the quantity. While for India information on the quality of schooling is sparse, whatever has been presented here suggests an educational deficit in the country.

India's policymakers need to pay attention to the emerging knowledge on what advances educational quality. The centrepiece of this knowledge is that 'input-based schooling policies' have failed to produce acceptable quality, implying that resource-enhancement by itself is likely to be inadequate. In fact, econometric research[83] reveals the absence of a significant relationship between expenditure per student and PISA and TIMSS test scores even for the richer countries of the world. Of course, the researchers themselves acknowledge that resource inputs such as provision of individual text books and other facilities can and do make a difference at very low levels of spending. However, they remain sceptical of schemes such as across-the-board increase in teacher salaries, reducing class size, and generally spending more on schools without altering the institutional structure governing incentives for teacher performance. Substantial empirical research on this issue exists and points to three institutional features that characterize a successful system of imparting cognitive skills to school children. These are: (i) competition among schools, (ii) decentralization and autonomy in their administration, and (iii) accountability for the outcome. The contention is that in the absence of a right incentive structure conditioned by these features, the infusion of resources could be ineffective. On the relative role of resources vis-à-vis institutions, some light is cast by the knowledge that tilting public expenditure towards higher education in India historically has been able to do little for quality even vis-à-vis that in publicly provided schooling. On the other hand, the importance of accountability for outcomes has been fully grasped in China where a hectic effort is on to align higher education in that country with that in the rest of the world.[84] Considering that China, unlike India, has for long been isolated from the mainstream of the world, the early results are very impressive at least on some indicators. In India, on the other hand, progress in education still tends to get associated with expanding numbers alone.[85] This is related to a reluctance to restructure the institutional terrain.[86] However, it is unlikely that the task can be postponed much longer. We have seen here how for a meaningful educational development in this country, the need to alter fundamentally the institutions that deliver education is inescapable. In the frontline of the global research effort on education a consensus appears to be emerging that institutional structure rather than resources is the binding constraint to higher educational attainment, especially in the poorest parts of the world. India's policymakers need to heed this advice.

Conclusion: Disappearing Restraints and Enduring Constraints

The history of the Indian economy since 1991 makes for a relatively straightforward narrative. In that year was initiated a package of liberalizing reforms that has unwound for over close to two decades by now. The economy has since then substantially changed from the point of view of its trade and industrial policy regime. Faster growth has been slow to appear, but from the year 2003–4 there has been unprecedented growth for five years. However, the average annual rate of growth of the Indian economy since 1991 is yet to match the double-digit rates aspired to by India's policymakers, and implicitly assumed to be achievable given the reforms programme.

An appropriate characterization of where the economy is today would be that while the reforms have significantly relaxed restraints on the private sector, the economy appears to be held back in some old ways. Based on the history of growth across nations, presented in Chapter 1, we had identified the most significant constraints on accelerated growth in India today as slow progress in agriculture and a lack of educational preparedness. These constraints were described and analysed at some length. Our conclusion is that the factors constraining agricultural growth and responsible for the poor outcomes in education are more likely related to better governance than increased public expenditure. This even though, historically in India, both education generally and knowledge generation in agriculture in particular have been under-funded by international standards. Agriculture is also challenged by a shrinkage of farm size, a problem that cannot be solved by financial resources alone. The natural resource aspect of Indian agriculture has no solution within the framework of liberalization per se. In general, the environmental constraint to growth has been more or less ignored in the writing on India's prospects.[87]

In this chapter, we have also highlighted another aspect of the recent growth. It was that growth since 1991 has been most pronounced in the services sector than elsewhere in the economy. This feature assumes relevance when it is recognized that the reforms had mostly addressed the manufacturing sector, having been inspired by the narrative of an inefficient inward-looking industrialization being the defining reality of post-Independence India. Based on the idea of structural transformation with growth in the work of Kuznets, in this chapter we have presented an alternative view of the slow industrialization of India.

By now we have reason to be sceptical of the exhortation often heard in public fora that what we need for accelerated growth is 'more reforms'.[88] Purely liberalizing reforms appear to have run their course and it is effective governance of the supply side in both agriculture and education that is pivotal to bringing about the double-digit growth rates targeted by India's policymakers. Our emphasis on agriculture and education is not meant to trivialize the importance of attending, even urgently at times, to other areas of the economy. In fact, we can think of several areas requiring immediate attention. These range across the economy from the public finances to the interest-rate regime, extending even to privatization and labour legislation. However, our own intention here has been to try and reduce the elements that go into the growth rate to their most basic.[89] Ambitious as the project may appear, we believe that the constraints on accelerated growth posed by agriculture and education are reducible to a common factor. Towards this, the findings in this chapter are of likely to be of some value. They suggest a recursive structure when it comes to the factors that are basic to accelerated growth in India today. First, raising the standard of education is fundamental to agricultural growth, both directly in terms of innovation and indirectly by enabling a significant part of the agricultural labour force to shift out of the sector. In turn, raising the educational standard would require improved governance of the public schooling and vocational training network. Indifferent governance can nullify the windfall of higher funding that rapid growth delivers into the hands of a government. Now, effective governance appears as the binding constraint on the future of growth in the Indian economy.

In the 1950s, perceptions on the future of the economy in India were divided broadly in two. There were those who believed that the fundamental constraint on growth was that of foreign exchange and those who saw it as constituted by the availability of wage goods. Till about the late 1970s, when analytical approaches to studying the Indian economy gave way to a more pragmatic 'policy-oriented' approach that often was ad hoc, it was the former idea that had prevailed. The Green Revolution had very likely contributed to a complacency on the food front. Into the twenty-first century, with India's reserves having crossed $250 billion in 2009, there is no longer a shortage of the foreign exchange.[90] On the other hand, the dwindling per capita availability of foodgrains in India after 1991 and the continued high share of food in household budgets suggest that the wage goods constraint is yet with us. The arguments in this chapter amount to saying that something more than liberalizing reform is needed to tackle this. In the permanent elimination of the wage goods constraint, governance—encompassing both the design and implementation of policy—matters more than any other factor.

Notes

1. See Panagariya (2005), Rodrik and Subramanian (2005), Nayar (2006), and Nayyar (2006) for differing perspectives on this issue.

2. It may be mentioned that the collapse was also somewhat in defiance of the Marxian dictum on the dependence of the political 'superstructure' on the

economic 'base'.

3. See Table 2.2 in Chapter 2.

4. Admittedly, the usage is found more often in the media than among academic economists, but in India by now the media can no longer be ignored as an important influence on public opinion.

5. These were to come almost a decade and a half after 1991, in the form of the Sarva Shiksha Abhyan and the National Rural Employment Guarantee Scheme, respectively.

6. See Kohli (2006b).

7. See especially Kohli (2006a, 2006b), Pedersen (2000), and Sengupta (2008).

8. See Sengupta (2008).

9. Though reference is made to the source of the idea in political theory, no evidence is advanced of an argument in the Indian context that answers to such a description.

10. However, her characterization of the essence of the regime change is worth noting: 'This was far more than a transition from "state" to "market", since much "market reform" had occurred prior to 1991. The most significant aspect of the 1991 reforms is that they signaled a transition to the political ideology of neoliberalism, and to its attendant assumption of a benign (liberal-capitalist) global order' (Sengupta 2008: 39).

11. See Rodrik and Subramanian (2005).

12. See Balakrishnan (2009).

13. Growth had figured prominently in Prime Minister Manmohan Singh's defence in Parliament of his government's record on the occasion of the confidence motion in July 2008 (see M. Singh 2008).

14. See *Economic Survey 1991–92*, p. 23.

15. This high-growth phase was aborted in 2008–9 due to India's exposure to the global financial crisis, and growth is expected to remain depressed in 2009–10 due to the deficient rainfall. See Table 4.1 for annual growth rates since 2003–4.

16. Extension of the data series to the year 2006–7, the terminal year for which final estimates of the CSO were available as this book went to the press, did not alter the result. The rationale underlying the choice of the size of interval is discussed in the Appendix.

17. Recall that within the framework of testing for breaks adopted here, an estimated breakpoint is the terminal year of a growth regime, implying a shift in the rate of growth from the following year. As for the feature that the year 2002–3 thus arrived at precedes by a year the onset of high growth observed when the data is merely eye-balled, note that the breakpoints are estimates and, therefore, come along with confidence intervals. Details of results referred to in this section that are not included in Tables A4.3 and A4.4 of the Appendix are available from the author upon request.

18. For official references to the East Asian record and its attainability, see *Economic Survey 1991–92* and Planning Commission (2006).

19. See Table A4.3 of the Appendix.

20. The methodology is described in the Appendix.

21. The regression results are not presented here but are available from the author upon request.

22. See Jha (1980).

23. The case of software, included under 'Business Services' in the *National Accounts Statistics*, is very likely *sui generis* though, and an identifiable part of the long-term cumulative expansion that may be imagined for much of the rest of the services sector. Here it was the commercialization of the Internet in the mid-1990s that enabled the leveraging for global deployment of an India-specific resource, namely, English-speaking, technically-skilled labour. Neither the technology nor the resource was parasitic on the reforms. But the reforms created an enabling climate—including the idea that the government was expected to facilitate commerce—in which the business opportunity was seized upon. See Balakrishnan (2006) for an economic analysis of the growth of the Indian IT industry.

24. I thank Vinoj Abraham for advice on the data and method that has gone into this exercise.

25. See Panagariya (2005).

26. See Kochhar et al. (2006).

27. See Gopinath and Roe (1997). See also the comment on the global 'agflation' since 2005 in *The Economist* (2007) magazine: 'For as long as most people can remember, food has been getting cheaper and farming has been in decline. In 1974–2005 food prices on world markets fell by three-quarters in real terms.'

28. This is an average; the figure for the poorest households is close to 80 per cent. See the data for the 61st Round—July 2004 to June 2005—in NSS Report No. 508, *Level and Pattern of Consumer Expenditure*, New Delhi, CSO, 2005.

29. Note that for India the absolute value of the share of food in the household budget reported in Table 4.5, though high by comparison, is substantially less than what we have mentioned earlier in this passage. This originates in the diversity of data sources.

30. See Table 1.2 of Chapter 1.

31. Chaudhri (1979: 80–1) reports that schooling had an impact on the Green Revolution in the Punjab–Haryana region. He has concluded categorically from his field studies that mere literacy or even primary schooling is insufficient, stating that 'sustained rural education upto secondary school level is required'.

32. We have by now at least indicative evidence on this. From NSS data on the distribution of wages, employment, and education levels across the economy, Eswaran et al. (2009: 52) infer that while it pays rural workers to get non-farm jobs, the probability of their finding one is directly related to the level of their education. Though the authors are themselves interested in the contribution of growth in the non-farm sectors to poverty removal, their findings have a direct bearing on the question of what governs the transfer of labour from agricultural activity into gainful employment elsewhere in the economy. They pose the question: '[W]here is the bottleneck—in the rate at which the educated are being

generated or in the rate at which employment opportunities are being created?' (p. 52). By tracking the movement over time of the educational premium that attaches itself to the non-farm wage rate, they conclude that it is the former, that is, the supply of educated rural labour, that is the constraint.

33. See Balakrishnan (2009) and *Economic Survey 2007–08*, respectively, for the evidence on investment rates and the annual growth rates.

34. See Balakrishnan (2009).

35. Our own search for a structural break in growth does not reveal any statistically significant break for agriculture after 1991, for which see Table 3.1 of Chapter 3. However, it cannot be ruled out that this is related to our requirement that a growth regime must last for eight years to be treated as distinct. As we will see shortly, when a less formal approach is adopted, a deceleration is discernible after 1991, for which see Table 4.6. At the same time, we know that in the first half of the 1990s, agricultural growth actually accelerated, signalling that the reforms themselves may not have been so malign towards agriculture as believed. See Table 8.3, *Economic Survey 2005–06*.

36. See Planning Commission (2006: 76), for a proposal to double its rate of growth.

37. There is a body of opinion which holds that agricultural performance continues to be important for overall growth of the Indian economy even after the rise of dynamic new segments in the services sector. See, for instance, Chand (2004). Consider also the following evidence. For the first seventeen years since 1991, the direction of change in the annual growth in GDP is correlated more closely with the direction of change in annual agricultural growth than with that of manufacturing and two out of the three segments of services at the two-digit level. Only the growth of 'community and personal services' was more closely linked to the change in the rate of growth of GDP. However, as neither theory nor history suggests any significant role for this segment when compared to that of agriculture, I ignore the correlation observed as without explanatory content. The pattern alluded to points to a continued importance of agriculture for growth in India.

38. In any case, the method we have adopted here can also serve, quite effectively, as a framework for the study of Indian agriculture at a more disaggregated level.

39. See Little et al. (1970) for the original statement; Gulati and Purcell (1993) for a re-statement; Singh (1995) for an exposition; Nayyar and Sen (1994) for a critique of the view; and Balakrishnan (2000) for an examination of its validity in the Indian context. Note that as Singh was finance minister of India in 1995, we would be right to assume that the view was broadly in accordance with the strategy being pursued by the Government of India at that stage.

40. For a perspective, early on in the reform process, that trade liberalization would be good for Indian agriculture, mainly via growth of exports, see Rao and Gulati (1994).

41. In the language of the global trade negotiations that ended somewhat inconclusively at Doha in 2008, 'market access' would be another.

42. See Misra (2004) for evidence.

43. As observed by Srinivasan (2007).

44. See *Economic Survey 2008–09*, Appendix Table 5.1.

45. The attention itself has been related to the spate of suicides among cotton farmers, especially in the Vidharba region of Maharashtra around 2005. It has strongly been suggested that this is related to low prices following import liberalization.

46. See *Economic Survey 2006–07*, Statistical Appendix, Table 1.12.

47. See Sud (2008a) for a report of field studies reviewing the results of adopting Bt-cotton, which has been replacing the traditional strain unexpectedly fast.

48. See Nayyar and Sen (1994).

49. See 'Situation Assessment Survey of Farmers: Some Aspects of Farming', NSS 59th Round, January–December 2003, Ministry of Statistics and Programme Implementation, Government of India, 2005.

50. See Fan and Gulati (2008).

51. See Alagh (1994).

52. 'Apart from the prosperous farmers, many in the government and among the international financial institutions strongly believe that opening-up trade through deregulation and the consequent rise in farm prices will give a fillip to agricultural growth in this country through increased private investment' (Rao 2005: 56).

53. It has been estimated by Vaidyanathan (2007) that almost all of the increase in agricultural production in the last three decades of the twentieth century has come from expansion of irrigated area and the increase in yields that this enables.

54. See World Development Indicators 1998, The World Bank.

55. A feature highlighted in the Year 2007 Report of the Economic Advisory Council to the Prime Minister.

56. See Vaidyanathan (2007).

57. We have stressed irrigation. However, governance issues in agriculture are spread over a wider canvas, for which see Ballabh (2007).

58. Pal and Singh (1997) cite several studies that establish this.

59. See Farrington et al. (1998). As an indication of the weakness of the research and extension effort in Indian agriculture, they point out that wheat cultivars in India are on average three times older than those in the UK, the economy with the highest wheat yields globally. A 'cultivar' is a plant variety produced from a naturally occurring species that has been developed and maintained by cultivation. Continuously recorded yield increases usually require planting younger cultivars, in turn requiring greater research and extension effort.

60. As may be gathered from the data in Tables 4.6 and 4.13c taken together.

61. Of course, the data in Table 4.13b pertains only to *public* expenditure. However, according to Pal and Singh (1997), it accounted for 85 per cent of total spending on research in India in the early 1990s.

62. See Ministry of Human Resource Development (2005).

63. Being the sum of expenditures on 'Research and Education' and 'Extension and Training'.

64. This interpretation of the Indian experience has been inspired by the review of Balakrishnan et al. (2008) by Sud (2008b).

65. See Mohan (1974) for an appraisal of the Programme, though with a focus on the research and extension package embedded in it.

66. Interestingly, a similar pattern has also been observed with respect to the incidence of hunger. While all three economies from Sub-Saharan Africa included in Table 1.1 have a per capita income lower than India's, only Ethiopia records a higher index of hunger. See the Global Hunger Index of the UN presented in Menon et al. (2008). Their association of hunger with malnutrition may be questioned, but the lack of a relation between food deprivation and per capita income is evident in the data they present.

67. Of course, by evaluating commitment in terms of outcomes we are ignoring good intentions that may not have fructified.

68. See Table 1.1 for the original list of countries.

69. This validates Naik's assessment that India has committed too few resources for education, interestingly, made by the eminent educationist even without the comparative international data to which we have such easy access today. Or, it may be said, to the international evidence by now commonplace that the returns to primary education, whether social or private, are the highest across all educational levels. For the latter, in particular, see Psacharapoulos (1980).

70. Defined as the percentage of enrolment in primary school (Classes I to V) to the estimated child population in the age group 6 to less than 11 years. Note that the indicator can yield figures exceeding 100 as enrolment includes that of children outside the specified age range.

71. See Hanushek and Wosmann (2007). I am grateful to Anit Mukherjee for drawing my attention to this work.

72. See Barro (2001).

73. See, for instance, Mehta (2007).

74. To see the US experience in perspective would be vital from every point of view, that is, on the importance of education to economic progress and the role of government in promoting it. And for both these we may turn to Krugman (2009): 'If you had to explain America's economic success with one word, that would be "education". In the 19th century, America led the way in universal basic education. Then, as other nations followed suit, the "high school revolution" of the early 20th century took us to a whole new level. And in the years after World War II, America established a commanding position in education. But that was then. The rise of American education was, overwhelmingly, the rise of public education—and for the past 30 years our political scene has been dominated by the view that any and all government spending is a waste of taxpayer dollars. Education, as one of the largest components of public spending, has inevitably suffered.'

75. For a discussion of the history and nature of the educational deficit in India and the issues related to its redressal, see Balakrishnan (2007).

76. Reflected in the highly publicized announcement in 2008 of an expansion in the number of central universities, IITs, IIMs, and Institutes for Science Education and Research.

77. See Mehta (2009).

78. See Ministry of Human Resource Development (2005).

79. Surely, there is something cultural in this. For we know that the leading educational foundations of the West have always prized learning in the non-scientific disciplines.

80. Public Report on Basic Education; see De and Dreze (1999).

81. The notable exceptions are Dreze and Sen (1995), though they have stressed social opportunity more than growth.

82. See Hanushek and Wosmann (2007).

83. See Hanushek and Wosmann (2007).

84. The innovations in the structuring of universities in China, as described in Lee et al. (2008), are truly radical in the sense of constituting a break from the past.

85. We have already referred to the move to increase, at short notice, the number of central institutions in higher education.

86. This had been well understood by Naik (1975) over thirty-five years ago when he observed that 'a major reason for the failure to improve standards' is the unwillingness to provide investment in 'the human' inputs, preferring to rely on 'financial inputs alone'. What the programmes for expansion need is expenditure on salaries, buildings, and equipment. All these can be had for money. However, in Naik's view, improving standards requires human inputs. These he saw as 'human effort and intellectual inputs' comprising able teachers, committed students, and engaged parents. What do the latter have to do with 'institutional terrain'? They do the following. Motivation and performance on the part of teachers, students, and to an extent even parents reflect the norms, incentives, and performance-enforcement mechanisms prevalent in our educational institutions.

87. For rare exceptions, see Pachauri (2004) and Roy (2007).

88. See, for instance, *The Hindu* (2009a).

89. In the context, the following observation by a former civil servant and current parliamentarian is apposite: 'It would be naïve to believe that some pending legislation in the areas of insurance, pension and banking hold the key to India's growth [strategy]' (see N.K. Singh 2008).

90. I am indebted to Arunava Sen for this perspective on thinking about the Indian economy.

Epilogue
Inclusive Growth as Unfinished Business

If I were making a country, I'd get the sewage pipes first, then the democracy, then I'd go about giving pamphlets and statues...

—Balram Halwai *alias* Munna to Wen Jiabao, Prime Minister of China, Arvind Adiga (2008), *The White Tiger*

A decade and a half into the reforms that had liberalized its trade and industrial policy regime, India has been at the top of the league of fast-growing economies of the world. However, it is now officially acknowledged that this growth has not been sufficiently inclusive. The goal of inclusion has been explicitly entered in the Approach[1] to the current Eleventh Five Year Plan, for the period 2007–12. No criterion has been offered, though, by which we may judge a growth process for its inclusiveness. There is instead only a suggestion in the document that the route to inclusiveness is via a higher rate of growth. This view is explicit in the official pronouncements of the architects of the reforms. Thus, we have the statement by Prime Minister Manmohan Singh in Parliament, mentioned at the beginning of Chapter 4. To this may be added the following statement by the then Finance Minister P. Chidambaram: 'India must touch a 10 percent growth and sustain it for 10, 20 and 30 years' to make poverty part of India's history. The minister had gone on to say that growth was not an end in itself but a strategy to 'raise resources and acquire the capacity to spend more money on the provision of goods and services that will mitigate the hardship of millions of poor people and bring some cheer in their lives'.[2] In this epilogue to our study we consider two issues pertaining to the idea of inclusive growth, namely, how best it can be understood so that economic policy can address it and whether we may reasonably expect that high growth *per se* will deliver it within an acceptable timeframe.

Criteria of Inclusiveness

To assess the prospects for inclusive growth in India today we need an understanding of what it entails. Two criteria are proposed here. First, for growth to be considered inclusive, it must carry with it the largest number. With a view to concreteness, we may reduce this to the criterion of employment. For, though individuals benefit in various ways from faster growth, in an economy where welfare is yet to be institutionalized, gaining employment is the surest way to be included. Note that the criterion proposed here is extremely mild. We could, for instance, have adopted 'maximin', which would imply that growth is inclusive only when it maximizes the income of the worst off.

A reasonable second criterion for inclusiveness would be that growth should cater to a wide range of our material needs, implying that growth is spread across the various sectors of the economy. From such a perspective we would be sceptical of a high growth achieved by turning the Indian economy into some kind of gigantic back-office to the rest of the world. Indeed, we are unlikely to find this edifying even if the export of software or information technology–enabled services (ITES) were to allow us to consume whatever we may need through imports. In any case, trade is unlikely to give us roads and parks, or, as eponymous hero of the novel *The White Tiger* (Adiga 2008) suggested, even sewage pipes. So an all-round development of the economy emerges as an additional criterion for judging inclusiveness. This is not much encountered in the public debate on inclusiveness in India today, which is mainly confined to the first criterion proposed here, but it must come across as equally important upon reflection. Aware of these two criteria, we are better placed to identify the factors that would make for an inclusive growth process.

We can see immediately that if a growth impulse is present in agriculture, it would come closer to satisfying both the criteria of inclusiveness adopted here. On the first count, as the largest share of the Indian workforce is rural, it is growth of this sector that, in the first instance, would carry along with it the largest possible number of workers. At the same time, going by the second criterion of inclusiveness—as India's households devote a far greater share of their budgets to food than the global average—cheaper food via faster agricultural growth is essential if growth is to cater to the most pressing of our material needs. The performance of the agricultural sector since the mid-1990s has been somewhat lacklustre. Specifically, the production of foodgrains has barely kept abreast of population growth. Though food requirement varies across the climatic zones of the globe, for perspective we may return to the cross-country data presented in Chapter 1. We would find there that the rate of growth of per capita production of food was 2 per cent per annum in South Korea for three decades from the mid-1960s. This had been a period of exceptional dynamism for Korea's economy as a whole. Interestingly, while references to the East Asian experience abound in official statements, as we have seen in Chapter 4, the agricultural aspect is ignored. With the increase in the real price of food since the reforms, documented in Chapter 4, and the close to 20 per cent year-on-year food-price inflation[3] registered in December 2009, it is not too early to take a fresh look at the strategy that has been pursued in India since 1991.

So we can identify a dynamic agriculture as one pillar of the strategy for inclusive growth today. However, acquiring this dynamism would require some non-trivial interventions. Faster agricultural growth requires an educational preparedness for the reasons discussed in Chapters 1 and 4. Again from Chapter 4, we know that improved agricultural productivity today requires an educated farmer to be able to face greater ecological adversity and deal with the opportunities and the threats as trade liberalization extends to his/her sector. Second, in order to reduce the overcrowding that leads to shrinkage of farm size, a shifting of labour from that sector to the rest of the economy is needed. Actually, these potential non-agricultural workers would not only have to be educationally prepared but also professionally trained. Other instances can be imagined. Suppose the liberalization pursued thus far were to generate greater opportunities for export of goods. To the extent that the production of goods for export requires a more educated workforce, the uneducated cannot take advantage of the opportunities that are presented. Now greater integration with the world economy, a goal of the reforms initiated in 1991, cannot contribute to an inclusive growth even if it can contribute to its acceleration. This would lead us to identify education as a necessary component of an inclusive growth strategy.

Thus, attaining the goal of inclusive growth, viewed from diverse angles, requires a concerted effort to raise the level of educational preparedness of the Indian population. A discussion of the issues involved has appeared in Chapter 4. Here it need only be stated that given the education deficit in the country and the extreme inequality in its distribution across the population, the excessive focus recently on the very limited number of Indian Institutes of Technology and of Management (IITs and IIMs) may yet amount to no more than a matter of toying with the tip of the iceberg.[4] Indeed this may well be the moment to grasp the opportunity hitherto missed of generally improving schooling and vocational training in the country.[5]

Both the theoretical and empirical literature on growth point to the need for greater focus on agriculture if inclusive growth is to be attained. The issue of the distributional impact of different types of growth has mostly been analysed within the standard two-sector model familiar since the work of Lewis (1954). In an influential contribution, Eswaran and Kotwal (1993) have shown that for a closed economy, technical progress in agriculture raises industrial production, enabling workers to shift out of agriculture, and increases the real wage, lowering poverty. On the other hand, technical progress in industry has no such impact. In an open economy, of course, industry can grow without support from domestic agriculture as food can be imported. However, for this, domestic industry must not only first gain an international competitiveness but retain it by ensuring productivity growth faster than that of its trading partners. The importance of education and continuous training for competitiveness is now apparent. And, though reduced in the model of an open economy, agriculture's importance cannot be obscured in practice it seems, as it is difficult to imagine a country of over a billion persons relying permanently on the global market for its food requirement.

For India, therefore, technical progress in agriculture as a major source of growth is likely to remain relevant for some time. Next, it has been demonstrated by Temple (2005) that capital accumulation or technical progress in agriculture can shift the Lorenz Curve inward—that is, it can reduce inequality. More interestingly, the effects of a similar development in 'non-agriculture' are ambiguous from this point of view. Finally, empirical investigation by Ravallion and Datt (1996) has shown that rural growth in India has benefited the urban poor as well as the rural poor, while urban growth is less inclusive, though this is not the term that they use.[6] These cases focus exclusively on agriculture while we have here also emphasized the role of education. Somehow, the role of education has been modelled far less within a macroeconomic framework that allows us to draw conclusions relevant to the issue of inclusive growth. For instance, the endogenous growth model of Lucas (1988), which is centred on schooling, has no room for distributional questions. On the other hand, the idea of education being important for both national wealth and social mobility, at the same time, was already present in Marshall (1890). Empirical work on the role of education in India is relatively scarce. However, the evident pattern of a better educated west and south of this country growing faster than the rest is indicative of its centrality to both growth and development.

The Question of the Market

Since Keynes, we know that the true significance of a 'market' economy is not so much that there is little or no government intervention as much as that the level of production, and therefore employment—the demand for labour being a derived demand—is determined by the aggregate demand for goods, or what we generally refer to as 'the market'. For a national economy then there are two sources of demand, namely, the domestic and the external. It would appear that as India is among the poorest economies of the world, the rest of the world is naturally a market for its lower-cost goods. Something close to this seems to have been the premise underlying the reforms of 1991 that integrated India with the world economy, so that a growth through trade may be initiated. While the opening up of the economy may have contributed to the growth of exports, this has been far from sufficient to make a dent on unemployment in the country, as we can by now see. This has to do with the feature that since the mid-1990s software products and services and ITES have come to account for a large part of India's exports. These exports rely on skilled labour. On the other hand, manufactures mostly rely on less-skilled manual labour. However, as far as the potential for exports from this sector is concerned, India faces strong competition from China. So the mere fact of a large supply of manual labour cannot assure India of success automatically upon opening up to trade. The poor educational level and low vocational training of its labour are as much constraints to raising manufactured exports as is the inadequacy of supporting infrastructure such as power, roads, and ports.

The question of the market, as in the source of demand, has not been adequately faced up to in the context of setting high growth targets. Once again, it was simply assumed that opening up of the economy will leave the global market for India's taking. At the same time, the potential of the domestic economy as a market for its goods appears to have been ignored, though perhaps more by default rather than by design. A fundamental distinction between the domestic and foreign economies as markets is that a country has, via its national government, some control over the determination of the former but none whatsoever over the latter.[7] The near instantaneous collapse of India's exports following the global slowing of 2007–8 points to this quite conclusively.[8] It reveals the limits of a strategy of relying on the world market for India's sustained growth. Clearly, at this stage of its economic development, its aim should be to grow its domestic market while at the same doing everything within its means to benefit from the access to the foreign. In such a scenario, the role of trade reforms is limited, and a policy of releasing constraints on domestic production asserts a priority. This need hardly be viewed as a particularly radical solution. Since the global financial crisis, it is actually one recommended by the global multilateral agencies.[9]

What is of interest for us here is the existence, if any, of a link between the internal market and inclusive growth. From this point of view, currently for India, it is the growth of agriculture that is likely to best serve the cause of a growing domestic market. A rupee of growth in agriculture is spread over a larger number of workers than growth elsewhere in the economy and, at current income levels, more likely to be spent on goods produced by manual labour in the non-agricultural sector. This mechanism boosts both demand and employment in the latter. The experience of Indian manufacturing in 2008–9 when the global slowing impacted it proportionately less than the slowdown in exports, due to the unexpected cushion provided by public spending under the National Rural Employment Guarantee Scheme (NREGS), is a case in point. Note that the NREGS is a limited scheme of employment generation in that it presently entitles one person in every family to 100 days of manual labour in one year. On the other hand, faster agricultural growth may be expected to spread incomes much more widely among rural households, with implications for the growth of the internal market. Thus, an agricultural expansion led by productivity growth, especially in the production of food, is particularly conducive to inclusive growth.

In the first round of such an expansion, being rural biased, the largest number of households in the country benefit due to rising incomes. In the second round, this raises the demand for manufactures from these households. The significance of a productivity-led agricultural expansion, especially in the production of food, is that it makes a declining relative price of food compatible with growing farm profitability, a condition for sustained expansion of the agricultural sector. A declining relative price of food leaves urban households with greater purchasing power over manufactures. This is likely to lead to a secondary expansion of the demand for the products of the manufacturing sector, the first having come from rising incomes in the agricultural sector. We have discussed this route to growth in Chapter 1. Indeed, it has been the history of most of the high-income countries of the world, except perhaps of the oil-rich kingdoms of the Middle East.

This is not a route that India has explored seriously enough, even though it was not inconsistent with pursuing the Nehru–Mahalanobis Strategy overall. Growth by expansion of the domestic market assumes relevance not only at the time of my writing this in 2009, when the effects of the financial meltdown are all too evident, but also in the foreseeable future, when the OECD (Organisation for Economic Co-operation and Development) economies are likely to grow only very slowly due to slowing demand from a slowing population growth. The latter implies a slow-growing market for goods in the West. However, the prospect of a declining relative price of food from rising agricultural productivity, a central element in this strategy, would require a departure from the current practice of the Indian government. For over three decades it has been evident that governments are loathe to allow a decline in agriculture's terms of trade irrespective of the profitability of farm production. This is incompatible with the type of agriculture-led expansion that has been proposed here. That would require a far more flexible form of government intervention in the grain markets than has been the practice for a long time in India. Politics impinges directly upon the possibilities here.[10]

We have argued that a growth strategy that creates a domestic market for mass consumption goods is the one most likely to be inclusive, as the employment generated will be directed towards less-skilled workers. Two points about this strategy may be noted. First, even if it is geared towards absorption of less-skilled labour, the requirement of generally upgrading education and training in India cannot be done away with. As the data in Chapter 4 reveal, current levels of human resource development in India are low. Nor are there signs of a hasty rectification of the situation in sight. UNESCO's 'EFA Development Index' meant to capture a country's progress towards the goal of 'education for all' (EFA) by 2015 indicates very slow progress in India, which is ranked 105 out of 129 countries.[11] Second, a strategy of growth via an expanding domestic market need not in any way imply a neglect of the opportunities offered by the foreign market. Indeed, effective participation in the two markets can be complementary. A large domestic market affords a size of operation that enables the exploitation of potential economies of scale which can only help Indian firms to compete in the global market.

Historically, from Britain to Japan, the main exporters of manufactures have also been great manufacturing nations to start with. This recognition had led Kaldor (1989) to propose that, on account of the importance of static and dynamic economies of scale, a country with a large home market may acquire an automatic advantage in exports. Note that here the causation is seen as running from the efficiency of domestic production, via economies of scale, to global competitiveness. The same holds for upgradation of skills of the labour force. Even when intended to enable an expansion of production in response to domestic demand, competing on the global market is aided by a better human resource base. We might say that historically the great exporters of the world, coming from distinct geographies and cultures, have also had the most educated and skilled workers. In the absence of a trained workforce, an open trade regime is not of much use from the point of view of growth through exports.[12]

So what stands in the way of the adoption of a growth strategy such as the one outlined here? First and foremost is a failure to appreciate its relevance. For instance, while the Approach Paper to the Eleventh Plan does speak of the need for both inclusion and a higher agricultural growth, it fails to develop an organic link between the two. The general premise appears to be that a higher growth rate is needed for inclusiveness to be attained, and faster agricultural growth is seen as the route to achieving the higher economy-wide growth. As for the reforms of 1991, their adoption was influenced by the historical moment in which they were launched. The end of East European communism had led to the unthinking rejection of any government intervention in the growth process, the market outcome being assumed to be optimal and best left untampered with. So, the main task for India, it was interpreted, was to unleash competition within the economy while at the same time integrating it with the rest of the world.

After close to two decades of this, we can see that while much of the liberalization was needed, timely, and has borne fruit, it yet does not constitute a *growth strategy*, leave alone guarantee inclusion. On the other hand, an agricultural expansion is constitutive of such a strategy and stands a better chance of carrying along with it the largest numbers. A belated recognition of its importance appears to have been instigated by the outcome of the general elections of 2009. It seems the result has been interpreted as a case of the rural voters rewarding the incumbent government for attention to their welfare. However, this overlooks the fact that though the NREGS was in place, GDP in the agricultural sector had grown by a whopping 4.7 per cent in the year 2007–8, and this itself had followed two years of very high growth.[13] Moreover, globally the allure of the American Business Model,[14] privileging the claims of the corporate sector, had dimmed after the financial meltdown that originated in the United States. The meltdown revealed the claims for its efficacy as bankrupt and the governments that had championed it as seriously culpable. As India is a democracy, the lesson could not but have been learnt by the political class here, and quickly. Nevertheless, it is very likely high rural growth than merely the NREGS that held the incumbent government in good stead. This takes us to the second factor that stands in the way of the success of the strategy for inclusive growth sketched here.

While a productivity-driven agricultural expansion supported by a rising educational level will require funding, the last is unlikely to prove the binding constraint. The tax–GDP ratio for India has distinctly risen[15] since 2004–5. Anyway, some rationalization of expenditure on subsidies should yield finances for greater investment. However, even without the financial leeway this allows, our brief comparison in Chapter 4 of expenditure and outcome in the irrigation sector over the last decade had clearly indicated that the government's finances may amount to less of a lacking than a proper use being made of them. In another instance, the public expenditure per student in elementary schooling increased by 50 per cent in the decade since 1993–4 while the same index for secondary schooling and higher education either remained stable or actually declined.[16] However, the findings of Pratham's Annual State of Education Report (ASER) provided in Chapter 4 show that very poor learning outcomes continue in our schools. A general message from these examples is that while in most areas of the economy where the government intervenes, resources may no longer be the binding constraint, the capacity for effective governance very likely is. So long as a lack of accountability prevails, outcomes from more spending are likely to remain disappointing. From the findings of international health researchers we know that a third area of the Indian economy where outcomes remain poor despite high economic growth is nutrition. This has been explicitly put down to the lack of governance.[17]

If it is considered obligatory to provide a rank order of the areas where intervention is necessary to make growth more inclusive in the long run than it has been so far, the following suggests itself—governance, education, and agriculture, in descending order of their importance. With the largest number of Indians still engaged in agriculture,[18] any plan for making growth inclusive must start here. We have seen that faster agricultural growth requires a better educational preparedness in the countryside. This is also needed to shift labour out of agriculture into manufacturing and the services. While India has historically spent less on education than other countries, in an international comparison it is also clear that her public education system functions very poorly. Though he may have had the economy in mind, Prime Minister Manmohan Singh's observation about the economy being 'over regulated and under governed'[19] appears to be particularly true of this sector. Effective governance now assumes a priority on the policy agenda.

We have here attempted to reduce to their most basic the elements that go into an inclusive growth. The result may appear as offering a nicely ordered set of interventions. However, the world is more complex and what has been proposed is not the only plausible ordering. In reality, a more prosperous agriculture, however attained, may encourage the private adoption of higher educational goals, and a better educated populace is a force for more democratic governance. Now we have the sequence reversed. Nevertheless, in the event of a willing and capable government, the sequence of interventions starting with improved governance constitutes a feasible growth strategy. Moreover, it is likely to achieve quicker results than allowing for the alternative scenario sketched earlier to work itself out. More to the point, indications are that all the political parties that took part in the elections of 2009 have internalized the message that the people of India expect a government that functions and that providing one is crucial to their returning to power.

We have sketched the outline of a strategy which we have argued is more likely than others to generate growth with inclusion. However, though an agriculture-driven growth process supported by the necessary educational interventions can yield a higher growth rate while carrying the largest possible numbers with it, a high growth rate per se, when attained by other means, need not necessarily do so. We are able to state this with some confidence as we have some recent experience to go by. Indeed it is the fact of the very high growth over 2003–8 not being inclusive that placed the issue on the political agenda in the first place.

While the architects of India's reforms are evidently sincere in their desire to see an inclusive economy, their pronouncements—some of which have been reproduced earlier—indicate that they privilege high growth over other instruments as a means of bringing it about. This perspective may be contrasted with the view advanced by us that, at least within a range, the composition of growth may matter more for inclusion and that much can be achieved without additional resources so long as governance improves.[20] On the other hand, the data and arguments presented in this study suggest that mere injection of funds without improved governance could end up delivering neither higher growth nor inclusiveness.

THE CHALLENGE AT THE BOTTOM OF THE PYRAMID

For close to a decade now the idea of a 'fortune at the bottom of the pyramid' expounded by management thinkers[21] has found its way into the public discourse on growth in India. It refers to the potential market at the lower end of the pyramidal structure representing the distribution of income in the economy, the suggestion being that the poorest constitute a market that has hitherto been ignored. For the economist, this is somewhat counterintuitive, as the definition of poverty is an absence of purchasing power to start with. The confusion, however, is cleared when it is recognized that what is being suggested is that such demands as emanate from the poorest be catered to by appropriately placed products. This is unexceptionable. Nevertheless, from the point of view of the economy as opposed to the firm, the idea is to actually grow the market and the existence of very poor people does not by itself advance this cause. We are now back to the central problem in bringing about an inclusive growth, which is how to economically empower the poor. The strategy proposed here is directly addressed to the question of what is necessary for the poorest to earn permanently higher incomes on a sustainable basis. And the essential interventions needed have been specified by us.

For the poor to be lifted out of poverty, they need to be turned into producers. This requires both that they be equipped for the task and a market be created for what they produce. The objective of policy should be to engineer this joint outcome. It is clear that to successfully bring about inclusive growth in India today economic policy needs to be more focused on the domestic economy than it has been in the past two decades. Over this period, attention was largely on the interface between India and the rest of the world. While this site must continue to receive our fullest attention, it is of limited value when it comes to designing a programme for inclusion. Our analysis has reduced the elements that go into inclusive growth to effective governance, as educationally equipping the poor to be producers and ensuring a market for the goods that they produce, initially via accelerated agricultural growth, is very likely more constrained by governance than it is by resources.

Right now, with India's poorest being undernourished and barely educated, the policymaker in pursuit of inclusion is faced with a *challenge* at the bottom of the pyramid. The challenge is to feed and equip them appropriately. Fortune awaits us only when we surmount it.[22] Arguably, in the immediate future, prospects for inclusive growth of the Indian economy turn on reform of the machinery of government that is required for effective governance. Exhortation that the reforms should continue must henceforth be addressed to this aspect rather than mere liberalization of the policy regime, which in any case has gone some distance by now.

Arguments for Inclusion

We have thus far discussed inclusive growth without providing an argument for why it is necessary or even important, treating its value as axiomatic. But surely this will not do. I now offer two arguments for inclusion. The first of these is placed within the long-standing discourse on growth and development among India's economists. Bhagwati and Desai (1970: 500) conclude their study of industrialization in India with the observation that you cannot have growth first and efficiency later. They were referring to the Nehru–Mahalanobis Strategy, which in their view ignored efficiency criteria. Though the Indian economy was to enter a phase of accelerated growth even without a significant change in the development strategy within a decade of their making the observation, their claims for efficiency cannot be faulted in principle. In fact, recall from the discussion in Chapter 3 that the industrial recovery of the 1980s was accompanied by an improvement in the profitability of the public enterprises. Actually, the latter development had commenced in the late 1970s, enabling the revival of public investment which contributed to the recovery itself. Efficiency, it appears, can make a difference.

It may be argued, however, that exactly as you cannot pursue long-term growth without efficiency, one cannot ignore distribution and expect continued high growth either. The history of growth in India as revealed in this book strongly suggests that spreading it more widely, via the Green Revolution, actually contributed to the growth transition *circa* 1980. So, the Indian experience suggests that a trinity of 'growth, efficiency, and distribution' was present in the economy in the recent past. Within a range, these three elements are likely, via positive feedback, to reinforce one another even into the immediate future. Hence inclusion defined as the spreading of the effects of growth widely is likely to remain crucial for growth itself. While I am aware that this is a somewhat general statement, to seek precise formulations of the relationship between growth and distribution would be akin to searching for the Holy Grail. It suffices here to state that the fine art of nurturing growth entails not blunting efficiency by focusing exclusively on distribution, as politicians with short-term agendas do, and not ignoring the expansion of demand that comes with spreading growth, as privileging the supply-side can lead the policymaker to do.

My second argument for inclusion is unconcerned with the project of raising the rate of growth of the Indian economy. It originates in a social philosophy, but is no less important for that. Every Indian would recall the first line of Nehru's speech made on the occasion of Indian Independence. However, it is the subsequent ones that had contained the message of the moment. Nehru had imagined the birth of India as a chance:

> To bring freedom and opportunity to the common man, to the peasants and workers of India; to fight and end poverty and ignorance and disease; to build up a prosperous, democratic and progressive nation, and to create social, economic and political institutions which will ensure justice and fullness of life to every man and woman. (Nehru 1947)

Inclusive growth remains the unfinished business of Indian Independence.

NOTES

1. See Planning Commission (2006).
2. See the report on the minister's speech in Singapore (Rajamohan 2008).
3. See *The Hindu* (2009b).
4. On this, see also Thapar (2009).
5. We have already seen in Chapter 4 where India stands vis-à-vis the rest of the world on education. India's relative position on vocational training is less well known by comparison. For perspective, it may be noted that the proportion of the vocationally-trained workforce in India is about five times lower than in Mexico and sixteen times lower than in Korea. In Korea, a country superior on this attribute than Germany, over 95 per cent of the population aged 20–4 years has received vocational training (see World Bank 2007: Figure 3.4). While there

is no reason to believe that Korea is the proper model for India, these figures give some indication of the distance that needs to be traversed if the reforms agenda of integrating India with the world economy is to bear any fruit. On whether India should emulate Korea at all, see Pack (2009).

6. For a review of empirical work on India that points to a significant role for agriculture in reducing poverty, see Panda (2008). For a similar role for agriculture in countries quite different from India in terms of economic structure and history, as in Africa, see Dercon (2009).

7. I am indebted to Amit Bhaduri for this insight.

8. As an indication, note that by October 2009 exports had declined on a month-to-month basis for thirteen consecutive months. The magnitudes are significant too. Over the first six months of 2009–10, the decline in exports was of the order of 26 per cent compared to the same period of the previous year (see *The Hindu* 2009c).

9. See Yunwei (2009) for the report: 'The Asian Development Bank said in an August report that the emerging nations need to value the expansion of domestic demand in order to realize their economy's balanced development.'

10. See Mitra (1978).

11. See UNESCO (2007). The Republic of Korea is ranked fifth, indicating that there is more than just the level of the tariff rate that distances India from that country. I am grateful to R. Govinda of the National Institute of Educational Planning and Administration, New Delhi, for bringing this document to my attention.

12. In work done for the World Bank in the 1980s when the East Asian Tigers caught the imagination of economists, Wheeler has explicitly considered the question whether education and health matter 'beyond extraversion' or openness to trade. His econometric investigation yielded evidence of this, leading him to conclude that countries that ignore the development of their human resource 'will experience more difficulty in export expansion, with its attendant benefits, than their counterparts which have focused on human resources' (Wheeler 1984: 34).

13. See *Economic Survey 2008–09*. The figure for 2007–8 is a 'quick estimate' while the figure for growth in 2008–9 was not released by the Central Statistical Organisation (CSO) at the time of writing.

14. See Kay (2003).

15. See *Economic Survey 2008–09*.

16. See Mishra (2009); source cited 'Annual Financial Statistics of Education Sector 2003–04', MHRD, 2005. I am grateful to the author for permission to refer to his findings.

17. See Haddad (2009).

18. See Table 4.3.

19. See Singh (2004).

20. The emerging evidence that Bihar recorded the second highest rate of growth among the states over 2004–9 after decades of indifferent performance has been put down mainly to improved governance. See *The Times of India* (2009).

21. See Prahalad (2004).

22. Since Abramovitz (1989) pointed out the importance of 'social capability' for growth, much empirical work on the relationship has followed. Though not always faithful to the spirit of his argument, they are nevertheless instructive. For cross-country regressions on social arrangements as a predictor of growth, see Temple and Johnson (1998); for econometric evidence of the greater importance for the growth of per capita income in India of 'social'—health and environmental quality—over 'physical' infrastructure, see Nagar et al. (2008); for a statement of what India's social sector needs and the policy for attaining it, see Vijay Shankar and Shah (2009).

Appendix

A1. Estimating and Testing for Multiple Structural Breaks in the Rate of Growth of GDP

The growth rates of aggregate and sectoral gross domestic product (GDP) may be estimated using the exponential function $lnY_t = a + gt + u_t$, where lnY, g, t, and u denote the log of income, growth rate, time trend, and random disturbance term, respectively. The subscript t denotes time. The parameters of the aforementioned regression model—a and g—would vary from one growth regime to another, making it necessary to identify the change point. Therefore, we first estimate the break-dates of the aforementioned model for aggregate and sectoral GDP and accordingly partition the data to estimate the period-wise growth rates. The methodology for estimating the break-dates is explained in detail below.

The exponential growth model containing $m+1$ growth regimes and m break-dates ($T_1,\ldots, T_m$) can be written as follows:

$$\begin{aligned} \ln Y_t &= a_1 + g_1 t + u_t, & t &= 1,\ldots,T_1 \\ \ln Y_t &= a_2 + g_2 t + u_t, & t &= T_1+1,\ldots,T_2 \\ &\vdots \\ \ln Y_t &= a_{m+1} + g_{m+1} t + u_t, & t &= T_m+1,\ldots T \end{aligned} \qquad \text{(A1.1)}$$

Here we adopt the convention that $T_0 = 0$ and $T_{m+1} = T$ the total number of observations. The number of breakpoints m and the break-dates ($T_1,\ldots,T_m$) are treated as unknown and estimated from the data.

The conventional approach to establishing a structural break in a time series regression model is to perform the test for a statistically significant difference in its parameters across two periods. This is referred to as the 'Chow Test'.[1] In recent years, however, this approach has come under scrutiny.[2] The issue of concern is the method of identification of the break-date. One of two approaches is followed. The first is to identify the break-date based on some known feature of the data, such as an observed inflexion in the graph of a series. The other is to choose the break-date based on the occurrence of some exogenous event expected to cause structural change in the model. An example would be to treat the first oil shock of 1973 as signalling a break in the growth rate of the oil-importing OECD (Organisation for Economic Co-operation and Development) economies, and then proceeding to test for the same.

Both these procedures for choice of break-date are problematic. In the first case, the choice is correlated with the data, and the Chow Test is likely to validate a break-date when none in fact exists. The problem with the second method is that it assumes that the exogenous event has had an impact on the parameters of the model, and that at that point in time it is the only causal factor. When this is not true, an observed structural change may have little to do with the exogenous event itself. Moreover, it has been demonstrated that this procedure can lead to erroneous conclusions.[3] All of this points to the importance of the proper identification of the break-date. Continuing with the Chow Test, we may now apply the test at every possible point in a sample and to choose the data point corresponding to the maximum valued F-statistic as the break-date. While this does generate for us an endogenously identified break-date, the procedure can be used to estimate only one break at a time. Of course, the method may be applied repeatedly to estimate more than one break but this is cumbersome and the procedure non-standard. On the other hand, we now have a methodology that can estimate simultaneously multiple structural breaks in a series which is described in the following.

Bai and Perron (1998, 2003) have developed an approach to the problem of identifying breaks in a series based on the least squares principle common to regression analysis. Its superiority draws from the feature that it allows for the simultaneous estimation of multiple breaks. The break-dates are estimated as global minimizers of the sum of squared residuals from an OLS regression of (A1.1) using a dynamic programming algorithm (see Bai and Perron 2003). The procedure is as follows. Given the number of breaks m, for each partition $(T_1, \ldots, T_m)$ denoted $\{T_p\}$ the associated least squares estimates $\beta_p = (a, g)_p$ are obtained by minimizing the sum of squared residuals $\sum_{j=1}^{m+1} \sum_{t=T_{j-1}+1}^{T_j} [\ln Y_t - a_j - g_j t]^2$. The resulting estimates $\hat{\beta}_p$ are used to compute the sum of squared residuals—denoted $S_T(T_1,\ldots,T_m)$—associated with the partition $\{T_p\}$. Now the estimated breakpoints $(\hat{T}_1,\ldots,\hat{T}_m)$ are such that $(\hat{T}_1,\ldots,\hat{T}_m) = argmin_{T_1,\ldots,T_m} S_T(T_1,\cdots,T_m)$, where the minimization is over all possible partitions $(T_1, \ldots, T_m)$ such that $T_i - T_{i-1} \geq h$. Note that h is the minimum length assigned to a segment and T_i is the ith breakpoint. The procedure considers all possible combinations of segments and selects the partition that minimizes the sum of squared residuals. Thus, the least-squares estimates of break-dates are those that minimize the full sample sum of squared residuals in (A1.1).

As we are working with a trending series, the following may be noted. First, Bai (1997: 553) has demonstrated that stationarity of regressors or disturbances is not required for consistency of the breakpoints estimated under the aforementioned procedure. Second, the asymptotic distribution of the breakpoint estimator, needed for construction of the confidence interval, has been derived by the author without assuming stationarity of the disturbances.

The aforementioned procedure is used to sequentially estimate the optimal breakpoints for the series starting from one to the maximum allowed by T and h. The next step is to select the number of breaks in the time series. When the number of breakpoints is unknown, a test based on the *supF* statistic has been proposed (Bai and Perron 1998) to choose the number of breakpoints. This testing procedure assumes non-trending regressors and is therefore inapplicable in the present context. An alternative approach which accommodates trending regressors is to use the Bayesian Information Criteria (BIC). This has been demonstrated to be superior to other information criteria in the determination of the number of structural breaks (Wang 2006). Here the number of breaks selected is that for which BIC is at a minimum. We adopt this procedure to choose the number of breaks, starting from zero to the maximum.[4] The criterion is particularly appropriate when multiple breaks are considered because it introduces a penalty factor for additional breakpoints which necessarily reduces the sum of squared residuals,[5] as is apparent from the following:

$$BIC(m) = \ln \hat{\sigma}^2(m) + p^* \ln(T)/T$$

$$p^* = (m+1)q + m + p$$

$$\hat{\sigma}^2 = T^{-1}\sum_{t=1}^{T}\hat{u}_t^2$$

where m is the number of breaks, q is the number of explanatory variables whose coefficients are subjected to shift, and p is the number of explanatory variables whose coefficients are constant.

Before proceeding to the estimation, we consider another issue. This relates to the question of whether we are faced with, what has been referred to in the literature as, a 'partial' versus 'pure' structural break. In the present context this translates into the following question. We are concerned with a change in the rate of growth of output which implies a shift in the slope coefficient. When this is accompanied by an intercept shift in the data-generating process, it is important to allow for this level shift in the estimation of the break-date. Simulation results of Perron and Zhu (2005) show that incorporation of a level shift of more than 0.3 in absolute value improves the accuracy of break-date estimation. However, a practical problem is that the estimated change in the intercept cannot be a good guide due to contamination and feedback effects between the estimated level shifts and break-dates. Here, along with an examination of the estimated intercept shift, a visual comparison of the actual and fitted series has been suggested to verify whether the intercept shift is a true level shift rather than a random deviation away from the trend line (Perron and Zhu 2005). We adopt this approach.

In the estimation of the break-dates, the minimum length of a growth regime, h, has been fixed at 8. This implies a maximum of five breaks or six growth regimes in our sample extending from 1950–1 to 2003–4. The figure 8 follows from a 'trimming' of 0.15 applied to our time series of just over fifty years. This is based on the recommendation of Bai and Perron (2004). Their recommendation itself is based on the results of a simulation addressed to the issue of adequacy of the size and power of their proposed test for the existence of a structural break in a time series. At the same time, it appears to us as not unreasonable to insist in a study spanning half a century that a growth regime lasts for eight years to be considered as distinct. Note that now the search for a possible break would be confined to the period 1957–8 to 1995–6.

The estimation of the break-dates was performed with the package *strucchange*.[6] Next, the growth rate for each regime was estimated by the procedure due to Boyce (1986). This involves imposing kinks at the estimated breakpoints to maintain continuity of the exponential trend line at the breakpoints. The complete set of results is presented in Section A4.

A2. Computation of the Confidence Interval for the Estimated Break-date

Confidence interval for break-dates, where trended regressors are present, are computed using the procedure given in Bai (1997). This can be explained as follows. Let $\hat{T}_j$ be the jth breakpoint, $\hat{a}_j = (\hat{a}_j, \hat{g}_j)$, $\hat{\delta}_j = (\hat{\beta}_{j+1} - \hat{\beta}_j)$ and z_{tj} = (1, t_j), where t_j is the value of t at jth break. Define $\hat{L}_j = (\hat{\delta}_j z'_{tj} z_{tj} \hat{\delta}'_j) / \hat{\sigma}_u^2$, where $\hat{\sigma}^2 = T^{-1} \sum_{t=1}^{T} \hat{u}_t^2$ from (A1.1). Now the 100(1–α)% confidence interval is given by $[\hat{T}_j - (c/\hat{L}_j) - 1, \hat{T}_j + (c/\hat{L}_j) + 1]$ where c is the (1–α/2)th quantile of the distribution (at 5 per cent level c = 11). Note that it is assumed that the variance of the error term is the same across segments. It is of course possible to construct the confidence interval without this assumption of uniformity (see Bai 1997), but we have not done so to maintain computational ease.

A3. Estimating the Sectoral Contribution to the Change in the Growth Rate

Consider two periods 1 and 2, respectively consisting of $n1$ and $n2$ years. Denote aggregate gross domestic product (GDP) and primary, secondary, and tertiary sector incomes by Y, P, S, and T respectively. Let w_{it} denote the share of sector i ($i = P, S, T$) in Y in year t and g denote the growth rate. Y in year t can be written as follows:

$$Y_t = P_t + S_t + T_t \qquad \text{(A3.1)}$$

From (A3.1), the growth rate of Y can be written as:

$$g_{Yt} = w_{Pt} g_{Pt} + w_{St} g_{St} + w_{Tt} g_{Tt} \qquad \text{(A3.2)}$$

where $g_{Yt} = \left(\frac{Y_t - Y_{t-1}}{Y_{t-1}} \right)$ is the growth rate of Y in year t and g_{Pt}, g_{St}, and g_{Tt} are defined similarly. Using (A3.2), the average annual growth rate for the period 1 (g_{Y1}) can be written as follows:.

$$\overline{g}_{Y1} = \overline{w_{P1} g_{P1}} + \overline{w_{S1} g_{S1}} + \overline{w_{T1} g_{T1}} \qquad \text{(A3.3)}$$

where,

$$\overline{g}_{Y1} = n1^{-1}\left(\sum_{t=1}^{n1} g_{Yt}\right), \text{ and } \overline{w_{il}g_{il}} = n1^{-1}\left(\sum_{t=1}^{n1} w_{it}g_{it}\right).$$

Similarly, $\overline{g}_{Y2}$ can be written as

$$\overline{g}_{Y2} = \overline{w_{P2}g_{P2}} + \overline{w_{S2}g_{S2}} + \overline{w_{T2}g_{T2}} \qquad \text{(A3.4)}$$

In (A3.4), averages are taken over $n2$ observations in period 2. Subtracting (A3.3) from (A3.4),

$$(\overline{g}_{Y2} - \overline{g}_{Y1}) = (\overline{w_{P2}g_{P2}} - \overline{w_{P1}g_{P1}}) + (\overline{w_{S2}g_{S2}} - \overline{w_{S1}g_{S1}}) + (\overline{w_{T2}g_{T2}} - \overline{w_{T1}g_{T1}}) \qquad \text{(A3.5)}$$

Dividing (A3.5) throughout by the left-hand side value and multiplying it by 100 gives the percentage contribution of each sector to the change in the average growth rate of Y in period 2 over that in previous period.

A4. Estimated Break-dates and the Phases of Growth in India since 1950

Table A4.1 Break-dates: GDP in 1993–4 Prices

		First break	*Second break*	*Third break*	*Fourth break*
	GDP	1978–9 (+) [1977/8–1979/80]			
1.1	Agriculture	1964–5 (+) [1963/4–1965/6]			
1.2	Forestry and logging	1964–5 (+) [1963/4–1965/6]	1976–7 (–) [1975/6–1977/8]	1988–9(+) [1987/8–1989/90]	
1.3	Fishing	1958–9 (–) [1957/8–1959/60]	1973–4 (–) [1972/3–1974/5]	1982–3 (+) [1981/2–1983/4]	1992–3 (–) [1991/2–1993/4]
2	Mining and quarrying	1959–60 (+) [1958/9–1960/1]	1969–70 (–) [1968/9–1970/1]	1980–1 (+) [1978/9–1980/1]	1988–9 (–) [1988/9–1990/1]
3	Manufacturing	1965–6 (–) [1964/5–1966/7]	1982–3 (+) [1981/2–1983/4]	1994–5 (–) [1993/4–1995/6]	
3.1	Registered	1965–6 (–) [1964/5–1966/7]	1982–3 (+) [1981/2–1983/4]	1994–95 (–) [1993/4–1995/6]	
3.2	Unregistered	1964–5 (–) [1963/4–1965/6]	1986–7 (+) [1985/6–1987/8]	1994–5 (–) [1993/4–1995/6]	
4	Electricity, gas, and water supply	1957–8 (+) [1956/7–1958/9]	1967–8 (–) [1966/7–1968/9]	1983–4 (+) [1982/3–1984/5]	1991–2 (–) [1990/1–1992/3]
5	Construction	1969–70 (–) [1968/9–1970/1]	1981–2 (+) [1980/1–1982/3]		
6	Trade, hotels, and restaurants	1962–3 (–) [1961/2–1963/4]	1971–2 (+) [1970/1–1972/3]	1994–5 (+) [1993/4–1994/5]	
6.1	Trade	1962–3 (–) [1961/2–1963/4]	1971–2 (+) [1970/1–1972/3]	1994–5 (+) [1993/4–1995/6]	
6.2	Hotels and restaurants	1959–60 (–) [1951/2–1967/8]	1971–2 (+) [1970/1–1972/3]	1984–5 (+) [1983/4–1985/6]	1994–5 (+) [1993/4–1995/6]
7	Transport, storage, and communication	1961–2 (–) [1960/1–1962/3]	1973–4 (+) [1972/3–1974/5]	1993–4 (+) [1992/3–1994/5]	

(contd...)

Table A4.1 *(contd...)*

	First break	*Second break*	*Third break*	*Fourth break*
7.1 Railways	1961–2 (–) [1960/1–1962/3]	1984–5 (+) [1983/4–1985/6]	1992–3 (–) [1991/2–1993/4]	
7.2 Transport by other means	1957–8 (+) [1955/6–1959/60]	1973–4 (+) [1972/3–1974/5]	1993–4 (+) [1992/3–1994/5]	
7.3 Storage	1974–5 (+) [1973/4–1975/6]	1984–5 (–) [1983/4–1985/6]		
7.4 Communication	1962–3 (–) [1960/1–1964/5]	1987–8 (+) [1986/7–1988/9]	1995–6 (+) [1994/5–1996/7]	
8 Financing, insurance, real estate, and business services	1966–7 (+) [1965/6–1967/8]	1979–80 (+) [1978/9–1980/1]	1992–3 (–) [1991/2–1993/4]	
8.1 Banking and insurance	1965–6 (–) [1958/9–1972/3]	1979–80 (+) [1978/9–1980/1]	1995–6 (–) [1994/5–1996/7]	
8.2 Real estate, ownership of dwelling, and business services	1966–7 (+) [1965/6–1967/8]	1980–1(+) [1979/80–1981/2]	1993–4 (–) [1992/3–1994/5]	
9 Community and personal services	1961–2 (+) [1960/1–1962/3]	1976–7 (+) [1975/6–1977/8]	1992–3 (+) [1991/2–1993/4]	
9.1 Public administration and defence	1961–2 (–) [1960/1–1962/3]	1986–7 (–) [1985/6–1987/8]	1995–6 (+) [1994/5–1996/7]	
9.2 Other services	1957–8 (+) [1956/7–1958/9]	1968–9 (–) [1967/8–1969/70]	1980–1 (+) [1979/80–1981/2]	1992–3 (+) [1991/2–1993/4]

Notes: The reported break-date corresponds to the last year of a growth regime; for instance, as reported in the table, in the case of GDP a new growth regime commences in 1979–80. Ninety-five per cent confidence interval of the estimated break-date is provided in the brackets. The signs plus and minus, in parentheses, indicate acceleration and deceleration, respectively.

Table A4.2 Phases of Growth: GDP in 1993–4 Prices

	Sector	Period 1	Period 2	Period 3	Period 4	Period 5
	GDP	3.34 [1950/1–1978/9]	5.20 [1979/80–2003/4]			
1.1	Agriculture	1.73 [1950/1–1964/5]	2.78 [1965/6–2003/4]			
1.2	Forestry and logging	1.57 [1950/1–1964/5]	2.46 [1965/6–1976/7]	−2.31 [1977/8–1988/9]	1.33 [1989/90–2003/4]	
1.3	Fishing	5.63 [1950/1–1958/9]	3.93 [1959/60–1973/4]	2.14 [1974/5–1982/3]	6.18 [1983/4–1992/3]	5.10 [1993/4–2003/4]
2	Mining and quarrying	4.82 [1950/1–1959/60]	5.44 [1960/1–1969/70]	3.14 [1970/1–1980/1]	8.65 [1981/2–1988/9]	4.90 [1989/90–2003/4]
3	Manufacturing	6.27 [1950/1–1965/6]	4.26 [1966/7–1982/3]	6.76 [1983/4–1994/5]	6.07 [1995/6–2003/4]	
3.1	Registered	7.76 [1950/1–1965/6]	4.53 [1966/7–1982/3]	7.53 [1983/4–1994/5]	6.13 [1995/6–2003/4]	
3.2	Unregistered	4.63 [1950/1–1964/5]	4.09 [1965/6–1986/7]	5.96 [1987/8–1994/5]	5.83 [1995/6–2003/4]	
4	Electricity, gas, and water supply	8.51 [1950/1–1957/8]	12.21 [1958/9–1967/8]	7.03 [1968/9–1983/4]	9.23 [1984/5–1991/2]	5.64 [1992/3–2003/4]
5	Construction	6.59 [1950/1–1969/70]	2.00 [1970/1–1981/2]	5.05 [1982/3–2003/4]		
6	Trade, hotels, and restaurants	5.79 [1950/1–1962/3]	3.80 [1963/4–1971/2]	5.12 [1972/3–1994/5]	8.40 [1995/6–2003/4]	
6.1	Trade	5.71 [1950/1–1962/3]	3.84 [1963/4–1971/2]	5.10 [1972/4–1994/5]	8.23 [1995/6–2003/4]	
6.2	Hotels and restaurants	5.42 [1950/1–1959/60]	4.67 [1960/1–1971/2]	4.45 [1972/3–1984/5]	6.74 [1985/6–1994/5]	9.91 [1995/6–2003/4]

(contd...)

Table A4.2 *(contd...)*

		Period 1	*Period 2*	*Period 3*	*Period 4*	*Period 5*
7	Transport, storage, and communication	6.12 [1950/1–1961/2]	5.50 [1962/3–1973/4]	5.55 [1974/5–1993/4]	9.21 [1994/5–2003/4]	
7.1	Railways	5.81 [1950/1–1961/2]	3.68 [1962/3–1984/5]	4.01 [1985/6–1992/3]	3.78 [1993/4–2003/4]	
7.2	Transport by other means	5.94 [1950/1–1957/8]	6.16 [1958/9–1973/4]	6.21 [1974/5–1993/4]	6.85 [1994/5–2003/4]	
7.3	Storage	3.09 [1950/1–1974/5]	9.99 [1975/6–1984/5]	1.15 [1985/6–2003/4]		
7.4	Communication	7.13 [1950/1–1962/3]	6.17 [1963/4–1987/8]	7.41 [1988/9–1995/5]	19.41 [1995/6–2003/4]	
8	Financing, insurance, real estate, and business services	3.06 [1950/1–1966/7]	3.44 [1967/8–1978/9]	8.88 [1979/80–1992/3]	8.00 [1993/4–2003/4]	
8.1	Banking and insurance	6.65 [1950/1–1965/6]	5.83 [1966/7–1979/80]	11.01 [1980/1–1995/6]	9.19 [1996/7–2003/4]	
8.2	Real estate, ownership of dwelling, and business services	2.29 [1950/1–1966/7]	2.79 [1967/8–1980/1]	7.77 [1981/2–1993/4]	5.92 [1994/5–2003/4]	
9	Community and personal services	4.20 [1950/1–1961/2]	4.46 [1962/3–1976/7]	5.95 [1977/8–1992/3]	6.86 [1993/4–2003/4]	
9.1	Public administration and defence	6.53 [1950/1–1961/2]	6.23 [1962/3–1986/7]	4.96 [1987/8–1995/6]	6.48 [1996/7–2003/4]	
9.2	Other services	2.41 [1950/1–1957/8]	3.97 [1958/9–1968/9]	2.83 [1969/70–1980/1]	5.01 [1981/2–1992/3]	7.43 [1993/4–2003/4]

Notes: All estimates are significant at the 1 per cent level. Period of growth is in parentheses.

Table A4.3 Estimated Break-dates: GDP at 1999–2000 Prices

		First break	*Second break*	*Third break*	*Fourth break*	*Fifth break*
	GDP	1978–9(+) [1977/8–1979/80]	1990–1(+) [1989/90–1991/2]			
1	Agriculture, forestry, and logging	1987–8(+) [1986/7–1995-6]				
1.1	Agriculture	1964–5(+) [1958/9–1965/6]				
1.2	Forestry and logging	1964–5(+) [1963/4–1966/7]	1976–7 (–) [1975/6–1977/8]	1988–9(+) [1987/8–1991/2]	1996–7(+) [1995/6–1997/8]	
1.3	Fishing	1958–9(–) [1957/8–1959/60]	1973–4(–) 1972/3–1974/5]	1982–3(+) [1981/2–1983/4]	1992–93(–) [1990/1–1993/4]	
2	Mining and quarrying	1959–60(+) [1958/9–1960/1]	1969–70(–) [1968/9–1970/1]	1980–1(+) [1979/80–1983/4]	1988–89(–) [1987/8–1989/90]	
3	Manufacturing	1965–6(–) [1964/5–1966/7]	1994–5(+) [1993/4–1996/7]			
3.1	Registered	1965–6(–) [1964/5–1966/7]	1982–3(+) [1981/2–1984/5]			
3.2	Unregistered	1964–5(–) [1963/4–1966/7]	1977–8(–) [1974/5–1978/9]	1994–5(+) [1993/4–1996/7]		
4	Electricity, gas, and water supply	1957–8(+) [1956/7–1959/60]	1967–8(–) [1966/7–1968/9]	1975–6(–) [1974/5–1977/8]	1983–4(+) [1982/3–1985/6]	1995–6(–) [1994/5–1996/7]
5	Construction	1969–70(–) [1968/9–1970/1]	1981–2(+) [1980/1–1983/4]	1997–8(+) [1996/7–1998/9]		
6	Trade, hotels, and restaurants	1962–3(–) [1961/2–1963/4]	1971–2(+) [1970/1–1972/3]	1994–5(+) [1993/4–1995/6]		
6.1	Trade	1962–3(–) [1961/2–1963/4]	1971–2(–) [1970/1–1972/3]	1993–4(–) [1992/3–1994/5]		
6.2	Hotels and restaurants	1959–60(–) [1954/5–1960/1]	1980–1(+) [1979/80–1981/2]	1994–5(+) [1993/4–1996/7]		

(contd...)

Table A4.3 *(contd...)*

		First break	*Second break*	*Third break*	*Fourth break*	*Fifth break*
7	Transport, storage, and communication	1957–8(+) [1956/7–1964/5]	1965–6(–) [1964/5–1966/7]	1973–4(+) [1972/3–1975/6]	1989–90(+) [1987/8–1990/1]	1997–8(+) [1996/7–1998/9]
7.1	Railways	1965–6(–) [1964/5–1966/7]	1985–6(–) [1982/3–1986/7]	1997–8(+) [1996/7–1998/9]		
7.2	Transport by other means	1957–8(+) [1956/7–1958/9]	1973–4(+) [1972/3–1977/4]	1989–90(+) [1987/8–1990/1]	1997–8(+) [1990/1–1998/9]	
7.3	Storage	1974–5(+) [1973/4–1975/6]	1986–7(–) [1985/6–1989/90]			
7.4	Communication	1962–3(–) [1960/1–1963/4]	1978–9(–) [1976/7–1979/80]	1989–90(+) [1988/9–1990/1]	1997–8(+) [1996/7–1998/9]	
8	Financing, insurance, real estate, and business services	1966–7(+) [1964/5–1967/8]	1979–80(+) [1978/9–1980/1]	1988–9(–) [1987/8–1989/90]		
8.1	Banking and insurance	1965–6(–) [1960/1–1966/7]	1979–80(+) [1978/9–1980/1]	1996–7(+) [1995/6–1997/8]		
8.2	Real estate, ownership, and business services	1964–5(+) [1963/4–1965/6]	1979–80(+) [1978/9–1980/1]	1993–4(–) [1992/3–1994/5]		
9	Community and personal services	1957–8(+) [1956/7–1958/9]	1968–9 [1967/8–1969/70]	1981–2(+) [1980/1–1982/3]	1989–90(–) [1988/9–1990/1]	1997–8(+) [1996/7–1998/9]
9.1	Public administration and defence	1961–2(+) [1960/1–1963/4]	1973–4(–) [1972/3–1976/7]	1986/7(+) [1985/6–1987/8]	1996–7(+) [1995/6–1997/8]	
9.2	Other services	1957–8(+) [1956/7–1958/9]	1968–9(–) [1967/8–1969/70]	1981–2(+) [1980/1–1982/3]	1995–6(+) [1994/5–1996/7]	

Notes: The reported break-date corresponds to the last year of a growth regime; for instance, as reported in the table, in the case of GDP new growth regimes commence in 1979–80 and 1991–2. Ninety-five per cent confidence interval of the estimated break-date is provided in the brackets. The signs plus and minus, in parentheses, indicate acceleration and deceleration, respectively.

Table A4.4 Phases of Growth: GDP at 1999–2000 Prices

	Period 1	*Period 2*	*Period 3*	*Period 4*	*Period 5*	*Period 6*
GDP	3.48 [1950/1– 1978/9]	4.38 [1979/80– 1990/1]	5.89 [1991/2– 2005/6]			
1 Agriculture, forestry, and logging	2.30 [1950/1– 1987/8]	3.14 [1988/9– 2005/6]				
1.1 Agriculture	1.72 [1950/1– 1964/5]	2.77 [1965/6– 2005/6]				
1.2 Forestry and logging	1.58 [1950/1– 1964/5]	2.39 [1965/6– 1976/7]	−1.99 [1977/8– 1988/9]	1.46 [1989/90– 1996/7]	1.67 [1997/8– 2005/6]	
1.3 Fishing	5.66 [1950/1– 1958/9]	3.95 [1959/60– 1973/4]	2.01 [1974/5– 1982/3]	6.28 [1983/4– 1992/3]	4.45 [1993/4– 2005/6]	
2 Mining and quarrying	4.83 [1950/1– 1959/60]	5.44 [1960/1– 1969/70]	3.14 [1970/1– 1980/1]	8.76 [1981/2– 1988/9]	4.75 [1989/90– 2005/6]	
3 Manufacturing	5.93 [1950/1– 1965/6]	4.75 [1966/7– 1994/5]	6.59 [1995/6– 2005/6]			
3.1 Registered	7.77 [1950/1– 1965/6]	4.66 [1966/7– 1982/3]	6.89 1983/4– 2005/6]			
3.2 Unregistered	4.79 [1950/1– 1964/5]	3.83 [1965/6– 1977/8]	3.46 [1978/9– 1994/5]	5.18 [1994/5– 2005/6]		
4 Electricity, gas, and water supply	8.64 [1950/1– 1957/8]	12.20 [1958/9– 1967/8]	7.18 [1968/9– 1975/6]	6.91 [1976/7– 1983/4]	8.40 [1984/5– 1995/6]	4.99 [1996/7– 2005/6]
5 Construction	6.93 [1950/1– 1969/0]	4.81 [1970/1– 1981/2]	3.42 [1982/3– 1997/8]	7.41 [1998/9– 2005/6]		
6 Trade, hotels, and restaurants	5.79 [1950/1– 1962/3]	3.79 [1963/4– 1971/2]	5.12 [1972/3– 1994/5]	8.49 [1995/6– 2005/6]		
6.1 Trade	5.69 [1950/1– 1962/3]	3.91 [1963/4– 1971/2]	5.02 [1972/3– 1993/4]	8.12 [1994/5– 2005/6]		
6.2 Hotels and restaurants	5.72 [1950/1– 1959/60]	4.36 [1960/1– 1980/1]	5.94 [1981/2– 1994/5]	9.97 [1995/6– 2005/6]		

(contd...)

Table A4.4 *(contd...)*

	Period 1	*Period 2*	*Period 3*	*Period 4*	*Period 5*	*Period 6*
7 Transport, storage, and communication	5.08 [1950/1–1957/8]	6.65 [1958/9–1965/6]	4.81 [1966/7–1973/4]	5.93 [1974/5–1989/90]	6.03 [1990/1–1997/8]	10.75 [1998/9–2005/6]
7.1 Railways	5.22 [1950/1–1965/6]	3.58 [1966/7–1985/6]	3.39 [1986/7–1997/8]	5.02 [1998/9–2005/6]		
7.2 Transport by other means	5.97 [1950/1–1957/8]	6.13 [1958/9–1973/4]	6.51 [1974/5–1989/0]	6.79 [1990/1–1997/8]	7.91 [1998/9–2005/6]	
7.3 Storage	3.29 [1950/1–1974/5]	8.51 [1975/6–1986/7]	1.31 [1987/8–2005/6]			
7.4 Communication	6.98 [1950/1–1962/3]	6.38 [1963/4–1978/9]	5.51 [1979/80–1989/90]	10.71 [1990/1–1997/8]	21.08 [1998/9–2005/6]	
8 Financing, insurance, real estate, and business services	3.01 [1950/1–1966/7]	3.61 [1967/8–1979/80]	8.07 [1980/1–1988/9]	7.75 [1989/90–2005/6]		
8.1 Banking and insurance	6.58 [1950/1–1965/6]	6.04 [1966/7–1979/80]	9.69 [1980/1–1996/7]	8.24 [1997/8–2005/6]		
8.2 Real estate, ownership, and business services	2.42 [1950/1–1964/5]	2.69 [1965/6–1979/80]	7.29 [1980/1–1993/4]	6.59 [1994/5–2005/6]		
9 Community and personal services	2.78 [1950/1–1957/8]	5.23 [1958/9–1968/9]	3.85 [1969/70–1981/2]	5.83 [1982/3–1989/0]	5.47 [1989/90–1997/8]	6.80 [1998/9–2005/6]
9.1 Public administration and defence	6.00 [1950/1–1961/2]	6.95 [1962/3–1973/4]	5.55 [1974/5–1986/7]	5.59 [1987/8–1996/7]	5.98 [1996/7–2005/6]	
9.2 Other services	2.34 [1950/1–1957/8]	3.91 [1958/9–1968/9]	2.73 [1969/70–1981/2]	5.36 [1982/3–1995/6]	7.21 [1995/6–2005/6]	

Note: All growth rate estimates are significant at 1 per cent level.

NOTES

1. Decades ago Professor T.N. Srinivasan had pointed out to me that this is a misnomer as the test had been first devised by C.R. Rao.

2. See Hansen (2001).

3. See Ben-David and Papell (1998).

4. For an application, see Uctum et al. (2006).

5. See Bai and Perron (2003) for a comparison of the performance of the BIC and *supF* statistics.

6. See Zeileis et al. (2005).

Bibliography

Abramovitz, M. (1956) 'Resource and Output Trends in the United States since 1870', *American Economic Review*, 46: 5–23.

—— (1989) 'Thinking about Growth', in *Thinking about Growth and Other Essays on Economic Growth and Welfare*, pp. 3–79. New York: Cambridge University Press.

Acharya, S. (2002) 'India's Medium-term Growth Prospects', *Economic and Political Weekly*, 37: 2897–906.

Adiga, Arvind (2008) *The White Tiger*. Noida: HarperCollins Publishers India.

Ahluwalia, I.J. (1985) *Industrial Growth in India: Stagnation since the Mid-sixties*. Delhi: Oxford University Press.

Alagh, Y.K. (1994) 'Macro Policies for Indian Agriculture', in G.S. Bhalla (ed.), *Economic Liberalisation and Indian Agriculture*. New Delhi: Institute for Studies in Industrial Development.

All-India Manufacturers' Organisation (AIMO) (1944) *Reconstruction in Post-war India: A Plan of Development All Round, The Bombay Plan*. Bombay: AIMO.

AM (1964) 'We, the People of India', *Economic Weekly*, 16: 1195–8.

Amsden, A. (2001) *The Rise of the 'Rest': Challenges to the West from Late Industrialising Economies*. New York: Oxford University Press.

Anderson, C.A. and M.J. Bowman (1965) *Education and Economic Development*. Chicago: Aldine.

Arrow, K. (1962) 'The Economic Implications of Learning by Doing', *Review of Economic Studies*, 29: 155–73.

Arthur, W.B. (1989) *Increasing Returns and Path Dependence in the Economy*. Ann Arbor: The University of Michigan Press.

ASER (2005) *Annual Status Education Report*. Mumbai: Pratham.

Bagchi, A. (1972) *Private Investment in India, 1900–1939*. Cambridge: Cambridge University Press.

Bagchi, A. and P. Nayak (1994) 'Public Finance and the Planning Process', in A. Bagchi and N. Stern (eds), *Tax Policy in Developing Countries*. New Delhi: Oxford University Press.

Bai, J. (1997) 'Estimation of a Change Point in Multiple Regression Models', *Review of Economics and Statistics*, 79: 551–63.

Bai, J. and P. Perron (1998) 'Estimating and Testing Linear Models with Multiple Structural Changes', *Econometrica*, 66: 47–78.

——(2003) 'Computation and Analysis of Multiple Structural Change Models', *Journal of Applied Econometrics*, 18: 1–22.

—— (2004) 'Multiple Structural Change Models: A Simulation Analysis', unpublished, Department of Economics, Boston University.

Bairoch, P. (1973) 'Agriculture and the Industrial Revolution, 1700–1914', in C. Cipolla (ed.), *The Fontana Economic History of Europe*. London: Collins/Fontana.

——(1997) 'New Estimates on Agricultural Productivity Yields of Developed Countries, 1800–1990', in A. Bhaduri and R. Skarstein (eds), *Economic Development and Agricultural Productivity*, pp. 45–58. Cheltenham: Edward Elgar.

Balakrishnan, P. (1991) *Pricing and Inflation in India*. New Delhi: Oxford University Press.

—— (2000) 'Agriculture and the Economic Reforms: Growth and Welfare', *Economic and Political Weekly*, 18–24 March, 35: 999–1004.

——(2001) 'An Equal Governance', *The Hindu*, 11 July.

——(2006) 'Benign Neglect or Strategic Intent? The Contested Lineage of the Indian Software Industry', *Economic and Political Weekly*, 41: 2438–44.

——(2007) 'Higher Education in India: Will "Six Per Cent" Do It?', *Economic and Political Weekly, 42: 3930–4.*

——(2009) 'Macroeconomic Policy, Structural Reforms and Economic Growth', in Asian Development Bank, *Macroeconomic Management and Government Finances*. New Delhi: Oxford University Press.

Balakrishnan, P., R. Golait, and P. Kumar (2008) 'Agricultural Growth in India since 1991', DRG Paper No. 27, Reserve Bank of India, Mumbai.

Balakrishnan, P. and M. Parameswaran (2007) 'Understanding Economic Growth in India, A Prerequisite', *Economic and Political Weekly*, 42: 2915–22.

Balakrishnan, P. and K. Pushpangadan (2001) 'TFPG in Manufacturing: The 80s Revisited', *Economic and Political Weekly*, 37: 323–5.

Balasubramanyan, V.N. (2001) *Conversations with Indian Economists*. Delhi: Orient Longman.

Ballabh, V. (2007) *Institutional Alternatives and Governance of Agriculture*. New Delhi: Academic Press in Association with the Institute for Rural Management, Anand.

Bardhan, P. (1984) *The Political Economy of Development in India*. Delhi: Oxford University Press.

Barro, R. (2001) 'Human Capital and Growth', *American Economic Review*, Papers and Proceedings, 91: 12–17.

Basu, K. and A. Maertens (2007) 'The Pattern and Causes of Economic Growth in India', *Oxford Review of Economic Policy*, 23(2): 143–67.

Ben-David, D. and D.H. Papell (1998) 'Slowdowns and Meltdowns: Postwar Growth Evidence from 74 Countries', *Review of Economics and Statistics*, 80: 561–71.

Bhagwati, J. (1956) 'Deficit Financing and Economic Development', *Indian Economic Review*, 2: 40–60.

—— (1994) 'Splintering and Disembodiment of Services and Developing Nations', *World Economy*, 7: 133–43.

——(1998) 'India's Economic Reforms: Dismantling the Machine for Going Backwards', *Vikalpa*, 23: 5–7.

Bhagwati, J. and C. Calomiris (eds) (2008) *Sustaining India's Growth Miracle*. New Delhi: Stanza.

Bhagwati, J. and P. Desai (1970) *India, Planning for Industrialisation*. Delhi: Oxford University Press.

Bhargava, A. (1987) 'Indian Economy during Mrs. Gandhi's Regime', *Journal of Asian and African Studies*, 22: 194–217.

Bhat, P.N.M. (2001) 'A Demographic Bonus for India?', Keynote address at the symposium 'Our Common Future', Population Research Centre, University of Groningen, 22 November.

Blyn, G. (1966) *Agricultural Trends in India, 1891–1947: Output, Availability and Productivity*. Philadelphia: University of Pennsylvania Press.

Bosworth, B. and S. Collins (2003) *The Empirics of Growth: An Update*. Washington, D.C.: The Brookings Institution.

Boyce J.K. (1986) 'Kinked Exponential Models for Growth Rate Estimation', *Oxford Bulletin of Economics and Statistics*, 48: 385–91.

Byres, T. and P. Nolan (1976) *Inequality: India and China Compared*. Milton Keynes: The Open University Press.

Carlin, W. and D. Soskice (2006) *Macroeconomics: Imperfections, Institutions and Policies*. Oxford: Oxford University Press.

Castells, M. (2000) *The Information Age: Economy, Society and Culture, Volume 3: The 'End of the Millennium'*. Oxford: Blackwell.

Central Statistical Organisation (CSO) (1983) *Transactions of the Public Sector 1960–61 to 1979–80*. New Delhi: CSO.

——(2007) *National Accounts Statistics Back Series 1950–51 to 1999–2000*. New Delhi: CSO.

Chakravarty, S. (1979) 'On the Question of the Home Market and the Prospects for Indian Growth', *Economic and Political Weekly*, 14: 1229–42.

—— (1988) *Development Planning: The Indian Experience*. Delhi: Oxford University Press.

Chand, R. (2004) 'Agricultural Growth during the Reforms and Liberalization: Issues and Concerns', Policy Brief, National Centre for Agricultural Economics and Policy Research, Indian Council for Agricultural Research, New Delhi.

Chandra, B. (1992) 'The Colonial Legacy', in B. Jalan (ed.), *The Indian Economy: Problems and Prospects*. New Delhi: Penguin.

Chandra, B., A. Mukherjee, and M. Mukherjee (2000) *India after Independence 1947–2000*. New Delhi: Penguin.

Chang, H-J. (2003) 'The East Asian Development Experience', in Ha Joon Chang (ed.), *Rethinking Development Economics*. London: Anthem Press.

Chatterjee, P. (1979) 'Jawaharlal Nehru and the Decade after Freedom, A Review Article', *Indian Historical Review*, 6, 237–45.

Chaudhri, D.P. (1979) *Education, Innovations and Agricultural Development*. New Delhi: Vikas.

Chenery, H.B. and M. Syrquin (1975) *Patterns of Development, 1950–70*. Oxford: Oxford University Press.

Chibber, V. (2003) *Locked in Place: State-Building and Late Industrialization in India*. Princeton: Princeton University Press.

Crafts, N. (1985) 'Income Elasticities of Demand and the Release of Labour by Agriculture during the British Industrial Revolution: A Further Appraisal', in J. Mokyr (ed.), *The Economics of the Industrial Revolution*, pp. 151–63. London: George Allen and Unwin.

—— (1996) 'The First Industrial Revolution: A Guided Tour for Growth Economists', *American Economic Review*, Papers and Proceedings, 86: 197–200.

Crocker, W. (2008) *Nehru: A Contemporary's Estimate*, first published in 1966, reissued with a foreword by Ramachandra Guha. New York: Random House.

Dantwala, M.L. (1967) ' The Growing Irrelevance of Economics in Planning: The Case of Procurement Prices', *Economic and Political Weekly*, 2: 1945–7.

De, A. and J. Drèze (1999) *Public Report on Basic Education in India*. New Delhi: Oxford University Press.

DeLong, B. (2003) 'India since Independence: An Analytic Growth Narrative', in D. Rodrik (ed.), *In Search of Prosperity, Analytic Narratives on Economic Growth*. Princeton: Princeton University Press.

Deng, A. and P. Perron (2005) 'A Comparison of Alternative Asymptotic Frameworks to Analyse a Structural Change in a Linear Time Trend', Working Paper, Department of Economics, Boston University.

Dercon, S. (2009) 'Rural Poverty: Old Challenges in New Contexts', *The World Bank Research Observer*, 24: 1–28.

Desai, M. (1998) 'Was There an Alternative to Mahalanobis?', in Isher Judge Ahluwalia and I.M.D. Little (eds), *India's Economic Reforms and*

Development: Essays for Manmohan Singh. New Delhi: Oxford University Press.

——— (2007) 'Our Economic Growth: 1947–2000', *IIC Quarterly*, Winter 2006–Spring 2007, 33: 34–44.

Dhar, P.N. (2003) *The Evolution of Economic Policy in India: Selected Essays*. New Delhi: Oxford University Press.

Dobb, M.H. (1946) *Studies in the Development of Capitalism*. London: Routledge and Kegan Paul.

Dreze, J. (2009) 'Employment Guarantee or Slave Labour?', *The Hindu*, 19 September.

Dreze, J. and A. Sen (1995) *Economic Development and Social Opportunity*. New Delhi: Oxford University Press.

Durlauf, S.N. (2003) 'Comment on "The Empirics of Growth" by B.P. Bosworth and S.M. Collins', *Brookings Papers on Economic Activity*, 2: 180–9.

Dyson, T. (2008) 'India's Demographic Transition and Its Consequences for Development', Third Golden Jubilee Lecture, Institute of Economic Growth, New Delhi, 24 March.

Easterly, W. and R. Levine (2000) 'It's Not Factor Accumulation: Stylized Facts and Growth Models', *The World Bank Economic Review*, 15: 177–219.

Economic and Political Weekly Research Foundation (2004) *National Accounts of India 1950–51 to 2000–02*. Mumbai: Economic and Political Weekly Research Foundation.

The Economist (2007) 'The End of Cheap Food', London, 6 December.

Eswaran, M. and A. Kotwal (1993) 'A Theory of Real Wage Growth in LDCs', *Journal of Development Economics*, 42: 243–69.

Eswaran, M., A. Kotwal, B. Ramaswami, and W. Wadhwa (2009) 'Sectoral Labour Flows and Agricultural Wages in India, 1983–2004: Has Growth Trickled Down?', *Economic and Political Weekly*, 44: 46–55.

Fan, S. and A. Gulati (2008) *The Dragon and the Elephant: Agricultural and Rural Reforms in China and India*. Washington, D.C.: International Food Policy Research Institute.

Farrington, J., V.R. Sulaiman, and S. Pal (1998) 'Improving the Effectiveness of Agricultural Research and Extension in India: An Analysis of Institutional and Socio-economic Issues in Rainfed Areas', Policy Paper No. 8, National Centre for Agricultural Policy, New Delhi.

Felipe, J. and F.M. Fisher (2003) 'Aggregation in Production Functions: What Applied Economists Should Know', *Metroeconomica*, 53: 208–62.

The Financial Times (2008) 'East Asia Must Tackle Inflation', 25 July.

Fisher, F.M. (1969) 'The Existence of Aggregate Production Functions', *Econometrica*, 37: 553–77.

Gopal, S. (1975, 1979, 1984) *Jawaharlal Nehru: A Biography*, in 3 volumes. Delhi: Oxford University Press.

Gopinath, M. and T. Roe (1997) 'Sources of Sectoral Growth in an Economy Wide Context: The Case of US Agriculture', *Journal of Productivity Analysis*, 8: 293–310.

Gordon, J. and P. Gupta (2004) 'Understanding India's Services Revolution', Working Paper No. 04/171, International Monetary Fund, Washington, D.C.

Gordon, R.J. (2004) *Productivity Growth, Inflation, and Unemployment: The Collected Essays of Robert J. Gordon*. Cambridge: Cambridge University Press.

Government of India (1967) 'Growth Rates in Agriculture, 1949–50 to 1964–65', Office of the Economic and Statistical Adviser, Directorate of Economics and Statistics, Ministry of Food and Agriculture.

Guha, R. (2007) *India after Gandhi: The History of the World's Largest Democracy*. New Delhi: Picador India.

Guhan, S. and M. Shroff (1986) *Economic Progress and Welfare: Essays in Honour of I.G. Patel*. Delhi: Oxford University Press.

Gulati, A. and G. Purcell (1993) 'Liberalizing Indian Agriculture', Policy Research Working Paper No. 1172. The World Bank, Washington, D.C.

Habib, I. (1975) 'Colonisation of the Indian Economy, 1757–1900', *Social Scientist*, 3: 25–53.

Haddad, L. (2009) 'Economic Powerhouse or Nutritional Weakling?', *The Hindu*, Kochi, 15 September.

Hankla, C.R. (2006) 'Party Linkages and Economic Policy: An Examination of Indira Gandhi's India', *Business and Politics*, available at http://www.bepress.com/bap/vol8/iss3/art4.

Hansen, B.E. (2001) 'The New Econometrics of Structural Change: Dating Breaks in US Labour Productivity', *Journal of Economic Perspectives*, 15: 117–28.

Hanushek, E.A. and L. Wosmann (2007) *Education Quality and Economic Growth*. Washington, D.C.: The World Bank.

Harcourt, G.C. (1972) *Some Cambridge Controversies in the Theory of Capital*. Cambridge: Cambridge University Press.

Hatekar N. and A. Dongre (2005) 'Structural Breaks in India's Growth: Revisiting the Debate with Longer Perspective', *Economic and Political Weekly*, 41: 1432–5.

Hayami, Y. (2001) *Development Economics: From the Poverty to the Wealth of Nations*, Second Edition. Oxford: Oxford University Press.

Helpman, E. (2004) *The Mystery of Economic Growth*. Cambridge, MA: Harvard University Press.

The Hindu (2009a) 'Reform Process Should Continue: Montek', *The Hindu*, Kochi edition, 2 December.

—— (2009b), 'Food Inflation Soars Again', *The Hindu*, Kochi edition, 18 December.

—— (2009c), 'Exports Continue to Decline in October', *The Hindu*, Kochi edition, 2 December.

Hirschman, A.O. (1958) *The Strategy of Economic Development*. New Haven: Yale University Press.

Huang, Y. (2008) *Capitalism with Chinese Characteristics*. Cambridge: Cambridge University Press.

Hulten, C.R. (2000) 'Total Factor Productivity: A Short Biography', NBER Working Paper Series Number 7471, Cambridge, MA.

Jeromi, P.D. (2007) 'Impact of Agricultural Trade Liberalisation: Farmers' Indebtedness and Suicides in Kerala', *Indian Journal of Agricultural Economics*, 62: 159–75.

Jha, P.S. (1980) *The Political Economy of Stagnation*. Delhi: Oxford University Press.

Johnston, B.F. and J.W. Mellor (1961) 'The Role of Agriculture in Economic Development', *American Economic Review*, 51: 566–93.

Joshi, P.C. (1982) 'Dimensions of Agricultural Planning: Reflections on the Mahalanobis Approach', *Man and Development*, 4: 9–31.

Joshi, V. and I.M.D. Little (1994) *India: Macroeconomics and Political Economy: 1961–1991*. Washington, D.C.: The World Bank.

Kahan, A. (1965) 'Russian Scholars and Statesmen on Education as an Investment', in C.A. Anderson and M.J. Bowman (eds), *Education and Economic Development*. Chicago: Aldine.

Kaldor, N. (1958 [1961]) 'Capital Accumulation and Economic Growth', in F.A. Lutz and D.C. Hague (eds), *The Theory of Capital*, Proceedings of a Conference held by the International Economic Association at Corfu in August 1958. New York: St. Martin's Press.

—— (1966) *Causes of the Slow Growth of the United Kingdom*, An Inaugural Lecture at the University of Cambridge. Cambridge: Cambridge University Press.

—— (1972) 'The Irrelevance of Equilibrium Economics', *The Economic Journal*, 82: 1237–55.

—— (1989) 'The Role of Increasing Returns, Technical Progress and Cumulative Causation in the Theory of International Trade and Growth', reprinted in F. Targetti and A.P. Thirlwall (eds), *Further Essays on Economic Theory and Policy*. London: Duckworth.

Kalecki, M. (1976) 'Observations on Social and Economic Aspects of "Intermediate Regimes"', in *Collected Works of Michal Kalecki, Volume 5: The Developing Economies*. Oxford: The Clarendon Press.

Kay, J. (2003) *The Truth about Markets*. London: Penguin Books.

Kim, L. (1995) 'Absorptive Capacity and Industrial Growth: A Conceptual Framework and Korea's Experience', in B-H Koo and D.H. Perkins (eds), *Social Capability and Long-Term Economic Growth*. New York: St. Martin's Press.

Kochhar, K., U. Kumar, R. Rajan, A. Subramanian, and I. Tokatlidis (2006) 'India's Pattern of Development: What Happened, What Follows', *Journal of Monetary Economics*, 53: 981–1019.

Kohli, A. (2004) *State-directed Development: Political Power and Industrialization in the Global Periphery*. Cambridge: Cambridge University Press.

——(2006a) 'The Politics of Economic Growth in India, 1980–2005, Part I: The 1980s', *Economic and Political Weekly*, 41: 1251–9.

——(2006b) 'The Politics of Economic Growth in India, 1980–2005, Part II: The 1990s and Beyond', *Economic and Political Weekly*, 41: 1361–70.

Krishna, R. (1979) 'The Nehru–Gandhi Polarity and Economic Progress', in B.R. Nanda, P.C. Joshi, and Raj Krishna (eds), *Gandhi and Nehru*. Delhi: Oxford University Press for Nehru Memorial Museum and Library.

——(1980) 'Assessing India's Economic Development—Part 1', *Mainstream*, 25 October, pp. 28–30.

——(1988) 'Ideology and Economic Policy', *Indian Economic Review*, 23: 1–26.

Krugman, P. (1994) 'The Myth of Asia's Miracle', *Foreign Affairs*, November/December, 73: 62–78.

—— (2009) 'The Uneducated American', *The Hindu*, Kochi edition, 10 October.

Kurosaki, T. (2007) 'Land Use Changes and Agricultural Growth in India, Pakistan and Bangladesh, 1901–2004', paper presented at the 'Conference on Comparative Development', Indian Statistical Institute, Delhi Centre, December 2007, available at http://www.isid.ac.in/~planning/ComparativeDevelopmentConference.html.

Kuznets, S. (1966) *Modern Economic Growth: Rate, Structure, and Spread*. New Haven: Yale University Press.

——(1982) 'The Pattern of Shift of the Labor Force from Agriculture, 1950–70', in M. Gersovitz, C.F. Diaz-Alejandro, G. Ranis, and M.R. Rosenzweig (eds), *The Theory and Experience of Economic Development: Essays in Honor of Sir W. Arthur Lewis*. London: George Allen and Unwin.

Lal, D. (1979) 'The Continuing Hangover', *Seminar*, 244: 17–20.

——(1999) *Unfinished Business: India in the World Economy*. New Delhi: Oxford University Press.

Lee, Y., J. Whalley, S. Zhang, and X. Zhao (2008) 'The Higher Educational Transformation of China and Its Global Implications', NBER Working Paper 13849, March.

Lewis, A. (1954) 'Economic Development with Unlimited Supplies of Labour', *Manchester School of Economic and Social Studies*, 22: 139–91.

Lipsey, R.G. and K.I. Carlaw (2004) 'Total Factor Productivity and the Measurement of Technological Change', *Canadian Journal of Economics*, 37: 1118–50.

Little, I., T. Scitovsky, and M. Fg. Scott (1970) *Industry and Trade in Some Developing Countries*. Paris: OECD.

Lucas, R.E. (1988) 'On the Mechanics of Economic Development', *Journal of Monetary Economics*, 22: 3–42.

Maddison, A. (1995) *Monitoring the World Economy 1820–1992*. Paris: OECD Development Centre.

Mahalanobis, P.C. (1955a) 'The Approach of Operational Research to Planning in India', *Sankhya: The Indian Journal of Statistics*, 16(1&2): 3–62.

——(1955b) 'Draft Plan Frame for the Second Five-Year Plan 1956–57 to 1960–61', *Sankhya: The Indian Journal of Statistics*, 16(1&2): 63–110.

—— (1961) *Talks on Planning Studies Relating to Planning for National Development*. Calcutta: Indian Statistical Institute.

Malhotra, I. (2007) 'Nehru's Luminous Legacy', *IIC Review*, Winter 2006–Spring, 33: 22–33.

Marathe, S.S. (1986) *Regulation and Development: The Indian Policy Experience of Controls Over Industry*. New Delhi: Sage Publications.

Marshall, A. (1890) *Principles of Economics*. London: Macmillan.

Mathrubhoomi (2007) *Vikassanathine Panam Ilya* ('No Money for Development'), Report, Kozhikode, 1 January.

Mehta, A.C. (2007) *Elementary Education in India*. New Delhi: National University of Education Planning and Administration.

Mehta, P.B. (2009) 'Universal Grabbing Commission', *The Indian Express*, 23 February.

Menon, P., A. Deolalikar, and A. Bhaskar (2008) *The India State Hunger Index*. New Delhi: International Food Policy Research Institute.

Ministry of Agriculture (2003) *Agricultural Statistics at a Glance*. New Delhi: Ministry of Agriculture, Government of India.

Ministry of Finance (1981) *Economic Survey 1980–81*. New Delhi: Ministry of Finance.

——(2005) *Indian Public Finance Statistics 2004–2005*. New Delhi: Ministry of Finance, Government of India.

Ministry of Food and Agriculture (1967) *Growth Rates in Agriculture 1949–50 to 1964–65*. New Delhi: Office of the Economic and Statistical Adviser, Ministry of Food and Agriculture.

Ministry of Human Resource Development (2005) *Report of the Committee on National Common Minimum Programme's Commitment of Six Percent of GDP to Education*. New Delhi: NIEPA.

Ministry of Industry (1982) 'India, Industrial Policy Statement, July 23, 1980', in *Guidelines for Industries*. New Delhi: India Investment Centre.

Mishra, A.D. (2009) 'Financing of Higher Education: A Shifting Pattern', paper presented at the Fifth Young Scholars' Programme, Mumbai: UNDP and IGIDR, mimeo, National University of Educational Planning and Administration, New Delhi.

Misra, V.N. (ed.) (2004) *The State of the Indian Farmer: A Millennium Study, Volume 15: Terms of Trade*. New Delhi: Academic Foundation and Ministry of Agriculture.

Mitra, A. (1978) *Terms of Trade and Class Relations*. London: Frank Cass and Company.

Mohan, R. (1974) 'Contribution of Research and Extension to Productivity Change in Indian Agriculture', *Economic and Political Weekly*, 9: A97–104.

—— (2008) 'The Growth Record of the Indian Economy 1950–2008: A Story of Sustained Saving and Investment', Keynote Address at 'Conference on Growth: Macroeconomic Issues and Challenges in India', Institute of Economic Growth, Delhi, 14 February, mimeo.

Mohan, R. and V. Aggarwal (1990) 'Commands and Controls: Planning for Indian Industrial Development, 1951–1990', *Journal of Comparative Economics*, 14: 681–712.

Mokyr, J. (ed.) (1985) *The Economics of the Industrial Revolution*. London: George Allen and Unwin.

—— (2005) 'The Intellectual Origins of the Industrial Revolution', *The Journal of Economic History*. 65: 285–351.

Morris, M.D. (1992) 'Indian Industry and Business in the Age of Laissez-Faire', in R.K. Ray (ed.), *Entrepreneurship and Industry in India, 1800–1947*. New Delhi: Oxford University Press.

Myrdal, G. (1957) *Economic Theory and the Underdeveloped Regions*. London: Methuen.

Nagar, A.L., A. Ray, A. Sawhney, and S. Samanta (2008) 'The Interface between Economic Development, Health and Environment in India: An Econometric Investigation', mimeo, Jawaharal Nehru University, New Delhi.

Nagaraj, R. (1991) 'Public Sector Performance in the Eighties: Some Tentative Findings', *Economic and Political Weekly*, 26: 2877–83.

Naik, J.P. (1975) *Policy and Performance in Indian Education (1947–74), The Dr. K.G. Saiyidain Memorial Lecture 1974*. Hyderabad: Orient Longman.

Nair, V.R.P. (2009) 'Financial Liberalisation, Capital Structure and Investment: A Study of the Private Corporate Manufacturing Sector', dissertation awarded the Ph.D. by Jawaharlal Nehru University.

Nayar, B.R. (2006) 'When did the 'Hindu' Rate of Growth End?', *Economic and Political Weekly*, 41: 1885–90.

Nayyar D. (2006) 'Economic Growth in Independent India: Lumbering Elephant or Running Tiger?', *Economic and Political Weekly*, 41: 1451–8.

Nayyar, D. and A. Sen (1994) 'International Trade and the Agricultural Sector in India', in G.S. Bhalla (ed.), *Economic Liberalisation and Indian Agriculture*. New Delhi: Institute for Studies in Industrial Development.

Nehru, Jawaharlal (1947) Speech in the Constituent Assembly, 14–15 August, reprinted as 'Tryst with Destiny', in *Jawaharlal Nehru's Speeches*, Volume 1, 1949. New Delhi: Publications Division, Ministry of Information and Broadcasting, Government of India.

—— (1952) Speech in the Lok Sabha on 15 December 1952, reprinted as 'Economic Democracy', in *Jawaharlal Nehru's Speeches*, Volume 2,

1954. New Delhi: Publications Division, Ministry of Information and Broadcasting, Government of India.
—— (1954) Speech in the Lok Sabha on 21 December 1954, reprinted as 'Progress by Consent', in *Jawaharlal Nehru's Speeches*, Volume 3, 1958. New Delhi: Publications Division, Ministry of Information and Broadcasting, Government of India.
—— (1956) Speech initiating the debate on the Second Five Year Plan in the Lok Sabha on 23 March 1956, reprinted as 'The Second Five-Year Plan', in *Jawaharlal Nehru's Speeches*, Volume 3, 1958. New Delhi: Publications Division, Ministry of Information and Broadcasting, Government of India.
—— (1957) Letter to Bisnuram Medhi, 13 June 1957, reprinted in *Selected Works of Jawaharlal Nehru*, Second Series, Volume 38, 2006. New Delhi: Jawaharlal Nehru Memorial Fund.
—— (1958) 'On Doctrinaire Philosophy and the Role of the Private Sector', in *Jawaharlal Nehru's Speeches*, Volume 3. New Delhi: Publications Division, Ministry of Information and Broadcasting, Government of India.
—— (1961) Speech at the inauguration of the second Hindustan Machine Tools Factory at Bangalore, reprinted as 'A Gift to the Nation', in *Jawaharlal Nehru's Speeches*, Volume 4, 1965. New Delhi: Publications Division, Ministry of Information and Broadcasting, Government of India.
—— (1963a) Response to the 'No Confidence' motion against the Government, Lok Sabha, 22 August 1963, reprinted as 'Our Policies Justified', in *Jawaharlal Nehru's Speeches*, Volume 5, 1968. New Delhi: Publications Division, Government of India.
—— (1963b) Speech to the National Development Council, New Delhi, 8 November 1963, reprinted as 'Agriculture—Basis of Economic Development', in *Jawaharlal Nehru's Speeches*, Volume 5, 1968. New Delhi: Publications Division, Ministry of Information and Broadcasting, Government of India.
—— (1964) Speech to the Conference of Ministers of Irrigation and Power, New Delhi, 3 January 1964, reprinted as 'Irrigation and Power', in *Jawaharlal Nehru's Speeches*, Volume 5, 1968. New Delhi: Publications Division, Ministry of Information and Broadcasting, Government of India.
Nelson, R. (1973) 'Recent Exercises in Growth Accounting: New Understanding or Dead End?', *American Economic Review*, 63: 462–8.
—— (1998) 'The Agenda for Growth Theory: A Different Point of View', *Cambridge Journal of Economics*, 22: 497–520.
Nelson, R. and E. Phelps (1966) 'Investment in Humans, Technological Diffusion, and Economic Growth', *The American Economic Review*, Papers and Proceedings, 56: 69–75.
Pachauri, R.K. (2004) 'India's Economic Growth: The Natural Resources and Energy Dimension', *Futures*, 36: 703–13.

Pack, H. (2009) 'Should South Asia Emulate East Asian Tigers?', in E. Ghani and A. Sadiq (eds), *Accelerating Growth and Job Creation in South Asia*. New Delhi: Oxford University Press.

Pal, S. and A. Singh (1997) 'Agricultural Research and Extension in India: Institutional Structure and Investments', Policy Paper No. 7, National Centre for Agricultural Policy, New Delhi.

Panagariya, A. (2005) 'The Triumph of India's Market Reforms: The Record of the 1980s and 1990s', Policy Analysis No. 554, Cato Institute, Washington, D.C.

Panda, M. (2008) 'Country Case Studies: India', in F. Bresciani and A. Valdes (eds), *Beyond Food Production: The Role of Agriculture in Poverty Reduction*. Cheltenham, UK: Edward Elgar and FAO.

Papola, T.S. (2005) 'Emerging Structure of Indian Economy: Implications of Growing Inter-sectoral Imbalances', Presidential Address to the 88th Conference of the Indian Economic Association, Vishakapatnam, 27–29 December, mimeo, Institute for Studies in Industrial Development, New Delhi.

Pedersen, J.D. (2000) 'Explaining Economic Liberalisation in India: State and Society Perspectives', *World Development*, 28: 265–82.

Perron, P. and X. Zhu (2005) 'Structural Breaks with Deterministic and Stochastic Trends', *Journal of Econometrics*, 129: 65–119.

Planning Commission (1955) 'The Second Five-Year Plan: Basic Considerations Relating to the Plan Frame, Memorandum Prepared by the Panel of Economists', *Sankhya: The Indian Journal of Statistics*, 16(1&2): 111–30.

——(2006) *Towards Faster and More Inclusive Growth: An Approach to the 11th Five-Year Plan*. New Delhi: Planning Commission.

Pradhan, B.K., D.K. Ratha, and A. Sarma (1990) 'Complementarity between Public and Private Investment in India', *Journal of Development Economics*, 33: 101–16.

Prahalad, C.K. (2004) *The Fortune at the Bottom of the Pyramid*. Philadelphia: Wharton Paperbacks.

Price, R.B. (1967) 'Ideology and Indian Planning', *American Journal of Economics and Sociology*, 26: 47–64.

——(1968) 'Reply: "On 'Ideology and Indian Planning'"', *American Journal of Economics and Sociology*, 27: 217–18.

Pritchett, L. (2004) 'Access to Education', in B. Lomborg (ed.), *Global Crises, Global Solutions*. Cambridge: Cambridge University Press.

Psacharapoulos, G. (1980) 'Returns to Education: An Updated International Comparison', in T. King (ed.), *Education and Income*', a background study for the World Development Report 1980, World Bank Working Paper No. 402, World Bank, Washington, D.C.

Raj, K.N. (1954) 'Definition and Measurement of Deficit Financing', *Indian Economic Review*, 2: 34–51.

——— (1965) *Indian Economic Growth: Performance and Prospects*. New Delhi: Allied Publishers.

———(1967) *India, Pakistan and China: Economic Growth and Outlook*. Bombay: Allied Publishers.

———(1976) 'Growth and Stagnation in Indian Industrial Development', *Economic and Political Weekly*, 11 (Annual Number): 223–36.

———(1979) 'Prospective Changes', *Seminar*, 244: 12–16.

——— (1982) 'Problems of Plan Implementation: Resource Mobilisation', *Mainstream*, 26 January: 24–8.

———(1984) 'Some Observations on Economic Growth in India over the Period 1952–53 to 1982–83', *Economic and Political Weekly*, 19: 1801–4.

Rajamohan, C. (2008) 'If Poverty Has to Go, Growth must Touch 10 Percent and Continue: FM', *The Indian Express*, 27 March.

Rakshit, M. (2007) 'Services-led Growth: The Indian Experience', *Money and Finance*, February, 3: 91–126.

Rao, C.H.H. (1964) 'Letter to the Editor', *The Statesman*, New Delhi, 26 August.

——— (2005) *Agriculture, Food Security, Poverty, and Environment—Essays on Post-reform India*. New Delhi: Oxford University Press.

Rao, C.H.H. and A. Gulati (1994) 'Indian Agriculture: Emerging Perspectives and Policy Issues', 29: A158–69.

Rao, G. and K. Rao (2006) 'Trends and Issues in Tax Policy and Reform in India', *India Policy Forum 2005/6*, 2: 55–122.

Rao, M.G. and T.K. Sen (1995) 'Public Finance and Economic Development: Lessons from India', *Asia Pacific Development Journal*, 2: 25–44.

Rao, S.K. (2004) 'Indian Development Strategies and Policies, 1945–70', paper presented at the Wassenar Conference on 'The Development of Development Policies: Theories, Actors and Structures, 1945–1970', mimeo, Hyderabad: Administrative Staff College of India.

Rao, V.K.R.V. (1952), 'Investment, Income and the Multiplier in an Underdeveloped Economy', *Indian Economic Review*, 1: 55–67.

———(1971) *The Nehru Legacy*. Bombay: Popular Prakashan.

Ravallion, M. and G. Datt (1996) 'How Important to India's Poor is the Sectoral Composition of Economic Growth?', *World Bank Economic Review*, 10: 1–25.

Ray, D. (1998) *Development Economics*. New Delhi: Oxford University Press.

Reddy, B.V.R.M. (2006) 'The New High-Growth Sector', *The Hindu*, 24 August.

Rodrik, D. (2003) *In Search of Prosperity: Analytic Narratives on Economic Growth*, Princeton: Princeton University Press.

———(2006) 'Goodbye Washington Consensus, Hello Washington Confusion? A Review of the World Bank's *Economic Growth in the 1990s: Learning from a Decade of Reform*', *Journal of Economic Literature*, 44: 969–83.

Rodrik, D. and A. Subramanian (2005) 'From "Hindu Growth" to Productivity Surge: The Mystery of Indian Growth Transition', *IMF Staff Papers*, 52: 193–228.

Romer, P. (1986) 'Increasing Returns and Long-Run Growth', *Journal of Political Economy*, 94: 1002–37.

—— (1990) 'Endogenous Technical Change', *Journal of Political Economy*, 98: S71–S102.

—— (1996) 'Why, Indeed, in America? Theory, History and the Origins of Modern Economic Growth', *American Economic Review*, Papers and Proceedings, 86: 202–6.

Rosenberg, N. (2000) 'American Universities as Endogenous Institutions', in *Schumpeter and the Endogeneity of Technology*, The Graz Schumpeter Lectures. London: Routledge.

Rosenstein-Rodan, P.N. (1943) 'Problems of Industrialisation of Eastern and South Eastern Europe', *The Economic Journal*, 53: 202–11.

—— (1963) 'Notes on the Theory of the "Big Push"', in *Economic Development for Latin America*, Proceedings of a Conference held by the International Economic Association in Rio de Janeiro in August 1957. London: Macmillan.

Roy, T. (2007) 'A Delayed Revolution: Environment and Agrarian Change in India', *Oxford Review of Economic Policy*, 23: 239–50.

Schultz, T.W. (1961) 'Investment in Human Capital', *American Economic Review*, 51: 1–17.

—— (1970) 'Foreword' in K. Ohkawa, B.F. Johnston, and H. Kaneda (eds), *Agriculture and Economic Growth: Japan's Experience*. Princeton: Princeton University Press and Tokyo: Tokyo University Press.

Scott, B.R. (1997) 'How Do Economies Grow?', *Harvard Business Review*, May–June: 156–64.

Self, S. and R. Grabowski (2003) 'Education and Long-Run Development in Japan', *Journal of Asian Economies*, 14: 565–80.

Sen, A. (1999) *Development as Freedom*. New York: Alfred Knopf.

Sen, A. and M.S. Bhatia (2004) *The State of the Indian Farmer: A Millennium Study*, Volume 14: Cost of Cultivation and Farm Income. New Delhi: Academic Foundation and Ministry of Agriculture.

Sen, K. (2007) 'Why Did the Elephant Start to Trot?', *Economic and Political Weekly*, 42: 37–47.

Sengupta, M. (2008) 'How the State Changed Its Mind: Power, Politics and the Origins of India's Market Reforms', *Economic and Political Weekly*, 43: 35–42.

Sharada Prasad, H.Y. (1979) 'Children's Nehru', *Mainstream*, 17 November.

Shenoy, B.R. (1955) 'A Note of Dissent on the "Memorandum of the Panel of Economists"', Papers Relating to the Formulation of the Second Five Year Plan, Planning Commission, New Delhi, available at http://www.indiapolicy.org/debate/Notes/shenoy.PDF.

Singh, M. (1995) Inaugural Address, Fifty-Fourth Annual Conference of the Indian Society of Agricultural Economics, Kolhapur, 26 November 1994, reprinted in *Indian Journal of Agricultural Economics*, 50: 1–6.

——(2004) Prime Minister's Address, All-India Conference of Lokayuktas and Uplokayuktas at Dehradun, 29 September, Press Release of the Government of India, available at http://pib.nic.in/release.

——(2008) Prime Minister's Reply to the Debate on the Motion of Confidence in the Lok Sabha, 22 July 2008, available at http://pmindia.nic.in/speeches.htm.

Singh, N.K. (2008) 'A Reminder of the Promises to Keep', *The Hindu*, Kochi edition, 21 August.

Sivaraman, B. (1991) *Bitter Sweet: Governance of India in Transition*. New Delhi: Ashish Publishing House.

Sivasubramonian, S. (2000) *The National Income of India in the Twentieth Century*. New Delhi: Oxford University Press.

Solow, R. (1957) 'Technical Change and the Aggregate Production Function', *Review of Economics and Statistics*, 39: 312–20.

Spear, P. (1967) 'Nehru', *Modern Asian Studies*, 1: 15–29.

Srinivasan, T.N. (1996) 'Professor Mahalanobis and Economics', in A. Rudra (ed.), *P.C. Mahalanobis: A Biography*. New Delhi: Oxford University Press.

—— (2005) *Eight Lectures on India's Economic Reforms*, fourth impression. New Delhi: Oxford University Press.

—— (2007) 'Development Strategy, the State, and Agriculture since Independence', Address to the Plenary Session, International Conference on Comparative Development, 18–20 December, Indian Statistical Institute, Delhi Centre, available at http://www.isid.ac.in/~planning/ComparativeDevelopmentConference.html.

Srinivasan, T.N. and N.S.S. Narayana (1977) 'Economic Performance since the Third Plan and Its Implications for Policy', *Economic and Political Weekly*, 12: 225–39.

Subramanian, D. (2008) 'Labour Relations in Public-Sector Companies during the Long 1950s: The Case of ITI, Bangalore', paper presented at the Conference 'The Long 1950s', Centre for Studies in the Social Sciences, Kolkata, March.

Sud, S. (2008a) 'The Rise of Bt-cotton', *Business Standard*, 29 January.

——(2008b) 'Reaping What You Sow', *Business Standard*, 26 August.

Sundriyal, G.B. (1996) *Industrial Policy in India: From Licencing to Deregulation*. New Delhi: Radiant Publications, for the Birla Economic Research Foundation.

Sundrum, R.M. (1990) *Economic Growth in Theory and Practice*. London: Macmillan.

Swaminathan, M.S. (2007) 'Ensure Remunerative Price to Farmers', *The Hindu*, 2 October 2007.

Syrquin, M. (1988) 'Patterns of Structural Change', in H.B. Chenery and T.N. Srinivasan (eds), *Handbook of Development Economics*, Volume 1, pp. 203–73. Amsterdam: Elsevier.

Temple, J.R.W. (2005) 'Growth and Wage Inequality in a Dual Economy', *Bulletin of Economic Research*, 57: 145–69.

Temple, J.R.W. and Johnson, P.A. (1998) 'Social Capability and Economic Growth', *Quarterly Journal of Economics*, 113: 965–90.

Thapar, R. (2009) 'Conversations about History, An Interview with Kalpana Sharma', *The Hindu*, 25 January.

Thorner, D. (1976) *The Agrarian Prospect in India*. New Delhi: Allied Publishers.

The Times of India. 2009. 'On the Move: Bihar's Economy Takes Off', *The Times of India*, New Delhi edition, 6 January.

Timmer, P. (1988) 'The Agricultural Transformation', in H. Chenery and T.N. Srinivasan (eds), *The Handbook of Development Economics*, Volume 1. Amsterdam: Elsevier Science.

Toner, P. (1999) *Main Currents in Cumulative Causation: The Dynamics of Growth and Development*. London: Macmillan.

Uctum, M., T. Thurston, and R. Uctum (2006) 'Public Debt, the Unit Root Hypothesis and Structural Breaks: A Multi-Country Analysis', *Economica*, 73: 129–56.

UNESCO (2007). *EFA Global Monitoring Report 2008*. Paris: UNESCO.

Vaidyanathan, A. (2007) 'Water Policy in India: A Brief Overview', Occasional Paper Number 6, Centre for Public Policy, Indian Institute of Management, Bangalore.

Vasudevan, A. (1968) 'On "Ideology and Indian Planning"', *American Journal of Economics and Sociology*, 27: 214–16.

Vijay Shankar, P.S. and Mihir Shah (2009) 'Rethinking Reforms: A New Vision for the Social Sector in India', paper prepared for the project 'Poverty Reduction and Policy Regimes' funded by UNRISD, Village Jatashankar, M.P: Samaj Pragati Sahayog, mimeo.

Virmani, A. (2006) 'India's Economic Growth History: Fluctuations, Trends, Break Points and Phases', *Indian Economic Review*, 41: 81–103.

Visvesvaraya, M. (1936) *Planned Economy for India*, second edition. Bangalore: The Bangalore Press.

Wade, R.H. (1990) *Governing the Market: Economic Theory and the Role of Government in East Asian Industrialisation*. Princeton: Princeton University Press.

Wallack, J.S. (2003) 'Structural Breaks in Indian Macroeconomic Data', *Economic and Political Weekly*, 38: 4312–15.

Wang Z. (2006) 'The Joint Determination of the Number and the Type of Structural Changes', *Economic Letters*, 93: 222–7.

Wheeler, D. (1984) *Human Resource Policies, Economic Growth, and Demographic Change in Developing Countries*. Oxford: The Clarendon Press.

Williamson, J. (1990) 'What Washington Means by Policy Reform', in J. Williamson (ed.), *Latin American Adjustment: How Much has Happened?* Washington, D.C.: Institute for International Economics.

Winchester, S. and R. Winchester (2004) 'Calcutta: A Brief History', in *Simon Winchester's Calcutta*. Footscray, Victoria, Australia: Lonely Planet Publications.

World Bank (2007) *Skill Development in India: The Vocational Education and Training System*. Washington, D.C.: Human Development Unit, South Asia Region, The World Bank.

——— (2008) *The Growth Report: Strategies for Sustained Growth and Inclusive Development*. Washington D.C.: The World Bank.

Young, Allyn (1928) 'Increasing Returns and Economic Progress', *The Economic Journal*, 38: 527–41.

Young, A. (1995) 'The Tyranny of Numbers: Confronting the Statistical Realities of the East Asian Growth Experience', *Quarterly Journal of Economics*, 110: 41–68.

Yunwei, F. (2009) 'Emerging Economies Strive for Development Amid Challenges', *The Hindu*, Kochi edition, 16 September.

Zachariah, B. (2004) *Nehru*. London: Routledge.

Zeileis, A., F. Leisch, K. Hornik, and C. Kleiber (2005) 'Strucchange: An R Package for Structural Change in Linear Regression Models', available at http://www.R-project.org/.

Index